STUDIES IN BAPTIST HISTORY AND THOUGHT

# A Distinctive People

# STUDIES IN BAPTIST HISTORY AND THOUGHT

Series Editors

| | |
|---|---|
| Anthony R. Cross | Bath, England |
| Curtis W. Freeman | Duke University, North Carolina, USA |
| Stephen R. Holmes | King's College, London, England |
| Elizabeth Newman | Baptist Theological Seminary at Richmond, Virginia, USA |
| Philip E. Thompson | North American Baptist Seminary, Sioux Falls, South Dakota, USA |

Series Consultants

| | |
|---|---|
| D.W. Bebbington | University of Stirling, Stirling, Scotland |
| Paul S. Fiddes | Regent's Park College, Oxford, England |
| Stanley J. Grenz | Carey Theological College and Regent College, Vancouver, British Columbia, Canada |
| Stanley E. Porter | McMaster Divinity College, Hamilton, Ontario, Canada |

STUDIES IN BAPTIST HISTORY AND THOUGHT

# A Distinctive People

## Aspects of the Witness of Baptists in Scotland in the Twentieth Century

Edited by
Brian R. Talbot

Copyright © Brian R. Talbot 2014

First published 2014 by Paternoster

Paternoster is an imprint of Authentic Media
52 Presley Way, Crownhill, Milton Keynes, Bucks, MK8 0ES, UK

www.authenticmedia.co.uk
Authentic Media is a division of Koorong UK, a company limited by guarantee

09 08 07 06 05 04 03   8 7 6 5 4 3 2 1

The right of Brian Talbot to be identified as the Editor of this Work
has been asserted by them in accordance with the Copyright, Designs
and Patents Act 1988.

*All rights reserved. No part of this publication may be reproduced, stored in a retrieval system, or transmitted, in any form or by any means, electronic, mechanical, photocopying, recording or otherwise, without the prior permission of the publisher or a license permitting restricted copying. In the UK such licenses are issued by the Copyright Licensing Agency, 90 Tottenham Court Road, London W1P 9HE.*

**British Library Cataloguing in Publication Data.** A catalogue record for this book is available from the British Library

ISBN 978–1–84227–851–2

Printed and bound in Great Britain
for Paternoster
by Lightning Source, Milton Keynes

# Series Preface

Baptists form one of the largest Christian communities in the world, and while they hold the historic faith in common with other mainstream Christian traditions, they nevertheless have important insights which they can offer to the worldwide church. Studies in Baptist History and Thought will be one means towards this end. It is an international series of academic studies which includes original monographs, revised dissertations, collections of essays and conference papers, and aims to cover any aspect of Baptist history and thought. While not all the authors are themselves Baptists, they nevertheless share an interest in relating Baptist history and thought to the other branches of the Christian church and to the wider life of the world.

The series includes studies in various aspects of Baptist history from the seventeenth century down to the present day, including biographical works, and Baptist thought is understood as covering the subject-matter of theology (including interdisciplinary studies embracing biblical studies, philosophy, sociology, practical theology, liturgy and women's studies). The diverse streams of Baptist life throughout the world are all within the scope of these volumes.

The series editors and consultants believe that the academic disciplines of history and theology are of vital importance to the spiritual vitality of the churches of the Baptist faith and order. The series sets out to discuss, examine and explore the many dimensions of their tradition and so to contribute to their on-going intellectual vigour.

A brief word of explanation is due for the series identifier on the front cover. The fountains, taken from heraldry, represent the Baptist distinctive of believer's baptism and, at the same time, the source of the water of life. There are three of them because they symbolize the Trinitarian basis of Baptist life and faith. Those who are redeemed by the Lamb, the book of Revelation reminds us, will be led to 'fountains of living waters' (Rev. 7.17).

To Scottish Baptists
whose names may not be acknowledged in this book, but whose service for God in the twentieth century was also greatly valued as we worked together in His service.

# Contents

**Contributors** ix

**Foreword**     David W. Bebbington     xi

**Introduction** xiii

### Part One: The People

**Chapter 1**     1
*Without a vision the people perish*:
The distinctive contribution to Scottish Baptist life
by key leaders of the Baptist Union
*Edward Burrows*

**Chapter 2**     24
*Equipping God's people for works of service:*
Baptist laymen in the life of the denomination
*Derek Murray*

**Chapter 3**     47
*Her children arise and call her blessed*:
The place of women in Scottish Baptist life
*Christine Lumsden*

### Part Two: Relationships with Others

**Chapter 4**     80
*Blest be the tie that binds*
Scottish Baptists and their Relationships with other
Baptist Churches, 1900-1945
*Brian Talbot*

**Chapter 5**     99
*There is one body*
Scottish Baptist Ecumenical Relations in the
Twentieth Century
*Watson Moyes*

**Chapter 6**     128
*Your word is truth:* Theological developments among
Twentieth Century Scottish Baptists
*Kenneth B.E. Roxburgh*

**Chapter 7**   151
> *Pour out Your Spirit*
> Experiences of the Holy Spirit amongst Scottish Baptists
> in the Twentieth Century
> *Alasdair Black*

## Part Three: Mission

**Chapter 8**   178
> *Fighting the good fight*
> Changing attitudes to War in the Twentieth Century
> *Neil Allison*

**Chapter 9**   203
> *First in Jerusalem*
> Scottish Baptist Home Mission work in Twentieth
> Century Scotland
> *Brian Talbot*

**Chapter 10**   228
> *Be not Conformed, but Transformed*
> Scottish Baptists and Social Action
> *Derek Murray*

**Bibliography**   248

# Contributors

**Revd Dr Neil Allison** C.F. is a chaplain serving in the British Army. He has been awarded three post-graduate degrees for theses related to Military Chaplaincy and has written articles for a variety of journals in this field. His published works include: N.E. Allison, *The Clash of Empires 1914-1939: The Official History of the United Board Volume One* (2008); *The Clash of Ideologies 1939-1945: The Official History of the United Board Volume Two* (2012); and 'Free Church Chaplaincy in the First World War', in Michael Snape & Edward Madigan (ed.), *The Clergy in Khaki: New Perspectives on British Army Chaplaincy in the First World War* (Ashgate Studies in First World War History), 2013.

**Professor David W. Bebbington** is Professor of History at Stirling University. He has written or edited many books, including: *The Nonconformist Conscience Chapel and Politics 1870-1914* (1982); *Baptists in Scotland: A History* (1988); *Evangelicalism in Modern Britain: A History from the 1730s to the 1980s (1989); The Mind of Gladstone: Religion, Homer and Politics* (2004); *The Dominance of Evangelicalism: The Age of Spurgeon and Moody* (2005); *Baptists Through the Centuries: A History of a Global People* (2010); and *Victorian Religious Revivals: Culture and Piety in Local and Global Contexts* (2012).

**Revd Dr Alistair Black** is the minister of Stirling Baptist Church. Alistair has research interests in a variety of historical and theological fields. He is currently working on a book entitled: *History, Myth and the Birth of Jesus.*

**Revd Dr Edward Burrows** taught for many years at the Scottish Baptist College in Glasgow and Paisley until his recent retirement. He has written histories of a number of Baptist Churches including *From Faith to Faith: Kirkintilloch Baptist Church 1887-1987* (with James Leitch 1987) and *Change at Springburn: Springburn Baptist Church 1892-1992* (1992). He is also the author of *For Me To Live is Christ, A Biography of Peter H Barber* (2005).

**Dr Christine Lumsden** is the secretary of the Scottish Church History Society. In addition to various articles and book chapters, her publications include: *A Centenary History of Edinburgh and Lothians Baptist Association* (1995); *Rich Inheritance: Sir William Sinclair and Keiss Baptist Church* (2013) and *Church and Society in Edinburgh 1850-1905* (2013).

**Revd T. Watson Moyes**, until his retirement had served as the pastor of Pitlochry, Tullymet, and Viewfield, Dunfermline, Baptist Churches. His published work in Baptist history includes 'Scottish Baptist relations with the Church of Scotland in the Twentieth Century', published *The Baptist Quarterly*, 33.4 (October1989). He has also written a book, *Principled Denominationalism: Our Place among the Churches* (Glasgow: SBHP, 2013).

**Rev Dr Derek Murray** has lectured at the Scottish Baptist College and the University of Edinburgh. He has written articles on a number of subjects, primarily in church history. His books include: *The First Hundred Years: The Baptist Union of Scotland* (1969); *Scottish Baptist College Centenary History 1894-1994* (1994) and *Faith in Hospices: Spiritual Care and the End of Life* (2002). His most recent publication is 'The Scotch Baptists and the Birth of the Churches of Christ', in D.W. Bebbington & M. Sutherland (eds), *Interfaces Baptists and Others* (2013).

**Revd Professor Kenneth B E Roxburgh** is the St Louis & Ann W. Armstrong Professor of Religion at Samford University, Birmingham, Alabama. He has written articles on various subjects in church history, including: 'Robert James McCracken: Theology of Mission' in the *Baptist Quarterly* (2008); and 'The Mission of the Protestant Church in Scotland 1940-1960', in the *Welsh Journal of Religious History*(2008); His major publication is *Thomas Gillespie and the Origins of the Relief Church in $18^{th}$ Century Scotland* (1999).

**Revd Dr Brian Talbot** is the minister of Broughty Ferry Baptist Church, Dundee; and a tutor at Greenwich School of Theology & Extraordinary Associate Professor, Department of Theology, North West University, South Africa. He is a Fellow of the Centre for Baptist Studies, Regent's Park, College, Oxford and a Fellow of the Royal Historical Society. In addition to various articles and book chapters, he is the author of *Search for a Common Identity: The Origins of the Baptist Union of Scotland 1800-1870* (2003); *Standing on the Rock: A History of Stirling Baptist Church 1805-2005* (2005); and a biographical study: *A Man Sent from God: The Life and Ministry of John T. Hamilton 1916-1999* (2011). His most recent publications are 'The King James Bible and Baptists over 400 Years', in the *American Baptist Quarterly,* 30.1 / 30.2 (Spring / Summer 2011); 'Baptists and Other Christian Churches in the First Half of the Twentieth Century', in D.W. Bebbington & M. Sutherland (eds), *Interfaces Baptists and Others* (2013)

# Foreword

The Baptists are of long standing in Scotland. Originally they arrived among the troops of Oliver Cromwell in the mid-seventeenth century, but their small churches seem not to have survived the Restoration of 1660. Subsequently the first church to be founded was at Keiss in Caithness, where in 1750 Sir William Sinclair, the local laird, gathered a body of baptised believers from among his tenants. From 1765 a number of churches usually called Scotch Baptists arose. Their first congregation began in Edinburgh in 1765 under Robert Carmichael, a former Presbyterian minister, and from the following year they boasted in Archibald McLean a prolific theologian. These 'McLeanite' Baptists held very distinctive principles, upholding the conviction that New Testament church order must be followed rigorously with a plurality of elders presiding at a weekly communion service. During the nineteenth century, however, they gradually abandoned their special views, and the last church adhering to their position, at Lower Largo in Fife, closed in 1927 – though a small number of churches still called Scotch Baptists survives in North Wales.

The brothers Robert and Alexander Haldane were responsible for initiating another strand of Baptist life. Engaging in vigorous home missionary work in the 1790s, they embraced believer's baptism in 1808 and many of the Independent churches they had founded followed their lead. In the same year Christopher Anderson created Charlotte Chapel in Edinburgh as a Baptist church of the 'English order', with a single minister. That pattern gradually prevailed as the nineteenth century advanced and the number of churches grew, not least because both the Haldanes and Anderson organised agencies to spread the gospel in the Highlands. In the 1840s Francis Johnston, who adopted more revivalist practices, initiated a fresh attempt at co-ordinated church planting. Congregations of the various streams came together in 1869 to form the Baptist Union of Scotland, giving the denomination a much greater sense of cohesion. A magazine was launched five years later, a college established in 1893 and from 1880 into the twentieth century George Yuille, the indefatigable secretary of the Union, fostered a range of measures to promote church growth. The common thread in these various ventures was a strong commitment to spreading the gospel. The evangelistic imperative was a hallmark of the Baptists in Scotland.

That remained so, as this volume reveals, during the twentieth century. A review of recent denominational history published in the 1920s commented that the Baptists owed a great deal to their prominent figures. 'The distinguishing feature of their character and labours', wrote the author, 'was zeal for God and the promotion of His cause.'[1] That reasonable judgement held true in subsequent generations too. Nevertheless, as the various essays in this collection also show, the Baptists played a full part in the ecclesiastical and social life of Scotland from 1901 onwards. They did not come to dominate in any branch of either: in the mid-1980s their members still formed no more than around 0.5% of the adult population.[2] Yet they produced men and women who were notable for their loyalty to Christian convictions. While they themselves recognised that they shared that role with other churches, they would have been pleased to be called a distinctive people for that reason.

David Bebbington
*July 2013*
*University of Stirling*

---

[1] A.T. Richardson, 'The Later Advance: 1850 to 1925' in George Yuille (ed.), *History of the Baptists in Scotland from Pre-Reformation Times*, 2nd edn (Glasgow: Baptist Union Publications Committee, 1927), p. 87.

[2] I.L.S. Balfour, 'The Twentieth Century since 1914' in D.W. Bebbington (ed.), *The Baptists in Scotland: A History* (Glasgow: Baptist Union of Scotland, 1988), p. 86.

# Introduction

The idea for this publication first began in conversations I had with Professor David Bebbington in April 2005. Over the next two years discussions with a number of colleagues regarding the themes to be covered and possible contributors led to the firm proposal being accepted by Paternoster for inclusion in the Studies in Baptist History and Thought Series in April 2007. Dr Anthony Cross has been a constant source of encouragement regarding this project since our first conversations with Paternoster in 2006. His assistance in completing the final stages of the production of this book has been most welcome. I am also grateful that when more recently publishing recommenced under new ownership that we have had the full support of Dr Mike Parsons, the Paternoster Commissioning Editor, for the continuation of this work and its publication under the auspices of Authentic Media Limited. His encouragement has been appreciated over the last couple of years.

It has been unfortunate that some intended contributors had to withdraw from this project. This has meant that potential chapters on 'Work amongst Children and Young People' and 'Scottish Baptists and Overseas Mission' were not able to be included in this book. However, two contributors completed a second chapter to allow other themes to be covered. As editor I want to acknowledge the hard work and patience of the different contributors as we have progressed slowly with this book. We have also appreciated the comments and feedback from members of the Scottish Baptist History Project, at whose meetings most of these chapters were first given as papers.

We are grateful to a number of people who consented to interviews or who provided information that has enabled each contributor to complete their particular chapter. It is important to note that each author has been given the freedom to express their own opinions in the writing of this book. The purpose behind the production of *A Distinctive People* was to enable Scottish Baptists in particular to reflect more deeply on what happened in their ranks over the century so recently concluded. This book is intended to initiate a conversation about our past and our identity as we continue our Christian service in Scottish Baptist Churches in the twenty-first century. Each reader will come to their own conclusions concerning how well we have covered the chosen themes.

Brian Talbot
September 2013

## CHAPTER 1

## *Without a Vision the People Perish*: The Distinctive Contribution to Scottish Baptist Life by Key Leaders of the Baptist Union

### Edward Burrows

#### Introduction

Over the course of the twentieth century there were eight General Secretaries of the Baptist Union of Scotland, though the first was appointed in 1880 and served for thirty-nine years and the last was appointed in 1995, holding this office until he returned to the pastoral ministry in a local congregation in 2009. In 1983 the office was divided and a separate Superintendent was appointed. There were two Superintendents in the twentieth century, each serving for ten years. This is an account of the distinctive contribution each made to Scottish Baptist life, not only in the periods of their Union offices, but in their whole ministry.

#### George Yuille (1845-1935; Secretary 1880-1919)

Of the ten leaders, the one that had by far the greatest impact on the Baptist denomination in Scotland was the first.[1] George Yuille, born in 1845, was present at the inauguration of the Baptist Union of Scotland in 1869 and every subsequent Assembly up to 1935, when he died at the age of ninety. He was born in Irvine, Ayrshire, and his father John was secretary of Irvine Baptist Church. After their building had to be sold in 1840 the few members held their meetings in the Yuille family home for fourteen years, while George was growing up. The wave of revival that came from Ulster and swept parts of Scotland in 1859 led to a full church again and to George's conversion at the

---

[1] Two accounts of Yuille have appeared in recent local church histories: Brian R. Talbot, '"Jealous for the honour of his Lord": The Ministry of George Yuille, 1870-1913', in his *Standing on the Rock: A History of Stirling Baptist Church 1805-2005* (Stirling: Stirling Baptist Church, 2005), chapter 3, pp. 51-68; Christine Lumsden, 'George Yuille "Grand Old Man" of Scottish Baptists', in David Polland and Ron Polland, *Great is Your Faithfulness: A History of Irvine Baptist Church* (Irvine: Irvine Baptist Church, 2006), chapter 9, pp. 160-76.

age of fourteen. In due course he was baptized by Dr James Paterson in the Hope Street Baptist Church, Glasgow (later known as Adelaide Place Baptist Church). Following his call to ministry he studied concurrently for five years at Glasgow University and the Baptist Association theological classes, which were tutored by Dr Paterson. His first and only charge was Stirling Baptist Church, where he was pastor for forty-three years (1870-1913), but he was also appointed part-time Secretary of the Union in 1880 and served for thirty-nine years, until 1919. For three years he was also the Secretary of the Baptist Home Missionary Society (1913-1916), when in his seventies he travelled extensively across the highlands, islands and lowlands of Scotland. Many wondered how he maintained a dual role as pastor of a local church and leader of the denomination for so long. As one writer put it after his death:

> Blest with a tenacious memory, a gift for method, and an ardent liking for hard work, he was, for many a year, our very efficient secretary, the while he carried on the duties of a busy pastor with unremitting faithfulness. How he managed it no one knows. There was no Church House in those days; the secretary lacked even the assistance of a typewriter, and wrote his letters with his own hand. Yet there was no better and prompter correspondent, and his characteristically clear and legible script, which to the last showed hardly a sign of failing firmness, was a joy to read.[2]

His early years in office as Secretary saw a series of controversies on ministerial education, which finally ended with the foundation of the Baptist Theological College of Scotland in 1894. Although he could not be neutral and openly expressed his opinions, he gained the confidence of all parties by his unfailing courtesy and scrupulous fairness.[3] At Stirling he was known as 'George the peacemaker' because of his gift for bringing reconciliation.[4]

He had a vision for the growth of Baptists in Scotland and saw much growth during his time as Secretary. There were only eighty churches in the Union when he began in 1880, with a total membership of 8,500. In 1919 there were 140 churches and a total membership of 21,000.[5] There was particular growth from revival early in the twentieth century. Yuille had been Union Secretary for twenty-two years when special circumstances led to his being appointed President too for the year 1902-1903. In his address at the 1902 Assembly, entitled 'The Place of the Holy Spirit in our Union, Fellowship and Work', he

---

[2] The anonymous writer of 'The Outlook', *SBM*, 62.1 (January 1936), p. 5.
[3] *SBM*, 21.8, (August 1895), p. 202; 45.11 (November 1919), p. 124; 62.2 (February 1936), p. 3.
[4] *SBM*, 62.1 (January 1936), p. 3.
[5] *Scottish Baptist Yearbook* (*SBY*), 1937, p. 161, quoted in Talbot, *Standing on the Rock*, p. 63. In his Jubilee Address Yuille said: 'The Union, which began with 51 Churches and 3,688 members, now consists of 140 churches with 21,400 members.' *SBM*, 45.11 (November 1919), p. 125.

called for the planting of more churches in areas of growing population and asked for more committed, Spirit-filled pastors, men of faith and courage to lead their people, and Spirit-filled members. A couple of years later he visited Wales at the time of the revival there and at the Annual Church Meeting of the Stirling Church expressed the hope that the Welsh revival would be extended to Scotland and to Stirling in particular.[6] The Stirling Church certainly experienced unusual growth at this time,[7] as did other Scottish churches, notably Charlotte Chapel, Edinburgh.[8]

Following his retirement from the secretaryship in 1919 Yuille remained constantly active in the service of the Union until his death. He was made a member of all the Union committees and served as Convener of the Ministerial Recognition Committee from 1920 until his death. He continued to preach and to write articles on a wide range of subjects for the *Scottish Baptist Magazine*; he collected material for and edited the invaluable book *The History of Baptists in Scotland from Pre-Reformation Times* (Glasgow: Baptist Union of Scotland, 1926); he gave support to his successors. Yuille was renowned as a champion of doctrinal orthodoxy and Baptist convictions, though R.W. Waddelow, his minister in his later years at Adelaide Place, wrote in his memorial tribute:

> Those who think of him merely as a champion of rigid orthodoxy do him injustice, for so long as his beloved Lord was honoured he was the most liberal-minded of men.[9]

Among the many tributes upon his death in 1935 was this assessment by D. Merrick Walker:

> George Yuille was in spirit what he was in body - princely. As a lad it was my privilege, occasionally, to attend Baptist Union Meetings in Dublin Street Church. There I saw the old stalwarts, and among them a younger man sitting at the Secretary's table, saying little but quietly helping to lay the sure and steadfast foundation of the Baptist Union of Scotland. Without depreciating the efforts of any other man, one may boldly say that George Yuille, to a greater extent than recent comers can appreciate, was the soul of our Baptist Union.[10]

### William Browne Nicolson, M.A. (1860/61-1920; Secretary: 1919-1920)

When Yuille submitted his resignation in October 1918 the Assembly unanimously invited the Rev. Thomas Stewart of Marshall Street, Edinburgh 'to

---

[6] Lumsden, 'George Yuille', p. 163.
[7] Talbot, *Standing on the Rock*, p. 53.
[8] See the bicentenary history by Ian L.S. Balfour, *Revival in Rose Street: Charlotte Baptist Chapel, Edinburgh, 1808-2008* (Edinburgh: Rutherford House, 2007).
[9] *SBM*, 62.2 (February 1936), p. 4.
[10] *SBM*, 62.2 (February 1936), p. 6.

take up the twofold task of Secretary of the Union and Superintendent of the Settlement and Sustentation Scheme',[11] but he asked for time to consider the invitation.[12] In a letter read to the Council in November he declined, whereupon Yuille agreed to serve until the 1919 Assembly.[13] An approach was then made to the Rev. W.B. Nicolson, who accepted the post.

Nicolson was very well known and had been contributing to the life of the Union for many years. He was born in Leith of godly parents. On leaving school he entered the business of a wholesale fish merchant, where he gained valuable experience in business, which developed his orderly, methodical approach.[14] He was baptized by Rev. John Murray of Madeira Street, Leith in 1877 and under his guidance began studying with a view to the ministry at Edinburgh University. He also did three summer sessions of training organized by the Baptist Union of Scotland.[15] He served in three pastorates in quite different areas: Broughty Ferry for four years (1886-1890), Kirkintilloch for seven years (1890-1897), Bristo Place, Edinburgh for 22 years (1897-1919).

He was appointed Convener of the Evangelistic Committee of the Union in 1893 and served for ten years 'with tact and efficiency' at a time when several new churches were planted. He was responsible for the minutes of the annual Council and Assembly for several years and was appointed Convener of the Ministerial Recognition Committee in 1918.[16] He was elected President of the Union for 1912-1913 and his Assembly address was entitled: 'The Ministry of the Word'.

Principal Coats wrote:

> Mr Nicolson is a man of proved worth, and needs no introduction to our Scottish Churches. He is known to all throughout the Union, and the fine record of efficient service behind him is sufficient surety for the labours of the future.[17]

But he was not a well man. The previous year he had been away from the pastorate for several months. Tragically after only five months as Union Secretary he took a seizure in a Finance Committee meeting and died four days later on 7 May 1920 at the age of fifty-nine.[18] This tragedy was mourned by his widow Margaret, his four daughters and the whole denomination.

---

[11] *SBM*, 44.11 (November 1918), p. 162.
[12] *SBM*, 44.11 (November 1918), p. 173.
[13] *SBM*, 45.1 (January 1919), p. 10.
[14] *SBM*, 45.11 (November 1919), p. 122; 46.6 (June 1920), p. 68.
[15] *SBM*, 45.11 (November 1919), p. 122.
[16] *SBM*, 45.11 (November 1919), p. 122.
[17] *SBM*, 45.11 (November 1919), p. 122.
[18] *SBM*, 46.6 (June 1920), pp. 68, 70; *Bristo Place Church Notes and News*, June 1920 (Bound with *SBM* in Baptist Union of Scotland archive copies).

We get a glimpse of Nicolson's character in the *Scottish Baptist Magazine* tribute:

> The ministry of Mr Nicolson was virile, stimulating, educative, provocative, strongest in exposition of Scripture, into which he poured a force of sound and fresh thought, while it was by no means deficient in evangelical appeal…In temperament he was a guarded soul that did not welcome intrusion, yet rich in the fine qualities of brotherliness and absence of jealousy, while in sorrow or distress his sympathy was prompt and full.[19]

## Thomas Stewart, M.A. (1879-1932; Secretary: 1920-1930)

Following Nicolson's death Thomas Stewart served as Secretary and Superintendent on an interim basis. He was then appointed on a full time basis by the Assembly in October 1920, though he did not close his ministry at Marshall Street, Edinburgh until the end of February 1921.

He was born in Glasgow in 1879 and brought up in the Bridgeton (Sister Street) Church. In his address to the Baptist World Congress in Toronto in 1928 he said that he had been brought up under the education system dominated by the Presbyterian majority in Scotland and had been withdrawn by his parents under the conscience clause from learning the Shorter Catechism at school because of its Calvinism and its teaching about baptism.[20] He gave himself to Christ as a boy and devoted himself to Christian service. In his teens he was known as the 'boy preacher' as he spoke at open air and gospel meetings.[21] He came from a poor family and left school early, but he had an acute mind and after a few years in business he entered the Baptist Theological College of Scotland and was able to take his degree at Glasgow University.

He became minister of the Pitlochry Church in 1904, went on to West Dunfermline in 1907 and then to Marshall Street, Edinburgh in 1911, where he became increasingly known in the wider denomination. In 1919 he was appointed by the College as part-time Tutor in Pastoral Theology, Homiletics and Church History with special reference to the Baptists.[22] As Secretary of the Union he was able to bring the College and the Union closer together.[23] His students remembered him as a strict disciplinarian, but the most approachable of men, with ready wit and humour.[24] His concern for Baptist theological education and knowledge of its history in Scotland is seen in his article for the

---

[19] *SBM*, 46.6 (June 1920), p. 68.
[20] *SBM*, 54.10 (October 1928), p. 113.
[21] *SBM*, 58.6 (June 1932), p. 88.
[22] Derek B Murray, *Scottish Baptist College Centenary History 1894-1994* (Glasgow: Scottish Baptist College, 1994), p. 41.
[23] Murray, *Scottish Baptist College Centenary History*, p. 43.
[24] *SBM*, 58.6 (June 1932), p. 89.

first issue of *The Baptist Quarterly* in 1922, entitled 'Theological Education among Scottish Baptists'.[25]

Thomas Stewart had many gifts that were used in the service of the denomination.

> He had a tremendous capacity for hard work. He was an eloquent preacher and continued to make that a priority, however busy he was in other ways. He had business acumen and brought a systematic approach to his tasks. He had a care for the churches and acted as peacemaker, able to diffuse difficult situations in the churches. He must have rejoiced when as a result of negotiations that he initiated two churches in Coatbridge agreed to unite in 1924.[26] He edited the *Scottish Baptist Magazine*.

He saw his work as 'largely pioneering work'[27], being virtually the first full-time Secretary. He advocated and administered various funds that vastly improved the situation of ministers and their families. In 1917 he had been appointed by the Council to renew the campaign for the Sustentation Fund, which had been interrupted by the war.[28] He raised the target from £30,000 to £50,000[29] and the fund closed with £52,000 in 1920.[30] The United Fund for Home and Foreign Work of over £20,000 was raised. The Ministers' Provident Fund was organized.[31]

Stewart was one of the prime movers of the plan to purchase a permanent office for the Union. The College joined in the appeal and the resultant purchase of 113 West Regent Street. Only one floor of the building was used by the Union and College at first, but there were great expectations that the rest of the building, currently let as offices, would be employed in due course for ministry to the denomination. Only two floors were actually ever used.

In the later years of his secretaryship moves were made for the Home Mission,[32] which had been formed in 1827, to be amalgamated with the Union. This finally took place in October 1930. It was not done without opposition and Holms Coats called it 'mainly a monument to his persistence and driving

---

[25] Reprinted in *SBM* issues 49.7,(July), 49.8 (August), 49.10 (October) 1923, pp. 87-88, 99-100, 127-128. It forms the basis of his chapter 'Education for the Ministry', in Yuille (ed.), *The History of the Baptists in Scotland* (Glasgow: Baptist Union of Scotland Publications Committee, 1926), pp. 250-259.
[26] *SBM*, 50.10 (October 1924), p. 118.
[27] *SBM*, 56.11 (November 1930), p. 174.
[28] *SBM*, 56.6 (June 1930), p. 84.
[29] *SBY 1933* p. 122.
[30] Derek B. Murray, *The First Hundred Years* (Glasgow: Baptist Union of Scotland, 1969), p. 92.
[31] *SBM*, 56.6 (June 1930), p. 84.
[32] Its full title was: 'Baptist Home Missionary Society for Scotland, chiefly for the Highlands and Islands'. See Murray, *First hundred Years,* pp. 83-85.

power'.³³ He also advocated church planting in the new housing areas of the cities, particularly around Glasgow, and the Extension Fund that was to be launched in 1931 to help build new churches.³⁴

Sadly his health was poor. In 1929 he was told that he had an incurable illness and was given three months' leave of absence. He resigned in 1930 and was given a standing ovation at the Assembly in November. He served for eighteen months as moderator, then pastor of the Bridgeton Church, where he had been brought up. When he died on 10 May 1932 at the age of fifty-two, there was an outpouring of grief and appreciation from the denomination.

He was remembered as one who had a frail body but a powerful personality, who was a hard worker, with a distain for ministerial laziness, who had a touch of melancholy that did not often show itself and was able to relax with friends away from Glasgow on the beach or on the golf course. He was orthodox without narrowness; he was no sectarian and was on intimate terms with those of other denominations. He made his impact on the wider church and society in Scotland.³⁵

### James Scott, M.A., Ph.D. (1878-1976; Secretary: 1930-1949)

James Scott, like two of the later Secretaries, was a product of Charlotte Chapel. Born in 1878, he was in his early twenties when he sat under the ministry of the Rev. Joseph Kemp and was influenced by the revival taking place at the Chapel.³⁶ He trained for full-time service at the Moody Bible Institute in Chicago and on his return to Edinburgh spent some time in business before becoming Kemp's assistant from November 1906. He was described as 'an indefatigable worker'³⁷ and as 'humble, helpful and hopeful'.³⁸ He took the pastor's place when he was away. He served during the years of the most rapid expansion and took over the leadership of the open-air meetings that were held every night at the corner of Charlotte Street and Princes Street. He wrote an article for the church magazine, *Record*, in 1912 on 'Five years of Soul Winning'.³⁹ In that year there was disappointment at the Chapel when he accepted a unanimous call to New Prestwick Baptist Church. Again he saw

---

[33] *SBY 1933*, p. 123.
[34] *SBY1933*, p. 123; *SBM*, 57.3 (March 1931), p. 35.
[35] *SBM*, 58.6 (June 1932), *In Memoriam* reports and tributes, pp. 83-91.
[36] See the biography by Kemp's widow, Winnie Kemp, *Joseph W. Kemp:The record of a Spirit-filled life* (London: Marshall, Morgan & Scott, n.d. [1936]) and Balfour, *Revival in Rose Street*.
[37] Kemp, *Joseph W. Kemp*, p. 41.
[38] Balfour, *Revival in Rose Street*: 'CD Additional Information –James Scott'.
[39] Balfour, *Revival in Rose Street*: 'CD Additional Information –James Scott'. One source recorded by Balfour places the training at Moody Bible Institute, Chicago, later in 1912.

growth. The membership was only fifty when he went there and when he left after ten years of diligent pastoral work in 1922 it had doubled. His next pastorate at Wishaw was brief, only three and a half years. His stamina was severely tested there, at a time of much unemployment and emigration, yet 140 had been added to the church roll when he left for Kirkintilloch in 1926. The congregation there found him to be a kindly, fatherly man who endeared himself to them by his gentle and caring manner. He was a quiet but forceful preacher with a scholarly approach to any theme.[40] He was there for five years and the membership was at its highest point to date when he was called to the Union office in October 1930.[41] The Scotts continued to live in Kirkintilloch, but transferred membership to Adelaide Place, Glasgow. During his time at New Prestwick he took the opportunity to begin enlarging his education. He attended the special war-time course for ministers at the Baptist College and took the Arts Course at Glasgow University, graduating M.A. in 1924 when at Wishaw. He was then encouraged by the Scots History Professor to do research in Scottish Baptist History and in 1927 was awarded a Ph.D. for his thesis on 'The Baptists in Scotland: An Historical Survey'.[42]

Introducing the new Secretary in the *Magazine* James Hair says that he did not come to prominence in the denomination until after his settlement in Wishaw. Then he found his rightful place in the Councils of the Union. The opportunity came with the production of the *History* edited by Yuille, to which he contributed a chapter on 'Baptist Witness during the Commonwealth' and two appendices. His thoroughness and diligence were soon recognized and in 1926 he became a most effective and knowledgeable Convener of the Sunday School Department.[43] He also took charge of the Baptist Union library as it moved to Church House. Two articles on the Library in the *Magazine* show that he had a great love for theological and wider literature.[44] James Hair gives a list of features of his character and spirit that led to his appointment:

> For all who have been in close touch with Dr Scott know how genuinely modest and gracious are his temper and bearing, how wise and discriminating he is in his contacts with men and affairs. In all his churches he has been conspicuous for his charity and tolerance, and his ability to grasp the other man's standpoint. Along with this there is a gentle firmness in a cause that he believes to be right, and a capacity for taking endless pains in its advocacy and defence. His uncompromising stand on No Licence and the strenuousness of his service to that unpopular cause are evidence of this. And underneath all else, there is an

---

[40] James Leitch and Edward Burrows, *From Faith to Faith: Kirkintilloch Baptist Church 1887-1987* (Kirkintilloch: Kirkintilloch Baptist Church, 1987), p. 45.
[41] *SBM*, 56.12 (December 1930), p. 196.
[42] *SBM*, 53.12 (December 1927), pp. 149-150; 56.12, (December 1930), p. 196.
[43] *SBM*, 56.12 (December 1930), p. 196.
[44] *SBM*, 52.8 (August 1926), pp. 116-117 'The Baptist Union Library'; 53.4 (April 1927, p. 46, 'The Baptist Union Library: The Value of Books'.

evangelical passion which links up and kindles all his interests and activities with the glow of concentrated purpose.[45]

Derek Murray commented: 'His tenure of the secretaryship was marked by denominational, and indeed international unrest, but he set a good example of devotion and gave his wisdom freely to the Churches and ministers.'[46] There was theological controversy between the Union and the College, including the trials of E.J. Roberts in 1932 and 1933. The Second World War affected him personally, for his own son, James Cameron Scott, was serving with the BMS in China, at Shantung Christian University, Tsinan. He, his wife Carrie and their three children were interned by the Japanese for three and a half years. It was a great relief when they arrived home safely after the cessation of hostilities late in 1945.[47]

On leaving office James Scott lived in quiet retirement. His wife Sophia died in 1960 and he died at the age of ninety-eight in 1976. James Dick had served with him as Union Treasurer for sixteen years. In his tribute he wrote:

> In his experience of the grace of Christ he found the secret of both poise and power. Sometimes, in the sphere of leadership, power is allowed to supplant poise, but not in Dr. Scott's life and service. A real humility of spirit often won through to success in some difficult assignment where much was 'at risk'. Dr. Glover wrote, "Seek power of soul not place, grace not dignity, usefulness not honour". Dr. Scott certainly never sought place or honour – for honour's sake – only that he might be useable by the Saviour he loved passionately and to whom he dedicated his life, his all.[48]

**George Macfarlane Hardie, M.A., B.D. (1901-1971; Secretary: 1949-1966)**

George Hardie was the son of Mr and Mrs John Hardie, members of the Kirkintilloch Church. He was baptized in August 1915 by the Rev. Joseph Burns. He fought in the Great War, but sustained a bad wound in an arm and was invalided out of the army. He responded to the call to the ministry and despite his disability became a prize-winning student. He trained at the Baptist Theological College of Scotland and at the same time obtained the M.A. degree from Glasgow University. During his first pastorate in Peebles (1926-1930) he continued his studies at Edinburgh University and obtained the B.D. degree in 1930.[49] He moved to the Wishaw Church in 1930 and served there until 1943, exercising a strong and effective ministry and becoming well known in the

---

[45] *SBM*, 56.12 (December 1930), p. 197.
[46] Murray, *First Hundred Years*, p. 99.
[47] Leitch and Burrows, *From Faith to Faith*, p. 48.
[48] *SBM*, 102.4 (April 1976), p. 3, reprinted in *SBY 1977*, p. 163.
[49] Leitch and Burrows, *From Faith to Faith*, p. 36.

denomination.[50] He is remembered as being always the gentleman. He preached in a frock coat, as was the custom, and cut a handsome figure, his wounded arm being out of sight.[51] He then went to Cathcart in the difficult days of the Second World War and helped rebuild the fellowship there (1943-1949).[52] In 1945 he was appointed by the College to teach Old Testament subjects, which he did until 1950.[53]

At the Assembly in October 1949 he was appointed to the office of 'Secretary and Superintendent of the Sustentation Scheme'. He served the denomination faithfully for seventeen years, which saw steady growth in Union activities, especially in financial matters and church extension. They were also years of controversy. Derek Murray comments:

> His tact, careful accuracy and attention to detail helped greatly to hold the diverse elements of Baptist life together in the critical years of the Ecumenical controversy.[54]

Several Assemblies included turbulent debates on membership of the ecumenical bodies. In October 1948 the Assembly voted to affiliate with the World Council of Churches and the British Council of Churches by a very small majority. In 1951 there was a motion asking for immediate withdrawal from the World Council, but the status quo was upheld by a two to one majority. In 1956 the Union withdrew from the World Council, but remained in the Scottish Churches' Council, leading to the withdrawal from the Union of Charlotte Chapel. In 1965 motions calling for withdrawal from the British Council of Churches and the Scottish Churches' Council were defeated, as a result of which Harper Memorial Baptist Church, Glasgow, left the Union.[55]

After Hardie's death in 1971 Andrew MacRae commented in his tribute:

> During days of dispute, and fierce debate, and threatening fragmentation, George Hardie maintained, probably more than any other man, the harmony of the denomination. He never allowed himself to be thrown off balance by difficulties which would have led a lesser man to despair. In Council, I have frequently marvelled – as a young minister – at his grasp of detail, patience with difficult situations and people, and his meticulous handling of Union affairs.[56]

Eric Watson came to Scotland in 1964 and became a Council member in 1965. He did not find George Hardie easy to get to know, though he was welcoming

---

[50] Tribute by Andrew D. MacRae, *SBM*, 96.5 (May 1971), p. 8.
[51] Information from Mrs Margaret Buchanan
[52] Tribute by Andrew D. MacRae, *SBM*. 96.5 (May 1971), p. 8.
[53] Murray, *Scottish Baptist College Centenary* History, p. 47.
[54] Murray, *First Hundred Years*, p. 122.
[55] Murray, *First Hundred Years*, pp. 113-119.
[56] *SBM*, 96.5 (May 1971), p. 8.

to him and glad to have testimony from further afield. Watson felt that Hardie was utterly engrossed in his job and that he was not often out of his office. He was rigid: everything had to be done according to the rules. As Secretary he strove to be impartial and kept his own counsel: he strongly held that anyone appointed to office should speak on behalf of the whole denomination. His external persona was severe, but at heart he was a kindly and sensitive man.[57]

Douglas Hutcheon similarly remembers George Hardie as a clear thinker, slow and deliberate in speech and communication. He was both gentle and severe at the same time. He did not smile readily. He was a man of great patience and was never angry. He did not get heavily involved with his own opinions, but would moderate, giving a more peaceful aura to the most tense situations.[58]

## Andrew Donald MacRae, M.A., B.D., Ph.D., D.D., (1933- ; Secretary 1966-1980)

In 1966 the Union was ready for a radical new start. The man for the hour was Andrew MacRae.[59] He was only thirty-two when first approached. He protested that he was far too young and suggested three other people more suitable, but the Search Committee convinced him that he was God's choice and he received the unanimous approval of the Assembly in 1966 at the age of thirty-three. He was born and brought up in Edinburgh. Charlotte Chapel was his home church, where in his teens he served as leader of the Young People's Meeting. He took the M.A. and B.D. degrees at Edinburgh University, studied at the Baptist College for the ten week summer terms and was student pastor of Peebles Baptist Church (1954-1956). His full-time pastorates were Larbert (1957-1961) and Ward Road, Dundee (1961-1966). He soon came to be known as one who had a special interest in evangelism and in Christian education. He became the Convener of the Sunday School Committee and in 1963 was invited by the Southern Baptist Sunday School Board to visit extensively in the USA in order to examine their effective Sunday School programme. He got permission to adapt their materials for use in Scotland and Europe generally. He urged the churches of the Union to take up All-Age Christian Education on the American pattern. He became part of the BWA Commission on Christian Teaching and Training, being made Co-Chairman in 1965 and Chairperson from 1970 to 1975. He developed his interest further by beginning a Ph.D. at the University of St Andrews, which he finally obtained in 1984 for the thesis: *Principles and*

---

[57] Interview with Eric Watson, 4 April 2008.
[58] Interview with Douglas Hutcheon, 28 March 2008.
[59] Much of the material in this section was kindly supplied by Andrew MacRae himself in an email letter, his C.V., and a specially written unpublished paper entitled: 'Reflections on the Baptist Union of Scotland, 1966-1980' (January 2008).

*Practice of Christian Education in the Churches of England and Scotland, 1900-1965.*

It is not surprising that at the time of his nomination as Secretary he was described as 'a young minister of outstanding gifts'.[60] There was a strong feeling that the Union was ready for younger leadership, ready to take risks, ready for new things. There were new experiments in evangelism. A major effort was the simultaneous evangelism over three years, the middle one being the centenary year, 1969. There were over 4,200 people at a rally in Paisley. In the 1970s lay training programmes for Christian witness were introduced: the WIN programme led to dramatic growth in some churches and the WOW programme was geared for training young people. These were years of church planting: at least seventeen new churches were founded. There were pioneer ministries of various kinds. MacRae changed the church planting policy: rather than sending people in, erecting a building and then pulling people out, leaving the local people saddled with debts, he sent a minister in first to build up the local church fellowship. The first one to be sent was Bill Clark, to Alness. A constant theme in MacRae's annual reports was church growth. In 1977 he persuaded the Assembly to aim at a 10% growth in membership in the next year. He remembers:

> Understandably, one or two were disturbed that we may be trying to do the Holy Spirit's work for him, but at the next Assembly we learned of dozens of churches which had responded to the challenge, and had set firm goals for the year. Many of them increased in membership by more than 10%, and one church indicated a 58% growth in the year.[61]

Out of his experience of church growth and church planting he wrote the book *Your Church Must Choose - If It Wants to Grow* (London/Glasgow: Pickering & Inglis, 1982).

The Union was concerned at the development of the oil industry, in which many Americans were involved. MacRae explored the possibility of collaboration with the Southern Baptist Convention. They readily agreed and the Scotland Baptist Mission was developed. This included the launching of the International Baptist Church in Aberdeen under the leadership of the Southern Baptist missionary, the Rev. Jim Spaulding. It also led to the establishing of the church in Brechin and the enrichment of other churches by the participation of Southern Baptist workers.

MacRae was keen to move the Union office from 113 West Regent Street to larger premises. He found that the Building Advisory Convener, John Arton, and the Union architect, Robert Rankin, shared this view. He was delighted when 14 Aytoun Road, a villa in the Pollokshields suburb on the south side of

---

[60] 'Council Report', *SBM*, 92.5 (May 1966), p. 3.
[61] 'Reflections on the Baptist Union of Scotland, 1966-1980', section 7.

Glasgow, was purchased. It was opened in January 1971. This led to the development of departments. Among those who served were Ron Scott as Assistant Secretary, Gilbert Ritchie as Director of Christian Education, Robert Armstrong as Publications Secretary. Later he was a strong advocate of the joint purchase by the Union and the College of the house next door, 12 Aytoun Road. They took possession of it in 1981.

In wider Baptist circles Andrew MacRae played a full part in EBF and BWA activities. He served as the first Scottish Vice-President and then President (1970) of the EBF, appointments which took him all over Europe many times, including visits to the Communist bloc. For the BWA he continued to serve as Co-Chairman of the Commission on Christian Teaching and Training. In his wider ministry MacRae was involved in broadcasting as adviser and participant. He was one of a team of Religious Advisers to BBC TV, Scotland and then Religious Adviser to Scottish Television (STV), working very closely with the Rev Dr Nelson Gray. He made frequent broadcasts, including the *Late Call* feature and hosting some of the 'head to head' interview programmes. This opened up opportunities for other evangelicals in broadcasting and for some of the churches to feature in broadcast services. MacRae also found it useful for his international ministry, as he was often interviewed at length in other countries. He spent about three months each year overseas in meetings, evangelism, Bible teaching and guest lectureships in various seminaries, but he paid more than seventy visits to Scottish Baptist churches annually. He was able to be away so often because Eleanor Bernard had been made his 'Administrative Secretary' and he left administration in her hands. He was appointed at first as 'Secretary and Superintendent of Sustentation Scheme', but the Union later agreed to the job title 'General Secretary and Superintendent of the Baptist Union of Scotland.'[62]

In 1980 he was appointed Professor of Evangelism and Mission at Acadia Divinity College, Acadia University, Nova Scotia, Canada. He became Principal and Dean of Theology of Acadia University from 1985 to his 'retirement' in 1998. He was then appointed Professor-Emeritus of Evangelism and Mission of the Divinity College in 1998 and Director of Doctoral Studies from 2000. He continues to have a busy and fulfilling life.

Gilbert Ritchie reviewing his services to the Union in the *Scottish Baptist Magazine*, wrote:

> The Baptist Union, which he leaves this year, has undergone a quite remarkable transformation, and much of the change which has taken place is due to the dynamic leadership that Andrew MacRae has exercised during his period in office…As a Union we are deeply appreciative of all he has done for the churches. We may not always have agreed with him. Nevertheless, we recognised that the

---

[62] *SBY 1967*, pp. 18-19.

hand of God has been upon him. We have, as a Union, been immeasurable enriched by the service he has rendered.[63]

### Peter Horne Barber, M.A., B.D., D.D. (1930-1994; Secretary 1980-1994)

When Andrew MacRae resigned only one name came to people's minds: his great friend Peter Barber.[64] They had both attended Boroughmuir Secondary School and both studied at Edinburgh University, New College and the Baptist College. Barber had been brought up in a Glanton Brethren family, but in his late teens began attending Charlotte Chapel, where he succeeded MacRae in leading the Young People's Meeting. He had already had a big impact on the denomination in his first pastorate at East Kilbride (1955-1973). He pioneered the work there in the expanding new town and led a hard working fellowship to plant two other congregations in the town, at Westwood (1965) and Calderwood (1972), the three congregations comprising one church. He was known for his enthusiasm for innovation. Peter Blackwood, who served as church secretary wrote at the time of Barber's appointment as Secretary of the Union:

> Peter Barber's 18 years of ministry in the East Kilbride Church were thrilling. The church was never allowed to stand still – evangelistic, youth and stewardship campaigns, Bible vacation Sunday school, all-age Christian education, church extension exhibitions, church get-togethers, drive-in services, the one church concept and team ministry and so on. He is not one to spare himself.[65]

He became fully involved in Union affairs when he was chosen to be the Centenary President in 1969-70. Always an evangelist, he threw all his energies into the three year simultaneous evangelism campaign. His presidential address had the same title as the campaign: 'Jesus Christ: the Only Hope'. During his presidential year he visited all the churches in Scotland.

In 1973 he was called to Upton Vale, Torquay, where he exercised a notable pulpit ministry and led the church to be more involved with the community. His wider experience of church life in England and of the Baptist Union of Great Britain proved to be valuable for his leadership of the Scottish denomination. He has been the only Secretary of the Baptist Union of Scotland to have ministered in a church south of the border.

His appointment in 1980 was to be 'General Secretary and Superintendent' of the Union, but there was an increasing conviction that the two offices should be separated and in October 1982 the Assembly agreed to the appointment of a separate Superintendent to give pastoral care to ministers and their families, and

---

[63] *SBM*, 106.6 (June 1980), p. 1.

[64] For a full account see Edward W. Burrows, *'To me to live is Christ': A Biography of Peter H. Barber* (Milton Keynes: Paternoster, 2005).

[65] *SBM*, 106.6 (June 1980), p. 3.

advice to the churches. D. Eric Watson served with Barber in this role from 1983 to 1993, when he was succeeded by Douglas Hutcheon, who served with Barber for less than two years and then with his successor W.G. Slack until 2003. Eric Watson had a happy working relationship with Barber. They often prayed together, particularly when crises arose, but always maintained the confidentiality that their separate roles demanded. Wounds received in the course of their duties were healed.[66] In Douglas Hutcheon's view Peter Barber maintained the impetus of Andrew MacRae's ministry, but put his own style on it. He led from the front, but was happy to work with consensus. He worked with persuasion, based on his own convictions. He was a very loyal and gracious colleague to Hutcheon, both as a minister and later as Superintendent. He had a wicked sense of humour, but was wise and caring, with insight into people.[67]

One of Barber's main aims was to stimulate the denomination to more effective mission. Early in his secretaryship he planned three years of simultaneous evangelism similar to that of 1968-1971. It was called 'Scotreach' and comprised a year of Preparation (1984), a year of Mobilisation (1985) and a year of Consolidation (1986). The programme of church planting encouraged by the Union continued. There was a happy partnership between the Union and the College in these years, when they jointly owned 12 Aytoun Road, the house next door to Church House. Together they awarded the Diploma of Practical Theology. Barber contributed to its programme, giving the students 'the benefit of his considerable pastoral and preaching gifts in homiletics lectures, a preaching workshop and the sermon class'.[68]

Several controversial problems arose. It was Barber's way to face up to them, speak with directness about them and make his views clear, often with great courage. This was particularly true of the decision that the denomination was called upon to make about the 'new ecumenical instrument', Action of Churches Together in Scotland (ACTS). This 'Inter-Church Process' began in 1982. Barber was sure that the denomination should continue to be involved with the 'new instruments' despite the fact that the Roman Catholic Church was to have full membership. There was strong opposition to his view. A lengthy afternoon debate took place in the Methodist Central Hall in Edinburgh on Thursday 26 October 1989. After a motion for full membership of ACTS was defeated by 345 votes to 152, Barber proposed the Executive's motion for associate membership. This was defeated by 261 votes to 222. Barber went down to the floor to support the third motion for observer status. There was a majority of 59.9% for it (287 for, 192 against), but a two thirds majority was required. Thus the Assembly failed to make any decision about ACTS and the Baptist Union of Scotland remained outside it, although individuals and

---

[66] Information from Eric Watson; See also Burrows, *'To me to live is Christ,'* p. 140.
[67] Interview with Douglas Hutcheon, 28 March 2008.
[68] Murray, *Scottish Baptist College Centenary History*, p. 52.

churches have been free to take part in it. During the years of discussion Barber had been subject to personal attacks, which perplexed and deeply hurt him and others.

Barber played a full part in the wider Baptist world. He was a driving force in the increasing co-operation of the Baptist Unions in Great Britain and the Baptist Missionary Society, which led to the formation of the Fellowship of British Baptists in November 1994, shortly after his death. He followed his predecessor in being fully involved with European and World Baptists. He became the second Scottish President of the EBF (two years 1989-91) and played a key role in the Ruschlikon funding crisis of 1991-1992. He was a member of the BWA Council and it was through his vision and drive that Scotland was chosen to host the BWA Youth Conference in Glasgow in July 1988. At the time of his death he had been nominated a Vice-President of the BWA from 1995. He was appreciated globally for his wise and innovative leadership.

There was much sorrow when he died of cancer on 1 September 1994, a week after his 64th birthday. The denomination's sympathy went out to his wife Isobel and their three children. He had carried on with his work, well beyond the call of duty, and had written his report for the October Assembly at his usual length and with his usual comprehensiveness and depth.[69] He drew strength from the fact that he was 'a man in Christ'.[70]

### William George Slack (1949-; General Secretary 1995-2003; General Director 2003-9)

For a few months after Peter Barber's death Ian Mundie was Acting Secretary, while the Search Committee interviewed candidates. They were ready to bring a nomination to the Council on 17 January 1995. The *Magazine* reported: 'Rev William Slack was commended to the Council as "God's man for the future"'. Part of the Committee statement read:

> The committee was impressed by Mr Slack's awareness of his gifts along with his strengths and weaknesses. He displayed vision and enthusiasm. They did not believe that the need of the times was for a theologian. Rather what was needed was one who would inspire the churches.[71]

Bill Slack, as he is called except on the most formal occasions, was brought up in Edinburgh until the age of thirteen, when his family moved to Hamilton.[72] He

---

[69] Burrows, '*To me to live is Christ*,' p. 217.
[70] Burrows, '*To me to live is Christ*,' p. 224.
[71] *SBM*, 121.3 (March 1995), p. 8.
[72] Information in this and the next three paragraphs was obtained from Slack's article in *SBM*, 121.3 (March 1995), pp. 4-5.

was a quiet and reserved teenager who found the change hard to come to terms with. His family was nominally Church of Scotland and he attended church and Sunday School, but he turned away from church in his early teens. Christian young people at school invited him to a youth Bible Study and to Hamilton Baptist Church, where he was converted at the age of sixteen and was baptized in 1965. His ideas of ministry were formulated under two ministers of Hamilton. He appreciated the pastoral care of people as exercised by John Dines (1951-1969); and the practical and passionate preaching of God's Word by Gordon Heath (1970-76). In the Christian Endeavour he first began to lead Bible studies and to preach.

After training at the Scottish Baptist College he was called to his first pastorate in Livingston (1974-1982), where Peter Blackwood, who had moved there from East Kilbride, was a 'spiritual father' to him. The church was young and vigorous, unafraid to experiment with new ideas and approaches. A new congregation was established in the town at Dedridge (1981) and the church was restructured as two congregations (Ladywell and Dedridge) in the one Livingston Baptist Church. In 1982 he was called to be the first Scottish pastor of the International Church in Cults, Aberdeen. At the time most of the congregation were American nationals in the oil industry, but by 1995 there were as many British members as internationals. Jim and Eileen Ralph commented on the way the two cultures were brought together: 'Even with God's help it takes a special kind of person to achieve this, and Bill has been God's man for this important task in Cults.'[73]

The Centenary Assembly (1969) was the first that Slack attended and it made a deep impression on him.[74] There was a family emphasis and a desire to work through differences within the family. However, the controversy that occurred in one of the business sessions deeply disturbed him. It made him determined to seek for ways of fostering the unity of the family. Because the ACTS debate in 1989 had been a particularly bruising one he made it his key priority as General Secretary to help the Union rediscover its confidence, to give it identity and purpose. He intentionally used the phrase 'Our family of Baptist Churches' a great deal and has continued to encourage this awareness, on the principle that diversity is good and healthy and the things all have in common are far greater that the things that divide.

The acceptance of women to the accredited list of ministers had been rejected by the Assembly in 1985. The subject was addressed again in 1997. Two viewpoints were put forward at a special weekend Assembly in May in Glenrothes. Slack feels in retrospect that this was not the best approach as it polarized opinion. The issue was voted upon at a two-day Assembly in November in Queen's Park Church, Glasgow. A majority was in favour of

---

[73] *SBM*, 121.3 (March 1995), p. 5.
[74] Information in this paragraph and the rest of this section is mainly drawn from interviews with Bill Slack on 17 and 25 January 2008.

accepting women on to the accredited list, but it was not a two-thirds majority. Slack believed that a Union of autonomous churches ought to be able to handle the issue for the sake of churches willing to accept a woman minister. At the 1999 Assembly the proposal based on this principle got the required two-thirds majority. Only the Stranraer Church withdrew from the Union following the decision.

Restructuring of the Union was on the agenda when Slack was appointed. There had been some restructuring in 1991, but this was reviewed in 1996, when there was a strong feeling that the structures were out of date and it was time for a radical new approach. However, the major restructuring took place later, with constitutional changes being accepted in October 2002. The 'General Secretary' then became the 'General Director'. Some of the business was shifted from the Assembly to the Council. The intention was to help the Union move away from bureaucratic approaches and become a more flexible spiritual movement able to meet the challenges of post-modern Scotland.

Slack was fully supportive of the wider Baptist fellowship. He has aimed to raise the profile of BMS World Mission and attends the meetings of the Fellowship of British Baptists, which are held annually. The Fellowship has enabled the unions and the BMS to benefit each other and enhance their united witness. The relationship between the unions is more harmonious, as they give help to one another. Some of the BUS publications have been republished by BUGB and Scottish ministers were generously allowed to join the BUGB pension scheme. Slack served on the Executive of EBF and was Chair of the Division of Communications. He has also given support to IBTS in Prague. In BWA he was Vice-Chair of the Division for Evangelism and Education and was also on the Baptist Heritage Group and the Church Leaders Group.

When he visited Croatia he was very moved by the devastation caused by the civil war and the way the churches had responded by bringing humanitarian assistance to all, whatever their ethnic or religious backgrounds. The Union provided funds for orphanages, property and the refurbishment of property for refugees. In 1996 the Union signed a partnership agreement with the Baptist Union of Croatia and there was a Christmas appeal for around 10 years.[75]

When Slack was appointed, Douglas Hutcheon wrote words that were prophetic of his continuing ministry to the Union:

> Bill has a fine preaching ministry, a strong passion for evangelism, a warm pastoral heart and has learned to administrate at the sharp end over the years. ... He will take a pro-active part in furthering our unity and deepening our faith and

---

[75] Reports on the work of Scottish Baptists in supporting the aid efforts in Croatia are held by Viewfield Baptist Church, Dunfermline, and in the Baptist Union archive in Glasgow.

love. I believe he will bring a very significant contribution to the development and maturing of the work and witness of the Baptist Union of Scotland.[76]

In the summer of 2009 Slack accepted a call to the pastorate of Culduthel Christian Centre, Inverness.

### Douglas Eric Watson (1928- ; Superintendent 1983-1993)

When the idea of appointing a separate Superintendent was being considered Peter Barber gave thought to a job description and consulted with Eric Watson because of his knowledge of superintendency in England. Neither of them at that time had any idea that Watson himself would be appointed as the first Superintendent in Scotland.[77]

Watson trained at Spurgeon's College, London and had two ministries in England: Fareham (1952-57) and Forest Hill, Sydenham (1958-1964). His call to Dennistoun (Glasgow) came about because he attended a BMS General Committee in Scotland and had hospitality with Vernon Colquhoun, a deacon of Dennistoun. He was asked later to preach there and quite unexpectedly received a unanimous call which, after some hesitation, he and Betty took very seriously as the call of God.[78] After six years in Dennistoun (1964-1970) he served the church in Rattray Street, Dundee for thirteen years (1970-1983). Soon after his arrival at Dennistoun, he was appointed in 1965 to the Council and the Ministerial Recognition Committee. He was President of the Union for the year 1977-1978. His presidential address, entitled 'Walk worthily: a Call to BE Christian', was based on Ephesians 4:1: *I, therefore, a prisoner of the Lord, beg you to live a life worthy of the calling to which you were called.* He chose the subject because: 'In far too many Churches – and Christians – a commendable orthodoxy of belief exists alongside an unpraiseworthy and even off-putting behaviour.'[79] Peter Barber commented: 'No one who sat under his chairmanship during his year of office will be in any doubt as to his business ability and administrative skill. Yet for all his disciplined and firm chairmanship there was a graciousness that is typical of all his dealings.'[80]

One important contribution that Watson made to the denomination over the years was as a member of the Joint Consultative Council. This had begun as the meeting of the office-bearers of the Baptist Unions and the BMS. Then two elected representatives from each body were added. The BUS Council appointed him in 1971 as one of the two Union representatives. He was regularly re-elected, and was the only person to serve on the JCC from its

---

[76] *SBM*, 121.3 (March 1995), p. 5.
[77] Burrows, '*To me to live is Christ*,' pp. 139-140.
[78] Interview with Eric Watson, 4 April 2008.
[79] *SBY 1978*, p. 7.
[80] *SBM*, 109.2 (February 1983), p. 10.

inception until it became the Fellowship of British Baptists in 1994. Having served on the JCC all its life representing the BUS, he signed the FBB covenant as President of the BMS! Over the years the JCC facilitated greater freedom of movement between the Unions and moved towards the mutual acceptance of one another's ministerial lists. They worked towards the acceptance of one another's pension schemes and parity in the setting of stipends and other allowances. Now there is mutual acceptance of ministers.

The tasks of the Superintendent, as outlined by Peter Barber, included interviewing those considering ministry; preparing applications to the Joint Ministerial Board; supervising probationary studies; arranging accreditation interviews; giving advice on retirement and the Provident Fund. It was expected that he would have time to visit manses and churches, in particular through local contact with vacancy committees and pastors in order to advise and share in pastoral settlements.[81]

The denomination took some time to adjust to the division of the roles between the General Secretary and the Superintendent, but looking back Eric Watson felt that the strength of what happened as he worked in close partnership with Peter Barber was the fact that their roles overlapped: they worked together and prayed together.[82]

The superintendency operated separately from the other departments in Church House. On at least three occasions it was proposed that the Superintendent should be an office-bearer, but Watson took the view that as an office-bearer he would be committed to take the Union's side and could be compromised in serving the ministers. He was, however, invited to office-bearers' meetings and was happy to attend them.

In his Assembly reports he did draw attention to important concerns for the ministry and the churches, but on some matters he remained neutral: he did not become involved in the women in the ministry and ecumenical debates, because he was serving people on different sides. A service in the Stirling Church on 2 April 1993 included a Farewell to Eric Watson and the Induction of Douglas Hutcheon as Superintendent. The *Magazine* report indicates that Watson opened up his heart:

> Reflecting on his time and tasks as Superintendent, Rev Watson spoke with dignity, balance and emotion. With honesty he expressed the times and occasions of disappointment when he had been "almost ashamed" to be called Baptist and those times and opportunities in which he had been "proud to be a Baptist Christian". "Who would *not* be proud", he asked, "to stand in the tradition of Helwys, Smith [*sic*], Spurgeon, Martin Luther King and Billy Graham?"

---

[81] *SBM*, 109.2 (February 1983), p. 10.
[82] This paragraph and the following two are based on my interview with Eric Watson, 4 April 2008.

He spoke too of the times in his decade of service when he had struggled with faith and for faith. There had been difficulties and depressions. "I was sustained by my two graces – Divine Grace and Elizabeth Grace". [Referring to his wife.][83]

Eric Watson has deep and firm convictions, states them clearly and stands by them. He magnified the office of pastor in the four churches he served and as Superintendent he both enabled others to magnify that office and magnified his own, new, wider office. Immediately after his 'retirement' he served the BMS as Vice-Chairman in 1993 during a time of fundamental change in the Society's structure, and in 1994 became its first President. He and Betty have a full and happy life in Broughty Ferry where they serve as active members of the local Baptist congregation.

### Douglas John Hutcheon (1938 -; Superintendent 1993-2003)

Douglas Hutcheon was brought up in the north-east of Scotland, in the Buckie area, and trained for the ministry at the Bible Training Institute, Glasgow. He served in a variety of pastorates: Dunrossnesss (Shetland) 1962-1967; St Kilda Road, Downfield (Dundee) 1967-1972; Dumbarton 1972-1981; Bridge of Don (Aberdeen) 1981-1993. It was while he was at the Bridge of Don Church that he became widely known.[84] The story of the founding and growth of the Church had a big impact on the denomination. It was planted by Loren Turnage, a missionary of the Southern Baptist Convention and constituted in 1980. Hutcheon was the first Scottish pastor. At the start of his pastorate the membership was between sixty and seventy people. They met at first in the Community Centre, but as numbers increased they had to move to Glashieburn Primary School and then to Olmachar Academy. In 1988 they opened their own building. It was the subject of an appeal by the Union to all the churches, which raised £50,000 for it. The land had originally been purchased by the Southern Baptists, at the time when Jim Spaulding was church planting, as a possible site for what became the International Church.[85] When that plan changed, the land was kept and in 1988 was generously offered to the Baptist Union of Scotland for the Bridge of Don Church. Membership was now around 200, with 300 attending on Sunday mornings and between ninety and 150 on Sunday evenings. At one time there were seventy students from various nationalities in the congregation: the Church arranged to pick students up in three buses from the halls of residence of Aberdeen University. The whole church had evangelistic passion. The pastor simply felt that he was caught up in something bigger than himself.

---

[83] *SBM*, 119.5 (May 1993), p. 4.

[84] Most of the information in the rest of this section is drawn from my interview with Douglas Hutcheon on 28 March 2008.

[85] See above, n. 72.

Douglas Hutcheon served as President of the Union in 1989-1990. His address was entitled: 'Tomorrow's Church - Coping with Change'. Churches were feeling the impact of the charismatic and ecumenical movements. Two days later he chaired the debate on membership of ACTS. It was a bruising experience. Sometimes he had to call for order. The General Secretary, Peter Barber, was heckled. Late in the afternoon four or five youngish men leant over the balcony of the Methodist Central Hall and shook their fists.

The appointment as Superintendent came to him as a surprise. He loved the situation in Bridge of Don, but was thinking that he should not remain there until retirement and was looking at the possibilities of overseas mission or parachurch ministry. He went to the appointments group interview with a degree of reluctance. He responded to their questions on the spot: he had not worked out any strategy.

At his Induction on 2 April 1993 Miss Marjorie McInnes made a statement on behalf of the Search Committee: it had recognized that he was 'calm and steadfast in crisis, a clear leader, sound in theology and a hard worker.' The 'Job Description' of the superintendency had run to twenty-one sections. It clearly required enormous tact and exceptional ability. She commented: 'The Superintendent of the Baptist Union of Scotland will need a backbone, a wishbone and a funny bone. Douglas has all three.' In reply Hutcheon said: 'God has not finished with me, so please be patient with me! I am still learning!'[86]

He does admit to being a hard worker. The typical north-east of Scotland work ethic was built into him; it was part of his culture. A 'Calvinistic' conscience, in which guilt plays a part from time to time, was a driving force for him in his younger days. The job was often trying. Many times he thought, 'I don't have an answer to this'. He has frequently said that churches ought to call the Superintendent in at an earlier stage, as with marriage guidance. More often than not he was able to give guidance towards an amicable parting, although there were several occasions when great difficulties were encountered. There were times when there would have been chaos if he had not kept his head and had control of his emotions. However, in a few instances he was asked by churches to give teaching over a period, with the result that the churches were able to overcome the problem.

He enjoyed preaching round the churches, though he really prefers regular preaching in one church to itinerary preaching. He was glad to be part of a team at Church House that was highly supportive and good-humoured. As in Eric Watson's time, the superintendency functioned separately from the other departments, partly because of the need for confidentiality. He continued Watson's policy of not being an executive office-bearer, but attending their meetings and speaking on superintendency matters.

---

[86] *SBM*, 119.5 (May 1993), p. 4.

He introduced retreats for small groups of ministers at Church House and latterly at Findochty, for forty-eight or seventy-two hours. They relaxed and shared in prayer. Day conferences were started for probationer ministers and their wives: these were separate from the usual ministers' and probationers' conferences and were held in different areas. He enjoyed all his churches and found a deep satisfaction in serving his colleagues and serving the churches. He experienced a degree of blessing beyond his wildest expectations. He and Helen are happily retired and still well occupied in Portlethen, Aberdeen, and are active members of the Crown Terrace Baptist Church, Aberdeen.

## Conclusion

The stability of the Baptist Union of Scotland has benefited from the long tenure of most of its General Secretaries and Superintendents. All of these men have possessed gifts amply suited to their office and all served diligently, bringing honour to their posts and to the Union they served.

CHAPTER 2

# *Equipping God's People for Works of Service*: Baptist Laymen in the Twentieth Century

## Derek Murray

### Introduction

Local Church Histories are often minister-centred, although there are sometimes lists of Church Secretaries, Treasurers and Sunday School Superintendents at the end of the volume, and occasional references to donors of windows, organs, or even church halls and manses. The value of the work of lay people often has to be deduced from reading between the lines of published material, and from other sources. One advantage of concentrating on ministers is that their number is finite, whereas choosing particular lay people involves a selection process which is almost certain to lead to accusations of bias, ignorance or worse! I intend in this chapter to commemorate some of the men of our churches (the women will be chronicled in another chapter) who have contributed to the life and work of our denomination and also those who made their mark on wider society.

I have adopted several criteria for selection: I will look at:

1. Men who were active members of Baptist Churches in Scotland between 1900 and 1999;
2. Men who were active on Union Committees and Council and some of those laymen who were elected President of the Union;
3. Men who were known publicly as Baptists in the wider society;
4. Men who were influential through Church and Para-church organizations, such as the Boys' Brigade, the Scouts, Councils of Churches, etc.

There are two organisations which have been influential in allowing and encouraging men in Christian service and fellowship, The Baptist Men's Movement, and the Lay Preachers' Association, although it must be noted that there are recognised women Lay Preachers also. Some notable men are bound to slip through and I have no wish to diminish the contribution of anyone. In the nature of our churches much pastoral, evangelistic and organisational work is done quietly, without fanfare and almost unnoticed, certainly in print, and tribute should be paid to the unsung heroes of these churches. From time to time there have been tensions between the ministry and the laity, and we may look at some of these. There have been some laymen who have set out to support and enrich the work of ministers, by personal encouragement, and sometimes by financial generosity.[1] There have been others who have insufficiently appreciated the calling and gifts of the minister and have wished to concentrate authority in the church in their own hands.

Our theology of ministry has developed and changed over the twentieth century, and social attitudes have in some ways demystified the ministry, blurring the lines that were taken for granted at least until the 1960s. Respect for the ordained ministry has not vanished, of course, but it has come to be demonstrated in different ways. As a young minister I was suitably humbled when the senior deacon of the church remarked at a business meeting, as he was proposing the re-election of the Church Secretary, that ministers were easy enough to find, but that a good Church Secretary was a rarity! My own view is that the real heroes are sometimes the property convenors.

### Baptists in Public Positions

Let us begin with those whose names have been quite widely known in public life, not because they are of any more importance in the Kingdom of God but because we must begin somewhere.

### *Land Owners*

Two members of land-owning families with Baptist connections may be mentioned first. Richard Burdon Haldane, later Viscount Haldane of Cloan, and twice Lord Chancellor, was a grandson of James Haldane and in his autobiography speaks highly of his Baptist forebears. 'I am a Baptist by descent and tradition.' He claims that he was persuaded to be baptized privately as a young man, and that emerging dripping from the font and facing the congregation, who had come despite the private nature of the ceremony, he told them that he had been baptized only to allay the anxiety of his parents, who were concerned that he had not been baptized as an infant; that he could not accept the doctrines of the church and regarded what had taken place as the merest external ceremony; and that for the future he would have no further connection with the church or its teaching or with any other church.[2] Now oral history must be called upon. It seems fairly sure that the Church was Dublin Street, Edinburgh, and I was assured by the oldest member, a lawyer, in the

---

[1] For example W.D. Beaton, MBE, for a time treasurer of Whyte's Causeway Church in Kirkcaldy, in the 1950s and 1960s made a point of giving new translations of the Bible to his ministers and to visiting students.

[2] R.B. Haldane, *Autobiography* (London: Hodder & Stoughton, 1929), pp. 22-23.

1970's, that the story is romanticised in the autobiography and that Haldane did not receive baptism, but made the statement and left. At any rate, Baptist blood in the Haldane family was running thin by this time, and the future Viscount had become a sceptic under the influence of German philosophy.

The other man was quite different. Alexander George Burnett, 6th Laird of Kemnay in Aberdeenshire, was the son of a friend of Christopher Anderson, and was himself baptised by Anderson in Charlotte Chapel. He is claimed in the history of Crown Terrace Church as 'the worthy and versatile Laird of Kemnay – an ardent Baptist,'[3] who married as his second wife the daughter of a previous minister of the church, Ebenezer Pledge. He was certainly a notable man and proclaimed himself a Baptist but not a denominationalist. He regarded the organisation of the Union as a great mistake, and appears not to have been a member of any Baptist Church. He had his own Chapel in Kemnay, where he preached to his tenants until the early twentieth century. Probably his last published sermon was on the death of Queen Victoria in 1901. In his many travels on the continent he sought out Baptists, and claimed a friendship with Scotland's 'second reformer'– James Haldane, and with Charles Spurgeon. A local history calls him 'the last of the old-time Lairds, with his own school and chapel.'[4]

## Scottish Baptists in the House of Commons

Many members of our churches have served in public office, locally and nationally. It seems appropriate to consider first those who reached the House of Commons. For this I am indebted to David Bebbington's articles in the *Baptist Quarterly*[5] on 'Baptist Members of Parliament 1847-1914', and 'Baptist Members of Parliament in the Twentieth Century'.

1. Sir Thomas Glen-Coats, Bart. (1846-1922) served as Liberal MP for West Renfrewshire from 1906 until 1910. He and his brothers and sisters built the Coats Memorial Church (Baptist) in Paisley in memory of their father Thomas Coats, and Sir Thomas is described, like his father, as a thread manufacturer. He was a member, though not a deacon, of the family church, although he chaired church meetings from time to time. He served as Lord Lieutenant of Renfrewshire from 1908, and on retiring from parliament in 1910 he was

---

[3] *The Centenary Brochure of the Free Communion Baptist Church, Crown Terrace,* Aberdeen, 1939, p. 12.

[4] Alan Cooper, *Old Inverurie and Kemnay in Pictures* (Catrine, Ayrshire: Stenlake Publishing, 2003), p. 13.

[5] See Bebbington, *Baptist Quarterly*, 29 (April 1981), pp. 64-76 'Baptist Members of Parliament 1847-1914', *Baptist Quarterly*, 31 (April 1986), pp. 252-87, 'Baptist Members of Parliament in the Twentieth Century', for all mentioned except Robert Gibson, for whom see *Baptist Quarterly*, 42 (April 2007), 'Baptist Members of Parliament, A Supplementary Note', pp. 155, 156.

appointed C.B. He was from the beginning of the century until 1920 treasurer of the Loan and Building Fund Committee of the Baptist Union of Scotland, and a member of the General Committee and its successor, the Council. He was a generous supporter of the schemes of the Union and particularly of the Baptist Theological College. His obituary in the Scottish Baptist Magazine reports a very impressive funeral, and speaks of his quiet witness and his healthy reticence about sacred things. 'He seldom spoke about his religion but he lived it.' At his death he left £1,651,000.

2. Sir John McCallum (1847-1920) a director of a soap manufacturing firm, was also a member of Coats Memorial Church and entered Parliament in 1906. He was Liberal MP for Paisley until 1920, and was knighted in 1912. Previously he had been a Town Councillor in Paisley, and was a deacon of his church taking charge of the YMCA Bible Class. He declined nomination as President of the Union, but served on the Sunday School, Total Abstinence Society and College Committees.

3. Sir Robert Pullar (1828-1912) was proprietor of famous dye works. He was a solicitor and a member of Perth Baptist Church, and in his old age was Liberal MP for Perth from Feb. 1907 until Jan 1910. He had 'strong temperance and missionary interests'[6] and was generous to the Perth Church and to various funds of the Union, but was not a committee member.

4. Dr William Chapple (1864-1936) represented Stirlingshire 1910-1918, and Dumfriesshire 1922-1924 as a Liberal. He had been a physician in New Zealand and Bebbington suggests that his Baptist membership remained there.

5. Rt. Hon. William Adamson (1863-1936)[7] was Labour MP for West Fife from 1910-1931. He was twice Secretary of State for Scotland and the only Scottish Baptist to gain Cabinet office. His family, including his mother, were miners and he moved from the Liberal party to Labour as a young man. He became secretary of the Fife, Kinross and Clackmannan Miners' Association in 1908,and was elected to Parliament in the second election of 1910 by 703 votes, remaining in the House until 1931, when he lost his seat to the Communist William Gallacher. He was on the right wing of his party, and as Communist influence grew and mining politics became complicated in the 1920's Adamson led a right-wing breakaway from the Miners' Union. He was leader of the Labour Party in the Commons 1917-1921, and, in Ramsay MacDonald's minority governments, Secretary for Scotland in 1924, and Secretary of State for Scotland from 1929-1931. He backed devolution for Scotland and delivered an oration at William Wallace's birthplace in Elderslie in 1924, declaring 'I

---

[6] A. Slaven and S Checkland, *Dictionary of Scottish Business Biography*, Volume 1, (Aberdeen: Mercat Press, 1986), pp. 393-95.

[7] See W. Knox (ed.), *Scottish Labour Leaders 1918-1939* (Edinburgh: Mainstream, 1984), pp. 58-60. Also, R. Page Arnott, *History of the Scottish Miners* (London: Allen & Unwin, 1955), p. 180, for Adamson's Breakaway Union.

look forward to the time when Scottish legislation will be enacted by Scotsmen in a Scottish Assembly.'

He is described by contemporaries variously as 'a real canny Scot, an engaging personality, simple, straightforward and friendly,' by a friend, and as 'too patient, too little revolutionary, the soul of loyalty and of good companionship,' by his colleague Tom Johnston. Beatrice Webb was much less flattering: 'he has an instinctive suspicion of all intellectuals or enthusiasts. He is slow and careful in speech, a total abstainer, and I am told domesticated and pious. He has neither wit, fervour nor intellect, he keeps himself to himself, making no enemies and never giving himself away.' Emmanuel Shinwell wrote that Adamson 'was a dour and phlegmatic Scottish Miners' leader very much out of his depths in the Commons.' In David Torrance's recent book on the Scottish Secretaries of State he is described as 'old Willie'.[8]

Adamson was a lifelong Baptist and was member, Deacon, Secretary and Sunday School Superintendent of the West Baptist Church, Dunfermline. Although his name does not appear in Union Committee lists he was instrumental in setting up the very effective Fife Joint Committee on Church Extension and in 1925 he gave an address at the Edinburgh BMS Exhibition. In his obituary in the Yearbook his Pastor praises his unspoilt Christian character and his work on behalf of widows and orphans during the Great War. His portrait, by Tom Curr, hangs in St Andrews House, Edinburgh.

6. Robert Gibson, KC (1886-1965), who appears on Bebbington's supplementary list, was a member, deacon and Sunday School Superintendent in Dublin Street Church in Edinburgh for many years although in his last years he moved to a distant suburb and joined the Church of Scotland. He was an Edinburgh lawyer and member of the Labour Party who stood unsuccessfully for parliament several times before being elected MP for Greenock in 1936. He resigned from the Commons on appointment as Chairman of the Scottish Land Court in 1941, as Lord Gibson. He is noted as serving during the 1930's and 1940's on several Union Committees, including the Council, the Ministerial Recognition Committee, the Social Service Committee and the Sunday School Committee. By 1955 as Lord Gibson, he was a member of the Sunday School Committee, and still a recognised Lay Preacher.

7. One other MP should be noted. Rt.Hon. Ernest Brown, (1881-1962) a member of Bloomsbury Central Baptist Church, London, was Liberal then Liberal National member for Leith from 1927-1945, and took some part in local life especially through the Brotherhood Movement.

8. There were also two Scotch Baptist Labour MPs in Wales, the brothers James Idwal Jones (1900-1982) and Thomas William Jones, Lord Maelor, (1888-1984.)

---

[8] David Torrance, *The Scottish Secretaries* (Edinburgh: Birlinn, 2006), p. 103. See also his entry in H.C.G. Matthews & Brian Harrison (eds), *Oxford Dictionary of National Biography* (Oxford: Oxford University Press, 2004), Vol. 1, p. 293-95.

So far as I know they had no direct connection with Scotland.[9]

9. In 2008, John Mason, member of the Easterhouse Church, was elected Scottish Nationalist MP for Glasgow East. He had previously been an active Councillor in Glasgow, and is well known as a Baptist.[10]

*Municipal Leaders*

In the days before the Kilbrandon Report of 1972 and the reform of Scottish local government, there were many Baptists who served on Town and Burgh Councils. One of the best known was Tom Curr, MBE, (died 1958) an Edinburgh printer, lithographer and artist who became Senior Bailie of Edinburgh in the early 1950s. Besides his fame as an artist, with a special love for paintings of Clydesdale horses, some of which can be seen in the Sitting Room of the 'Tor' Christian Nursing Home, he was football cartoonist for the Edinburgh Evening News, and delighted audiences of Sunday School children with his 'lightning artistry' illustrating Bible stories. An early work, 'The Baptist Road,' was viewed by the Library and Publications Committee of the Union in 1924, and 100 copies ordered, presumably for churches' use. His more famous painting of Jesus, surrounded by Boys' Brigade lads, was found in Baptist Church halls for many years, and reflected the great work he did as Captain of the Edinburgh $46^{th}$ B.B. Company, which met in the Canonmills Hall of Dublin Street Church. It was said that when boys were brought before him as he sat as a magistrate he would sentence them to join the Brigade! In 1947 he delivered the only illustrated Presidential Address to the Union. He was one of the founders of the Scottish Baptist Men's Movement. His son, Duncan, determined to be different, became a Boy Scout, and went on to give a lifetime of service to the Church and to represent the Union on the Scottish Christian Aid Committee.

John Young J.P. (died 1951) of the Rutherglen Church served for twenty years on the Council of that Burgh when it was still separate from Glasgow. John McAslan, OBE, D.L. J.P. (died 1956) was also a member of the Rutherglen Church until 1950 when he moved to Queen's Park Church. He was Bailie of the City of Glasgow from 1942-1953, Deputy Lieutenant, and Justice of the Peace. He served the Union, the Baptist Theological College, the Sunday School Union and the Glasgow City Mission, and his most valuable contribution to the religious life of Scotland was as Convenor of the committee that made it possible for Billy Graham's 1955 All-Scotland Crusade to use the Kelvin Hall.

James Faichney was Provost of Cupar and for a time treasurer of the Church there and Bailie Taylor (died 1952), grandfather of Dr Alastair Brown, served

---

[9] Welsh Scotch Baptists, who still meet for worship in four congregations, were strongly influenced by Archibald McLean, hence their designation.

[10] See article: 'An Independent Christian', *Life and Work*, November 2008, pp. 23-26.

with him on the Council. In the 1940s Thomas Blaney of Cowdenbeath Church was Provost of that Burgh.

Other Baptist men served as officials in local Government. John Noble, converted through the preaching of Jock Troup was Secretary of the Church and Burgh Chamberlain of Fraserburgh for many years and Treasurer of the Union from 1964 until his death in 1967. Andrew Balfour Gray, Treasurer of the Falkirk Church until his death in 1939, had been Town Clerk of the Burgh since 1899.

## Some Business Leaders

David Jeremy[11] remarks that Baptists attracted industrial and commercial men, and we can look more closely at some of them. The Nimmo family of coal-owners were intimately bound up with Union and Church life in the earlier part of the century. James Nimmo,[12] who died in 1912, was the founder of the family firm based in Slamannan, and, having been brought up in the Churches of Christ, he became a member of the Stirling Baptist Church. His daughter married George Yuille, the remarkable minister of that church, and his son, Adam (1867-1939), educated in Edinburgh and was a member until 1889 of Marshall Street Church. He transferred to Adelaide Place Church and was by 1912 chairman of James Nimmo and Son, and Director of the Fife Coal Company, one of the largest colliery combines in the United Kingdom. In the negotiations preceding the 1926 General Strike he was the most intransigent of the Mining Association's Central Council. The Fife Coal Company was losing between £10,000 and £15,000 per month, yet he pressed the case for lengthening the working day in the mines with extreme vigour and determination in the hope of dividing the executive of the Mining Federation of Great Britain by minimising the extent of wage reductions. It is not unlikely that the well-known comment of Lord Birkenhead after a meeting with mining trade unionists in 1926 that 'I should call them the stupidest men in England had I not previously had to deal with the owners'[13] was inspired by his earlier confrontation with Adam Nimmo. Did he ever confront his fellow Baptist William Adamson?

By 1934 he, now Sir Adam Nimmo, KBE, was Chairman of a conciliation Board exploring the question of a new wages agreement for coalminers. He was still Chairman of the Fife Coal Company and on the boards of the Shotts Iron Company, Ailsa Investment Trust and the Scottish Boiler and General Insurance Company. Besides all these responsibilities, he found time to be a loyal member, deacon and Treasurer of Adelaide Place Baptist Church in Glasgow, to serve on the Council of the Union, the Loan and Building Fund Committee, (as

---

[11] David Jeremy, *Capitalists and Christians* (Oxford: Clarendon Press, 1990), p. 383.
[12] Slaven and Checkland, *Dictionary of Scottish Business Biography*, Vol.1, pp. 59-60.
[13] Slaven and Checkland, *Dictionary of Scottish Business Biography*, Vol. 1, pp. 57-59.

Convenor for forty-two years) and the Ministerial Recognition Committee. He also held the office of Secretary of the Baptist Theological College of Scotland, jointly with Charles Bowser from 1894 to 1912, and then as sole Secretary from 1912 until 1939. In his obituary in the yearbook, his minister speaks of him as respected even by his opponents. 'He was as excellent in virtue as he was eminent in affairs.'

Adam Nimmo, JP, (1865-1927) who was also brought up in the Churches of Christ, and became around 1907 a member of Morningside Baptist Church, Edinburgh, was his cousin and contemporary. He was Treasurer of the Union from 1913 to 1922, and on even more committees than his namesake. When he resigned as Treasurer in 1922 he was appointed Convenor of the Twentieth Century Fund and of the Ministers' Provident Fund, and made an honorary member of all Union Committees. Neither Nimmo however was called to be President.

John T. Tulloch, (1880-1943) of the Hillhead Church was a member of a family that had given great service to the churches in Home Mission and Union. He was a senior partner in Moores, Carson and Wallace, chartered accountants, in Glasgow, and a director of several companies, including the Royal Bank of Scotland. He inherited the Scottish Baptist Magazine from his father and his grandfather, William Tulloch, the first Secretary of the Union, and shortly before his death he handed it and all its assets to the Union. From 1929 until 1942 he was Treasurer of the College.

Joseph T Lockhart belonged to one of the earliest families to become Baptists in Kirkcaldy. He was related to many of the older Baptist leaders, some of whom were prominent in Dublin Street, Edinburgh, and Whyte's Causeway, Kirkcaldy. He was a member and Secretary of Queen's Park Church and an earthenware manufacturer by trade. Much involved in College life, he was also a leader of the Scottish Baptist Men's Movement, and in 1958 he was President of the British Baptist Men's Movement.

The Bowser family of Adelaide Place Church played a leading part in the founding of the union in 1869, and in the early years of the College. Charles Bowser, married to a daughter of David Lockhart of Dublin Street, Edinburgh, was the first Secretary of the College, and before his departure for London was Treasurer of the Union from 1905 to 1913. The family lived in the West End of Glasgow, and were neighbours of Rev George Reith. The close friendship between Charles Bowser's son, also Charles, and John, later Lord, Reith is chronicled in several lives of the first Director General of the BBC.

Thomas Hadden was born in Hamilton in 1871, and trained as a metalworker, the family trade. In 1901 he set up a business in East Silvermills Lane, Edinburgh, with his brother, Robert, a woodcarver. In due course Robert's son, also Robert entered the business and his daughter, Winnie, became a missionary with the BMS. The family was connected with both the Portobello Baptist Church and with Charlotte Chapel, where Robert jnr became an elder. The firm worked on many architectural projects with Sir Robert

Lorimer, and specimens of their work are to be found in many Country Houses throughout Scotland. The most outstanding examples were the wrought-iron screens in the Thistle Chapel in the High Kirk of St Giles in Edinburgh, completed in 1911, and the gates and steel casket in the shrine of the Scottish National War Memorial in Edinburgh Castle, completed in 1927. In that year Thomas Hadden resigned as superintendent of Charlotte Chapel's Jamaica Street Mission, and the business moved to Roseburn, and in 1940 Robert took over on his uncle's death. His work includes the memorial gates at Glasgow University and tercentenary gates at Heriot's School in Edinburgh.

Many other examples of outstanding craftsmanship are to be found in Scotland and beyond. Jack Oliphant, also a Charlotte Chapel member, was responsible for the finials that can be seen on the houses at Ramsay Gardens above Princes Street Gardens. When Robert Hadden retired in 1975, the business came to an end. Perhaps for us the chief memory of Robert and his wife Jean may be their faithfulness in conducting open-air meetings at the foot of the Mound for many years in all weathers, occasionally supported by young people from the Chapel. Casual passers-by listening to a small rather nervous man playing his concertina can scarcely have been aware of his importance to Scottish craftsmanship and to our architectural heritage.[14]

Charlotte Chapel had a variety of business people in its ranks in the middle of the century. R.D. Clark was head of a large fruit business, prosperous enough to allow him to drive to church in a Bentley. The Ewing family who owned the 'Buttercup' Dairies were generous givers to all evangelical causes. In 1940 Andrew Ewing gave a former hen hut to be the first building of the Granton Church, and for many years he gave all the eggs his hens laid on Sunday to his church for distribution among the poor.[15] Robert Aitken, the Sunday School Superintendent, Treasurer and Group Scoutmaster for many years, and Jack Cochrane, Junior Sunday School Leader, Secretary and Scoutmaster, were mainstays of the outfitters, Aitken and Niven. William Niven Aitken, Robert's younger brother, was superintendent of Charlotte Chapel's High Street Mission for several years in the 1940's, while working in business, and then became minister at Burra Isle and Glasgow's John Knox Street churches before moving to Jarrow on Tyne and then to Canada. The Rae family were well-known builders, and George Rae took over from Robert Aitken as Sunday School Superintendent in 1942. The Tullises were housepainters. The Murrays were bakers and the McGregors were fishmongers with their own businesses, and it is partly because of several generations of these business folk remaining in central positions in the Church that it has been such a large and stable fellowship.

---

[14] Elizabeth F Wright, *Proceedings of the Society of Antiquaries of Scotland*, 121 (1991), pp. 427-35, 'Thomas Hadden: Architectural Metalworker', where there are also illustrations of the firm's work.

[15] I.L.S. Balfour: *Revival in Rose Street* (Edinburgh: Rutherford House, 2007), p. 257.

In Dublin Street Church two families of Coal Merchants, the Sharps of Bruce Lindsay and the Paul family of Gavin Paul's Coal firm occupied opposite back corners of the old church for many years. Indeed the church connection with Bruce Lindsay Waldie and the Sharp family continued to the end of the century. The Woykas, immigrants from Hungary, conducted a merchant and haulage business for several generations in Glasgow and Gustav Woyka was a stalwart of John Street Church. J.M. Bryden of the New Prestwick Church was a generous supporter of Union causes and with his wife endowed the Bryden Fund.

### Architects

The greatest architectural achievement to bear the name Baptist, the Thomas Coats Memorial Church in Paisley was designed by Hippolyte Blanc, not a Baptist but a Scot despite his name, and was opened in 1894. William Thomas Oldrieve, a contemporary architect who was prominent in our churches, was not among the eminent practitioners who were invited to submit designs in the architectural competition held in 1885. His main work was in civic buildings. Oldrieve was baptised in Duncan Street Church in Edinburgh and served as an elder in Charlotte Chapel from 1884 until 1887. He went to work in London and returned to Edinburgh in 1904 when he joined Morningside Church, where he became an Elder. He served on the Committee of the National Bible Society of Scotland and was Chairman of Carrubbers Close Mission. In 1915-16 he was President of the Union, choosing as his subject for the presidential address 'The Church in Emergency.' In 1904 he was appointed Principal Architect to His Majesty's Board of Works and retired in 1914. He designed Post Offices and other municipal buildings, including the magnificent former GPO in Crown Street in Aberdeen.[16]

Andrew Black FRIBA was born in 1862 and died in 1927. He was a member of Stirling Street, Galashiels and John Knox Street, Glasgow, and designed several Baptist Churches in the early part of the Century. He was responsible for Bridgeton, (1905), Hamilton (1909), Bellshill (1910) Harper Memorial, Glasgow (1922), Cathcart, Glasgow, (1925), Mosspark, Glasgow (1925), and Partick, Glasgow, (1927) amongst other churches, including St Andrews, Colombo, Sri Lanka.[17]

He had a practice in Galashiels from 1891-1899, and then set up a partnership in Glasgow. He is described as a fine draughtsman, who has a place in history as an influential teacher of Charles Rennie Mackintosh. There seems to be no record of his activities in Baptist churches, but the fine buildings mentioned above are a continuing memorial to his skill.

---

[16] www.scottisharchitects.org.uk/index.php
[17] ibid.

George Cassells, who died suddenly and prematurely in 1960, was a member in Portobello and then Bristo Churches in Edinburgh, and designed the churches at Glenrothes, Glenburn, Paisley and Girvan and he devised schemes for the reconstruction of several other churches. Robert Rankin of the Renfrew and Ayr churches designed several of our more recent church buildings, and was responsible for the conversion of 12 Aytoun Road for the use of the College and the Union. He was member of a notable family in the Renfrew Church, and his brother, Dr Harry Rankin, was secretary for many years of the Larkhall Church.

## Journalists, Scholars and Authors

From the days of William McCombie of Crown Terrace, who founded and edited the *Aberdeen Free Press* in the mid-nineteenth century, there have been men in our churches who have found their career in journalistic writing. Hamish Coghill, secretary of the Church that used to meet at Dublin Street and now gathers in Canonmills, spent his whole working life with the *Edinburgh Evening News*. When he retired he was Deputy Editor, and he was able to give more time to his interests in the history of his native City. *Discovering the Water of Leith*, published in 1988, and *Lost Edinburgh- Edinburgh's Lost Architectural Heritage* published in 2003 are two of his best-known books. Brewis Anderson, also of Dublin Street, and a collateral descendant of Christopher Anderson, published a farming newspaper[18] for many years and seemed to know every farm and farmer in Scotland. George Hogg of the Granton Church was a Sports Journalist with the same paper, and Ian Swanson of Canonmills, son of Rev Jack Swanson, also works for the Evening News as religious and now as political correspondent. Probably the best known Baptist journalist in recent years is Graham Speirs of Hillhead Church, son of Rev T. Kerr Speirs. He has written on sports matters for several newspapers, including the London-based Broadsheets, and has often appeared on sports programmes on television.

There would be no writing without printers, and Alex Sturrock of Ward Road Dundee, who died in 1977, was Managing Director of G.E. Findlay and Co., Ltd, who produced a great deal of material for the Union and individual churches over several years. Material for the Simultaneous Evangelism enterprise, pamphlets on Baptism and Church Government, and the first 'Baptist Anthology of Verse' are some of the results of his Christian service. The Kirkcaldy firm of Allen Litho, owned for several generations by the Whyte's Causeway family of Allen printed the *Scottish Baptist Magazine* for several decades, and George Allen was senior Deacon of the Church in the 1960s and 1970s. He was also a president of the Rotary Clubs of Scotland at an earlier date.

---

[18] *The Baptist Who's Who* (London) n.d. [but probably 1934], p. 85.

## Scholars

Dr Duncan Heriot, (1896-1967) began work before the first war as a banker, and returned from active service to study English at Glasgow University. He taught at Hamilton Academy, and was awarded a Glasgow PhD for work on the sources of Bunyan's *Pilgrim's Progress*, some of which he traced to the writings of the Anabaptists. For further work on Anabaptism in England he was made a fellow of the Royal Historical Society. In 1937 he moved to Aberdeen for the rest of his teaching career. There he joined Crown Terrace Church and became Secretary, until in 1963-64 he was elected president of the union after he had survived a serious heart attack. He produced a small and valuable *Hospital Bedside Book*, arising from his experiences as he recovered. He was a strong supporter of the Baptist Men's Movement and a regular at their St Andrews Conference. His conducted tour of the city was an annual highlight of the Conferences for many years.

Donald Meek, Professor of Scottish and Celtic Studies in the University of Edinburgh, is the son of Hector Meek who was Baptist Home Missionary in Tiree and other Hebridean churches. He is known as one of Scotland's foremost Celtic scholars and has published widely on Highland matters and the Gaelic language. Many articles have appeared on Highland missions and missionaries. He has produced histories of the Tiree and Mull Baptist Churches, and he was chosen to give the Public Lecture, on the Gaelic hymns of Peter Grant of Grantown-on-Spey, at the first International Conference on Baptist Studies at Regent's Park College in Oxford in 1997. He has been a staunch supporter of Gaelic-speaking work in evangelism and history. He served for some time as an elder of Charlotte Chapel and edited the 'Record.'

David Bebbington, Professor of History at the University of Stirling, came to Scotland in 1976 with an established reputation as a scholar of the Nineteenth Century, especially of the life and work of W.E. Gladstone, and of nonconformity. He immediately identified himself with our Scottish denomination and helped to found and organise the Scottish Baptist History Forum, which has met twice a year since 1977. He edited the 1988 volume *The Baptists in Scotland* and he has encouraged Baptist historical scholarship and research in Scotland with gentle rigour ever since. In 1989 he published *Evangelicalism in Modern Britain* and his definition of Evangelicalism, with its four characteristics of conversionism, activism, biblicism, and crucicentrism, has become the template for much recent scholarship on the Evangelical Movement.

Other notable educators with strong Baptist connections have been David Sked, of Morningside and Viewfield, Dunfermline, who was head of the Classics Department at Moray House College of Education, and President of the Union in 1988-1989, and James Jardine of Hawick and Dublin Street, Head of Physics at Moray House and author of the popular textbook *Physics is Fun*. David Cook, also from Hawick and later a member at Abbeyhill, Edinburgh, as a philosopher achieved fame as a panellist on the BBC Programme 'The Moral Maze', and, before his departure to the USA was often to be heard giving a Christian insight into moral questions in various broadcasts. Deryck Lovegrove, also of Abbeyhill and later of St Andrews Church, taught Ecclesiastical History at St Andrews for many years and became well known for work on the Haldanes, and on Itinerancy. John Barclay, for many years in Morningside, Edinburgh, was President of the Union in 1994-1995 and has been Secretary of the Edinburgh Medical Missionary Society, Chairman of the BMS and an enthusiastic historian and supporter of the Baptist Men's Movement.

Bob Holman, a member of Easterhouse Church, came to that vast and needy area of Glasgow after leaving the post of Professor of Social Administration in the University of Bath, to engage as a Christian with many of the problems of the housing schemes, caused by poverty and sometimes by government policy. He has been variously described in the Press as a Christian Socialist and as 'the Good Man of Glasgow', and has been in a strong position to speak out against injustice. One fruit of his work has been his biography of F.B. Meyer.[19]

## Medical Men

Scottish Baptists entered the century with a medical man, Dr Robert Somerville of Galashiels, as President (1899-1900), and he is only one of the many doctors and surgeons who have contributed to our Union and churches. Dr Maxwell Williamson and Dr John Gray were Charlotte Chapel elders who were Medical Officers of Health for the City and kept Baptist people aware of the social implications of the gospel. Dr John Guy, also an elder of Charlotte Chapel from 1919 until 1932 was MOH for Edinburgh from 1930 until 1938.[20] Quite a different sort of medical man was John Cameron of Spean Bridge, a shepherd and 'friend of almost every form of Christian work at home and abroad,' who died in 1906. He was a preacher at cottage meetings and widely known as a bone-setter and as such had a marvellous record of successes.[21] Ramsay Small of Broughty Ferry, President of the Union (1972-73) was MOH in Dundee and a friend to all the local churches. J.N. Tennent, of Kirkintilloch and Adelaide Place churches became an eminent eye specialist. He was President of the Union when he was still a young man in 1935-36. In later years he was closely involved with the College and with inter-Church Relations, representing the Union at the Nottingham Faith and Order Conference in 1964. Staunch in his Baptist Principles, he was not always comfortable in ecumenical company. His wife came from the farming and teaching family of Garden, closely associated with the St Fergus and Peterhead churches.

---

[19] Bob Holman, *F.B. Meyer, If I had a Hundred Lives* (Fearn: Christian Focus, 2007).
[20] Balfour, *Revival in Rose Street*, p. 199.
[21] *SBYB 1907*, p. 57.

H.J. Fraser is mentioned among Lay Preachers. Charles Anderson, brought up in John Knox Street, a member at Hillhead for many years, and then pioneer Secretary at Drumchapel, Glasgow, made outstanding contributions to the Union both in his work in the churches, and as an adviser and confidant of many ministers, especially those suffering from the stresses of the work. He was a popular speaker at Student meetings and Conferences on subjects of faith and medicine, and was President of the Union in 1982-83. W.W.W. McNeish, MD, who died in 1970 was a founder member of the Royal College of General Practitioners and for many years a member of Viewfield, Dunfermline. Hugh Kennedy of Queen's Park, Glasgow, for many years a Missionary with the BMS, was President in 1992-93. Jack Leng, son of Rev John Leng, was a Missionary in what is now West Irian, and on returning to Scotland worked as a GP in Kirkintilloch, served the church as Secretary, and was a valued member of the Board of Ministry. These are only a few of the doctors who have served in our churches and in the wider community.

Sometimes career moves facilitated the founding of churches. Peter Blackwood, of Ayr, was appointed as Senior Surveyor to the New Town Development of East Kilbride in 1952. He was instrumental in the beginning of what has become East Mains Church there and was Secretary when Peter Barber came to be minister in 1955[22]. In God's Providence he moved to Livingston, another New Town, in time to help found the first Baptist Church there in 1968. His devoted service to these two new ventures must be one of the reasons for the growth of our churches in these communities.

Ian McRae from Charlotte Chapel pursued a career in Airport management, which took him to Kirkwall at a time when a number of families from the Westray Church had moved to Orkney Mainland, and he was one of those responsible for the founding of the Kirkwall Church in 1959.

John Dick, a Banker, of Queen's Park Church, was a lay preacher, Treasurer of the Union from 1933-1964, architect of many denominational projects and policies, and a notable open-air evangelist for many years on Sunday evenings at Queen's Park Gates.

Jack Carr from the Gorgie, Edinburgh and Stirling churches was a Tax Inspector who was Treasurer of the Union from 1967-70, and was involved with interesting bi-lateral talks between Roman Catholics and Baptists in the 1970s.

Lawyers are of course useful in our work, and the Union Law Agent has been an important advisor to the Office-Bearers. It was Andrew Urquhart, SSC, who was one of those who had faith that Charlotte Chapel could be revived at the beginning of the Century and his son W. Macduff Urquhart was Secretary of the Chapel in his turn. Later Ian Balfour succeeded to that office. Not only is he a solicitor and a former Senior Partner of a large Edinburgh Law firm, but he has gained the London external BD and also an Edinburgh PhD with a Thesis on

---

[22] E.W. Burrows: *'To Me to Live is Christ': A Biography of Peter H Barber* (Carlisle: Paternoster Press, 2005), pp. 32-36.

another lawyer of an earlier day, Tertullian. Through this work he has become a well-known patristic scholar, and recently he has published surely the Rolls Royce of local Church histories, *Revival in Rose Street*, (2007). He has been Law Agent of the Union, Treasurer and then Secretary of the College, and President of the Union in 1976-77, when his subject was 'The Peril of Taking a Lawyer's Advice'.

## Lay Pastors/Elders

It was the Scotch Baptist tradition to appoint elders who had other callings to the Pastorate of the churches. By the twentieth century this custom had almost died out as trained ministers were appointed and Scotch churches came into the mainstream of Baptist life. Sir Charles Barrie, a Dundee businessman, was a Pastor at Rattray Street Church in the late nineteenth century before 'the church changed its policy'[23] and continued a benefactor of the Church, buying the Manse and in 1916 giving the Church building to the members, amongst other acts of generosity.[24]

Academy Street the Scotch Church in Aberdeen, continued with lay pastors, until its dissolution in 1920, but it is suggested that the reason for this was lack of money to pay a minister.[25]

The last of the Lay Pastors was the formidable Percival Waugh of Bristo Church, Edinburgh, who served from 1903 until 1923 alongside stipendiary Pastors, and kept alive the tradition of this, the first of the Scotch Churches. He was born into a Church of Ireland family, and by the time he came to Edinburgh, where he rose to high position in the Scottish Office, he was a convinced Baptist. He was a devoted supporter of the Baptist Home Missionary Society of Scotland, with an intimate knowledge of its churches in the highlands and islands, and of their pastors. He collected Baptist literature and old Baptist Hymnals, contributed to and for a time edited the *Scottish Baptist Magazine*, and supplied much information to the 1926 *History of the Baptists in Scotland*. It was said that government ministers bowed before him in the Scottish Office, and certainly he was a formidable and tenacious debater. By 1928 he was an honorary member of the Home Mission Committee. Urging the seniority of the Mission to the Union and the interests of churches and missionaries in danger of being swallowed up in a larger body, he led the opposition to the amalgamation of the Union and the Mission, unsuccessfully moving the rejection of the Report of the Joint Committee which recommended the acceptance of a new scheme at

---

[23] G. Yuille (ed.), *History of the Baptists in Scotland* (Glasgow: Baptist Union of Scotland Publications Committee, 1926), p. 162.

[24] D.W. Bebbington (ed.), *The Baptists in Scotland, A History* (Glasgow: Baptist Union of Scotland, 1988), p. 244.

[25] A Gammie, *The Churches of Aberdeen* (Aberdeen: Aberdeen Daily Journal Office, 1909), p. 270.

the Assembly of 1929. Peter MacKenzie, another lawyer from Bristo Church, was Secretary of the Mission at this time, and urged a peaceful outcome to the dispute. After Counsel's opinion had been taken the amalgamation took place by deed of incorporation in 1931. At that same 1929 Assembly he asked if the advisability of uniting the College and the Union and the bringing the *Scottish Baptist Magazine* under denominational control had been taken into consideration.[26] He died in 1934, before the vexed question of Union-College relationships could be raised as it was in the 1940s.

## The Scottish Baptist Lay-Preachers' Association

While the Association has had and has now distinguished women on its list, the preponderance of members over the last eighty-three years have been men. Some of them are mentioned because of their other activities, but it seems fitting to honour our Lay Preachers in a special section.

The Association was formed on 12 May 1925 with Rev R.F. Conway as Convenor and G.S. Kirby as Secretary, with the object of preparing a list of names of lay preachers to be submitted to the Union. Any preacher who had served the Scottish Baptist churches with acceptance for at least two years could be considered eligible given the further recommendation of the committee.[27] The Association was formally constituted on 19 October 1927 and in 1928 Alexander McKinlay of the Morningside Church was appointed Treasurer and Supply Secretary. During the first year preachers, hitherto accepted without examination, were offered various training courses. By 1927 there were forty-nine recognised preachers on the list and several in training, including one lady. The Association has always been closely connected to the Union and to the Lay Preachers Federation in the South, later the Federation of Lay Ministries.

Unlike the Methodists, Baptists have not expected their future ministers to cut their teeth as local preachers. Nevertheless a number of our Lay Preachers have proceeded to ministry, sometimes serving as Lay Pastors before ordination. John McKendrick of Hamilton completed the normal three-year course of study in two years, and later went as Lay Pastor to Lochgelly before becoming the honoured and much loved Pastor of South Leith and Ayr. Archibald MacNicol went to Bowmore initially as Lay Pastor, and then as pastor, going on to other churches in the North and to Girvan. Among well-known men on the first list were Tom Curr, John Dick, Dr Harold Fraser, James Paterson, driver of the Royal Train, and Charles Welch.

Thomas Ramsay, a shoe manufacturer in Maybole, nurtured a church there from its foundation in 1900, and became pastor-emeritus in 1919 when a full-time pastor was appointed. He died in 1934. Several small churches such as Ratho and Millport were served by Lay Preachers until they ceased to meet, just

---

[26] *SBYB 1930*, p. 115.
[27] http://sblpa.co.uk/history.html

before the Second World War. There have been faithful Lay Pastorates at Dalkeith and Selkirk, conducted by Tom Nisbet of Abbeyhill Church, at Peebles, by Jack Speirs of the Portobello Church, by Hamish McRae of Charlotte Chapel who served in Bo'ness and much more recently in Newburgh, and others. There have also been several Lay Pastors who had no direct connection with the Association such as Walter Maxwell of Clydebank and A.M Ferguson of Cleland. Neil Macdonald of Tiree who died in 1957 gave many years' service as a Lay Assistant to the Missionary there. He was a poet as well as a preacher, and some of his Gaelic hymns were published. He was also an island Councillor.

In later years Dalkeith and the long running attempt to begin a cause at Moredun, Edinburgh, were also taken under the wing of the Association, and there was considerable involvement with the new churches at Broxburn and Bathgate. At times, as in the 1980s, a place on the accredited list of Pastors has been given to some Lay Pastors.

Until 1978 there was a Lay Preachers Committee answerable to the Union Council. In that year the Union was restructured and the Association became a Core Group within the department of Church Life. At the next rearrangement the Association became autonomous, and nominally independent of the Union. Over the years different training schemes have been in use, with an increasing emphasis on courses drawn up and tested in Scotland.

Several notable men have served the Association as Office Bearers, some of whom will be referred to elsewhere. Charles Welch, MBE, (1895-1987) a Senior Civil Servant and brother-in-law of Tom Curr, joined the Association at the beginning, and with the exception of some years spent in London, served as supply Secretary for the West of Scotland, until he retired to Grantown-on-Spey in 1967, where he continued to serve the local church and others in the North in many capacities until his death.

Dr H.J. Fraser, who attended Bristo and Granton churches in Edinburgh, was a Medical Officer of Health for Midlothian. He joined the Association in 1929 and succeeded as Convenor from 1946 until 1957. He became Lay Pastor at Broxburn in 1954 and died in 1964. He was President of the Union from 1951-52.

W.A Hunter, Secretary of the Cowdenbeath Church, succeeded Dr Fraser as Convenor in 1957, and served until he was killed in a road accident in 1973. He was succeeded as Convenor by J.M. Grant M.A., of Glenburn Paisley, one of the six founding elders of that church, and Headmaster of Stanely Park Approved (List D) School, for many years. He had already been Secretary and Treasurer for a number of years. John Grant was a man who thoroughly knew his Bible, and, being a mathematician by training, had a sharp and precise mind, and also a good sense of humour. He helped more than one inexperienced minister to grow in understanding and experience.

His namesake, John Grant of Morningside, who died in 1982 at the age of 90, was an equally devoted preacher and church worker. He was in charge of the Sunday School at Morningside for many years and was reputed to remember every child who had passed through it. He was a carpenter by trade, coming from an honoured Baptist family, including among his ancestors Peter Grant of Grantown, the Gaelic hymnwriter. He moved into teaching of Technical Subjects for many years, and was mentioned in the Guinness Book of Records as the longest serving teacher in the UK. He retired from teaching in Darroch School in 1953 and then continued there part time for many years, and taught sight and hearing impaired children until 1973. In his last days he brought a special spiritual flavour to the community of the Tor, now the Tor Christian Nursing Home, Edinburgh, where he ended his days.

John Lockie, who was converted during the Revival in Charlotte Chapel at the beginning of the century, became an industrial chemist in Coats Mills in Paisley and was a member of Victoria Place Church for many years before becoming another of the founding elders of Glenburn. Beyond Baptist circles he is still honoured as the expert on Scottish Communion Tokens and Beggar's Badges, which he collected and annotated over many years. Most of his collection of tokens is now in the Royal Museum of Scotland in Chambers Street, Edinburgh, and with a colleague he published the definitive lists and descriptions of Tokens in the Proceedings of the Society of Antiquaries of Scotland.[28]

Michael Campbell, of the Stenhouse Church, was a Lay Preacher for many years, and was particularly interested in work in Saughton Prison, for which he was awarded the B.E.M. Philip Staley, M.A. a member of Pitlochry and Morningside churches, and latterly of Charlotte Chapel, was the son of a Church of England clergyman, who trained in Classics and worked for many years as a master in a Boarding School. He brought to his work as Secretary of the Association, 1974-1992, a careful mind and a great grasp of detail, besides a deep faith and much patience.[29] He also served a Secretary of the Edinburgh and Lothians Baptist Association in the 1980s.

Addresses given to the Association, usually by ministers, betray a certain ambivalence about the distinction between lay and ordained ministry amongst Scottish Baptists. Sometimes Lay Preachers have felt undervalued and underused in our churches, and indeed many of the preaching engagements listed each year have been in churches of other denominations and in Mission Halls. Sometimes it seems as if ministers are condescending to their lay brethren, whose training might seem to be belittled, in comparison with training for full-time work. Rev James Taylor's Presidential Address in 1971 entitled:

---

[28] PSAS 75, 1941, pp. 144-183, *Unpublished Tokens of the Church of Scotland, 17th and 18th centuries*; PSAS 77, 1943, pp. 48-147, *Tokens of the Church of Scotland, 19th and 20th centuries*; PSAS 79, 1945, pp. 26-81, *Tokens of the Free Kirk.*

[29] This section owes much to his paper: *The Scottish Baptist Lay Preachers' Association - A Historical Review*, which was published in 1993, with the approval of the Scottish Baptist History Project.

'The Ministry or the Abolition of the Laity' seeks to empower all Christians as ministers with a variety of gifts and to rediscover the New Testament concept of baptism as ordination. The church cannot leave everything to the 'ordained' ministry. While lay preaching is not mentioned, Philip Staley claims that the Address 'matched our thinking.' He also remarked that the idea that 'the mildly disparaging title "Lay"' might be removed, met with little response in the Association.[30]

Lay preachers continue to play an important part in the work of the Union and at the end of the century there were thirty-eight on the Active Roll, and seven on the Honorary Roll. They represent many occupations and many of our churches, and when those who preach but are not members of the Association are included, the Union is served by a remarkably diverse body of men and women, without whom several of our smaller churches would not be able to function, and through whom all our fellowships are blessed.

## Lay Evangelists

Many City Missions and independent mission Halls have been served by members of our churches, as preachers and leaders. Some years ago there were several Missions in Edinburgh and Leith whose leaders worshipped in Baptist Churches on Sunday mornings, and led evangelistic meetings on Saturday and Sunday evenings. The Merchiston Railway Mission, now the Merchiston Mission, was the special interest of the Cormack family of Duncan Street Church, and another notable family of Cormacks, members of Charlotte Chapel, sustained evangelistic activity over several generations. Donald Cormack (1), a former soldier, preached at the foot of the Mound in the early years of the century, and his son Donald[31] (2) worked for several spells with the Open-Air Mission, at street corners and race-courses throughout the land. His son Donald (3) was an Evangelist with the Heralds, the musical group founded in 1964. Both Donald Cormack and Ian Leitch achieved a national reputation as preachers and musicians, and Ian Leitch (who trained at Moody Bible Institute, Chicago) continues a world-wide ministry.

---

[30] Staley, *Historical Review*, p.9.
[31] Donald (2)'s brother John achieved unenviable fame as a Protestant agitator in the 1930's and after, before achieving respectability and becoming a senior member of the Edinburgh Town Council after World War Two. He seems to have no church affiliation in his years of notoriety. He had been associated with Alexander Ratcliffe, in 1915 secretary of Leith Baptist Church, who relocated to Glasgow and led a highly inflammatory anti-Catholic political movement for a few years in the 1930s. see Steve Bruce, T. Glendinning, Iain Paterson, Michael Rosie, *Sectarianism in Scotland* (Edinburgh: Edinburgh University Press, 2004), pp. 46-56. There is an entry for Cormack in the ODNB.

The Scottish Baptist Men's Movement was a local expression of the Laymen's Missionary Movement, later the Baptist Men's Movement in the South, which began in 1917. The first exploratory Conference in Scotland was held at Cove in 1947, and soon the annual Conference moved to St Andrews. Joseph T. Lockhart, a member of a family long associated with many aspects of Baptist work, was its secretary and guide until his death in 1964. For several years the Sunday morning service of the Annual Conference was broadcast by the BBC, and the Movement continues, with rather less local meetings than formerly but with still a well-attended Conference in St Andrews. The missionary enthusiasm of the Movement bought a Furlough House in Glasgow and provided the Scottish BMS representative with a car in the 1960s and has continued to this day, providing books and other support for missionaries and promoting interest in the worldwide mission of the Church. There are also fruitful contacts with Continental Baptists, and through its Book Project the Movement has been able to give valuable service to Baptist bodies in Europe and through the BMS to Christians in many other parts of the world and also to students of the Scottish Baptist College.

The Baptist Theological College of Scotland as it was until 1981, when it became the Scottish Baptist College, has been served by a succession of laymen from a variety of churches. Sir Adam Nimmo[32] was Secretary from 1894 until shortly before his death in 1939, and until 1912 he was assisted by Charles Bowser of Adelaide Place. Sir Adam was succeeded by T.K. Ward of Hillhead Church who guided the College through the difficult years of the 1940s, when war, shortages and theological and personal controversies troubled the College. Other secretaries have been Andrew Ralston of Denniston and Hillhead, and Ian Balfour of Charlotte Chapel, both lawyers. Raibeart Gillies of Adelaide Place, lawyer and banker, served from 1952 until 1978 as Treasurer, and he was succeeded first by Ian Balfour until 1983 and then by William Storm of Victoria Place, Paisley from 1983 into the new century.[33]

David Coats, CBE, DSc, a distinguished Civil Engineer returned from England to rejoin Queen's Park Church in Glasgow in the early 1960s and soon followed in the footsteps of his father and grandfather, both Principals of the College, in becoming involved in Union and College activities. D.S.K. McLeay, Secretary of the John Knox Street Church in Glasgow, and of the Band of Hope Union, was President of the Union in 1959-60. Theologically he moved from being one of the sponsors of the Evangelical Baptist College in the 1950s to being a strong supporter of the Baptist Theological College, as it was then, even encouraging some contact with the Student Christian Movement.

The roll of Committee members of the College contains the names of many prominent Scottish Baptists, and shows remarkable continuity over the years. In

---

[32] See the information on Sir Adam Nimmo on p. 6.
[33] D.B. Murray, *Scottish Baptist College Centenary History*, 1894-1994 (Glasgow: Scottish Baptist College, 1994), pp. 55-57.

a comparatively small Institution there has been a need for those who could give time and expertise to the work of training ministers, and occasionally lay preachers and others. Many more of our people have befriended and assisted students for the ministry by their generosity and their hospitality. Students of the College through many generations have been grateful for a warm meal and a bed for the night in some of the remoter parts of our Baptist family.

## Baptists in the World of the Arts

Archibald McLean, who was the leader of the Scotch Baptists in the eighteenth century, complained of the worldliness of the Glasites, from whom he drew much of his ecclesiology. He accused them of going to Balls and even to the Theatre when even respectable Presbyterians were very unfriendly to the Stage. Scotch Baptists certainly did not indulge in such frivolities, and this attitude has in some ways persisted. Joseph Kemp, minister of Charlotte Chapel at the revival, was firmly against 'worldliness' in any form, and in some of our churches even uniformed organisations were excluded, not only because they were apparently militaristic, but also because they were of 'the world' and would lead Christian young people into too close contact with unbelievers. Fortunately for many of us, Graham Scroggie had, in Charlotte Chapel, in the 1920s, encouraged not only Scouts and Guides but also a cricket club.

With this separatist teaching and practice a prominent part of our ethos, it is not surprising that there have been few Scottish Baptists in the Arts World. Music, since it is part of worship and outreach, is possibly an exception. Choirs and soloists have abounded over the century, and Baptist men have been the mainstays of many of the Male Voice Choirs which have flourished in several parts of our country. The Men of Orkney, brought together by Rev Bryden Maben when he was minister in Westray were much enjoyed, as about the same time was the Border Male Voice Quartet. In the 1960s two Whyte's Causeway, Kirkcaldy men, Bob Storrar, and Morris McMahon at the organ or piano, led a very successful Fife Baptist Young People's Choir, and several men were prominent in the Scottish Baptist Youth Choir. It would be invidious to list the men who have been Organists, Choirmasters and Praise leaders in our individual churches, but men have played a large part in fostering the musical tradition of our churches in changing times.

There have been poets amongst us. Books of verse by Baptist poets were published in the 1980s by the union, and Alexander Halden of Pitlochry is one man whose poetry has been commercially published. Stuart MacGregor was brought up in Charlotte Chapel in the mid-century, and in his teens became an effective open-air preacher, often at the Foot of the Mound. He studied medicine in Edinburgh and gradually was drawn into the folk-singing scene of the time. After qualifying he moved out of church circles, but became more widely known as a poet, songwriter and novelist. His Edinburgh Medical Novel, *The Myrtle and Ivy*, was published in 1967, and his *Poems and Songs*, posthumously, in 1974. He was killed in a road accident in Jamaica in 1973, and his memory lives in Scottish folk-singing circles.[34]

Eric Lomax, whose autobiography, *The Railway Man,* was published in 1995, was drawn into Charlotte Chapel through a common interest in train spotting with a man called Jack Ewart, (whom the writer remembers as rather frightening), who kept a boarding house for young single men. Eric Lomax gives a somewhat jaundiced but nevertheless revealing account of the Chapel, and therefore of some smaller Baptist churches of those days, all hell-fire preaching and petty squabbles, yet with a real welcome for a lonely young man. His book goes on to tell of his horrific experiences as a prisoner in a Japanese prisoner of war camp, his eventual return to good people who simply could not understand how war had changed him, and his gradual disillusionment with the church.[35]

George Bruce, the eminent Scottish Poet, whose collected poems[36] were published in 2001, and whose grandfather was one of the builders of Fraserburgh Baptist Church, attended Canonmills Church in his latter years, and hinted that he was really a Baptist at heart.

He was a friend of Tom Fleming CVO, OBE, a lifelong member of Dublin Street, now Canonmills Church, where his father, Peter Fleming was minister from 1922 until his death in 1939. Tom Fleming is one of the best known of Scottish actors, and perhaps even more widely known as a BBC commentator on state occasions such as royal weddings and the annual ceremony at the Cenotaph. His voice is familiar as the commentator on the Tattoo at the Edinburgh International Festival, and from many stage and Television plays. In 1956 he portrayed Jesus in a BBC Children's Television production of Jesus of Nazareth, filmed in Palestine, and noteworthy as the first time an actor had played the part of Jesus on British Television. Not surprisingly this event raised protest. In the 1940s Dorothy Sayers' *The Man Born to be King* had been broadcast on radio, and this had seemed blasphemous enough to many Christians. Now an actor was portraying Jesus on the screen! A contemporary article in the Radio Times says that 'the series made a tremendous impact on the viewing public and perhaps not least on the actor himself, for this, more than

---

[34] See John Beech, Owen Hand, Fiona MacDonald, Mark A. Mulhearn & Jeremy Weston (eds), *Scottish Life and Society, A Compendium of Scottish Ethnology,* Volume 10, *Oral Literature and Performance Culture,* (Edinburgh: John Donald, 2007) p. 386. Although Stuart MacGregor had apparently discarded his faith by the time he qualified as a doctor, it is intriguing that Charlotte Chapel creeps into his novel as 'City Baptist Chapel' full when summer church attendances elsewhere were low. S. MacGregor, *The Myrtle and Ivy* (Edinburgh: Macdonald, 1967), p. 42.

[35] Eric Lomax: *The Railway Ma,* (London: Vintage, 1995), pp. 35-36, 208-15. And Balfour: *Revival in Rose Stree*t, pp. 246-47.

[36] Lucina Prestige (ed.), *Today Tomorrow* (Edinburgh: Polygon, 2001).

anything that had gone before, was the crystallisation of his ideas about the relationship between his work as an actor and writer and his faith.'[37]

In the fifty or so years that have followed, Tom Fleming has faithfully served his church, the Baptist Men's Movement, and the public who have been moved by his portrayals of, among many others, Lord Reith, Hugh McDiarmaid, and George McLeod. He has been a key person in the life of the Canonmills Church, not least as its organist. During his time at the Gateway Theatre in Edinburgh he published a Nativity Play, *Miracle at Midnight,* and a little volume of poems, *So That Was Spring*. He has made a notable contribution to Scottish culture and remains a faithful member of one of our churches.

Other Baptist men have been involved in broadcasting at various levels. Brian Muir, of Hillhead Church, has had a long commitment to the Gospel Radio Fellowship, and several laymen have contributed to local and Hospital radio programmes both in the United Kingdom and through Gospel radio stations overseas.

As befits the heirs of Archibald Mclean and James Haldane, Scottish Baptists have stood in different relationships to wider society. Some of the men who have been mentioned have kept themselves aloof form wider society, holding that Christians should keep themselves unspotted from the world, and spent their live in Church related activities, while others have joined Political Parties, Trades Unions, Golf Clubs, and have mixed freely in local and national society. All those and those in between have enriched the life of our churches, the wider church and the nation.

And time would fail me to tell of the others who consoled the bereaved, built church halls, preached in mission halls, taught our children, drove trains, climbed mountains, played organs, edited church magazines, visited the sick, worked hard at their trades, were good husbands and fathers, lived in solitude, played golf, gave to all good causes and were and are examples of faith ...[38]

---

[37] *Radio Times*, 7 September 1956.
[38] Hebrews 11 vs 32ff adapted.

## CHAPTER 3

# *Her Children Arise and Call her Blessed*:
# The Place of Women in Scottish Baptist life

## Christine Lumsden

### Introduction

The twentieth century opened with the death of Queen Victoria on 22 January 1901, having acceded to the throne, a month after her eighteenth birthday, on 20 June 1837, on the death of her uncle, William IV. Thus her long reign of over sixty years came to an end. The Victorian age had witnessed the development of an ideology of 'separate spheres' with regard to appropriate behaviour for men and women, particularly for the middle classes. The male role was to work to provide for the family, while the female was to look after the home and comfort of all those in it. As well as fulfilling the roles of dutiful wife and caring mother, the responsibilities of the lady also extended to setting a moral example to her servants and to the poor families she might visit, so transmitting to them the Victorian values of respectability, serious character, and self-help.

Towards the end of the nineteenth century, this ideal was challenged as women gradually were admitted to the professions, such as medicine, and to the universities for higher education. Initial moves were made towards granting the universal franchise, since those women who met the property qualification in their own right could vote in local elections. From 1872, when school boards were established in Scotland to oversee the new education system, women could stand for election to these boards as well as vote for their members. A new age was indeed beginning. As this chapter will show, however, Scottish Baptists were slow to grant their women members full equality with men in the work of the church.

Where women played a central role, on the other hand, was as trainers of the young, whether children or servants, and as visitors to those less fortunate than themselves. Such philanthropy, at least in the earlier years of the twentieth century, provided an outlet for the energies of middle-class ladies, where paid employment was actively discouraged, as it implied that their husband or other male relative could not provide for them. Many less fortunate women, of course, had no choice but to work, often in unskilled, poorly-paid, menial employment. Such work was undertaken, for example, by single women or widows and those whose husbands' wages were insufficient to support the family. As the century progressed, improved female employment opportunities, especially since the 1950s, had an impact on church life as younger women were no longer available during the day to participate in activities like missionary support groups or women's prayer and fellowship meetings. These daytime meetings became more and more the preserve of the elderly until, in many cases, falling attendances meant that they were no longer viable.

With that background we will examine the contribution of a few Scottish Baptist women to church life at various stages throughout the twentieth century and consider how this impacted on the debates regarding women in ministry. Our first is a family who bridge the nineteenth to the twentieth century.

## A Dynasty's Daughters

Perhaps the most significant contribution to Scottish Baptist history continuously since the eighteenth century has been made by the Coats family of Paisley. They were descended from handloom weavers, one of whom, James, in 1827 founded the Ferguslie Mills, an early Scottish industrial enterprise, which, through his sons, became the famous firm of J. and P. Coats, thread manufacturers. The youngest son is remembered by the magnificent church, replacing the Storie Street building, opened in 1894 'erected through the munificent generosity of the family of the late Thomas Coats to his memory'.[1] This spirit of generous service to the Baptist cause is evident throughout the family's history, producing four Presidents of the Baptist Union of Scotland, both laymen and ministers, and two Principals of the Scottish Baptist College.[2] This section examines the contribution of three Coats ladies to twentieth century Scottish Baptist life, Mrs Joseph Coats and her daughters, Olive Mary and Victoria.

Their husband and father was Professor Joseph Coats, the youngest son of William Holms Coats, a grocer in Paisley and a cousin of the thread manufacturers. Joseph qualified as a doctor in 1867 at the age of twenty-one, becoming assistant to the pioneering Joseph Lister, Professor of Surgery at Glasgow Royal Infirmary.[3] Joseph Coats was appointed lecturer in pathology in 1870, and, in 1894, when Glasgow University founded the Chair of Pathology, became its first Professor.[4] He was a member of the newly built Adelaide Place

---

[1] George Yuille (ed.), *History of the Baptists in Scotland* (Glasgow: Baptist Union Publications Committee, 1926), p. 201.

[2] Information from the family tree published in Derek B. Murray, *Scottish Baptist College Centenary History 1894-1994* (Glasgow: Scottish Baptist College, 1994), p. 78.

[3] Olive Mary and Victoria Coats, *Dr and Mrs Joseph Coats: A Book of Remembrance compiled by their daughters* (Glasgow: Jackson, Wylie & Co., 1929), pp. 6 and 12. My thanks to Dr. David Coats for lending me this book.

[4] ibid. p.35.

Baptist Church, to which the former Hope Street congregation had moved, as the site of that building had been sold to the Caledonian Railway Company in 1874 for development, now part of Central Station.

Among the members of Adelaide Place was the Taylor family of four sisters and a brother. The second sister, Georgiana, caught Joseph's attention from his seat in the gallery looking down to the Taylor family pew, the fifth from the front. Their father, John Taylor, had been a prosperous Glasgow merchant but had died, aged seventy-two, when Georgiana was around thirteen years old, her mother, his much younger second wife, having predeceased him. Georgiana therefore became responsible for the family after the marriage of her elder sister, Sophia, to William Tulloch, another member of Adelaide Place.[5] Like the Coats family, the Taylors had a long Baptist heritage. Mr Taylor having been a member of John Street, founded as a Scotch Baptist Church in 1769 and thus the oldest Baptist church in Glasgow.[6] There is also a record that John Taylor's father, a Paisley weaver, was one of the co-pastors of the Scotch Baptist Storie Street Church, founded in 1795.[7]

Georgiana, born in 1852, had been educated at boarding schools and had spent time travelling abroad so had had a less sheltered upbringing than was usual for her class and time. In 1873 she accompanied overseas her younger sister, Victoria, suffering from tuberculosis, in an attempt to improve her health. Victoria's death in Malta that year at the age of nineteen gave Georgiana an even stronger awareness of her responsibilities towards her remaining sisters. In 1879 she finally agreed to marry Joseph Coats on condition that her two remaining younger sisters came to live with them. The wedding took place in December that year. In 1882 their elder daughter was born. She was named Olive Mary, after Joseph's sister, Mary, and after his brother-in-law, the Rev. Oliver Flett, Minister of Storie Street, Paisley from 1860 until 1894.[8] Their second daughter, born in 1885, was named Victoria Taylor in memory of Georgiana's sister. Such interlocking relationships among Scottish Baptist families were common in the nineteenth century.

Mrs Joseph Coats, as she was known after her marriage, in some respects is a transitional figure. She fulfilled the role of supportive wife in all her husband's activities, both professionally and in church, concentrating on home and family and remaining somewhat in the background. Yet, in accordance with their religious principles, there was a degree of equality in their relationship which was ahead of its time.

---

[5] ibid p.31.
[6] Yuille, *Baptists in Scotland*, p. 178. (John Street Church closed in 1969.)
[7] George H. Coats, *Rambling Recollections* (printed privately, 1920), p.74. (My thanks to Dr David Coats for this reference.) John Taylor is not listed among the Storie Street /Coats Memorial pastors in Yuille, *Baptists in Scotland*, pp. 201 and 287.
[8] Yuille, *Baptists in Scotland*, p. 287.

For some years the family lived at 31 Lynedoch Street, in the Claremont estate of mainly terraced houses built in the mid-nineteenth century to attract wealthier families from the crowded city centre. Several medical professors lived in the area, as well as merchants, lawyers, and other professional families.[9] Nevertheless, an important consideration in the Coats household, despite the move from the centre of Glasgow, Adelaide Place and the infirmary were within easy reach. In 1895 the family relocated to a new house at 8 University Gardens to be nearer Professor Coats' work, as by this time his health was failing.

Olive Mary and Victoria give us a glimpse of their childhood, with its privileged background. Victoria (Vicky) became ill with rheumatic fever at the age of nine so was never very strong. Thereafter she was taught at home by a governess. As might be expected, religious observances were an important part of family life. Every morning after breakfast there was family worship at which the Bible was read aloud and prayers said. The family attended the morning service where the children sometimes sat in the side pews to observe the weekly Communion service when Dr. Coats, as a deacon, led the prayers. They remembered the 'solemn, awed tones of his quiet voice in the opening words of his prayer, "Almighty God".'[10] Dr. and Mrs. Coats attended the afternoon service while the Sabbath ended with hymn singing round the piano, since there was no evening service then. The girls did not go to Sunday School but were taught the psalms and paraphrases by their mother.

By the spring of 1897 Joseph Coats had become seriously ill and was ordered to take a long sea voyage, then regarded as a possible cure for all manner of illnesses. In October that year, Professor and Mrs. Coats sailed for Australia and New Zealand, leaving their daughters in the care of their former 'mother's help' and family friend, Alison Waddell.[11] On returning to Glasgow some months later, Professor Coats resumed work but in November 1898 become seriously ill again. He died on 24 January 1899 at the comparatively early age of fifty-two. After this shock, Georgiana, never one to observe the protracted conventions of Victorian mourning, took her daughters abroad for a year or two, visiting Paris, Weimar, Italy and Switzerland. In this way their education was completed.

During her widowhood Mrs. Coats involved herself in Baptist causes, especially the work of the Baptist Theological College which her husband and Oliver Flett had promoted. Joseph Coats was appointed its first president in 1894 and his brother, Jervis, the first principal. Indeed, discussions about its foundation had taken place around the Coats' dining room table, which Mrs.

---

[9] Eleanor Gordon and Gwyneth Nair, *Public Lives: Women, Family and Society in Victorian Britain* (New Haven & London: Yale University Press, 2003), Appendix 1, pp. 237-40.

[10] O.M. and V. Coats, *Book of Remembrance*, p. 140.

[11] ibid, p. 37.

Coats gifted to the college in 1925.[12] Women were eligible to serve on the college committee from the beginning and among the first was Mrs. Coats.[13] Her lasting legacy to the College was the Book Fund, subscriptions to which provided a sum of money for each leaving student to begin his personal library. The collection and distribution of this money was a task Georgiana Coats fulfilled for many years to be succeeded by her daughter, Olive Mary, who administered the Fund for forty years.[14] Mrs. Hazel Coats, wife of Dr. David Coats, then took over until 1988 when responsibility transferred to the Baptist Union administrative staff.

The outbreak of war in August 1914 brought an opportunity for wider service. Almost immediately Mrs. Coats was appointed to represent Glasgow Baptists on the local executive of the Red Cross, the main work of which became the provision of 'comforts' for the troops. Her organisational skills were evident in the way she mobilised Scottish Baptist women to provide money and materials to make up these parcels. Mrs. Coats was also active in the wartime temperance crusade.

Years ahead of her time, Georgiana Coats also favoured the ordination of women. During a protracted visit to London in 1919 she listened to the Anglican Maude Royden preach in the City Temple, followed by a debate between Miss Royden and a clergyman on the 'rights of women to take holy orders'. Georgiana's vote was 'with Miss Royden.'[15] The first woman to be listed as a probationer minister by the Baptist Union of Great Britain was Miss Edith Gates in 1922. She had been appointed to Little Tew and Cleveley Baptist Church, Oxfordshire in 1918 'when normal procedures in the churches had been affected by the war'.[16] As will be seen below, Scottish Baptist women had to wait for many years before they were accepted for ordination on the same basis as men.

Mrs. Coats died while on holiday in Pitlochry on Sunday 19 June 1927, as quietly as she had lived. True to her upbringing as a wealthy Victorian lady, she saw her role as homemaker and support to her husband and example of Christian service for her daughters. Yet in other ways Georgiana Coats looked forward, as evidenced by the support she gave to women's work in the church. Her character is summed up in the anonymous obituary published in the *Scottish Baptist Yearbook* for 1928.

---

[12] ibid, p. 39.
[13] Murray, p. 58.
[14] Obituary 'Miss Olive Mary Coats' in *Scottish Baptist Year Book 1976* (*SBYB*), pp. 151-52 (p.152)
[15] Ibid, p.191
[16] Ian M Randall, *The English Baptists of the Twentieth Century* (Didcot: Baptist Historical Society, 2005), p. 71.

Hers was a radiant personality, an eager mind, a warm heart – and her faith in our Lord and Saviour and in His Church was at once a rebuke and an inspiration.[17]

It is in the lives of her daughters, however, that her influence is perhaps most apparent.

Professor and Mrs. Coats did not press their daughters to join the church but left them to make up their minds when they were old enough to appreciate the responsibilities that came with such a step in a Baptist church with its congregational form of government. Olive Mary was baptised and received into membership of Adelaide Place on 23 September 1900 and was to remain there for her long life. Among the duties she undertook in the church was the editorship of its magazine.

In 1933, after considerable discussion among deacons and members, it was agreed that any church member, male or female, could be nominated to serve as a deacon. Among the four lady deacons elected that year was Miss Coats. She served in that capacity until 1973 and was made a life member of the diaconate. However, under the rules covering membership of the Adelaide Place Deacons' Court, service was for a period of four years, after which s/he had to stand down and could not seek re-election until at least two years had passed. There would have been breaks, therefore, in Olive Mary's service as a deacon.[18] As a child she had stood beside her father when he was on duty at the church door and pretended to be 'a kind of deacon too'.[19] His example must have provided her with good training for the future.

Miss Coats' wider interests are revealed in her obituary. She was honoured among Scottish Baptists through life membership of the Baptist Union and its committees, to which she was elected on 23 October 1973, and also of the Baptist Theological College, fittingly given the role her family played in the College history. The Women's Auxiliary, too, elected her a life member. From 1915 Olive Mary had served the Auxiliary as assistant to the secretary, Miss Isabella Watson, and succeeded to this office in October 1919. She resigned in 1925 on health grounds but was elected national president in 1934. She was a steadfast supporter of the Baptist Missionary Society, perhaps recollecting her mother's open house for its missionaries when they visited Glasgow. She also introduced the Women's World Day of Prayer to Glasgow.

Olive Mary Coats died on 9 October 1975, aged 93, so achieving almost a century's association with Adelaide Place Baptist Church, a record which can rarely be equalled. Her unknown obituarist records her character as follows:

---

[17] Obituary 'Mrs. Coats' in *SBYB 1928*, p. 134.
[18] Personal information from Mrs. Frances Addis, archivist, Adelaide Place Baptist Church.
[19] O.M and V. Coats, *Book of Remembrance*, p. 139.

She was a Christian lady with the broadest sympathies with whom one never felt any generation gap but always a spontaneous and understanding fellowship. Richly endowed in the qualities of heart and mind it was at once a privilege and an inspiration to know her. Well read, widely travelled, kindly and very deeply spiritual, with an active enquiring mind and a puckish sense of humour she was indeed a lady of many gifts which were recognised and honoured not only in her own loved church but also in the wider sphere of Denominational life....Her work for her church and the Kingdom of Christ is incalculable. There is no doubt whatsoever that Jesus Christ was the central loyalty of her life...let us give thanks to God for a life so dedicated as hers.[20]

Victoria, too, joined Adelaide Place following her baptism in 1902 and 'was among its most loyal members'.[21] Both girls had attended classes at Glasgow University, particularly English literature 'under the inspiring teaching of Professor Walter Raleigh'.[22] These classes developed Victoria's writing gifts and she published privately a collection of poems, *Today and Yesterday*, which she dedicated to her father, 'a memory and a presence' and 'the one who gave the writer her first encouragement'. The poems show the influence of her governess who was 'a fan of Matthew Arnold' while Vicky herself preferred Christina Rossetti.[23]

Although the book is undated, many of the poems were written during the First World War. An example is 'Snow in Weimar', contrasting present enmity with past friendship.

> 'There's snow in Flanders,' papers said
> The other day. And is there snow,
> I wonder, falling soft and slow,
> In Weimar, while the sunset red
> Gilds and adorns the quaint old street,
> The gray Stadt Kirche, standing there,
> And Herder's statue, smiling fair,
> On Markt Platz, where his people meet
> After the service? Friend meets friend,
> Greetings are quickly given, for, see,
> The wind blows colder, anxiously
> Each wonders when the War will end.[24]

---

[20] Obituary 'Miss Olive Mary Coats', p. 152.
[21] Obituary 'Miss Victoria Taylor Coats' in *SBYB* 1941, p. 160.
[22] Letter from Olive Mary Coats to R.E.O. White, Principal of the Scottish Baptist College, 26 September 1972. The letter accompanied the gift of Vicky's poems to the College library. (My thanks to Dr. Edward Burrows for a copy of the letter and a few of the poems.)
[23] ibid, Letter.
[24] *Today and Yesterday*, p.14

Or, on a happier note, in 'The Story Room' we see a young child's imagination at work as she lies in bed before falling asleep.

> Even on nights of fog and gloom
> I'm happy in the Story-Room!
> For there each friendly Story's face
> Comes peeping from its hiding-place.
> And every silly, little thought,
> That the long, busy day has brought,
> Has taken wings to Storyland
> And come back with a joyful band.
> There, 'midst the curtain's wind-tossed lace,
> One Story grins with impish face.
> And, hiding near the mirror cool,
> A little Story sorrowful.
> Behind where the tall Wardrobe stands
> A happy Story claps its hands. [25]

Vicky's literary gifts were used in the service of the Baptist Union as Convenor of the Library and Publications Department from 1917 to 1930. These also found expression in her contributions to the *Scottish Baptist Magazine*, written 'in an attractive literary style with penetrating spiritual insight'.[26] She also tutored a four-year Bible study course for the BMS Home Preparation Union and compiled the syllabus for Every Woman's Bible Readings published by the Baptist Union of Great Britain and Ireland.[27] Vicky died on 4 January 1940 at the age of fifty-four. Olive Mary said of her sister, 'Hers was a rare spirit.'[28] Vicky's obituarist amplifies this simple, yet profound, statement:

> Her passionate belief in prayer, and her deep sympathy with the lonely and her very real gift of being able to encourage others made her the kind of church member whose loss will be felt increasingly with the passage of time. [29]

## Mrs George Yuille

One of the most significant figures in early twentieth century Scottish Baptist life was Mrs. George Yuille, wife of the pastor of Stirling Baptist Church, who

---

[25] Ibid, p.36
[26] Obituary, 'Miss Victoria Taylor Coats'
[27] ibid.
[28] Letter 26 September 1972.
[29] Obituary, 'Miss Victoria Taylor Coats'.

himself has a unique place in Scottish Baptist history.[30] Jessie Nimmo, daughter of a coal-master or mine owner, James Nimmo, was born in 1864 in Ceres, Fife, where her parents were visiting. She was brought up in the mining village of Slammanan and at the age of ten was sent to school in Edinburgh. Here, even at that early age, her Baptist convictions were evident. As was normal practice, the children were asked to repeat the Shorter Catechism which included the sentence: 'The infants of such as are members of the visible church are to be baptised. This young Jessie refused to repeat, saying in response to the teacher's prompting, "Please, ma'am, I don't believe it." The teacher replied, "My dear, you are too young to understand such things." [31]

When the family moved to Edinburgh in 1877, they joined the newly built Marshall Street Church where the Rev. Francis Johnstone was pastor for the second time.[32] Here Jessie was baptised and, exercising her gift for music, joined the choir. In due course she became organist and choir leader. In 1888 the family moved again, this time to Glasgow, becoming members of Adelaide Place where, in September of that year, the Rev. T.H. Martin was called as minister. She soon became involved in the life of the church and in the wider ministries which were becoming available to women. This was excellent preparation for her future role as wife of a very influential pastor, one which she filled very ably.

Among the causes Jessie espoused was that of the Baptist Zenana Mission, which was formed in 1858 under the auspices of the Baptist Missionary Society, to reach women in the zenanas (Hindu women's quarters) of India where men outwith their close family members were forbidden to enter. The Glasgow Auxiliary began in Adelaide Place on 20 September 1877, an Edinburgh Auxiliary having been set up two years earlier.[33] These were essentially fund-raising and support groups for the work among women. Jessie Nimmo served as honorary secretary for twenty years from 1881, continuing after her marriage, organising the annual sale of work in Stirling.

With her marriage to George Yuille on 1 June 1893 she entered upon what became her years of greatest achievement. George had been ordained to the pastorate of the Stirling church, his only charge, on 27 July 1870. So by the time of his marriage he was approaching his silver jubilee as pastor. While the

---

[30] For the life and ministry of George Yuille see Christine Lumsden, 'George Yuille "Grand Old Man" of Scottish Baptists' in David and Ron Polland, *Great is Your Faithfulness: A History of Irvine Baptist Church* (Irvine: Irvine Baptist Church, 2006), pp. 160-76; and Brian R Talbot, *Standing on the Rock: A History of Stirling Baptist Church 1805-2005* (Stirling: Stirling Baptist Church, 2005), pp. 51-68.

[31] 'In Memoriam Mrs George Yuille' in *The Scottish Baptist Magazine* (*SBM*), 51.4 (April1925), pp. 47-50 (p. 47).

[32] Yuille p. 131.

[33] Ibid, pp. 264-65. (These auxiliaries were the forerunners of the BMS Women's Links.)

church minutes record neither of these momentous events, the anniversary is reported in the *Scottish Baptist Magazine* in 1895 where the correspondent records that

> he still further extended his usefulness, consummated his happiness by marrying Miss Nimmo, the amiable and accomplished daughter of James Nimmo, Esq., of Glasgow, a sincerely sympathetic helpmeet in his spiritual work.[34]

Mrs. Yuille's lasting legacy from this period was the formation of the Women's Auxiliary of the Baptist Union.[35]

Mrs. George Yuille, as she was now known, was nineteen years younger than her husband, an age gap which was not unusual at that time. Her family, too, was wealthy whereas George, the son of an Irvine bookseller, had come from a humble background. Nevertheless, despite this social disparity, theirs was a true partnership of Christian service. Very little is known about their family life. They had three children, James Nimmo born 6 December 1894, Helen Mary Victoria, born 18 May 1897 (the Queen's diamond jubilee year), Jessie Olive, born 20 December 1901.

When Mr. and Mrs. Yuille moved to Glasgow in 1913, on his appointment as Superintendent of the Baptist Union Home Mission, they became members of Adelaide Place, the fellowship, then meeting in Hope Street, into which George had been baptised by Dr James Paterson. In that city environment, Mrs. Yuille continued her Christian service, now on a wider stage.

The church was not the only area in which Mrs. Yuille showed her leadership qualities. She had re-organised the Stirling branch of the British Women's Temperance Association, becoming its first president, both at town and district level. The family's move to Glasgow coincided with the passing of the Temperance (Scotland) Act 1913 which allowed local plebiscites to control the numbers of licensed premises in a ward, burgh or parish. At least 55% of those who voted had to be in favour of 'No licence', with a simple majority for no change or for limited licensing. However, this legislation did not come into effect immediately, but 'on the expiration of eight years from the first day of June nineteen hundred and twelve.'[36] This delay in the operative date had serious consequences, especially with the opening of hostilities in 1914, since the easy availability of alcohol leading to drunkenness was seen to undermine the country's war effort.

Founded that year by Miss Isabella Watson, a friend of Mrs. Yuille and the first secretary of the Women's Auxiliary, the grandly named 'Women's Patriotic Crusade for Prohibition during the War' united female leaders from all

---

[34] A. Wylie, 'The Rev. George Yuille' in *SBM*, 21.8 (August, 1895), pp. 201-03 (p. 203).

[35] The work of the Women's Auxiliary forms a separate section of this chapter.

[36] 3&4 Geo.V Ch.33 Temperance (Scotland) Act 1913 Section 1.

the churches with representatives of other women's societies in a campaign for war-time prohibition. Mrs. Yuille was one of the three presidents, the others being the Hon. Mrs. Campbell, wife of the Episcopalian Bishop of Glasgow, and Mrs. Noel Paton, wife of the Professor of Physiology at Glasgow University. The Women's Auxiliary office-bearers were members of the committee with Olive Mary Coats as secretary of the Crusade and then of its successor, the Glasgow Citizens' Committee.[37] Large gatherings, including prayer meetings, were held throughout the city at which political and religious leaders spoke.[38] Again Mrs. Yuille's considerable organisational skills were evident as she

> flooded the City with literature, organised the great women's procession and the petition to Parliament, and along with others interviewed Ministers in London.[39]

This 'great Procession and Demonstration' consisted of 30,000 women who marched from five districts of the city to Glasgow Green.[40] Among the marchers, proudly participating was Mrs. Joseph Coats who assisted her daughter in her work as Crusade secretary.[41] In addition to the demonstration, a 'Memorial urging War-time Prohibition' was signed by 142,500 women from Glasgow and its environs and submitted to the Secretary for Scotland.[42] Most of the work of organising the protest and drafting the memorial was done by Mrs. George Yuille.

A further aspect of national politics which gained Jessie Yuille's interest and support was the campaign for female parliamentary suffrage or 'Votes for Women'. In 1905 she led the local branch of the Women's Social and Political Union (WSPU) in Stirling.[43] This Union had been founded in 1903 in Manchester by Mrs. Emmeline Pankhurst, assisted by her daughters Christabel and Sylvia, who were frustrated by the failure of the National Union of Women's Suffrage Societies (NUWSS), which had been formed from two earlier societies in 1892.The NUWSS and its predecessors, whose supporters were known as suffragists, had campaigned to win women the parliamentary vote by constitutional means, such as petitioning Parliament, writing letters to the newspapers and holding peaceful demonstrations. Since such tactics had proven ineffectual, the WSPU, with the motto 'Deeds not Words', adopted a

---

[37] O.M.C. [Olive Mary Coats], 'After Twenty-One Years' in the *SBYB 1931*, pp. 1-15 (pp.5-6).
[38] 'In Memoriam', p. 49.
[39] Ibid, p.47.
[40] O.M.C., p. 6.
[41] O.M and V. Coats, *Book of* Remembrance, p. 189.
[42] O.M.C, p.6 (The office of Secretary for Scotland was created in 1885. The holder was allowed a seat in the Cabinet from 1892 and promoted to full Cabinet rank as Secretary of State in 1926.)
[43] Talbot, *Standing on the Rock*, p. 58.

more violent approach, encouraging acts of civil disobedience. These activists, known as suffragettes, broke lampposts and windows, chained themselves to railings, or interrupted public meetings, especially during elections when prominent politicians were targeted. Arrests and imprisonment were the inevitable results. Despite her association with the Pankhursts, Jessie Yuille would not have sanctioned law-breaking to achieve their aims.

With the outbreak of the Great War in 1914, the suffrage movement channelled its energies into the war effort. Women's service at home and overseas helped their cause more than the years of campaigning. The 1918 Representation of the People Act enfranchised women over the age of thirty and this was lowered to twenty-one, the same as for men, in 1928.

Jessie Yuille died on 24 February 1925 after a 'simple operation', an event which shocked the Scottish Baptist community.[44] The *Scottish Baptist Magazine* of April 1925, as has been noted, published extensive tributes from the Stirling church, and from the associations to which she had given unstinting support. A large congregation gathered in Adelaide Place for her memorial service arranged by her friend, Miss Watson. The service was conducted by the Rev. J.T. Forbes, Principal of the Scottish Baptist College, with the Rev. Thomas Stewart, Secretary of the Baptist Union, giving the address. In addition he read written tributes submitted by the Rev. Alexander Bremner, Union President, Mrs. Ramsay, President, and Mrs. Stott, former President, of the Women's Auxiliary. Poignantly the reporter notes: 'The presence of the Rev. George Yuille, surrounded by members of his wife's family, touched all hearts and sympathetic thoughts went out to his and her children, all three of whom are abroad.'[45] The anonymous obituary in the 1926 *Scottish Baptist Yearbook* describes her life of service to the Scottish Baptist cause as follows:

> The unexpected death of Mrs. Yuille removed one of the most vital and radiant personalities ever given in the Providence of God to our Denomination and it is impossible to chronicle here her manifold services for our Baptist Churches and for our Union. Her faith in them was not only unwavering but unlimited, and the fruits of her service will not only continue for many days, but will increase. To a remarkable degree she combined the gifts of advocacy and leadership with a genius for detailed organisation and her chief monument is the Women's Auxiliary with its splendid record of work already done, and its far reaching plans for future service. As minister's wife in Stirling, as secretary of the Women's Missionary Association for the West of Scotland and as founder and leader of the Women's Auxiliary…she lived a full life, and gave a full day of notable service….Her passionate devotion to evangelical and Baptist principles, and her constant faith in their present power and future triumph were the mainsprings of

---

[44] 'In Memoriam', p. 47.
[45] Ibid, p. 48.

her ungrudging labours, and a constant inspiration to all who were privileged to know her. [46]

Somehow, we have the impression that George Yuille's last years must have been very lonely. He died on 18 December 1935 aged ninety.

## The Women's Auxiliary

Following that brief look at the life of Mrs. George Yuille, we will now consider the work of the organisation with which her name will always be associated, the Women's Auxiliary to the Baptist Union of Scotland. The objectives Mrs. Yuille had in proposing the formation of a Women's Auxiliary at the 1908 Baptist Union Assembly were:

> to organise the women of the churches for the spread of evangelical truth and Baptist principles; to assist the Union in promoting any Scheme for the advance of the Denomination; to appoint and support Deaconesses; and to organise women's work generally in the churches. [47]

The Auxiliary was constituted and approved by the following Assembly with Mrs. Yuille as its first national president. Its organisational structure mirrored that of the Union with president, vice-president, secretary and treasurer at national and district level. The presidential office alternated between a minister's wife and another lady, married or single, so mirroring the Union practice of pastor followed by layman. However, Mrs. Yuille's term as president lasted from 1909 until 1920, with Miss Isabella Watson, secretary, serving one year less. Mrs. Yuille was succeeded as president by Mrs. Stott from Dundee, who held office for three years. Thereafter one year in post became the norm. The annual public meeting of the Women's Auxiliary still forms an important part of the Baptist Union Assembly, since it is at that meeting the new president is installed and gives her address.

Miss Watson's final report summarises the first ten years of the W.A. By the end of the first year eighteen churches had branches, while by 1919 these had increased to sixty. In other churches, while no branches were formed, the women 'manifested a strong sympathy with its aims'.[48] The women met for prayer and fellowship, taking account of the spiritual needs of their district, which they were encouraged to evangelise, leaflets and other materials being provided. At local W.A. branch level, the pastor's wife was often the leader.

Nationally, in February 1914 the Union appealed to the Auxiliary to support the Sustentation Scheme which was established to supplement pastors' incomes with the aim of securing a minimum annual salary of £120 for single men and

---

[46] Obituary 'Mrs. George Yuille' in *SBYB 1926*, p. 121.
[47] Yuille, *Baptists in Scotland*, p. 245.
[48] I. Watson, 'Tenth Annual Report' in the *SBYB 1920*, pp. 60-64 (p. 61).

£150 for married.[49] The capital suggested for this fund was £40,000 and the W.A. resolved to raise £10,000 as their share, afterwards increased to £12,500. This pledge was met in full.

The outbreak of war brought further demands. In the autumn of 1914 the Union asked the W.A. to organise Red Cross work. Mrs. Yuille suggested that funds for motor ambulances for the wounded were the most urgent need. Within a month, £980 was raised and our two "Scottish Baptist Ambulances" were sent forth on their mission of mercy'.[50] This war gave women wider opportunities for service both at home and overseas. In the churches, the older women adapted their Ladies' Working Parties for Red Cross Work. For younger women, serving overseas provided very different experiences, as those of two members from Bristo Place, Edinburgh show.

> Miss Ina Stewart has been accepted as a nurse under the Scottish Women's Hospitals for Home and Foreign Service and has left for Russia. She is well qualified for the post having gone through a thorough training as a nurse.[51]
>
> Sister C. Florrie Forbes had been absent from this country for 22 months….She had spent nearly all the time in hospitals in Malta, whence it was difficult and dangerous to get passage. Now she has been appointed to hospital service in the Riviera (South of France) to attend to patients from Italy. May her work be light![52]

What can be more of a contrast than nursing in revolutionary Russia or in the balmy climate of the French Riviera, the favoured resort of those who were able to escape the chill damp of the British winter! As the magazines record nothing further about Ina or Florrie, they presumably returned home safely at the end of the war.

Another initiative by Mrs. Yuille, just before Christmas 1914, was to establish the Manse Fund which provided a small gift to the mothers 'in the manses of our churches where so much heroism is displayed and so much hardship silently endured.'[53] For three years in succession a small cheque was sent each Christmas to over thirty mothers. The total raised for the Fund was £1000.[54]

The following short extracts come from a sample of acknowledgement letters for the five pounds gifts distributed in the first year. They show how the gifts alleviated hardships at a difficult time and fostered a spirit of unity among Scottish Baptist women.

---

[49] Yuille, *Baptists in Scotland*, p. 244.
[50] Watson, 'Tenth Annual Report', p. 62.
[51] *Bristo Place Baptist Church Magazine*, August 1917.
[52] ibid, March 1918.
[53] Yuille, *Baptists in* Scotland, p. 245.
[54] 'Tenth Annual Report', p. 63.

> I thank the Women's Auxiliary for the gift most sincerely, and especially for the loving spirit of sisterhood it brought with it. It has given me a 'lift' in more ways than one. I can assure you that the gift is a real help in these trying times. Nearly all the men are away from their homes, engaged in work under the Admiralty. But the Lord is with us and our eyes are towards Him.[55]

The post war period saw an increase in the number of W.A. branches and more forming district associations but occasionally we have reports of branches withdrawing from the Auxiliary. Although the reasons are not given, the most likely cause is falling membership.

In accordance with their aim to assist the Union, the W.A. embarked upon another national fund-raising effort in October 1920 when the office-bearers of the Auxiliary and the BMS Women's Missionary Association appealed for a United Fund of £25,000. The Fund's purposes were:

> to augment the Sustenation Fund allowances because of the continued high prices; to make worthy superannuation provision for our ministers and their widows; to meet the emergency of the Baptist Missionary Society in view of the high rate of exchange.[56]

By spring 1923 the Fund was closed at £23,000 despite the difficult economic situation with rising unemployment. The W.A. stipulated that the money allocated to the BMS should be sent overseas for work among women.[57]

An innovation for the Auxiliary came on 11 February 1925 with the Rally and Thanksgiving Day. Among the speakers was Mrs. Yuille, less than two weeks before she died. Despite this sad beginning, the Thanksgiving Rally became an annual event. It provided 'an opportunity for fellowship, conference, and united worship.'[58] A high point of the Rally occurred when the roll was called and a representative from each branch brought forward its gift. The first weekend conference was held in Largs from 8 to 10 February 1930, when over sixty ladies were present. This conference, held annually in St. Andrews, is still an important event for Scottish Baptist women.

The Second World War and its aftermath brought major changes in British society, which had a long-term effect on the role of women. Churches were disrupted with both men and girls serving in the armed forces. This war had a greater effect on the civilian population too, as the 'home front' became a battle field, with communities, particularly in the west of Scotland, devastated by bombing raids. Nevertheless, the war-time W.A. reports are quite restrained in their descriptions of life for the women at home.

---

[55] I. Watson, 'The Women's Auxiliary Seventh Annual Report' in the *SBYB 1917*, pp. 1-5 (p. 3).
[56] O.M.C., 'After Twenty-one Years', p. 7.
[57] ibid, p. 10.
[58] ibid, p. 12.

> Almost all branches are doing some kind of war work, supplying comforts, parcels, letters and social evenings for the Forces, visiting the sick and wounded in hospitals, and staffing canteens and Rest Centres.[59]
>
> Vital links are being maintained between the churches and the increasing numbers of young men and women who are serving in H.M. forces, letters and parcels being sent...from time to time. Our President sent a gracious letter to all our chaplains at the beginning of this year expressing the appreciation of the women at home for their splendid work.[60]

The 1945 annual rally, the date having been arranged some time previously, took place on 9 May, the day after victory in Europe was achieved.

> The Morning Session became a service of Thanksgiving and Re-dedication... Our Sympathy and prayers went out to all who had suffered the loss of homes and loved ones....The address given by Mrs. Gibb, a chaplain's assistant, was of great interest describing her work amongst the girls in the Forces. She appealed to church workers to help the girls find real and satisfying fellowship in the churches when they return.[61]

The girls were returning to a changing society. Within the next generation, wider educational and employment opportunities for women meant that no longer were wives prepared to stay at home, looking after their families. While formerly, in professions such as teaching, nursing and the civil service, women were required to resign on marriage, this restriction was removed gradually. This cultural change affected the membership of the Women's Auxiliary. Because more women were working outside the home, fewer could attend meetings.

A milestone in the history of the Women's Auxiliary was reached in 1959 when it celebrated its jubilee. Fittingly, the spring rally that year took place in Stirling, where the organisation had begun. In the morning Miss M.C. Wright, a former secretary and life member, addressed the meeting, while at the afternoon session two young members spoke: 'Mrs. W.S. Christie, [Bristo] Edinburgh a lay lady, and Mrs. A.D. MacRae, the wife of the esteemed minister at Larbert.'[62] In this way each generation of the membership played its part.

The main celebration, however, took place in October as part of the Assembly programme 'in which both the Auxiliary and the Union shared'.[63] Edinburgh's Usher Hall was crowded. A choir of 270 voices led the praise. Almost £6,000 was raised for the jubilee thank-offering. On the following

---

[59] 'Women's Auxiliary Report' in the *SBYB 1944*, p. 79.
[60] Report in the *SBYB 1945*, p. 78.
[61] Report in the *SBYB 1946*, p. 89.
[62] 'Fiftieth Annual Report' in the *SBYB 1960*, pp. 186-87 (p. 187).
[63] 'Fifty-first Annual Report' in the *SBYB* 1961, pp. 190-91 (p. 191).

Sunday, the B.B.C. broadcast a special service from Adelaide Place, again making history.

In 1969 the diamond jubilee of the Auxiliary coincided with the centenary of the Union and the 75$^{th}$ anniversary of the Scottish Baptist College. To celebrate their anniversary, Glasgow's Tent Hall was the venue for an afternoon thanksgiving rally and evening festival of praise 7 May, while on 24 September the ladies presented a pageant in the Church of Scotland Assembly Hall, Edinburgh. Entitled 'Judged to be Faithful', this outlined the history of the Auxiliary in relation to its areas of social concern and Christian service. To mark their jubilee, at the annual meeting in October, the women gave the Union £10,000 towards its Centenary Fund. Andrew MacRae, General Secretary, paid tribute as follows:-

> Through the W.A. God has been pleased over the years to strengthen greatly the work of our Union, and by a variety of means, spiritual and practical, has used the Auxiliary for the enrichment of our common life in Christ. May God continue to use the Auxiliary as a blessing to churches and Union alike in days to come.[64]

In 1996, recognising that membership was falling and that many women in Baptist churches were not associated with the Auxiliary, a Review Group was formed to consider how women could work and serve the churches together. After three years deliberation, their proposals were taken to members for discussion but did not obtain the two thirds majority vote necessary for approval.[65] Following a period of reflection on the future of the Auxiliary, in 2002 it was renamed the Scottish Baptist Women's Fellowship. However, the structure and annual programme is similar to the earlier format.

So after one hundred years, the Women's Fellowship, as we must now refer to it, continues to serve Scottish Baptist churches in Christian witness locally and in supporting the Union. However, with the notable exception of Miss Jane Henderson, the Women's Auxiliary failed to meet one of their original aims, to appoint and support deaconesses. We now consider the role of deaconesses in Scottish Baptist churches and reasons for this failure.

## Deaconesses

There is considerable uncertainty about the function and appointment of deaconesses within Scottish Baptist churches. Whyte's Causeway, Kirkcaldy, held their first election of deacons in November 1852, four months after it was founded in a secession of thirty-four members from the Scotch Baptist Church then meeting in Rose Street. This new fellowship also operated on Scotch Baptist principles in its early years. Three men were set apart as Elders, four as

---

[64] Andrew MacRae, in *SBYB 1970*, p. 15.
[65] 'Woman's Auxiliary' in *SBYB 2000*, pp. 204-207 (p. 204).

Deacons 'and Mrs. William Murray and Mrs. Ninian Lockhart as Deaconesses.'[66] Mrs. Lockhart was the wife of a prominent linen manufacturer in the town. As there was no further reference to these ladies in the church records, we can only speculate on their work. The author of the Church's centenary history notes, 'The precedent set up in those early days has not, so far, been followed.'[67] Whyte's Causeway did not admit women to the diaconate on the same basis as men until the 1970s.[68]

By 1890, the Baptist Union of Great Britain had established an Order of Deaconesses. In that year a Baptist Deaconess Home and Mission was founded under the direction of the Rev. F.B. Meyer, Regent's Park Chapel, and the London Baptist Association, focussing mainly on medical, social and evangelistic work.[69] This precedent suggests that Mrs. Yuille may have proposed a similar Order, although the concept of an 'Order' would not find much favour in a predominately Presbyterian Scotland. However, deaconesses had been appointed in Dennistoun, Glasgow during the ministry of J.W. Ashworth (1870-1875).[70] There were also deaconesses working at St. Andrews; although no dates are given 'but for these women there would have been no Baptist Church in St. Andrews today.'[71] These confused origins suggest that deaconesses had been active in some Baptist churches at an early date. Charlotte Chapel appointed its first deaconess, Miss Elizabeth Boyle, in 1907, '...an Edinburgh businesswoman, a member of the Chapel, already active as a worker and soul-winner.'[72] Miss Boyle served the church for thirty-six years, with visiting the sick and needy in the area and conducting women's meetings her main duties. As Miss Boyle left Edinburgh in 1916, her successor Miss E. Tipper, from Cardiff City Mission, was appointed. She found the work too onerous, however, and resigned in 1920. Meantime, Miss Boyle had returned home and the Chapel 'called' her to resume her former post, which she did in April 1921. She retired in 1948.[73] In all, Charlotte Chapel had nine deaconesses serving for various periods. The last, Miss Eilish Agnew, was appointed in 1995. During her eleven years in post, it was renamed 'pastoral assistant', a title

---

[66] Matthew McLachlan, *Whyte's Causeway Baptist Church: The First Hundred Years, 1852-1952* (Kirkcaldy: For the Church, 1952), p.5 (My thanks to Dr. Helen Wishart for this reference.)
[67] ibid.
[68] Personal information from the Rev. Dr. Derek Murray, a former minister of the church.
[69] Ian M. Randall, *English Baptists of the Twentieth Century* (Didcot: The Baptist Historical Society, 2005), pp. 44-45.
[70] Yuille, *Baptists in Scotland*, pp. 174 and 281.
[71] ibid, p. 158.
[72] Ian L.S. Balfour, *Revival in Rose Street: Charlotte Baptist Chapel, Edinburgh 1808-2008* (Edinburgh: Rutherford House, 2007), p. 113.
[73] ibid, p. 187.

more expressive of her work. She retired in 2006, returning to her home in Northern Ireland.[74]

The Scotch Baptist Church meeting in Bristo Place, Edinburgh agreed in 1911 that ladies be appointed to act as visitors to female members.[75] In this respect, therefore, their duties were similar to those of the Charlotte Chapel deaconesses. The 'lady visitors' were allocated to the districts covered by the deacons for their oversight, but the ladies were not eligible to take part in the deacons' meetings, where the spiritual and business affairs of the church were discussed. They could, however, draw attention to any particular need among those they visited so that help could be given. As they were in most cases the wives and daughters of the existing deacons, the visitors came from the same narrow background. It was not until 1956 that the first lady deacon, Miss Marjory Pringle, was elected on equal terms as the men.[76]

The Women's Auxiliary appointed Miss Jane Henderson as their first deaconess in 1913.[77] While they intended to engage another two years later, wartime conditions meant that 'further action was deemed inexpedient'.[78] However, lack of finance also proved a hindrance, as the following extract makes clear:

> We have always hoped to be able to help struggling churches to support their own deaconesses but further development on these or other lines is impossible until we have adequate support for our present work. The sum required is not large, but friends forget that it is double what it was in pre-war days.[79]

In 1924 the Auxiliary consulted the ministers of churches with over two hundred members to ascertain their views on using trained women workers. Thirty-eight were contacted and all except four replied. Twenty were 'entirely in favour', several of these 'felt there was a crying need', while others, who approved in principle, urged care over training and conditions of service. Six ministers disapproved. In the circumstances the Union was asked 'to consider the advisability of preparing a scheme for training and employing deaconesses as soon as practicable.'[80] In January 1928 W.A. branches voted on a scheme which had been sent to them for consideration. Fifty-four cards were returned of which only eleven were in favour. Accordingly the proposed scheme lapsed. [81]

---

[74] ibid, pp. 436-37.
[75] 'A Journal of Proceedings in connection with Bristo Place Baptist Church Edinburgh' Minute 15 May 1911. (This somewhat grandiose title simply contains the minutes of the church business meetings and is held by Bristo Baptist Church.)
[76] ibid, Minute 14 May 1956.
[77] Miss Henderson's life and work is considered below.
[78] 'The Women's Auxiliary' in *SBYB 1915*, pp. 69-71 (p. 70).
[79] 'Twelfth Annual Report' in *SBYB 1922*, pp.146-47 (p. 147).
[80] 'Fifteenth Annual Report' in *SBYB 1925*, pp. 153-55 (p. 154).
[81] 'Eighteenth Annual Report' in *SBYB 1928*, pp. 158-59 (p. 158).

This vote suggests that the ordinary members themselves were not ready to accept trained women to work in churches. Following Miss Henderson's resignation, she was succeeded in 1927 by Miss E.C. Dillon as W.A. 'sister'. Her appointment ended in March 1930, since the branches felt that her work of visitation and evangelism was something which they themselves should be doing.[82]

In England, on the other hand, the work of deaconesses had increased due to both World Wars. There, the equivalent to the Women's Auxiliary was the Baptist Women's League, which had been formed in 1908.[83] In 1947, concerned that the demand for deaconesses in England exceeded the numbers available, to make this career better known the Women's Auxiliary co-operated with the League in arranging meetings in Aberdeen, Edinburgh and Glasgow. Sister Helen Graham was the speaker and, as a result, several young women enquired regarding training in the Baptist Women's Training College in London.[84] How successful this initiative was is not recorded.

## Jane Henderson, Deaconess, Missionary and Pastor

As already noted Miss Jane Henderson was the first and best known deaconess supported by the Women's Auxiliary. Born in Anstruther, in the East Neuk of Fife, in 1881, at the age of fifteen she was baptised and became a member of the Baptist Church there, where she immediately 'gave herself to service.'[85] Later, sensing a call to missionary service overseas, she trained at the Lady Missionary Training Home in Glasgow, taking courses in theology, medicine and general education. However, an accident to her knee meant that she was no longer fit for overseas work. Jane's missionary service was to take a different form.

Appointed as deaconess by Stirling Baptist Church in November 1908, her work for the church involved door-to-door evangelism, visiting homes in the town and also in the neighbouring country districts.[86] However, the Lord had prepared an additional sphere of service for Jane, and it is this work with which her name is most closely associated.

In 1906 the Baptist Church Christian Endeavour Society had issued a call, through the Rev. T.W. Govenlock, pastor of Lerwick Baptist Church, to the Baptist Union Home Mission Committee for a lady 'deputy' to work among the fisher girls.[87] In response the Committee sent Mrs. William Cooper, a former missionary in China, to work there for the month of August. Her report describes the situation as follows:

---

[82] O.M.C., 'After Twenty-One Years', p. 11.
[83] Randall, *English Baptists*, p. 75.
[84] 'Women's Auxiliary Report' in *SBYB 1948*, p. 137.
[85] Obituary, 'Miss Jane Henderson' in *SBYB 1933*, pp. 150-51 (p.150).
[86] Talbot, *Standing on the Rock*, p. 58.
[87] 'Report on Mission to Fisher Girls at Lerwick' in *SBYB 1911*, pp.149-51 (p. 149).

> In Lerwick there were between 2000 and 3000 girls assembled. These girls live in wooden houses erected for their benefit by the masters. These 'huts' are like bathing boxes, with a stove at one end, and four beds ranged round one above the other like berths in a steamer. Six or eight girls live in each hut. [They] have few comforts and little privacy.[88]

The other 'deputies' were Miss Pollock, from the United Free Church, and Sister Jeanie Banks, a Wesleyan Methodist nurse. As nothing had been settled for Mrs. Cooper's arrival, she arranged for a local joiner to build a little wooden hut, where she could meet the girls for advice or simple medical attention. The joiner charged a reduced price of £6. So the famous 'Pearl Hut' came into being.[89] Obviously a more permanent arrangement was required for this work, as Mrs. Cooper appeals:

> I feel very keenly that we should not let this work drop [---] but take it up as a permanent work. Let the Christian Endeavour societies promise to support one deputy each year.[90]

The challenge was met and the main support of the Lerwick Fisher Girls' Mission, as it came to be known, was through the churches' Bible classes and Christian Endeavour societies, the young members collecting willingly for this outreach. A small grant for the Lerwick work was provided by the Evangelistic and Preaching Circuit Committee, an offshoot of the Scottish Baptist Christian Endeavour Committee, in the early years. However, in 1913 Mrs. Yuille proposed that Jane become the Women's Auxiliary deaconess and responsibility for the Mission passed to that organisation in 1914.

The fishing industry, particularly herring, was very seasonal, depending as it did on the movements of the shoals around UK waters. Boats followed the fish round the east coast from Lerwick to Yarmouth. Catches fluctuated from year to year and often there were periods of famine, while a glut of fish meant prices were reduced. The 'fisher lassies', too, migrated from various island and mainland communities, following the boats to their port-based curing stations.

What was work like for these girls in the early twentieth century? First the fishing boats would come into harbour, laden with herring. The men carried their catch ashore and dumped it into large wooden troughs known as 'farlins'. Waiting, in groups of three, were the girls, wearing black oilskin aprons over thick woollen jumpers. They gutted the fish, (apparently) averaging one per second, then packed them in barrels, alternating layers of herring and coarse salt. The gutters bandaged their fingers to protect them from cuts but, because of the speed at which they worked, injuries were nevertheless frequent. The packers, too, wore bandages for protection from the water and salt, exposure to

---

[88] 'Evangelistic and Preaching Circuit Report' in *SBYB 1907*, pp. 108-10 (p. 108).
[89] Ibid, p. 109.
[90] Ibid, p. 109.

which injured the skin. Although cuts were an occupational hazard, other ailments treated were sunburn, blisters, boils, sprains and splinters from the wooden barrels. Initially the girls worked twelve to fifteen hours per day but in 1913 these were regulated to ten and thirteen hour shifts, alternately. Wages averaged 25/- (£1.25) weekly but this was drastically reduced as time went on. By 1918 first aid stations had become compulsory.[91]

With her fishing community background, nursing qualification and missionary training, Jane Henderson was the ideal choice for the permanent 'deputy', to which she was appointed in 1909, the Stirling Church releasing her during the summer months. She served in this dual capacity until 1913 when she became lady agent of the Baptist Union 'to help the churches in evangelistic and social work'.[92] Annual reports published in the *Scottish Baptist Year Book* present a picture of hard, intensive labour during the months of the northern summer, generally May to September, but sometimes less depending on the herring. Nevertheless there were also times of great blessing.

The Committee's report for 1911 shows some concern that 'the risk in sending Miss Henderson to Lerwick was greater than on any former occasion'.[93] This unease was due to the resignation of Mr. Govenlock as pastor, just as arrangements for the Mission were about to be made. As Jane herself was willing to go and the deacons of the church promised to support her work, the Committee agreed to 'increase the grant by £5, and send their deputy to the far north again'.[94] Jane's own report for that year illustrates the hazardous economics of herring fishing, yet shows how even these setbacks can be used for good.

> After the first month, the fishing became very poor, and during July and August, the outward aspect of things was anything but cheering. To those of us who were Christian workers, it was most discouraging, but by the grace of God, we were enabled to turn the time of material depression into a season of very real and definite spiritual blessing. During these weeks there was not so much hand-dressing, so we determined to do something more than usual for the conversion of the girls. We did what in previous years, owing to the nature of the work, had been an impossibility, viz., we arranged and conducted special meetings for the girls on their own curing stations.[95]

---

[91] This description is based on an undated document about life in early twentieth-century Lerwick written by Mrs. Cheryl Nicholson. (My thanks to the Rev. Dr. Brian Talbot for a copy of this item and also for reports of the Lerwick Mission to Fisher Girls from various *SBYBs*.)

[92] Yuille, *Baptists in* Scotland, p. 245.

[93] 'Mission to Fisher Girls at Lerwick' in *SBYB 1912*, pp. 150-52 (p. 150).

[94] ibid.

[95] ibid, pp. 150-51.

In these evening meetings Jane was assisted by Miss Munro, a deputy from the United Free Church and Miss Lawson, a Christian Endeavour member from Pittenweem (another East Neuk fishing community) and a few local workers. However, the meetings were difficult to arrange as they depended on the volume of the herring catch. Several girls from throughout Shetland came to faith in Christ as a result of these extra week-day meetings. They were not the only fruit, however, as Jane relates:

> Before shutting up the 'Pearl Hut' for the season, there was one more remarkable scene witnessed. An old man, who had been a regular attender at my Sunday afternoon meeting, and who had wandered far from God, got down on his knees and asked forgiveness for the sins of a lifetime. God grant that his end may be peace! [96]

The following year's report indicates that the Pearl Hut was too small for the Mission's needs and the Rev. James Dunlop, who had succeeded Mr. Govenlock at Lerwick, promised a new building for which the girls, too, would raise funds from their knitting. [97] The new Mission Hall was opened in June 1913, the start of a poor season lasting only until the end of July. The cyclical nature of the fishing industry proved a constant problem, exacerbated during the Great War when the Mission ceased, resuming again in 1920. The War and its aftermath was a time of crisis in the entire Scottish fishing industry as the Russian revolution of 1917 'brought an end to the hitherto vast East European export trade in herring'.[98] This was a market on which the Shetland Islands were particularly dependent.

The fishing did not improve until 1922 when the work was heavy and difficult. Unusually that year, among the Shetlanders, Highland and lowland Scots, the fishing girls included people from Ireland, England, Holland and Sweden, adding an international dimension to the meetings. As Jane reported:

> We had several Dutch-English meetings with our good friends, the staff and crew of the Dutch Mission Hospital ship, "De Hoop", when first Dominie Jansen and then Dominie Stoppeler addressed us in both languages. We learned our mutual hymns, and we sang them together to the same tunes, but each in our own tongue, with wonderful harmony. Never shall we forget the glory of these meetings![99]

Jane's work was not easy, despite the optimism of her reports. Occasionally the stress shows, as in the 1926 report given by Catherine Stott, convener of the W.A. evangelistic committee.

---

[96] ibid, p. 152.
[97] Report *SBYB 1913*, pp. 150-53 (p. 153).
[98] T.C. Smout, *A Century of the Scottish People 1830-1950* (London: Collins, 1986), p. 77.
[99] 'Annual Report of Evangelist' in the *SBYB 1923*, pp. 144-45 (p. 145).

> After a fortnight's restful holiday Miss Henderson set out for Lerwick on June 9th, and after experiencing one of the most terrible passages lasting nineteen hours, arrived in a very exhausted state. She has had a great season of "Blessed results."...Never has Miss Henderson had such a strain of work as this year, yet with it all she has been wonderfully restored in her health. By request she gave two Sundays to Lerwick and Burra churches respectively.[100]

In 1927 Jane relinquished her relationship with the Auxiliary to concentrate on itinerant evangelism, a work in which she had already been engaged for some time. Miss Dillon and volunteers from the churches carried on the Mission to the fisher girls. With the years of economic depression, however, problems were becoming too great. Yet, despite the difficulties, the 1939 Assembly business meeting voted by a decisive majority to continue the work. The herring fishing that year had been a complete failure. The secretary of the Auxiliary, Mrs. Henderson, visited to discuss the situation with the minister and deacons of Lerwick Baptist Church but 'was unable to come to any satisfactory arrangements with them'.[101] So another war and the decline of the herring industry brought this work to an end.

Jane Henderson's work among the Shetland fishing girls occupied only part of her year. With her appointment as the W.A. deaconess from 1913, her service to Scottish Baptists consisted of assisting churches throughout the country, from large city congregations to small rural communities, conducting evangelistic campaigns, including home visiting and gospel meetings. Often she was assigned to a church for a week or two to give the pastor a holiday, or, for a longer period when a church was vacant. This could lead to contrasting situations within a very short time, as her report for 1916 indicates.

> After a holiday in June, I was dispatched to another vacant charge (Peterhead) where I enjoyed a month's hard, stiff work in a cause sorely hit by the war. Then came the call of the far north and I was asked by the Home Mission to go to Burra Isle, Shetland, for two and a half months...For several weeks I was the only resident spiritual ministrant on the island, the one settled minister being on holiday.[102]

In the midst of all this, Burra Isle experienced a measles epidemic and as the nearest doctor, in Scalloway on the Shetland mainland, had been called away, Jane also was the island's only medical attendant, assisted occasionally by a doctor from Lerwick. All over the island she travelled, 'sometimes pressing through a heavy gale' to nurse the sick of all ages. She continues her report:

---

[100] 'Evangelistic Report' in the *SBYB 1927*, pp. 152-53 (p. 153).
[101] 'Women's Auxiliary Thirtieth Annual Report' in the *SBYB 1940*, pp. 211-13 (p. 213).
[102] 'Miss Henderson's Report' in *The Women's Auxiliary Report 1917*, pp. 7-8 (p. 7). This report is included in the *SBYB 1917*.

> The empty church was a great grief. One Sunday a few of us could only meet for prayer, and the following Sunday we had no services at all. But the gratitude of the people, and their kind words of appreciation, were sweet reassurances to the tired worker.[103]

These years of varied, tireless work were preparation for another area of service for Jane Henderson, as the first woman to pastor a Scottish Baptist church. She was called to the church at Lossiemouth in 1918 and served there until 1921.[104] This call was a response to the shortage of men as a result of the war, but Miss Henderson's record of unstinting service to Scottish Baptists proved that she was able for the task. Lossiemouth was also a fishing community, so this would make her ministry more acceptable to them. After this pastorate ended, Jane resumed her work as an itinerant evangelist, supported by the Women's Auxiliary.

Jane Henderson died on 4 January 1932 at the age of 51. Her obituary records:

> There are few Baptist Churches in Scotland that have not had the services of Miss Henderson. One report of her work said, 'Wherever she goes, young hearts are yielded to their Lord'…As years go, she did not live long…But as service goes, she lived well.[105]

Another lady pastor who came to the aid of the churches was Mary Flora MacArthur, whose father, Donald, had been an itinerant evangelist with the Tiree Church. Miss MacArthur ministered in Tobermory from 1938 to 1941 and in Colonsay from 1945 to 1947. These pastorates were in areas where there was a shortage of male ministers, especially Gaelic speakers. Mary Flora had also worked with the fisher girls at Lerwick in the early 1930s and was a missionary in the Orkney islands of Sanday and Eday between 1943 and 1945.[106]

## Muriel's Story[107]

A step towards the full ordination of women as ministers in Scottish Baptist churches came with the appointment of Mrs Muriel McNair as Secretary of the Department of Church Life from 1981 until 1985, for the first year on a part-

---

[103] Ibid, pp. 7-8.
[104] Yuille, *Baptists in Scotland*, pp. 98 and 286. (Only the dates of her pastorate are given.)
[105] Jane Henderson, 'Obituary', *SBYB 1933*, pp. 150-51.
[106] D.E. Meek 'The Highlands' in D.W. Bebbington (ed.), *The Baptists in Scotland: A History* (Glasgow: The Baptist Union of Scotland, 1988), pp. 280-308 (pp. 298 and 307).
[107] This section is based on a conversation with Mrs McNair on 16 May 2008 and a follow-up letter to the author 31 July 2008.

time basis. So far, Mrs McNair is the only lady to have served in a senior capacity on the staff of the Baptist Union of Scotland. The Department of Church Life was established by the Rev. Andrew McRae, then General Secretary, in 1979 with the Rev. William Wright as its first secretary, a post he held for two years.

Muriel McNair had been born into a Christian family, her parents having been missionaries with the Baptist Missionary Society. She had qualified as a teacher of English, graduating from Edinburgh University, and taught for three years before her marriage to Jim. They went abroad for some time and on their return to Scotland, she looked after her small children, at the same time serving her church as family demands permitted. In 1973 Jim and Muriel helped to start the new Baptist Church at Bearsden. This experience deepened Muriel's interest in study of the Christian faith with a view to gaining a qualification in Religious Education as a second subject, should she resume her teaching career in the future.

On her application to the Scottish Baptist College, her acceptance as a student by its Committee in 1977 was on the strict understanding that she could not enter the ministry but could only undertake the academic work required for the four-year London B.D. course. However, Dr. R.E.O. White, then Principal, invited Muriel to sit in on the Pastoral Theology classes whenever she wished and she also participated in leading the college prayers. Thus Muriel was the first lady to take the same course as men preparing for the ministry in the Scottish Baptist Church. (Two female students had been accepted by the College before Muriel; Miss Florence Stewart joined in 1930 with a view to missionary service overseas and in 1976 Janice Sneddon was accepted for the London Diploma in Theology as a qualification to teach religious education.[108]) Muriel's appearance as a student in the Scottish Baptist College at first puzzled the men but later they worked well together. She successfully completed the course, graduating BD in 1981.

With the Rev. William Wright's call to St Andrews Baptist Church that year, the College was asked to recommend a possible successor as secretary of the Department of Church Life. It was suggested that Muriel might 'help out' for six months or so. The Department had four aspects, all established from its inception: Christian Education, Youth, Denominational Training, and Ministry, each represented by a small committee of five. The Youth Choir was an important part of their remit, as was also the Youth Night at the annual Assembly.

Muriel's duties as Department Secretary were as they had already been established. This involved considerable administration, including organising the annual ministers' conference and others on an *ad hoc* basis. Responsibility for the Youth Choir involved organising weekend visits to churches and summer

---

[108] Derek B. Murray, *Scottish Baptist College Centenary History: 1894-1994* (Glasgow: Scottish Baptist College, 1994), p. 72.

tours. A significant event was the Choir's visit to the European Baptist Federation (EBF) youth conference in Hamburg in 1984. This experience together with the good relations previously established with EBF youth secretaries, led to the request to hold the EBF Youth Conference in Glasgow in 1988, the year of the city's Garden Festival.

Occasionally Muriel was asked to take church services. Some congregations were helpful and welcoming but others did not wish a woman to take services or preach. While there was little direct confrontation with the ministers, the fact that during the period of Muriel's service the Secretary of the Department of Church Life was a lay person and a woman was difficult for some to accept. Yet it was during her tenure that the report of the Joint Ministerial Board "Women in the Ministry" was brought to the Baptist Union Council.[109] The progress and outcome of this long-standing debate will be examined in due course.

## A Lady President

Tuesday 23 October 1990 was a significant date for Scottish Baptist women. In the City Hall, Glasgow, at the Baptist Union Assembly opening rally that evening Miss Marjorie McInnes was installed as President. With the reconstruction of the Union in 2002, that office no longer exists. Miss McInnes therefore holds a unique position in the history of the Baptist Union of Scotland as its only lady president.

Miss McInnes was baptised and received into membership of Adelaide Place Baptist Church, Glasgow on 29 May 1932 and remains a member of that church.[110] She had served the Union in various ways, as a member of Council and on the Ministerial Recognition and Scottish Baptist College committees, in particular. She was therefore well-known to the denomination. Miss McInnes had a distinguished career in social work, latterly holding a senior position in the then Scottish Office. In this role she was used to public speaking, had a natural concern for people and an appreciation of their pastoral problems. This combination of practical and spiritual experience fitted her for the task ahead. Appropriately, given her professional background, Miss McInnes chose as her theme during the presidential year 'Called to Care'. In her address to Assembly she linked our love for Christ with His command to love our neighbour however that term may be interpreted. Caring was not an optional extra but part of our daily lives. She challenged us, as Scottish Baptists, to face up to the implications in society and in our churches.[111]

In conversation, I asked Miss McInnes to describe her year as Baptist Union president. Her first reaction on being nominated was to be overwhelmed at the

---

[109] Minutes of Baptist Union Council, 17 May 1983, paragraph 24, in *SBYB1984*, p. 93.
[110] Information from Mrs Frances Addis, archivist, Adelaide Place Baptist Church.
[111] Presidential Address, published in *SBYB 1991* (Glasgow: Baptist Union of Scotland, 1991), pp. 89-94.

immensity of the task, not only because she was a woman but also a lay person. She knew that those with strong views against women in leadership would not invite her to preach in their churches, a situation which she accepted. On the other hand, those who did invite her, from Shetland to Dumfries, were very supportive, as were the Union office-bearers with whom she worked closely throughout her term of office. Miss McInnes did not see her role as one in which she overtly sought to break down barriers.[112] On the specific question of whether her presidency had an impact on the debate regarding ministerial ordination of women in Scottish Baptist churches Miss McInnes did not feel able to comment. However, the Rev. Douglas Hutcheon, then superintendent of the Union, considers that her presidency was 'much more influential than some would have believed possible' and boosted the credibility of women in leadership.[113]

## Towards Equality?

These case studies spanning most of the twentieth century show the gradual acceptance of women in leadership of Scottish Baptist churches. The pastorates of Jane Henderson and Mary Flora MacArthur were short-lived in the extraordinary circumstances of war. Thereafter Scottish Baptist women faced a long struggle to achieve equality with men in the pastoral office and some doubt whether true equality has yet been reached.

In 1911 the second Baptist World Alliance Congress met in Philadelphia. One of the three British women who addressed the Congress was Mrs. D.M. Scott from Bearsden, who later held office as vice-president of the Women's Auxiliary. In her address to Congress Mrs. Scott declared:

> No nation can be happy or great except as their women are the honoured partners and fellow workers with the men. When the woman is either the slave or plaything of man, the men and the nation are degraded.[---] our understanding of Christianity and the teaching and spirit of our Lord Jesus Christ is still far from being truly enlightened and complete, for he has swept away all such distinctions, distinctions of race, of speech, of color (*sic*), and also distinctions of sex.[114]

With these words Mrs. Scott affirmed the true equality which informed the Reformation doctrine of 'a priesthood of all believers', as no other mediator safe Christ was required to give the believer access to God. Although this concept was fundamental to Baptist theology, for women the ideal and the reality were somewhat different.

---

[112] Personal conversation with Miss McInnes 19 October 2007.
[113] Personal letter to author 2 May 2008.
[114] Quoted by Karen E. Smith, 'British Women and the Baptist World Alliance' in *Baptist Quarterly*, 41 (January 2005), pp. 25-46 (p. 36).

In 1910, a Miss Clark, then a first-year student at Glasgow University intending to graduate MA and BD, wrote to J.H. Shakespeare, General Secretary of the Baptist Union of Great Britain, enquiring about 'future settlement as a Baptist minister'. In reply, she was informed that the Ministerial Recognition Committee could only consider those who were actually engaged in pastoral work.[115] Given this lack of encouragement Miss Clark did not pursue her case. This brief reference is all we know of Miss Clark. However, by electing to study the MA and BD, she was following the requirements for ministerial candidates at the four Scottish university divinity faculties. In keeping with their tradition of a broad-based education, an arts degree was a necessary prerequisite before specialised theological study. To undertake this six or seven years' course Miss Clark must have been very sure of her call to the ministry.

In England, the first woman student at Regent's Park College was Violet Hedger who, on graduating BD, was settled as a probationer minister in 1926 in Derbyshire.[116] She saw a need for women ministers, suggesting that churches should have both male and female pastors. However, between 1927, when women were first placed on the BUGB ministerial list, and 1975, they were shown separately from the men.[117] Also in 1975, recognising that all their serving deaconesses were exercising a pastoral function, the BUGB transferred them to the amalgamated list of accredited ministers.[118]

Other denominations in Scotland, however, were ordaining women as ministers. In 1963, Mary Lusk, a graduate in divinity, who had been commissioned as a deaconess and licensed to preach the gospel, petitioned the General Assembly for ordination as a minister following her appointment as assistant chaplain at Edinburgh University. She considered that this constituted a call to the ordained ministry and wished the Assembly to test her call. After a series of reports on the subject of women's ordination and consultations with presbyteries, in 1968, the General Assembly passed an act allowing 'the ordination of women to the ministry of Word and sacrament on the same basis as men'.[119] Although she herself was not ordained until 1978 Mrs. Mary Levison, as she was by then, had paved the way for others, who in fact were ordained ahead of her.

---

[115] Randall, *English Baptists*, p. 71.
[116] Ibid, p.142
[117] Jane Craske, 'The Grounds of Dispute: Theologies of Leadership, Ministry and Ordination and Women's Ministry' in Janet Wootton (ed.) *This is Our Story: The Free Church Women's Ministry* (London: Epworth, 2007), pp. 11-29 (p. 20).
[118] Randall, pp.389-90
[119] L.O. Macdonald, 'Women in Presbyterian Churches' in Nigel M. de S. Cameron et al (eds), *Dictionary of Scottish Church History and Theology* (Edinburgh: T&T Clark Ltd, 1995), pp. 883-88 (p. 887).

The 'first woman ordained to a pastoral charge in a Scottish mainstream denomination' was Mrs. Vera Kenmure (nee Findlay). [120] Miss Findlay studied at the Scottish Congregational College and was called to Partick Congregational Church, Glasgow, before she completed her BD. She was ordained to that charge on 1 November 1928 and in April 1929 the Congregational Union of Scotland amended their constitution, allowing the designation 'minister' to apply equally to women as well as men. Objections were raised by a minority of the Partick congregation when she married, especially after the birth of her first child. She resigned her charge and those who agreed with her started a new church, which she led.[121] Mrs. Kenmure's experience shows an inherent prejudice against female ministers then, but this must be seen in the context of the time, when, as previously indicated, professional women were required to resign on marriage.

Scottish Baptist women who were called to the pastoral ministry therefore had two difficult choices, to train and work in England or to leave their church and join one which recognised female ordination. Both courses were followed and, although numbers were not great, the result was a loss of talent within the churches the women had left. Yet, there was a contradiction in the Union's failure to grant these women ministerial recognition, as the Scottish Baptist Lay Preachers' Association had accorded equality to men and women since its inception in 1926.

The question of women in the ministry was debated at the Baptist Union Assembly in October 1985, to which Hillhead Baptist Church, Glasgow, had submitted the motion:-'That women should be accepted for training for the Baptist ministry and in due course be placed on the accredited list on the same terms as men.'

Because of its importance, it was decided that a majority of two-thirds of the delegates present should vote in favour. After lengthy debate, the result of the ballot was 231 votes in favour and 235 against the motion out of 466 votes cast. The motion failed but the result showed how narrowly opinion was divided.[122]

In May 1996 a letter was submitted to the Baptist Union Council by one of its members requesting that 'fresh consideration be given to the "Women in Ministry" issue'. It was agreed that the matter should be referred to the Ministry Study Review Group and the Doctrine and Inter-Church Relations Committee, with seminars at the Assembly in May 1997 for discussion, followed by a special 'one-day' Assembly on 1 November 1997 for decision.[123] As the

---

[120] Elizabeth Ewan, Sue Innes and Sian Reynolds (eds), *The Biographical Dictionary of Scottish Women* (Edinburgh: Edinburgh University Press, 2007), p. 191.

[121] ibid.

[122] 'Assembly Report Third Session' in *SBYB1986*, pp. 102-106.

[123] Digest of Council Minutes 14 May 1996 para.24 in *SBYB 1997*, p.176. For the report of the seminar in May 1997 see 'Minutes of Assembly Business Sessions' in *SBYB 1998*, pp. 197-206.

proposal again failed narrowly to reach the required two-thirds majority in favour, the question was brought to Assembly again in October 1999. The motion to amend the Union's recognition and accreditation procedures to include women as well as men was agreed with a majority of 68.6%, just over the two-thirds required.[124] This illustrates the deep division among Scottish Baptists over the leadership of women in their churches, yet we continue to work together in fellowship.

## A Pioneer Ordinand[125]

A few years after Muriel McNair, the Scottish Baptist College admitted another lady who became a pioneer in the movement towards women's ordination. In 1987 Mrs. Marjorie Taylor was accepted to study for the College's Christian Service Certificate and the Cambridge Certificate in Religious Studies, at that time the only courses available to women. During her second year, Marjorie, sensing a call to Christian service, asked her tutor, Dr. Burrows, whether she could proceed to the Diploma in Practical Theology. This course, operated jointly by the College and the Baptist Union, was designed for men who intended to become full time ministers in our churches. Marjorie was referred to the then superintendent, the Rev. Eric Watson, who thought her request unlikely to be allowed, as this could be regarded as permitting women to enter the ministry 'by the back door'.

Meanwhile, the Union had withdrawn from involvement in the Diploma course, which then became the sole responsibility of the College. In these circumstances Marjorie was allowed to begin her studies for this in 1989. The course involved practical work in various aspects of ministry, including hospital chaplaincy. While preparing for a meeting with the chaplain at Glasgow Royal Infirmary, one of her fellow students asked Marjorie whether she had thought of this as an area of Christian service. Immediately she sensed without any doubt that this was the Lord's call to her. Supported by the College, she undertook a practical placement at Gartnavel Royal, a psychiatric hospital in Glasgow, alongside students for ministry in the Church of Scotland.

Appointments to hospital chaplaincy were made by the Church of Scotland on behalf of the National Health Service, with posts advertised at the local Presbytery meetings and in their newsletters. This made it difficult for candidates from other denominations to access information. However, on completing her course in 1991, undeterred, Marjorie approached the Chaplain's Convener at her local hospital, Hairmyres, East Kilbride, who was very sympathetic. A part-time post was available and the other chaplains were keen to have a woman and someone who was not a member of the Church of

---

[124] For the report on this debate see 'Minutes of Assembly Business Sessions' in *SBYB 2000*, pp. 236-44.

[125] Based on personal information from Mrs. Taylor to the author 17 January 2009.

Scotland. Nevertheless, there was a problem. Before she could take up the post, Marjorie had to be ordained. Was this a stumbling block or a testing of her call?

Marjorie approached Eric Watson again. He advised that there was provision to ordain women for specialist ministries, including hospital chaplaincy. Although the Baptist Union office-bearers had supported Marjorie throughout her studies, the Union could not undertake her ordination. Either her own church or the Scottish Baptist College would be responsible. So on 30 November 1991 Marjorie was ordained in Westwood Baptist Church, East Kilbride. Her minister, the Rev. Trevor Miller, chaired the service; Dr. Burrows ordained her, and the Rev. William Clark, Director of Pastoral Studies at the College, preached.

Marjorie has worked as a hospital chaplain since then and in 2001, with full accreditation for women as ministers in Scottish Baptist churches now possible she applied, only to be told that she would be required to undertake the three years probationary studies required of newly settled ministers on leaving College. For Marjorie this was especially stressful as by now she was wheel chair dependent because of multiple sclerosis.

On reflecting on her situation, Marjorie admits, that while the Union and College staffs had supported female students throughout, it was very much a learning process on both sides. Particularly difficult was the lack of credit given for practical experience to those who applied for retrospective accreditation. This was possibly due to prejudice expressed by a fear that women ministers would 'bring down the standards'. Despite her struggles and setbacks as she pursued her calling, Marjorie counts it a privilege to have pioneered the ordination of women although that was never her intention.

Another lady who was seeking accreditation 'with great grace and humility' was Miss Beth Dunlop, a former Salvation Army Officer, who had been appointed associate pastor of Dumfries Baptist Church in 1997. In 2000, the Rev. Douglas Hutcheon ordained her and preached at the service.[126] However, Beth too had to complete the probationary studies. Finally, at the Baptist Union Assembly in Inverness in October 2003 Marjorie and Beth were the first women to be fully accredited as Ministers by the Baptist Union of Scotland. As is still the case in England, the numbers of women in pastoral ministry in Scotland is likely to remain small and probably concentrated in specialist areas such as hospital chaplaincy.

## Conclusions

Because of the sources available, this study has concentrated on the more influential women in Scottish Baptist churches. History does not record those who quietly and faithfully serve the Lord as Sunday School teachers, leaders of other organisations or in music ministries. Many now serve as deacons, a few as

---

[126] Letter to author, 2 May 2008.

secretaries and treasurers. Statistically, women form the majority of our members and adherents. They work behind the scenes at social gatherings, often unnoticed, and in many other ways.

Despite the constraints of their lives in the earlier twentieth century, Scottish Baptist women led in campaigns for political change and social improvement. They met the challenges of two world wars, which gave them greater opportunities for Christian service and witness. This paved the way for the acceptance of women into the pastoral ministry, although it is too early to say what the long-term results will be in our churches. These will be for a future generation of historians to consider.

CHAPTER 4

## *Blessed be the Tie that Binds*: Scottish Baptists and their Relationships with Other Baptist Churches, 1900 to 1945

### Brian Talbot

#### Introduction

Scottish Baptists began the twentieth century in good heart. The Baptist Union of Scotland (BUS) formed in 1869 with fifty-one churches and 3,700 members,[1] had increased, by 1900, to 113 churches with 15,137 members.[2] Growth was to continue in the number of affiliated churches until 1937 when 158 congregations had declared their allegiance,[3] though, it was a figure that was to decline to 151 churches by 1945.[4] Total membership of these bodies peaked at 23,190 in 1935,[5] a figure reduced to 20,760 by 1945.[6] This paper will examine one aspect of the collective life of this group of Baptist congregations, in the period 1900 to 1945, namely its relationships with other Baptist Churches. First there will be an examination of ties with other British Baptists, especially those associated with the Baptist Union of Great Britain and Ireland (BUGBI). Secondly, the development of relationships with other Baptist bodies, especially, but not exclusively, with those in Europe and North America. Of necessity this study of the life of a denomination over five decades of the twentieth century can at best provide only an introduction to this subject.

---

[1] *Scottish Baptist Yearbook* (SBY) (Glasgow: Baptist Union of Scotland, 1899), p. 8.
[2] D. Hunt, *Reflections on Our Past: A Statistical Look at Baptists in Scotland, 1892-1997* (Hamilton: Hamilton Baptist Church, 1997), Appendix 2, 'Table of Annual Statistics', n.p. [NB 1901 *SBY* unobtainable, and membership total is for reporting churches.]
[3] *SBY*, 1938, p. 79.
[4] *SBY*, 1946, p. 51.
[5] *SBY*, 1936, p. 79.
[6] *SBY*, 1946, p. 51.

## Scottish Baptists and the Baptist Union of Great Britain

In order to understand more fully the relationship between the BUS and BUGBI it is helpful to relate a brief outline of their historical interaction in the period prior to the twentieth Century. From the inception of the movement, through the influence of Baptists in Cromwellian armies, in the seventeenth century,[7] Baptists in Scotland have normally had good relationships with other British Baptists. In the eighteenth and nineteenth centuries the Scotch Baptists, who insisted on the plurality of the eldership in their congregations, usually had regular fellowship with their brethren in England and Wales.[8] 'English' Baptists in Scotland, those who held to a sole pastor and deacons model of leadership, by contrast, had strong links to BUGBI. This fellowship had been strengthened significantly in the early nineteenth century through the agency of Andrew Fuller, Kettering minister and first secretary of the Baptist Missionary Society (BMS), who obtained funding from London Baptists to encourage home mission work by his Scottish colleagues.[9] The extent of the ties between Scottish Baptists and BUGBI can be seen in the response of the latter denomination to the decision of the former body to establish the Baptist Union of Scotland in 1869. It was assumed that the Scottish Union was affiliated to the larger organisation, rather than established as a separate denomination. The 1872 BUGBI Assembly motion declared: That the Union recognises the

> Baptist Unions of Wales and Scotland as affiliated to the Baptist Union of Great Britain and Ireland, and resolves that the Chairman, Secretary and Treasurer of each of these Unions be entitled, ex officio, to seats on the Committee of this Union.[10]

This assumption irritated the independent-minded Scots. The 1872 Scottish Assembly ensured that this false perception was graciously corrected. The minute, dated 24 October 1872, stated:

---

[7] D.B. Murray, 'The Seventeenth and Eighteenth Centuries', in D.W. Bebbington (ed.), *The Baptists in Scotland: A History* (Glasgow: Baptist Union of Scotland, 1988), pp. 9-13.

[8] B.R. Talbot, 'Unity and Disunity: Scotch Baptists, 1765-1842', in R. Pope (ed.), *Religion and National Identity: Scotland and Wales, c.1700-2000* (Cardiff: University of Wales Press, 2001).

[9] B.R. Talbot, *Search for a Common Identity: The Origins of the Baptist Union of Scotland 1800-1870* (Carlisle: Paternoster, 2003), pp. 153-55.

[10] BUGBI, Committee Meeting, 21 November 1871; Annual Session, 22 April 1872, MS in Angus Library, Regent's Park College, Oxford; *Baptist Handbook* (London: Yates and Alexander, 1873), p. 41.

> The Session whilst grateful for and most desirous to reciprocate the practical courtesy of the Baptist Union of Great Britain and Ireland is doubtful of the propriety of affiliation with the larger society.[11]

The Scots did not wish their friendship with the larger body to be taken for granted and wished to work together as equal partners. The motion was followed up by the BUS Executive Committee, in July 1873, who were determined to ensure that 'our relation to that Union should be more clearly defined.' The secretary was instructed to inform BUGBI that they ought to consider changing 'the name of the larger Union' to 'The Baptist Union of England and Wales.'[12] The younger body was grateful for assistance from their British colleagues, but had a strong sense of their distinct identity in the last quarter of the nineteenth century.

This assertion of the autonomy of the small body was continued in the twentieth Century. The consistent references to BUGBI as the 'English Union',[13] with the exception of formal citations from documents, had arisen as a result of the larger body assuming that the BUS was a branch of its own operations. The Scotch Baptists in particular, though largely identified with the BUS, were less than happy at the prospect of unduly close ties with BUGBI, when at the same time they had retained their affection for Scotch brethren outside of Scotland in the United Kingdom, and did not want to see a weakening of that relationship.[14] The particular focus of their grievance, on that occasion, was over plans for a scheme of Ministerial Recognition.[15] The Baptist Union of Scotland was interested in participating in the scheme established by BUGBI, but sought a number of changes in its regulations prior to recommending the proposals to its own constituency. There was a determination to retain control over the accreditation of its own ministers and to avoid being swallowed up by a numerically larger body. The areas of concern included the need for the examiners of Scottish candidates for accreditation to be independent of BUGBI[16] and the need for a BUS representative on the British Union's committee setting the examination papers for ministers seeking

---

[11] Annual Session, 24 October 1872, Baptist Union of Scotland Minute Book, 1869-1880, n.p. MS in the Historical Archive of the Baptist Union of Scotland, Baptist House, Glasgow (as are all BUS Minute Books).

[12] Executive Committee of BUS, Minutes, 8 July 1987, BUS Minute Book, 1869-1880, n.p.

[13] BUS Council, 23 October 1923, BUS Minute Book, 1915-1926, p. 530, is a representative example.

[14] BUS Council, 30 October 1901, BUS Minute Book, 1896-1906, n.p.

[15] Details of this scheme are given in P. Shepherd, *The Making of a Modern Denomination: John Howard Shakespeare and the English Baptists 1898-1924* (Carlisle: Paternoster, 2001), pp. 53-91.

[16] BUS General Committee, 12 May 1903, BUS Minute Book, 1896-1906, n.p.

recognition.[17] General agreement was reached over the operation of a joint Ministerial Recognition Scheme, even though the Scots continued to refer to it as 'the new scheme of the English Union.' Adam Nimmo, Convener of the Scottish Ministerial Recognition Committee, believed that despite its deficiencies this common approach to accrediting ministers would 'promote unity and facilitate ministerial transfers between England and Scotland.'[18] He persuaded the BUS Council that 'we should utilise the impulse of the larger movement in order to strengthen our position in Scotland.'[19] The Annual Assembly that year, October 1912, also accepted his advocacy of this cause.[20] Preservation of a distinctive Scottish identity within a British Baptist context was a prominent theme in the first quarter of the twentieth century.

The confidence of the BUS appeared to grow in the next few decades as a sense of apparent 'inferiority' to the larger body diminished. There were, though, still occasional concerns expressed in its ranks. At the BUS Council in November 1927 there was discussion over the appointment of the BUS President as the Scottish representative to BUGBI, in particular 'the desirability of some recognition being given him in the annual assembly was emphasized.'[21] After decades of Scottish appeals for changes to procedures in the British Union the tables were turned in 1942. It had been noted that the Scottish General Secretary had been entitled for over twenty years to an automatic seat on the BUGBI Council, but the honour had not been reciprocated on the BUS Council. This discrepancy was drawn to the attention of the Office-bearers of the Scottish Union who decided to rectify the situation, commending it to the Council who shared their favourable viewpoint.[22] At the end of our period, in 1949, Scottish Baptists were invited to send a representative to join the search committee of BUGBI who needed to replace their General Secretary, the Rev. M.E. Aubrey, who was due to retire in 1951.[23] However, it is probable that one of the greatest means of strengthening ties between these two bodies was the regular movement of ministers between churches in England and Scotland. On the occasion of the transfer of a minister from Scotland, a letter was sent commending him to the relevant Baptist Association.[24] A similar procedure was

---

[17] BUS General Committee, 9 February 1904, BUS Minute Book, 1896-1906, n.p.
[18] BUS Ministerial Recognition Committee, 23 January 1912, BUS Minute Book, 1906-1915, n.p.
[19] BUS Council, 13 February, 1912, BUS Minute Book, 1906-1915, n.p.
[20] BUS Annual Assembly, 24 October 1912, BUS Minute Book, 1906-1915, n.p.
[21] BUS Council, 29 November 1927, BUS Minute Book, 1927-1931, p. 144.
[22] BUS Office-bearers, 25 February 1942, BUS Minute Book, 1939-1942, pp. 696-97. BUS Council, 25 February 1942, BUS Minute Book, 1939-1942, pp. 707-708.
[23] BUS Finance and Business Committee, 9 February 1949, BUS Minute Book, 1945-1950, p. 589.
[24] BUS Council, 8 September 1914, a letter to the Northern Baptist Association, BUS Minute Book, 1906-1915, n.p.; BUS Council 27 November 1923, a letter to the London Baptist Association, BUS Minute Book, 1915-1926, p. 607; BUS Council,

followed when an English minister moved to Scotland.[25] Ownership of the link between BUGBI and BUS had to be in the hands of the ordinary members. The acceptance of a steady transfer of ministers between English and Scottish Union churches implied that the ties between them were increasing in strength. Mutual respect and confidence in their respective identities characterised the relationship between these two Baptist Unions by the middle of the twentieth century.

## Other British Baptists and the Baptist Missionary Society

It was not surprising that the overwhelming number of references to other British Baptists in the minutes of the BUS committees and in the pages of the *Scottish Baptist Magazine* (*SBM*) concerned the largest of the British Baptist Unions. There were, though, some references to the bodies in Wales and Ireland. The Baptist Union of Wales received the least attention, with only a handful of references and these mainly to the movement of, ministers between Scotland and Wales,[26] but there was also an article in 1906 on the impact of the Welsh Revival on the statistics of the Baptist Churches in that land.[27] The attention given to Irish Baptists was mainly restricted to reports on the Annual Assembly of the Baptist Union of Ireland in the SBM,[28] though an article in 1910, with favourable comments, reported protests by Irish Baptists to their South African colleagues over a proposed ecumenical venture, in which the Baptist Union of South Africa was intending to participate.[29] It must be assumed that, though all the references to these two sister Unions were favourable, their affairs were not prominent in the list of priorities of Scottish Baptists.

One Baptist body around which most British Baptists united was the Baptist Missionary Society. Support for the BMS in Scotland had always been generous. Scotch Baptists, associated with Archibald McLean had given a gift of £151 as early as 1796 to support the work in India.[30] This tradition had been maintained amongst Scottish Baptists who shared with their fellow British Baptists in a 'wonderful' collection of £210,992 for the work of overseas

---

16 September 1931, a letter to the Yorkshire Baptist Association, BUS Minute Book, 1927-1931, p. 696, are examples of this movement.

[25] BUS Council, 25 February 1931, letters from London Baptist Association and the North East district of the Lancashire and Cheshire Association, commending English ministers moving to Scotland, BUS minute Book, 1927-1931, pp. 592-95.

[26] BUS Council, 6 May 1924, BUS Minute Book, 1915-1926, p. 642. BUS Council, 21 February 1928, BUS Minute Book, 1926-1931, p. 172.

[27] *Scottish Baptist Magazine* (*SBM*), 32.1 (January 1906), p. 3.

[28] *SBM*, 36.8 (August 1910), pp. 124-125; 59.5 (July 1933), p. 6, are examples.

[29] *SBM*, 36.8 (August 1910), p. 125; 36.9 (September 1910), pp. 140-41.

[30] W. Jones (ed.), *The New Evangelical Magazine*, Vol.2 (London: T. Tegg, 1816), p. 76.

mission in the year 1922-1923.³¹ The Foreign Mission sub-committee of the BUS decided in May 1941 to set a target of £10,000 for the Ter-jubilee celebrations of the BMS in 1943. The BUS Council accepted this challenge, but regretted that no appeal could be made prior to the 1942 Annual Assembly due to other heavy financial commitments, incurred as a result of the war in Europe.³² Scottish Baptists exceeded their target, reaching a total of £13,413 in 1943, a notable achievement given other necessary monetary demands. The income trends showed a continuing increase throughout the 1940s.³³ Scotland was to follow Wales in appointing a fulltime representative, in 1937, to encourage additional support for its work.³⁴ The level of financial assistance for any society is a good indication of the commitment of its professed supporters. Baptists in Scotland were clearly dedicated to the cause of the BMS in the first half of the twentieth century.

There were also regular features on the work of this mission agency in the *SBM*.³⁵ China received the most attention with fourteen major stories between 1900 and 1945. These accounts tended to focus on particular Scottish missionaries, for example, the Rev. and Mrs Moir Duncan who served mainly in the province of Shensi. Prior to his death in 1906 Moir Duncan was Principal of the University of Shensi.³⁶ There were also short biographical sketches of distinguished indigenous Christians such as Hannah Liu, the daughter of a Chinese Baptist pastor, who was one of the first women, in 1931, to be elected to the Chinese parliament.³⁷ India also featured prominently with stories about Medical Mission activities, for example, at the Moorshead Memorial Hospital, Kond Hills, North India³⁸ and Christian Education at the Serampore College, later University, founded by William Carey.³⁹ There was also a lesser focus on the indigenous Baptist work in India, for example, reporting on the formation of the All-India Baptist Union, comprising Baptist work in India, Ceylon and Burma, a body established to unite the existing Baptist Unions in that part of the world.⁴⁰ There was also a reference to other Christian bodies working in India,

---

[31] *SBM*, 49.5 (May 1923), p. 58.
[32] BUS Officebearers Meeting, 13 May 1941, BUS Minute Book, 1939-1942, p. 465.
[33] *Baptist Missionary Society: Ter-Jubilee Celebrations: 1942-44* (London: Baptist Missionary Society, 1945), pp. 14-16, cited by B. Stanley, *The History of the Baptist Missionary Society* (Edinburgh: T. & T. Clark, 1992), p. 392. See also *SBM*, 74.10 (October 1948), p. 9.
[34] Stanley, *Baptist Missionary Society*, p. 513.
[35] See also M. McVicar (ed.), *The Great Adventure: Scotland and the BMS* (Glasgow: Baptist Union of Scotland, 1992).
[36] *SBM*, 26.1 (January 1900), pp. 4-5; 28.2, (February 1902), p. 17; 29.6, (June 1903), p. 94; 32.10, (October 1906), pp. 178, 184-85.
[37] *SBM*, 57.8 (August 1931), p. 123.
[38] *SBM*, 62.3 (March 1936), p. 10.
[39] *SBM*, 35.2 (February 1909), pp. 32-33; 36.8, (August 1910), p. 140.
[40] *SBM*, 64.3 (March 1938), p. 8.

with a feature on New Delhi Free Church, an ecumenical congregation sponsored and attended by both Baptists and Methodists. This Church was established jointly by the BMS and the Methodist Missionary Society as a non-denominational church for all English-speaking Christians. Scottish Baptist minister the Rev. Norris Carpenter was appointed to serve this congregation in 1946.[41] The activities of the Baptist Zenana Mission, established to reach Muslim and Hindu ladies by other women, principally in India, though also operating in China, were also promoted.[42] Baptist work in Africa focused on the Congo,[43] and the Baptist Industrial Mission's work in Blantyre, Malawi,[44] of which the medical service was associated with Church of Scotland missionaries.[45] Interest in and support for the work in the West Indies was also evident. Details were given, through the BMS, for example, of an aid appeal by Jamaican Baptists after an earthquake had severely damaged Kingston in January 1907.[46] In the following year an article in the *SBM* revealed a link between Berwick Baptist Church and the West Indies.[47] The significance of the growth of Baptist causes in the West Indies and Central America, through missionary activity, was made plain in a lengthy article in 1935.[48] The work of the BMS and its associated societies received unrivalled prominence amongst Scottish Baptists through the pages of the *SBM*, in this period, in contrast to the multiplicity of evangelical mission organisations that would seek the support of Scottish Baptists, and the resultant publicity, in the second half of the twentieth Century.

## Baptists in Continental Europe

It was natural that the impact of the Baptist movement in Europe would also be of great interest to Scottish Baptists. The first significant article on European Baptists published in the BUS magazine in the twentieth century, appeared in 1905 and was a survey of the impact of Baptist witness in different parts of the world. It drew attention to a number of countries in Europe where progress was encouraging, especially Germany, Italy and Russia, but also mentioned other

---

[41] *SBM*, 72.10 (October 1946), pp. 1-2; McVicar, *Great Adventure*, p. 71.
[42] *SBM*, 28.6 (June 1902), pp. 90-91; 32.9 (September 1906), p. 158;
[43] *SBM*, 30.6 (June 1904), p. 102; 32.3 (March 1906), p. 42; 38.4 (April 1912), insert between pp. 72-73.
[44] *SBM*, 28.4 (April 1902), p. 53; 33.7 (July 1907), pp. 134-135; 33.10 (October 1907), p. 181; 31.11 (November 1907), pp. 203-204; 34.9 (September 1908), pp. 142-43.
[45] Some details of the Church of Scotland work in Blantyre are found in E.G.K. Hewat, *Vision and Achievement, 1796-1956: A History of the Foreign Missions of the Churches united in the Church of Scotland* (London: Thomas Nelson, 1960), pp. 222-31.
[46] *SBM*, 33.4 (April 1907), p. 66.
[47] *SBM*, 34.5 (May 1908), p. 70.
[48] *SBM*, 61.8 (August 1935), pp. 6-7.

places like Norway where persecution of Baptists had led many families to take the decision to emigrate to America.[49] The first European Baptist Congress in Berlin during 1908 was promoted earlier that year in the *SBM* It was noted that two Scots, Peter Campbell JP of Perth and the Rev. J.T. Forbes of Glasgow, would be amongst those individuals invited to address the assembled delegates. The former was President of the BUS and the later was minister of Hillhead Baptist Church in Glasgow.[50] Future Congresses were also brought to the attention of Scottish Baptists. The Second gathering in Stockholm, in 1913, for example, received noticeably more space in the *SBM* than the first in Berlin, indicating the growing importance of the Baptist cause in Europe to their colleagues in Scotland, despite the fact that no Scot had been invited to give a major address on this occasion.[51] There was also an attempt to build relationships between young people in the United Kingdom with others in mainland Europe. 'Fellowship Tours' were organised in 1934, for example, in order that:

> Young Baptists of different lands may discuss the new nationalisms - the British and Germans may, without heat or bitterness, speak about war guilt and Hitlerism...From such fellowship arises such mutual respect and affection that War between them would seem to be madness.[52]

The Baptist Union of Scotland had also put aside money for the support of Baptist mission work in Europe, for example in 1937 a figure of £200 was made available.[53] The European Committee of the Union kept colleagues aware of the changing situation in mainland Europe. The November Council in 1939, at the advent of the Second World War, was urged by members of this committee to remember in prayer, in particular, their Baptist colleagues in Europe.[54] It is evident that links between Scottish and European Baptists were not only maintained, but increasing in the twentieth Century. This pattern may be due in part to better communications and transport, but also in large measure to a growing desire for fellowship with fellow Baptists living on the same continent.

The majority of references to Baptist work in Europe, in Scottish Baptist literature and minutes of this period, however, referred to events in particular

---

[49] *SBM*, 31.2 (February 1905), pp. 21-22.
[50] *SBM*, 34.4 (April 1908), p. 50. Reports of their contributions are given in J.H. Rushbrooke (ed.), *First European Baptist Congress* (London: Baptist Union Publications Department, 1908), pp. 29, 75-79.
[51] *SBM*, 39.4 (April 1913), p. 58; 39.8 (August 1913), pp. 143-144; 39.9 (September 1913), pp. 158-59. See also B. Green, *Crossing the Boundaries: A History of the European Baptist Federation* (Didcot: Baptist Historical Society, 1999), pp. 3-4.
[52] *SBM*, 60.4 (April 1934), p. 2.
[53] Annual Meeting of BUS Nominees Ltd, 30 November 1937, BUS Minute Book, 1935-1939, p. 455.
[54] BUS Council, 29 November 1939, BUS Minute Book, 1939-1942, p. 122.

countries. Russia and Romania received the greatest attention, with more than twenty articles about the former and fourteen concerning the latter. The principal reason for the dominance of these countries was due to the regular waves of persecution that were visited upon Baptists and other Evangelical Christian bodies. Oppression of Russian Baptists had begun under the regime of the Czars.[55] Its extent usually depended on the local officials in any given part of the Russian Empire. In theory religious liberty for dissenters from Orthodoxy had been guaranteed after 1905, but the picture was somewhat different in practice.[56] The affliction of these Christians increased greatly with a famine that was brought to the attention of Scottish Baptists in February 1922. An open letter signed by the leaders of the 'Baptist Union of All Russia', P.V. Pavloff, M. Timoshenko and W.G. Pavloff, painted an appalling picture of mass starvation in their homeland.[57] British Baptists, led by J.H. Rushbrooke, the Baptist World Alliance (BWA) Commissioner for Europe, rallied to the cause, providing enough food for 'a Baptist Relief Train.' Most of the Scottish Baptist Churches took collections to assist this effort.[58] At the end of March 1922 Rushbrooke was able to welcome the relief train into Moscow. It would provide food for over 12,000 people until the next harvest. Aid appeals to Baptists in other parts of Europe and North America also produced large quantities of food supplies.[59] In addition to the stories of hardship from Russia there were also some good news reported such as the union of the two Baptist denominations in that country in 1944,[60] and the encouraging evidence of religious freedom in the immediate post-war period. Scottish Baptists would have been delighted to read statements such as these from their Soviet brothers: 'We do most gratefully report that we are now enjoying a measure of freedom unknown by Baptists in all the years of our witness in Russia.'[61] This information came from a group of Christians who had been almost totally cut off from the outside world since their last period of repression from 1928 to 1943.[62] Baptists in Scotland, in line with

---

[55] B. Green, *Tomorrow's Man: A Biography of James Henry Rushbrooke* (Didcot: Baptist Historical Society, 1997), pp. 153-54.

[56] C.T. Byford, *Peasants and Prophets: Baptist Pioneers in Russia and South Eastern Europe* (London: The Kingsgate Press, 2nd edition, 1912), pp. 82-87.

[57] *SBM*, 48.2 (February 1922), p. 14.

[58] *SBM*, 48.3 (March 1922), p. 30.

[59] Green, *Tomorrow's Man*, pp. 93-94.

[60] *SBM*, 70.4 (April 1944), p. 2.

[61] *SBM*, 73.1 (January 1947), p. 2. Caution must be expressed regarding the accuracy of this claim. No doubt the level of persecution had decreased, but by the mid 1940s the Government had imposed new restrictions on churches placing limitations on forms of worship and forcing baptistic churches to operate as one denomination. 'Baptists and Evangelical Christians in the USSR (1919-1991)', in A.W. Wardin, *Baptists Around The World: A Comprehensive Handbook* (Nashville: Broadman and Holman, 1995), p. 216.

[62] Green, *Tomorrow's Man*, pp. 156-57.

fellow Baptists in Europe, and some further afield, were grateful for opportunities to stand alongside their Russian colleagues in very practical ways.

Romanian Baptists also suffered severe persecution at the hands of their Government at the instigation of the Orthodox Church. This problem was at its most severe in the 1930s when, in spite of all their claims to be in favour of promoting religious tolerance, Archbishop Colan was the Minister of Cults and the Patriarch of the Orthodox Church was the Prime Minister.[63] This oppression culminated in the notorious 1938 decree enforcing the closure of all the approximately 1600 Baptist Churches in Romania, a policy enforced for over five months.[64] Baptist protests at this infringement of basic religious and civil liberties had some impact on the Romanian Government, especially when presented in person in Romania by J.H. Rushbrooke.[65] The Rev. James Hair, writing in the *SBM*, left no doubt about the strength of feeling in his own constituency about this appalling situation. 'There is a striking similarity between their actions and that of the Nazi Government in Germany, although the Romanians in their treatment of those outside the State Church, have out-Heroded Herod!',[66] Hair's remarks were put in a more succinct manner in the open letter sent to the Romanian ambassador in London on behalf of the BUS Council in September 1938. Scottish Baptists also sent a copy to the BWA to encourage them also to continue to work hard to resolve this difficult situation.[67] It was recognised that pressure from many bodies was required to bring about the necessary resolution to these problems. Baptists in Scotland had played a full part, both as a member of the BWA and as an independent Union in seeking to address this problem.

The Baptist witness in Bohemia, now the Czech Republic, was also strongly promoted in Scotland. Here there was a personal link with the Rev. Henry Novotny, now a Baptist minister, but formerly a Presbyterian, whose training for pastoral work had included time at the Free Church of Scotland College in Edinburgh. Novotny, while serving as a Free Reformed minister in Prague had become convinced of the need for believer's baptism and in 1885 had become a Baptist. His itinerant labours, prior to his death in 1912, had led to the planting of more than thirty churches. Scottish Baptist Churches were the principle source of external finance for Baptist work in Bohemia.[68] Novotny's tours of

---

[63] *SBM*, 64.3 (March 1938), p. 4.
[64] Decizie [Law] No.26, 208, cited by Green, *Tomorrow's Man*, p. 152. The BWA letter of protest at this Decizie is printed in the *SBM*, October 1938, p. 16.
[65] *SBM*, 61.11 (November 1935), p. 2; 64.5 (May 1938), p. 7, are examples.
[66] *SBM*, 65.1 (January 1939), p. 5.
[67] BUS Council Resolution to the Romanian Ambassador, London, BUS Minute Book, 1935-1939, pp. 632-33.
[68] Byford, *Peasants and Prophets*, pp. 15-25. J. Novotny, *The Baptist Romance in the Heart of Europe: The Life and Times of Henry Novotny* (East Orange, New Jersey: Czechoslovak Baptist Convention in America and Canada, 1939), pp. 126-27.

Scotland were promoted in the *SBM*, as were the reports of the progress of his labours at home.[69] After his death the work was led by his son Joseph, also a Baptist minister, who maintained the link with their Scottish supporters. There were two ministers, Revs George Yuille (Glasgow) and Alex Wylie (Edinburgh), who passed on the news of the work in what became Czechoslovakia, in the first three decades of the twentieth century, and two laymen, W.M. Urquhart S.S.C. of Edinburgh and Frank Ramsay from Glasgow, who co-ordinated the collection of finance to fund the work in that country.[70] It was no surprise, for example, when the political and social crisis in Czechoslovakia reached its height in 1939, due to Nazi German pressures, that Scottish Baptist Churches took up collections to alleviate the hardship being faced by their fellow Baptists.[71] It is certain that the spiritual and emotional ties for this group of Christians in Scotland were as great, if not greater, with their Czechoslovak brethren than with any other comparable Baptist body in Europe.[72]

It is probable that every Baptist Union or Mission operating in Europe at this time received some form of recognition in the *SBM*. Regular news came from Baptists in Italy,[73] Germany, whose Baptists received food parcels from Scotland, in 1947, after the war;[74] the Baltic States,[75] Scandinavia,[76] and Spain,[77] with occasional information from Portugal,[78] France,[79] Hungary,[80] Holland,[81] Poland[82] and Bulgaria.[83] After making allowances for the limited

---

[69] *SBM*, 27.10 (October 1901), p. 172; 28.1 (January 1902), p. 11; See also the notices of details of his death, 38.2 (February 1912), p. 24; 38.3 (March 1912), p. 52.

[70] *SBM*, 37.5 (May 1911), pp. 76-77; [The gap was due to the war in Europe] 45.7 (July 1919), p. 78; 46.3 (March 1920), pp. 28-29; 48.9 (September 1922), p. 106; 50.9 (September 1924), p. 109;

[71] *SBM*, 65.3 (March 1939), p. 21.

[72] *SBM*, 46.8 (August 1920), p. 101.

[73] For example: *SBM*, 31.10 (October 1905), p. 182; 59.8 (August 1933), p. 19; 60.6 (June 1934), p. 4; 73.5 (May 1947), p. 9.

[74] For example: *SBM*, 35.4 (April 1909), pp. 75-76; 35.8 (August 1909), pp. 163-64; 40.9 (September 1914), pp. 147-48; 48.9 (September 1922), pp. 106-107; 73.1 (January 1947), p. 4.

[75] For example: *SBM*, 48.9 (September 1922), p. 106; 49.10 (October 1923), pp. 121-22; 51.3 (March 1925), p. 36; 51.11 (November 1925), p. 153; 62.5 (May 1936), pp. 8-9.

[76] For example: *SBM*, 35.5 (April 1909), p. 76; 38.9 (September 1912), p. 158; 62.5 (May 1936), pp. 8-9; 63.4 (April 1937), pp. 6-7; 64.12 (December 1938), p. 3.

[77] For example: *SBM*, 37.5 (May 1911), p. 70; 63.6 (June 1937), p. 12; 71.1 (January 1945), pp. 1-2.

[78] *SBM*, 63.8 (August 1937), p. 14.

[79] *SBM*, 35.4 (April 1909), pp. 77-78.

[80] *SBM*, 35.4 (April 1909), p. 77.

[81] *SBM*, 35.4 (April 1909), p. 76; 70.12 (December 1944), p. 2.

space available each month for European news in this denominational periodical, it is obvious that Scottish Baptists, or at least those individuals in charge of producing the magazine, took a major interest in Baptist work and witness throughout the rest of the continent of Europe.

## Baptists in Other Areas of the World

The next area for consideration is the interest of this Scottish denomination in Baptist work in other parts of the world. It is appropriate to begin by looking at the association with the Baptist World Alliance. Minutes of the BUS Council, 25 October 1905, record that 'the General Committee take the steps necessary for associating this Union with the Alliance.... The Resolution was heartily adopted'.[84] The measure of support by Scottish Baptists for this organisation can be seen in the fact that between 1900 and 1945 there were more items published in the *SBM* with reference to this external agency than to any other Baptist body. There were detailed articles encouraging people to attend BWA Congresses and reports from those people who had attended as delegates.[85] The emergence of BWA Youth Congresses were also covered[86] and other international Baptist gatherings were noted, in other parts of the world, in which Scots had played no part.[87] This latter point indicates a genuine concern for wider Baptist work that went beyond activities and events in which Scots participated. Accusations of parochialism could not have been justifiably levelled at Scottish Baptist leaders in this era. Other aspects of BWA work

---

[82] *SBM,* March 1940, p. 6; BUS Officebearers, March 1940, BUS Minute Book, 1939-1942, p. 181.

[83] *SBM*, 75.7 (July 1949), p. 9.

[84] BUS Council, 25 October 1905, BUS Minute Book, 1896-1906, n.p.

[85] *SBM*, 31.8 (August 1905), pp. 133-34, 136-40; 37.4 (April 1911), pp. 54-55; 37.6 (June 1911), p. 91; 37.8 (August 1911), pp. 121-29; 49.7 (July 1923), p. 82; 49.8 (August 1923), p. 93; 49.9 (September 1923), pp. 105-106, 108, 112-15; 54.8 (August 1928), pp. 89-95; 60.9 (September 1934), pp. 1-2; 60.10 (October 1934), pp. 1-3; 61.6 (June 1935), p. 5; 65.9 (September 1939), pp. 1-3; 65.10 (October 1939), pp. 12-13; 73.4 (April 1947), pp. 6-7; 73.6 (June 1947), p. 8; 73.9 (September 1947), pp. 3-5; 76.9 (September 1950), pp. 3-4. Fuller details of these Congresses are found in the volumes published after each event and in F.T. Lord, *Baptist World Fellowship: A Short History of the Baptist World Alliance* (London: Carey Kingsgate Press, 1955).

[86] *SBM* [No reference to the 1st Youth Congress 1931], 63.3 (March 1937), p.11; 74.12 (December 1948), pp. 8-9.

[87] For example: The First Latin American Baptist Congress for Central and Southern America, *SBM*, 57.6 (June 1931), p. 4; and a Scandinavian-Baltic Baptist Youth Conference, *SBM*, 62.6 (June 1936), pp. 6-7.

covered included its aid work in Europe[88] and reports on the international tours of its leaders.[89] The BUS Council, on noting that Dr Rushbrooke was about to embark on a tour of Baptist work in the Far East, (during 1935), requested that the greetings of Baptists in Scotland be conveyed to colleagues in those countries.[90] There were also stories on the life and obituaries of the passing of BWA Presidents;[91] promotion of BWA Sunday in the Scottish congregations; the printing of the President's annual letter to member churches in the *SBM*[92] and the BWA contribution to the debate on peace and disarmament and its comments on the Second World War.[93] Dr Townley Lord, in his Jubilee history of the BWA, claimed that by 1955, the time of the writing of his book, that 'the Alliance could claim to be more deeply rooted than ever in the affections of its constituent Unions and Conventions.'[94] This interpretation of BWA history, for the first half of the twentieth century, was certainly true for Baptists in Scotland.

Transatlantic relationships were also greatly valued by this Scottish denomination. The regular news items and comments gleaned from America showed the respect in which the larger Baptist bodies in that country were held. It is probable that copies of *The Baptist Argus*, later called *The Baptist World*,[95] a Southern Baptist publication, were read by the editor of the *SBM*, as there were a number of occasions on which a recent issue of that American periodical was discussed. In February 1904, for example, there were comments in an *SBM* article on one entitled 'Baptist World Outlook', produced in America as recently as January that year. The editor of the Scottish magazine was delighted to pass on evidence of rapid church growth in many parts of the world, but less happy for Scottish Baptists to be described as "a feeble folk", on the grounds that numerical growth for Scottish Baptist Churches was modest. He was convinced that a more upbeat comment on his own denomination's progress was merited.[96] On a regular basis the Baptist numerical statistics from America were

---

[88] *SBM*, 46.8 (August 1920), pp. 100-101; 49.2 (February 1923), p. 18; 65.8 (August 1939), p. 3; 72.3 (March 1946), p. 2.

[89] *SBM*, 44.7 (July 1918), p. 98; 48.3 (March 1922), p. 30; 56.11 (November 1930), p. 179; 57.1 (January 1931), p. 4; 61.11 (November 1935), p. 9; 63.8 (August 1937), pp. 1-2, 12.

[90] BUS Council, 27 November 1935, BUS Minute Book, 1935-1939, pp. 11-12.

[91] *SBM*, 55.1 (January 1929), p. 8; 60.11 (November 1934), p. 2; 63.3 (March 1937), p. 5; 63.7 (July 1937), p. 6; 70.8 (August 1944), p. 1; 73.3 (March 1947), p. 2; 74.3 (March 1948), p. 5; 75.4 (April 1949), p. 9.

[92] *SBM*, 37.5 (May 1911), pp. 79-80; 63.2 (February 1937), p. 4; 66.2 (February 1940), p. 4; 72.2 (February 1946), p. 5.

[93] *SBM*, 57.8 (August 1931), p. 120; 65.12 (December 1939), pp. 3-4; 74.9 (September 1948), p. 6.

[94] Lord, *Baptist World Fellowship*, p. 153.

[95] Lord, *Baptist World Fellowship*, p. 2.

[96] *SBM*, 30.2 (February 1904), pp. 21-22. See also 30.5 (May 1904), p. 82; 42.8 (August 1916), p. 60.

brought to the attention of his readers, with the probable intention of encouraging them by the greater numerical growth in sister churches in the USA.[97] J.H. Rushbrooke, then General Secretary of the BWA, was invited to write an article in 1930 for the *SBM* reviewing the success of the work of American Baptist missionaries that were based outside their native land. The title of the article, 'An Impressive Missionary Report', reveals the attitude of the writer, and of the periodical editor, to the subjects under discussion.[98] The underlying attitude of admiration for American Baptists and their success in Christian work would have been evident to most Scottish Baptist readers of their denominational magazine.

Fraternal links with both the Southern Baptist Convention (SBC) and the Northern Baptist Convention (NBC) in America were sufficiently strong for an exchange of delegates to be proposed for annual assemblies or conventions. In October 1920 the SBC sent a delegate to convey greetings to the Baptist Union of Scotland.[99] This visit had been preceded by an invitation from Dr Love of the SBC to the BUS to send a representative to their annual meetings in the USA in May that year.[100] Enquiries were made, in February 1920, as to whether any Scottish Baptists, due to be in the USA in May 1920, would be able to attend on behalf of the Scottish Union, but unfortunately there was no-one available for that purpose. As a result of this difficulty, the BUS Council decided that the appropriate step was to send a letter of greetings instead.[101] In September 1934 Dr W.G. Lewis, European representative of the NBC, was a guest at the BUS Council. He was invited to address the assembled company over lunch, an engagement he was pleased to fulfil.[102] A further means of strengthening fellowship with American Baptists came with the transfer of ministers from Scotland to the USA. When Joseph Kemp moved from Charlotte Baptist Chapel, Edinburgh, to Calvary Baptist Church, New York, in 1915,[103] and Duncan McNeil of Bridgeton Baptist Church, Glasgow, also moved to New York, in 1927, letters of commendation were sent to the receiving Baptist Associations in New York.[104] There was also information in the *SBM* in August 1906 regarding earthquake damage to Baptist Churches in California, but it was assumed that financial assistance from outside the USA was not required on this

---

[97] For example: *SBM*, 30.7 (July 1904), pp. 123-24; 31.7 (July 1905), p. 119; 34.4 (April 1908), p. 50; 49.1 (January 1923), p. 8; 49.4 (April 1923), p. 52; 57.8 (August 1931), p. 119.
[98] *SBM*, 56.3 (March 1930), p. 39.
[99] *SBM*, 46.10 (October 1920), p. 110.
[100] BUS Council, 10 February 1920, BUS Minute Book, 1915-1926, p. 359.
[101] BUS Council, 4 May 1920, BUS Minute Book, 1915-1926, p. 378.
[102] BUS Council, 19 September 1934, BUS Minute Book, 1932-1935, p. 560.
[103] BUS Council, 14 September 1915, BUS Minute Book, 1906-1915, n.p. See W. Kemp, *Joseph Kemp: The Record of a Spirit-Filled Life* (London: Marshall, Morgan &Scott, n.d.), pp. 83-89, for details of his ministry in New York.
[104] BUS Council, 1 February 1927, BUS Minute Book, 1926-1931, p. 69.

occasion.[105] It was clear that fraternal links between American and Scottish Baptists were warm throughout the period 1900 to 1945.

Many Baptists in Scotland, though, were probably even more closely linked to their Canadian colleagues, due to a greater proportion of Scots choosing to emigrate to Canada rather than the USA when they moved to North America. Even in the pages of the *SBM*, for example, in April 1907, information is given of the warm welcome awaiting Scottish Baptist families who wished to emigrate to Canada. Hard-working men will be remunerated with 'wages [that] are the very highest that I suppose are paid in any country', and a certain Charles Brodie of Aberdeen 'is in a position to give [letters of] introduction' for such desirable young people.[106] This article followed one in December 1905 commending those Scottish Baptists who had accepted the challenge of life in Canada. Interest in Baptist work in that country was further stimulated by the visit of Rev. A.J. Vining, a representative of Canadian Baptist Churches, who was apparently 'making a deep impression' in the Scottish congregations he had visited in 1905. It was also important to note that, in addition to the American Baptist periodical mentioned earlier, the editor of the *SBM* also received a regular copy of the *Canadian Baptist*. It is unlikely that more than a handful of Scottish Baptists obtained this periodical however, regular information from Canada was obtained with a view to seeing 'a deeper interest in the Canadian enterprise awakened at home.'[107] This information from North America was supplemented by personal accounts of visits, for example, by the lengthy report from the Rev. W. Holmes Coats, Principal of the Baptist Theological College of Scotland, of his extensive tour of Baptist churches and academic institutions in Ontario and Quebec.[108] When this kind of information was combined with regular news from Scottish Baptist ministers who had moved to Canada, for example, the Rev. Edward Stobo in Quebec, then it is clear that this link across the Atlantic was strong. News was, however, a two-way process, as Stobo made plain in his lengthy letter. 'For over thirty years I have been kept in touch with Scottish brethren and largely through the Magazine reaching me once a month.'[109] In addition, a regular movement of Baptist ministers from their homeland to Canada ensured that the personal interest of many Baptists in Scotland remained strong.[110]

---

[105] *SBM*, 32.8 (August 1906), p. 138.

[106] *SBM*, 33.4 (April 1907), p. 70.

[107] *SBM*, 31.12 (December 1905), p. 214; see also 65.8 (August 1939), p. 6, for a further reference to the *Canadian Baptist* implying that the same editorial policy was in place.

[108] *SBM*, 65.8 (August 1939), pp. 1-3.

[109] *SBM*, 29.6 (June 1903), pp. 105-106; another example is the account of Dr C.C. McLaurin, a pioneer with strong Scottish connections, 66.6 (June 1940), p. 3.

[110] For example: *SBM*, Rev. W.G. Taylor, Keiss to Canada, 32.9 (September 1906), p. 158; Rev. John Elder, Scarfskerry to Canada, 34.9 (September 1908), p. 134; Rev.

The evidence from the *SBM* is clear in stating that ties with North American Baptists dominated articles about the international Baptist scene in this monthly magazine, however, it was not an exclusive interest in one part of the world. There were occasional reports from Asian Baptists in China,[111] Burma, where a Baptist Sydney Loo-Nee had been appointed Pro-Chancellor of Rangoon University in 1940,[112] and Japan.[113] Baptists in Central and South America also received some attention, with several reports on the work in Chile,[114] an appeal for aid to help distressed Baptists in Honduras,[115] and two reports about Brazil. The first story related to BMS plans to consider sending pioneer missionaries to work in the Amazon valley.[116] Proposals to send Brazilian Baptists to plant churches in Portugal was the other story from that country.[117] More information came from Africa, principally from South Africa, but with one other item from the German Baptist Mission in Cameroon.[118] The news from South Africa was offered occasionally from a personal account by a visiting minister, for example, Rev. Graham Scroggie in 1932,[119] but more frequently it was generated through continuing interest in Scottish Baptist ministers who had settled in that country. The January 1943 issue of the *SBM*, in an article based on a copy of the latest *South African Baptist*, referred to the high number of Scots now ministering in that country. The men listed were

> Rev.R.F.Lindsay M.A, formerly of Dunoon; Rev.Andrew McBeth, brother of Dr John McBeth; Rev.W. Morrow Cook, formerly of Johnstone and Partick; and Rev.Harold Herringshaw, son-in-law of the late P.T. McRostie, Tent Hall, Glasgow, who conducted successful evangelistic missions in Scottish Baptist Churches before proceeding to South Africa.[120]

A further article in February 1945 described a Scottish minister W. Morrow Cook, who had been appointed President of the Baptist Union of South Africa.[121] The minutes of the BUS Council also provide additional information of men who moved to serve churches in South Africa. The Rev. A.B. Jack, for

---

R.J. McCracken, Dennistoun, Glasgow, to the chair of Systematic Theology, McMaster University, Ontario, 63.9 (September 1937), p. 16.
[111] *SBM*, 62.6 (June 1936), p. 16; 62.8 (August 1936), p. 9.
[112] *SBM*, 66.3 (March 1940), p. 6.
[113] *SBM*, 66.4 (April 1940), p. 11.
[114] *SBM*, 30.4 (April 1904), p. 75; 35.11 (November 1909), p. 225; 40.3 (March 1914), p. 34.
[115] *SBM*, 62.10 (October 1936), p. 16.
[116] *SBM*, 34.2 (February 1908), p. 18.
[117] *SBM*, 63.8 (August 1937), p. 14.
[118] *SBM*, 66.4 (April 1940), p. 11.
[119] *SBM*, 58.9 (September 1932), p. 142.
[120] *SBM*, 69.6 (June 1943), p. 5.
[121] *SBM*, 71.2 (February 1945), p. 1.

example, moved from Irvine in 1915 to Cape Town. Jack, like Joseph Kemp, mentioned earlier and who had moved from Scotland to New York, was granted personal membership of the BUS.[122] This determination to retain formal links to the homeland was a significant factor in the retention of the affections of Baptists remaining in Scotland. It was also evident that the more Scottish emigrants became leaders in the Baptist circles in their new country, the more likely it became for significant coverage to be obtained in the pages of the *SBM*. The evidence from the high proportion of Scots in the small Baptist presence in South Africa provides firm support for this inference.

The final references to Baptist work overseas comes from Australia and New Zealand. Once again the emigration of Scottish Baptists provides the basis for building a relationship to sister churches in these countries. The Rev. Albert Bean moved from Kelvinside Baptist Church, Glasgow, to Tasmania in 1904,[123] closely followed by the Rev. George Menzies who moved from Arbroath to Freemantle Baptist Church, Western Australia.[124] Menzies was also helpful in providing reports of Baptist progress in Western Australia for the *SBM*.[125] The Rev. James Mursell, who left Dublin Street Baptist Church, Edinburgh, in 1905, for a temporary pastorate at Flinders Street Baptist Church, Adelaide, South Australia, was called to that Baptist congregation on a permanent basis in 1907.[126] William Allen was another Baptist minister leaving Arbroath for Australia, in his case accepting a call to Mount Morgan Baptist Church, Queensland, in 1908.[127] Some pastors served for a limited time in Australia before returning to Scotland. One example of this phenomenon was Peter Flemming who left Duncan Street Baptist Church, Edinburgh, in 1908, to replace James Mursell in Adelaide, before returning to Scotland in 1922 to become the pastor of Dublin Street Baptist Church, Edinburgh, after distinguished service amongst Australian Baptists for 14 years.[128] As in the case of Canada incentives were offered to increase the number of Baptist emigrants to Australia. A lengthy advert in the *SBM*, in October 1925, appealed for another eighty-four Baptist families to move from the United Kingdom under the auspices of the Baptist Colonial Society, a body dedicated to assisting British Baptists move to Commonwealth countries overseas.[129] References to New Zealand in this Scottish periodical were significantly less than to its larger neighbour. In part this fact is due to fewer Scottish Baptist ministers choosing to emigrate to that country. The Rev. William Hay moved from Grantown-on-Spey

---

[122] BUS Council, 14 September 1915, BUS Minute Book, 1906-1915, n.p.
[123] *SBM*, 30.2 (February 1904), p. 22.
[124] *SBM*, 30.10 (October 1904), p. 203.
[125] *SBM*, 31.5 (May 1905), p. 82; 34.1 (January 1908), pp. 7-8.
[126] *SBM*, 33.12 (December 1907), pp. 213-14.
[127] *SBM*, 34.12 (December 1908), p. 190.
[128] *SBM*, 48.2 (February 1922), p. 13.
[129] *SBM*, 51.10 (October 1925), p. 130.

to Dunedin in 1904 and reported back to Scotland a few years later on the progress of his work.[130] He was replaced in Grantown by James Ings, who ironically had been serving a Baptist congregation in New Zealand.[131] There were also several obituary notices in the *SBM* of Scottish Baptist emigrants who had died in New Zealand, but it was evident that ties with this country were not as strong as with Australia.[132] The quantity of Scottish emigrants was almost certainly the decisive factor here.

## Conclusions

In 1900 the Baptist Union of Scotland was a young denomination that had seen healthy growth in the previous decade and was enthusiastic about its prospects in the new century. It had taken some time for the relationship with the Baptist Union of Great Britain and Ireland to be recognised as two independent Unions working together, rather than the Scottish body being subsumed as a regional part of the larger British Union. Common ownership of a Ministerial Recognition Scheme played a part in uniting their respective leaderships and the agreement to exchange representatives at Baptist Union Councils ensured good communications. Official records make only a few references to the Welsh and Irish Baptist Unions, but they are cordial in tone. The main source of unity between British Baptists, however, was the Baptist Missionary Society. Scots showed the extent of their generosity by sometimes exceeding the financial targets given to them and the few articles in the *SBM* continued to feed the enthusiasm of supporters of overseas mission work. The twentieth century had seen closer fellowship between British Baptists and the Scots had played their part in. the development of this progress.

Interest in and support for Baptist work in Europe was high on the agenda of Scottish Baptists. The development of links with Continental Baptists went beyond promotional literature to the provision of financial assistance, campaigns against religious persecution, particularly in Russia and Romania, and the special relationship with Henry and Joseph Novotny, the leaders of the Bohemian Baptist Mission. The rise of the Baptist World Alliance enabled Scottish Baptists to share fellowship with an increasing number of Baptists around the world, through various Congresses and Conventions, both for adults and younger people. The transatlantic ties were strong with both America and Canada, with regular reports on events in those countries. The closest links were naturally with Scottish Baptists serving in those countries, especially Canada which many Scots had chosen for their new home. Asia, Africa and South America received some attention, but due to distance and an absence of Scottish correspondents in those countries the promotion of their work was modest in

---

[130] *SBM*, 30.9 (September 1904), p. 163; 34.5 (May 1908), p. 77.

[131] *SBM*, 29.7 (July 1903), p. 115.

[132] *SBM*, 57.7 (July 1931), p. 111; 64.9 (September 1938), p. 18.

scope. This point could not be said of South Africa, Australia and New Zealand where regular Scottish emigration in this period ensured a steady supply of information of Baptist work. This was especially true of Australia, the first choice for most Scottish Baptist ministers emigrating to the southern hemisphere. A charge of insularity could not have been levelled at Scottish Baptists in this era, as there was an eagerness to keep informed of Baptist progress outside their native land. In the period 1900 to 1945, Baptists in Scotland increasingly felt able to share with the wider Baptist family a growing sense of unity in the gospel.

CHAPTER 5

# *There is one body:*
# Scottish Baptist Ecumenical Relations in the Twentieth Century[1]

## Watson Moyes

### Introduction

Baptist communities in Scotland were formed in the eighteenth and nineteenth centuries[2], the context of their development being the fragmentation, re-union and re-fracturing of Presbyterian groups. The 'Church of Scotland' had emerged from the Scottish Reformation of 1560 and oscillated in church polity between Presbyterianism and Episcopalianism until, in 1690, the 'Church of Scotland', traditionally known as 'The Kirk', was finally established as Presbyterian. Dispute and division, however, continued among Presbyterians and was paralleled within non-Presbyterian dissenting groups including Baptists. There were three Baptist streams: the Scotch Baptists, who adhered to plurality of eldership; the Haldaneite congregations that emerged from the Independent tradition; and the 'English' Baptists who followed the principles and practices of the Particular Baptists of England.

Baptists came into being to bear witness to a set of inter-linked principles, which developed and clarified over an extended period of years and became focused in a Declaration of Principle that, with minor variations, forms the basis of union for Baptists worldwide. But Baptists also called themselves 'Evangelical'. D.W. Bebbington lists four 'special marks of Evangelical religion': conversionism, activism, Biblicism and crucicentrism.'[3] Baptists as

---

[1] This chapter is a précis of a fuller script, T.W. Moyes *Our Place among the Churches* (n.p.: Scottish Baptist History Project, 2013), describing Scottish Baptist twentieth century ecumenical relations, especially the issue of the Inter-Church Process of the 1980s. The title is taken from that of the Presidential Address of Walter Hankinson, *Scottish Baptist Year Book 1927*, pp. 120ff.

[2] The first Baptist congregations emerged during the 1650s in Scotland, but persecution from the Government and the Church of Scotland caused their public demise by the end of that decade.

[3] D.W. Bebbington, *Evangelicalism in Modern Britain* (London: Unwin Hyman, 1989), pp. 2, 3.

Evangelical Christians also accept this 'quadrilateral of priorities', but claim to do so in a distinctively Baptist way. As the century progressed, however, the denomination appeared to develop something of an identity crisis: which took precedence, Baptist principle or Evangelical solidarity? Was 'Evangelical' an adjective describing a quality of being Baptist or a noun contending with another noun, 'Baptist', for supremacy? Are Scottish Baptists a separatist Evangelical group identifying with other separatist Evangelical believers, or a denomination holding Evangelical convictions, identifying with those who share these convictions whatever denomination they belong to, but open to all believers who share the great creeds and respectful of their freedom of conscience to disagree with Baptist convictions?

Despite the history of fragmentation in Scotland, new attitudes were emerging both within Presbyterianism and in the wider Christian world. Presbyterian groups, especially in the later nineteenth century, sought union or re-union mainly on the basis of shared theological formulations. Baptists, driven partly by their priority of evangelisation, sought union on the basis of affirmation of a defining core and acceptance of differing traditions.[4] This process was paralleled south of the Border where the General Baptist and the Particular Baptist movements eventually came together on the Declaration of Principle.

### Our Place among the Churches 1900-1969

The twentieth century dawned with the coming together of the United Presbyterian Church and the Free Church of Scotland, to form the 'United Free Church of Scotland'. Dr Jervis Coats in his October 1900 Presidential Address, 'Christian Union and the Denominational Spirit', welcomed this union on behalf of Scottish Baptists. Given future Scottish Baptist attitudes, it is worth noting the principles he sets forth. He affirmed 'the spiritual union of all who love the Lord Jesus Christ' as 'the supreme purpose of all the Divine leadings'.[5] Secondly, he notes the Biblical principle of 'manifoldness in unity'[6] implied in the biblical concept of 'one body, many different parts'. He therefore dismisses as extremes both uniformity and 'blatant individuality ... in the name of liberty or independence'. In later twentieth century ecumenical discussion this concept of unity-in-diversity became important: diversity does not need to mean division[7]. His third principle, that uniting groups 'unite on the distinct and express understanding that neither Church surrenders or compromises anything

---

[4] B.R Talbot, *The Search for a Common Identity* (Carlisle: Paternoster Press, 2003).
[5] *Scottish Baptist Magazine* (*SBM*), 26.11 (November 1900), p. 171.
[6] *SBM*, 26.11 (November 1900), p. 173.
[7] Christopher J Ellis, *Together on the Way* (London: British Council of Churches, 1990), p. 60.

that has been characteristic of it'[8], assumed a defining role in the Inter-Church Process of the 1980s. Coats asked what Baptists have to contribute within this manifoldness-in-unity and raises, fourthly, the related issue of principled denominationalism. He asked what kind of unity is possible and consistent with those whose understanding of how salvation is appropriated is radically different from the Baptist understanding? 'The denominational spirit with us means the desire, the purpose, the endeavour to uphold the spirituality of the kingdom of God'.[9] The 'denominational spirit' is therefore a positive trait, arising from a desire for truth. Coats is able to envisage an expression of oneness among Churches that differ theologically, and indeed, believes that that oneness, the 'larger unity',[10] is God's will and is inevitable, but balks at formal union with those who take a radically different view of how salvation is appropriated. He distinguishes between principled denominationalism and separatism, which he calls 'blatant individuality'. These principles were recurring elements in Baptist conversations with other denominations in the twentieth century.

Meanwhile in the wider world of Christian Missions larger concerns were developing which were to have enormous influence on Christian thinking. The exigencies of the growing world mission movement had, during the latter part of the nineteenth century, forced the leaders of denominational missionary societies to begin a process of coming together. A major impetus featured a Scotsman, Alexander Duff of Pitlochry, as far back as 1854. Duff, an outstanding missionary thinker and practitioner, was in New York to receive an honorary doctorate. Christian leaders there saw an opportunity to arrange the first major world mission conference. This set in motion the series of interdenominational world gatherings that climaxed in the World Missionary Conference of 1910. Among the regulatory features of the conference was the requirement that, 'no opinion on ecclesiastical or doctrinal questions would be expressed by the Conference',[11] a different approach indeed from that among Scottish churches. A rallying cry for all English-speaking missionaries, young and old, on both sides of the Atlantic emerged: 'The Evangelization of the World in This Generation'. Implicit in the rallying cry was a call for unity among missionaries of the different Protestant denominations. Some believed that the greater success of Roman Catholic missionaries resulted from their being unified. Thus, alongside the movements towards unity within the Presbyterian community in Scotland and against their divisive and sectarian history, was a growing call to unity for the sake of the advancement of the Gospel worldwide. The 1910 Conference is referred to in 'Church Union in

---

[8] *SBM*, 26.11 (November 1900), p. 174.
[9] *SBM* 26.11 (November 1900), p. 176
[10] *SBM,* 26.11 (November 1900), p. 172
[11] *Burke Library Archives at www.Columbia.edu*: World Missionary Conference Records, Edinburgh 1910.

Scotland: the Truth in Love',[12] the Presidential Address of Scottish Baptist President, J.R. Chrystal, a former minister of the Church of Scotland, but his main concern was to comment on the formal negotiations that had begun in 1909 between the recently formed United Free Church of Scotland and the Church of Scotland. He spells out the two main reasons for Baptists' maintenance of a separate witness. These are the familiar principle of the spirituality of the church, that is, a believers' Church, and the conviction that the two ordinances, Baptism and Communion, are *Church* ordinances not *saving* ordinances and are likewise for believers alone. He respects the call for the oneness of God's people, honours 'many in all the Churches', even co-operating with them in good works, but 'the time has not yet come when we can safely withhold our witness'. Chrystal here is evincing the typical contemporary Scottish Baptist position: Scottish Baptists bear their witness and practice their faith 'among the churches' as a denomination. They are a denomination, not a sect; they stand among the Churches not over against them.

The advent of the Great War delayed ecumenical advance, but by 1920 movement was resumed. In this year, Thomas Stewart became Baptist Union Secretary and, as Editor of the *Scottish Baptist Magazine*, commented on wider church issues including what he saw as growing sacramentalism in the National Church and a preoccupation with their creed, the Westminster Confession. Stewart dismisses creeds as a 'fruitful source of schism' but welcomes the Church of Scotland Moderator's statement that 'personal loyalty to Christ must be the supreme test', appropriate to the Baptist principle of the spirituality of the Church.[13] The goodwill generated by the 1910 Conference and united missionary thinking enabled Baptists to participate in a number of further missionary gatherings during the 1920s and to play significant roles. Another prominent Baptist, Dr. John MacBeath, was secretary of the 1922 Missionary Congress of Scottish Churches. Baptists also shared in a consequent event held in Aberdeen which drew the following enthusiastic comment in the *Scottish Baptist Magazine*: 'The campaign ... succeeded in arousing interest in Aberdeen as no religious effort has done for the past decade . . . All the churches ... co-operated ... thus affording a superb demonstration of the unity that lies deeper than their differences.'[14] MacBeath's report records: 'it was the first effort in which all the Reformed churches united together. There were no precarious negotiations concerning union – there was rather the impulse of a great task that could best be done together.'[15] Baptists co-operate in advancing the Great Commission, but matters of union are 'precarious'. Ecumenism for Scottish Baptists is about co-operation, not structural union.

---

[12] BUS Presidential Address, *Scottish Baptist Year Book 1911* (*SBYB*), pp. 25-36.
[13] *SBM*, 46.7 (July 1920), pp. 75-76.
[14] *SBM*, 48.12 (Dec 1922), p. 48.
[15] *SBM*, 49.6 (June 1923), pp. 75-76.

Their co-operative spirit had the effect of bringing them into meaningful engagement with other Christians and the resulting fellowship among Christian leaders in Scotland led to the founding of the first 'Scottish Churches Council' in 1924. Most Protestant Churches, including the Scottish Baptists, came together in this body. Its aim was to extend the influence of the Churches through unified action on matters of national concern on behalf of Protestant Churches in Scotland. The Roman Catholic Church was not involved.

In 1920 the Rev. Alexander Paterson had taken 'Denominational Union' as the theme of his Presidential Address.[16] He spoke about the difficulties confronting the United Free Church and the Church of Scotland in their conversations about re-union. Two issues required to be resolved: Establishment and Endowments. While 'State entanglements' were odious to the UFC, the Church of Scotland's 'right and power, subject to no Civil Authority, to legislate, and to adjudicate finally, in all matters of doctrine, worship, government and discipline' was guaranteed in the passing by Parliament of 'The Declaratory Acts'. These 1921 Acts clarified the bases on which the Church of Scotland claimed to be the National Church in Scotland.[17] Scottish Baptists opposed 'a State Church', located their own authenticity in the apostolic Church of the New Testament, continued to claim their place among the Churches in Scotland and affirmed a deeply sensed call to make Christ known throughout the nation and the world, a task in which they had shown themselves ready to co-operate with other Christians.

But they also, along with other smaller denominations, had an interest in the matter of Endowments. Since the time of Charles I (1633), parish ministers had been maintained from the 'teinds' (tithes), a land tax paid by all in the parish whether of the Free Churches or the National Church. Paterson, on behalf of Baptists and the non-Presbyterian Churches, raised a number of questions. 'To whom do the revenues from the teinds belong? ... Can Parliament hand over to one Church, that no longer represents the majority if the Scottish people, monies that are held in national trust for the use of the whole country?'[18] Since the teinds were intended to support not only parish ministers but 'also the poor and the schools', it was a moot point. These matters of re-union, establishment and endowments were of sufficient concern to Scottish Baptists for them to appoint in 1920 a watching committee and, a year later, to add to its concerns the immediate question of the Church of Scotland Bill.

A Government committee, the Haldane Committee, had recommended that the teinds, which were *national* property, be transferred to the Church of Scotland as their *private* property. The Scottish Baptist Assembly of October 1923 reacted with vigour to this proposal, which was described as 'a gigantic

---

[16] *SBYB 1921*, pp. 43-51.
[17] See Alistair G. Hunter and Steven G. Mackie, *A National Church in a Multicultural Scotland* (Dunblane: Scottish Churches Council, 1986), p. 7.
[18] 'BUS Presidential Address', *SBYB 1921*, pp. 43-51.

act of robbery'[19] and adopted unanimously a resolution protesting against 'the principle of a State-established Church' and 'against the final appropriation of the National teinds to the exclusive advantage of one section of the people and for only one of the three purposes for which the teinds were originally designed.'[20] This illustrates that Baptists in this period were a Church among the Churches confidently playing a part in Christian witness and Christian concerns. In 1920, the Baptist Union Council had agreed to join with the Congregationalists in challenging the validity of 'National Church' status. At the same meeting they agreed to support the United Free Church in promoting the League of Nations, and the Wesleyan Methodists in their concerns about gambling.[21] However, despite the protests of Baptists and others, the Haldane proposals were accepted and in 1925 the *Church of Scotland (Property and Endowments) Act* was passed, transferring to the Church of Scotland as a Trust Fund the value of the teinds. This having been achieved, the way was now clear for the two Presbyterian giants to unite. Paterson welcomes the union but explains why Baptists see 'Denominational Union' differently:

> We, as Baptists …are not averse to co-operate with Christian brethren of all denominations in a unity of aggressive service and evangelical effort, but we cannot for a moment dream of watering down [sic!] the distinctive principle that is more than an ordinance of baptism of different mode and subject from that of our Presbyterian brethren …[22]

Here again we see the typical Baptist combination of principled denominationalism and inter-denominational co-operation, a stance that is seen to be more fruitful than that of formal union.

> I venture to think that a much closer bond of union between ourselves and other Churches is able to be attained with them in all that makes for the furtherance of the Gospel reclamation of men, rather than in any incorporation when our distinctive principles would be weakened …[23]

The Presbyterian Re-union took place in May 1929 and, in September, the Scottish Baptist Union Council received invitations from both the enlarged Church of Scotland and the United Free Church of Scotland (Continuing) to send representatives to their respective Assemblies. By a large majority, they

---

[19] *SBM*, 50.3 (March 1924), p. 34.
[20] Quoted in *SBM*, 50.3 (March 1924), p. 34.
[21] BUS Council Minutes, May 1920.
[22] BUS Presidential Address. *SBYB 1921*, p. 47.
[23] BUS Presidential Address, *SBYB 1921*, p. 51. See also T.G. Dunning, *SBM*, 47.9 (September 1921); *SBM*, 48.7 (July 1922), p. 78; Thomas Stewart, *SBM*, 54.12 (December 1928), p. 145; Walter Hankinson, BUS Presidential Address 1928, *SBYB 1929*, p. 120.

chose to send a representative only to the Continuing UF Church. Some thinkers in the enlarged Kirk were suggesting that 'baptism' might be offered to infants of non-church members. Baptist comment was that the Scottish Presbyterians had no consistent position on this matter, and that the problem arose from increasing 'sacramentarianism' in the National Church. 'There is still need', therefore, 'for Baptist witness in Scotland'.[24] During the 1930s the Baptist Union Council in Scotland received favourably reports from their representatives on the Scottish Churches Council, and took a positive interest in the Edinburgh Faith and Order Conference of 1937 through their representatives, Rev. John McBeath and Dr R.J. McCracken. Their report to the Baptist Union Council encouraged Baptist attendance at these conferences so as to bear witness to 'the truths we profess ... we have something to give and something to gain from the common stock of Christian experience'.[25] The issue of how salvation is communicated and appropriated was at the heart of their concerns. Also in 1937, a Church of Scotland booklet on Baptism was described as 'a well-phrased piece of adroit special pleading'.[26] The Church of Scotland however, suggested reciprocal Assembly visits by Baptist and Church of Scotland representatives and in 1940, sent their Moderator to the Baptist Assembly where he received 'an upstanding welcome'.[27] This happy state continued for a few years and there were reciprocal visits from Baptist Presidents. Thus the picture of Scottish Baptist life for most of the first half of the Century was of a sense of purposeful place among the Churches, bearing witness to Baptist distinctives, a concern to advance 'the Gospel' and to co-operate in this task across denominational boundaries.

There was, however, a sphere of activity for many Scottish Baptists other than that within and among Baptist Churches. The first half of the twentieth Century saw an enormous growth in evangelical para-church movements such as Christian Endeavour, Scripture Union, the 'mission hall' and City Missions movement, the Festivals of Gospel Male Voice Praise, the Saturday Night Gospel Tea Meetings and other nondenominational agencies and events. This very active and lively informal network was an alternative to the more formal ecumenical arrangements and played a very large part in the lives of the ordinary members of these fellowships. It brought together Christians from different streams and created a wide 'evangelical community'. This raises the question of how ordinary Scottish Baptist Christians regarded the issue of 'Christian Unity'. There is little doubt that for many Scottish Baptists this evangelical community was the true Christian community of Scotland; this was what true Christian unity was about and this was how it was best expressed.

---

[24] *SBM*, 58.2 (February 1932), p. 1.
[25] Derek Murray, *The First Hundred Years* (Glasgow: Baptist Union of Scotland, 1969), p. 104.
[26] *SBM*, 63.8 (August 1937), p. 2.
[27] Assembly Minutes, *SBYB 1941*, p. 142.

Being 'Evangelical' (adjective) or 'an Evangelical' (noun) was beginning to take precedence over being Baptist.

As a result the mood among Baptist people was changing, perhaps caused partly by the growing influence of this para-church life: 'principled denominationalism' and measured Baptist comment gave way to open attacks on the Christian integrity, even the Christian status, of Churches and Church leaders who were not part of the 'evangelical community'. More specifically, within the Baptist community a party spirit developed allowing attacks against some Baptist leaders, especially those who taught in the Baptist Theological College of Scotland who were accused of corrupting the minds of their students. One outcome of this was the development of a divide between ecumenical ('liberal') and evangelical ('conservative') that has persisted to the present day. Why did this develop? There are confusing and contradictory elements. The inter-War years had seen the rise of new theologies, variously described as rationalist, modernist or, more generally, liberal. Some Baptist ministers, including graduates from the College, saw positive elements in them causing concern to an emerging 'fundamentalist' and separatist group within the denomination. Yet alongside this, young men and women emerged from their Wartime experiences with a new and broader outlook on life. In the later 1930s a Commission of Enquiry had been set up to investigate the decline in Baptist life during the decade including the departure of a worryingly high number of able Scottish Baptist ministers to other denominations. Its analysis, reported to the 1943 Assembly, suggested that there existed now 'a generation that is impatient with denominational differences'[28] and, while it saw the need to continue to bear witness to Baptist distinctives, it encouraged moves towards Church Unity. This reflected a view quite contrary to the narrower conservative view just referred to. As the decline in Baptist numbers, in common with all Churches, accelerated during the War years and after, perhaps people were looking for reasons in different directions. One group saw the need for a wider, inclusive spirituality; another group saw the answer exclusively in the Gospel of personal salvation. For the latter this was the normative Christian experience and they found it hard to accept the validity of the different experience of others. It appeared that the two experiences clashed. Typically, many went on to think of other understandings not only as wrong but also as wickedly wrong. Anecdotal evidence suggests a further element in the post-War inclination to disunity within the denomination. There appears to have been an influx into the Baptist community in the post-War years of young men of Christian Brethren or Mission Hall provenance some of whom, while seeking a wider spiritual canvas than that provided in their Meetings retained a huge suspicion of 'The Churches'. Baptist life gave them the degree of freedom they sought within a framework that remained distinctive and separate.

---

[28] Murray, *First Hundred Years*, p. 113.

All of this was to come into sharp focus for Baptists in the moves towards a global forum for Christian Churches. Two world wars, vast increases in international trade and communication and the World Mission movement itself required Christians to think globally; Christian leaders of very different traditions had since Edinburgh 1910 increasingly seen the value of a representative world Christian body for mission, service, study and unity. World War II had delayed the formation of a global body but the separate strands of *Faith and Order* and *Life and Work* in which Scottish Baptists had been involved came together in the formation in 1948 of the World Council of Churches in Amsterdam. Great hopes were attached to the new body. The need to build bridges and create common ground among Christians was made even more urgent by the horrors of the Second World War including the Holocaust and the deployment, twice, of the atomic bomb. In addition to the call to the world's Churches to demonstrate the oneness of The Church, leaders of the World confessional bodies saw the importance of a Christian demonstration of global reconciliation and cooperation. Post-War, Christians cooperated in reaching out to the refugees and displaced persons created by the War in Europe through a new body, the Inter-Church Aid and Refugee Service. This agency became Christian Aid and functioned as a division of the British Council of Churches, which had been formed in 1942. Scottish Baptists had expressed their solidarity with other Churches in their active membership of the Scottish Churches Council, through their participation in the Faith and Order Conference in Edinburgh in 1937 and in preliminary meetings in advance of the 1948 formation of the World Council. But the growing fracture within the denomination was in danger of becoming a split in the face of a decision to join the global body. At the World Council itself Scottish Baptists were represented by Rev. Alexander Clark of Motherwell. He reported encouragingly to the 1948 Scottish Baptist Assembly and presented a motion from the Baptist Council that the Baptist Union of Scotland affiliate both with the WCC and with the British Council of Churches. This was carried by a majority of one vote (81 to 80). Many in the denomination were disturbed about this association with Churches holding diverse theologies. One church, the Union's largest, was particularly opposed, Charlotte Chapel in Edinburgh. They sought advice, not from Baptist sources, but from the International Council of Christian Churches, a fundamentalist evangelical movement in USA, another example, perhaps, of placing a type of 'evangelical' attitude above Baptist principle and ethos.[29] But concern was widespread. This unease led to the presentation at the 1951 Assembly of a motion for immediate withdrawal from the WCC, which was rejected by a two-thirds majority. The debate, however, indicated a need to examine the issue more comprehensively and a Committee of Enquiry was set up to investigate and report on 'the Constitution, objectives, practice and

---

[29] See Ian L.S. Balfour, *Revival in Rose Street: Charlotte Baptist Chapel, Edinburgh, 1808-2008* (Edinburgh: Rutherford House, 2007), p. 303.

achievements of the World Council of Churches'. The report came to the 1955 Assembly with a majority recommendation that affiliation should continue for a further seven years. The minority recommendation, signed only by two Charlotte Chapel members of the Committee, called on the Assembly to 'take all necessary steps to disaffiliate immediately'.[30] Ahead of the Report to the Assembly in 1955, Charlotte Chapel had intimated its intention to withdraw from the Union over the ecumenical issue. At the Assembly, the Report's majority recommendation to continue affiliation for seven years was narrowly defeated by an amendment to 'withdraw affiliation for seven years in the hope that the basis of the World Council of Churches be brought nearer our own faith and practice'. The Union therefore disaffiliated from the WCC but remained in the British Council of Churches and the Scottish ecumenical groupings. Charlotte Chapel, however, remained disaffiliated from the Union, on the grounds of the Union's continued affiliation with the other ecumenical bodies.

These events happened alongside lengthy inter-church preparations for the All-Scotland Billy Graham Crusade in 1955. Scottish Baptists worked with members and leaders of all the Scottish Churches in the administration and organisation of the great rallies in Glasgow's Kelvin Hall and in the meticulous and fully ecumenical follow-up arrangements for those who 'got up out of their seats'. Some Scottish Baptists were critical of these arrangements, preferring that 'contacts' be referred only to bona fide 'evangelical' churches. In 1961, the seven year period nearing its end, the Scottish Baptist Assembly empanelled a group to re-examine its relationship with the WCC. They reported in 1963. Their view was that though the WCC at New Delhi had added the phrase 'according to the Scriptures' to its basis, it was not yet sufficiently close to the Baptist position to allow the Union to re-join. The motion 'to continue in disaffiliation' was passed with a four-fifths majority. This was an emphatic voice for continued disaffiliation; Scottish Baptists were moving towards a separatist 'undifferentiated evangelical' position and Baptist historical practice and foundational principles were losing place as sources of guidance. A group of younger ministers, however, who had voted with the defeated fifth, formed themselves into a group which met for many years under the name, 'The Lower Fifth', as an open forum for exploring wider subjects.[31] Many others, the minority in most churches, also regretted the outcome.

The decision appears to have settled the WCC issue for the time being, but Scottish Baptists remained members of the British Council of Churches and the Scottish ecumenical agencies. Many Baptist Churches were also strong supporters of Christian Aid, which had become a 'Division' of the British Council of Churches. Local Baptist churches were active in local councils of

---

[30] For a detailed account of Charlotte Chapel's relations with the BUS on this issue see Balfour, *Revival in Rose Street*, pp. 302-307.

[31] An unpublished paper on 'The Lower Fifth' was delivered by Rev. Robert Armstrong to the Scottish Baptist History Project on 19 April 2008.

churches. Also, in 1964 the various Scottish ecumenical groups amalgamated in a new Scottish Churches Council, and Baptists were fully involved. Scottish Baptists were still short of the separatist position. When, however, the matter of continuing membership of the new body came for decision to the 1965 Assembly there were calls for withdrawal not only from SCC but also from the British Council of Churches. Both were defeated. This allowed some distinguished Baptists to serve in these bodies. Rev. Dr. Derek Murray and Rev James Taylor both held the Vice-Chairmanship of the Council. Andrew MacRae, General Secretary of BUS from 1966-80, Dr John Drane, a well-known Baptist writer and academic, and Rev. Donald McCallum, a much-loved pastor, had all been Chairmen of its Mission Committee. Therefore, though the move had begun towards a separatist position, Scottish Baptists were at this point still a denomination bearing witness 'among the Churches' and in membership with other Christians in ecumenical bodies both at Scottish and British level. To deal with all of this an Inter-Church Relations Committee was formed which developed into the 'Doctrine' and Inter-Church Relations Committee (DICR), a significant linking of subjects in contrast with other denominations.

A further issue was the Roman Catholic Church, which had been excluded by Reformed churches from the family of Christian Churches in Scotland. A new early twentieth Century factor was Irish immigration to the central belt of Scotland, especially around Glasgow, creating two distinct communities between which there has been greater tension than that found elsewhere in Scotland or south of the Border. An anti-Catholic attitude in Scotland generally was evident in 1923 when the Church of Scotland produced a highly controversial (and since repudiated) report entitled 'The Menace of the Irish Race to our Scottish Nationality'. It accused the Catholic population of subverting Presbyterian values and of causing drunkenness, crime and financial imprudence.[32] However, at the BUS Council, a motion proposing that a representative be appointed to co-operate with the Presbyterian Churches on this issue was 'negatived' by a large majority.[33] But in 1943, when Dr. W. Holmes Coats presented the Scottish Churches' Council Report referring to contact made by the Commission of the Churches with the Sword and Spirit Movement, a Roman Catholic organisation, several members objected to the reference and suggested its omission from the report. Then, in his impressive Presidential Address of 1962, the Rev George Young, former missionary to China and minister of Adelaide Place Baptist Church, Glasgow, referring to the 'challenge of world Communism' asserted that the answer was a revival of New Testament Christianity and declared: 'A frightened Church which seeks to unite with the powerful Roman Catholic Church in a holy crusade against

---

[32] See www.nationmaster.com/encyclopedia/Catholic-Church-in-Great-Britain.
[33] BUS Council, 27 November, 1923, BUS Minute Book 1915-1926, p. 605.

Communism is not the right answer'.[34] The Assembly responded with sustained applause. Strong suspicion of Catholicism was wide-spread among Scottish Baptists.

It was, of course, at this time that Rome was itself undergoing radical self-examination and was contemplating a fundamental reordering of its relations with other Churches. This arose within the Second Vatican Council, 1962 to 1965. The changed outlook, in turn, led these other Churches to reconsider meaningful relations with Catholic communities. The Scottish Churches Council therefore invited the Scottish Roman Catholics to become observers upon their deliberations. The Union had opposed this invitation. The matter came before the Centenary Assembly of 1969 when Peter Barber chaired the Assembly as Centenary President. By a two-thirds majority the Assembly decided to remain in membership of the Council. A further proposal that the Union withdraw in the event of the Roman Catholic Church becoming members of the Council was rejected, but by a smaller majority. The President and leaders brought a statement to the Assembly later in proceedings, concerned to clarify what these Assembly decisions implied.[35] The statement indicates a number of points. First, that Scottish Baptists at this juncture were wary of too close a formal association with Roman Catholic believers. Secondly, that a significant purpose, among others, of Scottish Baptist involvement with the wider Christian community was to bear a distinctive doctrinal witness. Thirdly, by implication, that Scottish Baptists were aware of developments in the wider Christian world and would therefore not prejudge the future. Two churches, Inverness and Hermon, Glasgow, withdrew from the Union over this decision.

Meanwhile, out in the wider world of Scottish, British, and global Church life ecumenical activity was gathering momentum. This included such seminal developments at the global level as Vatican II, the Conferences of the WCC and the strategic and extensive series of bilateral conversations between representatives of World Confessional Bodies[36]. Around the world, Church communities in Christian nations were forming United or Uniting Churches, for example in Australia and Canada. From 1962-65 the Second Vatican Council was held in Rome. Among the many documents issuing from this Council was *Unitatis Redintegratio* ('Restoration of Unity') which set out Catholic principles of ecumenism and Catholic practice in relation to 'separated brothers and sisters'. The 1964 BCC Faith and Order Conference held in Nottingham, England, gave added impetus to the ecumenical momentum within the home nations and led to the Multilateral Church Conversation in Scotland (1967),

---

[34] George Young, BUS Presidential Address 1962, *SBYB 1963*, pp. 5-16.

[35] E.W. Burrows, *'To me to live is Christ' A Biography of Peter H. Barber* (Carlisle: Paternoster, 2005), pp. 81-84.

[36] For an early survey of these Conversations, see N. Ehrenstron & G. Gassman, *Confessions in Dialogue: Survey of Bilateral Conversations Among World Confessional Families, 1959-1974* (Geneva: WCC, 1975).

launched by the Church of Scotland. At the local end of the scale, the Livingstone New Town Ecumenical Parish in West Lothian came into being in 1966 for which again the Church of Scotland provided the lead.[37]

The Multilateral Conversation produced a series of publications covering such matters as a *'Basis of Union', 'Witness and Service', 'Worship and Sacraments', 'the Faith of the Church'* including a *Statement on Baptism* and a 'final' Report of 1985. This latter disputed issue of Baptism earlier had brought Scottish Baptists and the Church of Scotland into close conversation. For many years Baptist ministers in Scotland had upset their Church of Scotland colleagues by baptizing, as believers by immersion, Church of Scotland members, often with no communication whatsoever with these Parish Church colleagues. However, in 1975, the 're-baptism' of two Church of Scotland members was brought by the Parish minister in Wishaw, Lanarkshire, to the General Assembly of the Church of Scotland. Wide media interest followed and, this being one among many similar 're-baptism' instances, demanded that the two denominations meet to consult. The outcome was a Joint Statement on Baptismal Practice.[38]

The fortieth anniversary of the founding of the British Council of Churches, 1982, was a significant year for ecumenical events and developments. This year the *Final Report* of the Anglican-Roman Catholic International Commission was published with this conclusion:

> The convergence reflected in our Final Report would appear to call for the establishing of a new relationship between our Churches as a next stage in the journey towards Christian unity.[39]

This year the World Council of Churches' Faith and Order Commission 'Lima Report' on *Baptism, Eucharist and Ministry* was published with its invitation to all Churches 'to prepare an official response to this text at the highest appropriate level of authority'. This generated an enormous volume of serious theological dialogue and debate between, among and within all the main Christian Communities around the world. The DICR for the Baptist Union of Scotland offered a largely critical response, particularly of its view of the issues concerning baptism. Peter Barber felt that, though the denomination was not a WCC member, 'BEM' was an important document and Scottish Baptists should respond; but it was submitted in the name only of the DICR.[40]

---

[37] Though Baptists in Livingston were moving towards the formation of a congregation at this time, they declined to be involved.

[38] For a full account of this episode and the joint statement see T.W. Moyes, 'Scottish Baptist Relations with the Church of Scotland in the Twentieth Century', *Baptist Quarterly*, 33.4 (October 1989), p. 174.

[39] *1982 Anglican-Roman Catholic International Commission, The Final Report* (London: CTS / SPCK, 1982), p. 99.

[40] DICR Minutes, 3 May 1983.

1982 was also the year of the visit of Pope John Paul to Scotland when, referring to 'the larger community of believers in Christ', he said:

> We are only pilgrims on this earth, making our way towards that heavenly Kingdom promised to us as God's children. Beloved brethren in Christ, for the future, can we not make that pilgrimage together hand-in-hand...doing all we can 'to preserve the unity of the Spirit by the peace that binds us together'? This would surely bring down upon us the blessing of God our Father on our pilgrim way.[41]

In this same year, the Autumn Assembly of the British Council of Churches responding to these and other factors, agreed the motion:

> The British Council of Churches is ready for change so as better to serve the growth into unity, and invites the Roman Catholic Church to share in the discussion of changes which might hasten the day when it can feel ready to be a member.[42]

It was also the year of the failure of the proposed Covenant in England between the Church of England, the Methodist Church, the United Reformed Church and the Moravian Church. The goal of Christian unity remained clear and immense effort was being applied to it across the Christian world but the methods currently employed were not all 'running smooth'. A new approach was needed.

Scottish Baptists were ambivalent about this ecumenical fervour yet Baptists worldwide and at every level were involved. Earlier, from 1973-77, the Baptist World Alliance and the World Alliance of Reformed Churches had extensive bi-lateral conversations and in 1983 all Baptist and Reformed Churches were asked to discuss the findings. The Union received an invitation from the Church of Scotland to engage in discussions and three senior Scottish Baptists were invited to represent the BUS in the talks.[43]

The Baptist World Alliance was also involved in talks with the Vatican in 1984-88, resulting in a report in 1990 entitled 'Summons to Witness to Christ in Today's World.' About the same time Scottish Baptists were engaged in informal talks with representatives of the Scottish Roman Catholic Church. The Baptists were the General Secretary, Dr. Andrew MacRae, Dr. Derek Murray and a leading layman, Mr Jack Carr.[44] Nor were Baptists alone among Evangelical Christians engaged in such talks. Pentecostals were in dialogue with

---

[41] *The Pope in Britain: Collected Homilies and Speeches* (London: St Paul's Publications, 1982), pp. 78-79.
[42] *SBM*, 109.1 (January 1983).
[43] DICR minutes 10 Nov. 1983.
[44] Derek Murray recalls that, as these were informal talks and not reported, they were accused of holding them 'behind closed doors'!

other World Confessions including Rome[45] and with the WCC. The latter talks have continued into the twenty-first century. In 1989 at the Manila Mission Conference (Lausanne II), the following statement was made: 'We affirm the urgent need for Churches, mission agencies and other Christian organisations to co-operate in evangelism and social action, repudiating competition and avoiding duplication.'[46] A few years later the World Evangelical Alliance itself was in active dialogue with Vatican representatives. These conversations also have continued into the twenty-first century.[47]

In addition to these developments, a number of Evangelical and Baptist writers had published books supportive of ecumenical dialogue including George Carey[48] who later became Archbishop of Canterbury, and David Coffey[49] who later became General Secretary of the BUGB and President of the Baptist World Alliance. At the 1977 National Evangelical Anglican Congress at Nottingham, David Watson, John Stott and Colin Buchanan, all leading evangelical Anglicans, spoke positively about ecumenical involvement.[50] Later, J.I. Packer, another leading evangelical Anglican, spoke positively about renewal in the Roman Church.[51] There was also a growing Evangelical presence at WCC conferences. Evangelicals produced their own separate report following the Vancouver Conference of 1983, as an 'open letter to fellow-evangelicals world-wide, calling them to put aside their previous theological reservations about the WCC and without compromise become involved in the ecumenical debate'.[52]

A further significant factor in the wider picture was the emergence of the 'Neo-Pentecostal Movement'. Lesslie Newbigin had already suggested that there were now three great Christian movements in the mid-twentieth century: the Catholic 'Sacramental' movement, the Protestant 'Word' movement, and the Pentecostal 'Spirit' movement. The Charismatic Movement was evident within all the mainstream denominations including the Roman Catholic Church so that Christians who were denied fellowship under old structures were now discovering common ground and an enriching shared experience.

Throughout this period of ecumenical initiative the Multilateral Church Conversation among the denominations of Scotland was in process. The

---

[45] Ehrenstron & Gassman, *Confessions in Dialogue*.
[46] Derek Palmer, *Strangers No Longer* (London: Hodder and Stoughton 1990), p. 130.
[47] World Evangelical Alliance Website, Theological Commission, Theological News, April 2001 Issue.
[48] George Carey, *The Meeting of the Waters* (London: Hodder and Stoughton, 1985).
[49] David Coffey, *Build that Bridge* (Eastbourne: Kingsway Publications, 1986).
[50] John Capon, *Evangelical Tomorrow* (London: Harper Collins, 1977), pp. 61, 62; Michael de Semlyen, *Ecumenism: Where is it leading us?* (Gerrards Cross, Bucks: Dorchester House, 1989).
[51] De Semlyen, *Ecumenism: Where is it leading us?* p. 6.
[52] David Coffey, *Build that Bridge*, p. 23.

Churches of Christ (later merged in the United Reformed Church), the Congregational Union of Scotland, the Methodist Church, the Scottish Episcopal Church, the United Free Church and the Baptist Union of Scotland had accepted the Church of Scotland's invitation to begin to work towards the unity of the Christian Church in Scotland. Baptists were full members until 1983, when they reduced to observer status because of the Conversation's goal of structural union. A 'final' Report entitled '*Christian Unity – NOW IS THE TIME* was published in 1985. The Basis of Union for participating Churches, though, was produced as late as 1992. But by then an alternative approach was in place, the outcome of the Inter-Church Process, 1984-90.

## 'Churches Together'

We must now to take space to describe this process because it led to the end of formal relationships between the BUS and the other Christian communions in Scotland.[53] What were the factors requiring a new approach to inter-Church life in the British Isles? We can only list them here.[54]

The British Council of Churches was not representative of the range of Christians of the British Isles: Charismatic, Black-majority (immigrant) Churches, the many Evangelical groupings, and specifically Roman Catholics were not in membership; the BCC appeared to operate separately from its parent bodies, the Churches; the implied goal of a single National Church was a stumbling-block to many Christians; and many felt the need to share resources

---

[53] [Note: In describing these events, I will adopt the first person. To take the conventional approach would be tedious and stilted. I was one of five people invited to represent the BUS at the Scottish Inter-Church Process Conference at St Andrews in 1987. I also represented the BUS at the British Isles discussions along with the General Secretary, Peter Barber, including attendance at the final conference at the Hayes Conference Centre, Swanwick, Derbyshire, in September 1987. I was appointed to the Scottish Inter-Church Process Steering Group and, within that Group, to the sub-group on Basis and Aims. I served later in the Process on the sub-group on Membership and represented the Scottish Steering group on occasions at joint meetings of the national Steering Groups. I served on the sub-group that drafted the job descriptions and terms of appointment for the General Secretary of ACTS and for the Director of Scottish Churches House. During the period of the Inter-Church Process I served on a BCC group that sought a better understanding between the Charismatic networks and the ecumenical movement. Having been appointed to represent the BUS on the British Council of Churches in 1983, I became automatically a member of the BUS Doctrine and Inter-Church Relations Committee, continued in membership through the ICP and beyond, and became its Chairman from 1992-1995. Within that Committee I served on the group that produced the booklet *Our Roman Catholic Neighbours*. I am, therefore, describing events and discussions in which I was fully involved.]

[54] For a full description, see *Our Place among the Churches*, pp. 123-36.

where Christians manifestly could do so. Also there were Irish, Scottish and Welsh ecumenical councils, but no English council; and there was a strongly felt need to involve the 'people in the pews'. A new vehicle for associating as Churches was needed. That new vehicle was set on course at the Spring Assembly of the British Council of Churches of March 1984, which passed the following resolutions:

> 1 (a) to consult the member Churches and other Christian bodies on their readiness to share in a process of prayer, reflection and debate together centred on the nature and purpose of the Church in the light of its calling in and for the world;
> (b) to consider whether the focus of this process should be a major conference by the end of this triennium [1984-87];
> 2. To consult the member Churches, national Councils of Churches in Scotland, Wales and Ireland, and other Christian bodies not yet in membership of the BCC about developments to provide an ecumenical instrument more broadly representative of the whole people of God in Britain and Ireland.

The Churches and Christian bodies of the United Kingdom and Ireland were informed and a quick response came from the Roman Catholic Bishops' Conference of England and Wales at the end of April 1984 when the initiative was endorsed. Broadly favourable responses came over the next few months from a wide range of Churches and other Christian bodies including the Scottish Baptists. The BUS Executive's recommendation to accept the invitation was overwhelmingly endorsed by the Council in September 1984.[55]

Meanwhile, a meeting of BCC leaders also in September 1984 created a Working Party that, with immense energy and creative imagination, devised a remarkable programme of consultation, investigation, study and prayer for implementation within the Christian communities of the UK and Ireland. Its title, *'Not Strangers but Pilgrims'*, intentionally reflected Pope John Paul's 'pilgrim' plea uttered in Glasgow in 1982. The Working Party brought these comprehensive proposals to a gathering of thirty-two church leaders and representatives at Lambeth Palace on 7 May 1985 at which the General Secretary, Peter Barber, represented the Scottish Baptists. This meeting launched the Inter-Church Process. This Process, the most comprehensive and radical approach to Church Unity ever attempted, began with a self-assessment programme which included inter-Church Lent courses in spring 1986 linked to local radio, and which resulted in three publications: *'Views from the Pews'*, the views of returned questionnaires from one million church people who met in 70,000 house groups; *'Reflections: How Churches View their Life and Mission'* which revealed real differences in understanding of such central doctrines as the Church, ministry, baptism and Communion; and *'Observations'* which gathered

---

[55] *SBM*, 110.9 (September 1984). Some requirements were added, see *SBYB 1986*, pp. 83-86, 90, 97-99; and *SBM*, 111.3 (March 1985), p. 10.

*A Distinctive People*

together responses from para-church organizations, theological colleges, the 'House churches', the Evangelical Alliance and Third World Churches, and many others, the purpose being to enable the Churches to 'see oorsels as ithers see us'. The substance of these three publications provided the starting point for discussions at a series of 'national' conferences for the constituent nations of the UK.

The Scottish event was held in St Andrews 3-5 April 1987 with 210 delegates. Roman Catholic delegates were included on an equal basis for the first time in Scotland. The Scottish Baptist representatives were Peter Barber, BUS General Secretary, Mrs. Muriel McNair, BUS Director of the Department of Church Life 1981-85, Rev. James Gordon, minister of Crown Terrace Baptist Church, Aberdeen, Mr. Brian Muir, a layman active in Christian radio, and myself, minister of Viewfield Baptist Church, Dunfermline. The purpose was to reflect together on 'the nature, purpose and unity of the Church' and to consider what structures might be devised to enable effective cooperation.

Our report notes that our presence ensured that the Evangelical voice had been heard and that we believed we could help in 'bridging the gap between many Scottish evangelical Christians and the Scottish Ecumenical Movement'; we experienced 'a oneness of spirit with other believers that transcended denominational barriers'; we felt a call to co-operation with those in whose life and witness we recognised a rich diversity of theology, worship, devotion and service from which we could gain immeasurably and which could only enhance Christian witness and mission in Scotland; and, while accepting there were reservations within our denomination about any ecumenical association, we recognised that radical changes were currently taking place in churches, in Scotland and more widely, calling urgently for 'openness, dialogue and co-operation'.

We asked and discussed a series of questions.[56] A summary[57] records the DICR's criticism of some aspects of the Conference Report but states that 'The Core Group, as a whole, favoured our denomination's continuing involvement in the Inter-Church Process', giving several reasons: an obligation to represent the evangelical community in Scotland to other churchmen, the opportunity to influence the Process and shape the new instrument, the obligation, not least to the Roman Catholics, to share our theology at what is a time of searching, and a Biblical duty to seek unity among the Lord's people. Were we to opt out now, we would give an impression of superiority and exclusivism.

Following these three regional conferences a final conference was held in the Hayes Conference Centre, Swanwick, Derbyshire, from 31 August to 4 September 1987, attended by over 330 representatives of thirty-three denominations from the four nations of Britain and Ireland. Scottish Baptists

---

[56] BUS ICP Consultation document 'ICP to ACTS' p. 7, DICR.
[57] DICR Minutes, 15 October 1987.

were represented by Peter Barber and myself, our status being that of 'Observers'.

These conferences were not plain sailing. Mistakes were made and regrettable attitudes were displayed but the dominant experience, especially at Swanwick, was of the presence of the Holy Spirit among the delegates, creating a 'spirit of acceptance and forbearance over a spectrum of churchmanship reaching from Christian Brethren and Salvationists to Anglicans and Roman Catholics.'[58] On the fourth day of the conference, following morning meetings in denominational groups, Cardinal Hume, made this significant statement, expressing the Roman Catholic Church's commitment to a new ecumenical partnership with other churches in Britain:

> I hope that our Roman Catholic delegates...will recommend to members of our Church that we move now quite deliberately from a situation of co-operation to one of commitment to each other... Christian unity is a gift from God and in these last few days I have felt He has been giving us this gift in abundance. It is also a process of growth ... one step at a time, and Swanwick has been a very decisive one.[59]

This statement transformed the mood and pace of the discussions, which now moved to conclusions 'with amazing speed and clarity'. Significant contributions were made by Baptist delegates notably Dr Paul Beasley-Murray of Spurgeon's College, London. His intervention secured a clear wording on evangelism in the Swanwick Declaration. What were the distinctive components in this new approach? It was to be a process of 'the Churches', *together* seeking the mind and purpose of God. This was definitive: not the Churches seeking formal unity; rather the Churches together seeking 'oneness' within which it could fulfil better 'its mission in and for the world'. This gave the phrase 'Churches Together'. There was no necessary connection between this 'oneness' and structural union. This 'oneness' was Christ's gift to his Church, a 'given', and therefore, if recognized, an existing basis upon which to meet, share and act together. How would it work? The principle was to operate together through simplified structures within which ideas, plans, projects, mission initiatives relevant to the common life of the Churches would be discussed centrally and commended to the member bodies *where authority would remain*. These member Churches would be free to consider them and make their own response. Some Churches would have greater expertise and experience in some areas and would take the lead; groups of Churches might work together on behalf of all the churches; resources would be shared, possibly including resource centres, offices, meeting rooms and personnel. This was

---

[58] Burrows, *'To me to live is Christ'*, p. 169, quoting Peter Barber, *SBM*, 113.10 (October 1987).
[59] Palmer, *Strangers No Longer*, pp. 64-65.

'Churches Together', a new concept and quite different from the old structures which acted almost as a parallel body to the life of the Churches. All of this was gathered into the Swanwick Report that was then sent to all participating Churches and groups.

The next step was to set up working parties for England, Scotland, Wales and 'Britain and Ireland'. The Scottish Inter-Church Process Steering Group was chaired by the Very Reverend Professor Robin Barbour, MC, Professor of New Testament at Aberdeen University, a former Moderator of the General Assembly of the Church of Scotland and Chaplain to the Queen in Scotland. The Secretary was Canon Kenyon Wright, a Scottish Episcopalian, gifted administrator and clear thinker with a great love for Scotland, and Warden, at that time, of Scottish Churches House, Dunblane. Peter Barber and I represented the Baptist Union of Scotland.

At the first meeting of the Scottish Steering Group on 22 September 1987 the main points of discussion were the basis, aims, principles and statement of commitment of the new Scottish ecumenical instrument. At the meeting I was appointed to a Basis and Aims sub-group along with Robin Barbour and James Quinn, SJ, a Roman Catholic theologian and hymn-writer. There is an interesting story here, which follows in outline.[60] Steering Groups had been advised informally that the Basis of Faith should be the same as that of the WCC and the BCC. James Quinn and I questioned this and wanted to consider a new Basis for Scotland. Robin Barbour was initially inclined towards a common Basis, probably that of WCC and BCC, but it was agreed that James and I would prepare, from our own perspectives, drafts of a possible Scottish Basis and Aims document, and send them to each other and to Prof. Barbour who would attempt to coordinate them. Vigorous debate followed. It had seemed to me three categories had emerged from Swanwick 'oneness in Christ', 'developing understanding' and 'unified action'. Preferences were agreed: full membership to be for 'Churches', para-church bodies being offered associate membership; the name should use 'Churches' rather than 'Christian', hence 'Churches Together' occurring in names of all national bodies; and that there be no reference to the sacraments/ordinances (here the Baptist prevailed over the Catholic!). A requirement to share papers resulted in all Groups' abandoning the WCC/BCC Bases, and largely adopting the Scottish approach and, indeed, the Scottish wording.

The outcome was a Basis and Aims document that included several points Evangelical people had requested and for which Baptist representatives had argued, including a clear reference to Scripture, the omission of any reference to 'one church', and a clear statement under *Unified Action* 'to co-operate as far as possible in proclaiming the Gospel so as to evoke a personal commitment to Christ and His Church'.

---

[60] A full account is given in *Our Place among the Churches*, pp. 79-84.

ACTS therefore remains Action of *Churches* Together in Scotland and includes only a small number of Associate Member Bodies. This demonstrates that there was openness to Baptist input on these issues and the result was a Basis and Aims document more congenial to Baptist thinking than otherwise might have been.[61]

## Scottish Baptists and 'Churches Together'

Peter Barber's first opportunity to report to the Denomination following Swanwick was the October 1987 *Scottish Baptist Magazine* where he wrote positively of the Conference. At the Assembly later that month he asked whether Scottish Baptists *want* greater Christian unity, and *want* Christ's prayer, that his people be one, answered. Despite some negative comment, the Assembly voted to continue in the Process.

As Scottish Baptists were generally poorly informed about the Process, the churches were encouraged to read the Swanwick Report, together with the BUS Statement on Unity, revised in 1987. Two of the St Andrews delegates, Brian Muir and myself, were charged with communicating the concept of *Churches Together* to the 1988 Assembly. We noted a striking parallel between the ACTS *modus operandi* and Baptist practice. Baptists combined two defining concepts, those of 'association' and 'autonomy'; ACTS also combined these two principles: working to fulfil the agreed aims of its members ('association'), authority remaining with the member Churches ('autonomy').

At the Assembly in Aberdeen, the General Secretary reminded delegates that at next year's Assembly we would decide on the issue of ACTS membership; at this Assembly our concern was to comment on the *modus operandi* for the new instruments. The Union had prepared a 'Response to the Proposals' and this Assembly would be invited to endorse it. My task was to outline the development of the Process, indicating the factors that lay behind this new initiative. The discussion reflected positive and negative views, sadly without reference to Baptist principle. In conclusion, the General Secretary argued that '... the new instruments did not materially change our present position as members of S.C.C.' The DICR Core Group would arrange a series of consultations around the country in spring 1989 and publish a booklet on Roman Catholicism by summer 1989. The 'Response' was approved by a large majority, but the negative concerns were important in preparing for the area consultations.[62]

By the first meeting of the DICR in mid-March 1989, it was becoming clear that the ecumenical temperature within Scottish Baptist life was rising. Negative attitudes were hardening and, significantly, a meeting of Scottish Baptist

---

[61] For the final agreed Constitution of ACTS see *Churches Together in Pilgrimage* (London: British Council of Churches, 1989).
[62] 'Assembly Minutes', 1988, *SBYB 1989*, pp. 103-105.

ministers had been held in February to discuss action to oppose ICP, followed by further meetings. Ecumenically supportive letters were also received but were the minority. The Committee, however, pressed on with the arrangements for the area consultations and agreed the procedure for bringing a proposal to the Assembly.

At its next meeting in May, the Committee learned that a letter had been prepared at the meeting of ministers opposed to ICP for publication in the Scottish Baptist Magazine; that Council and Assembly would probably require a two-thirds majority in voting on the issue; and that the area consultations, so far held, revealed predominantly negative viewpoints and an alarming degree of ignorance, specifically of Baptist principle and practice. However, the Committee agreed to recommend that the Union seek participant (or 'associate') membership and should ask that urgent consideration be given to four major issues – Protestant/Catholic relations, the nature of the Church, the nature of Christian unity and the nature of evangelism.

The promised letter appeared in the *SBM* of June 1989 subscribed by the names of thirty-five ministers, arguing for complete separation from ACTS (three subsequently denied any knowledge of the letter). We note here only its complete lack of reference to Baptist history and principles. They were writing, clearly, not as Baptists, but as a group of 'evangelicals', a further instance of 'evangelical loyalties taking precedence over Baptist history, practice and principle. Subsequent *Magazines* carried responses to the letter from both sides of the debate, including – unusually – one from Canon Kenyon Wright, Secretary of the Inter-Church Process in Scotland; my own response was a lengthy and detailed rebuttal of the Ministers' letter,[63] and making a crucial distinction between 'the *exercise* of faith upon which God recognises those who are His and the *profession* of faith upon which we recognise one another as His'.[64] There is only one Christ and all involved in the Inter-Church Process profess faith in him. This is the basis of Christian one-ness as Baptists have understood it. Summer saw the publication of the Viewpoint Booklet, *Our Roman Catholic Neighbours*. Then at the September Council meeting, proposals for full membership and observer status gained limited support while the proposal for associate membership was carried by a substantial majority and became the Council's recommendation to Assembly. The Council also agreed to require a two-thirds majority for this proposal despite concerns that a minority could thereby deny the freedom of a majority to have formal association with the new bodies.

Peter Barber continued his efforts to ensure that the Assembly decision would be well-informed and conducted according to Baptist practice. In the October SBM, immediately before the Assembly, he spelt out Baptist principles

---

[63] A critique of the letter and a survey of the signatories' views in 2008 can be found in *Our Place among the Churches*, pp. 90-95.

[64] *SBM*, 115.9 (September 1989), p. 2.

and our historic stance on 'liberty' expressing the hope that 'as we come to this year's Assembly we will again prove worthy heirs of our great heritage'.

## Assembly 26 October 1989

The Assembly took place in Edinburgh, ironically in the Methodist Central Halls. The proceedings of the afternoon session of Thursday 26 October 1989 deserve to be fully recorded with detailed critical analysis.[65] Here we have room only for an outline of the session and some brief comments. In the earlier days of the Assembly, the President, Douglas Hutcheon[66] the chief guest, Dr John Briggs, President of the BUGB, and David Neil, BUS Mission Fieldworker[67], spoke positively about the need to work together with other Christians. It appeared that leaders and the chief guest anticipated a positive decision. No fewer than six motions or counter-motions were presented to Assembly on this issue – for full membership, associate membership, observer status and non-participation, with two more consequent on the failure to make any decision! The four motions on membership were subject to a two-thirds majority. Introducing the issue on the Thursday afternoon, the General Secretary noted that all other member bodies of the ICP in Scotland had opted for full membership including the Roman Catholics.

What were the issues? Those in favour of some form of association argued on several levels. First, the Biblical call to unity among all believers and the linkage of oneness with mission; second, Baptist principle and practice flowing from the Declaration of Principle; third, Scottish Baptist history of unbroken participation in, and high-level contributions to, the modern ecumenical movement since Edinburgh 1910; fourth, pragmatic considerations internally, such as granting 'liberty' to individuals and churches, and externally such as avoiding isolation and a sectarian image. They spoke of positive experiences of unity with other Christians, the need for unity in presenting the Gospel in Scotland, the immense opportunities for evangelism and united social action, and of a sense that 'the Holy Spirit was urging us to step forward without fear as full members of this Process'. In statements against any form of association, anti-Catholic comments occurred in several contributions, the doctrinal purity or adequacy of the other Churches was questioned and fears of compromise were expressed.

Counter-motion 1 for full membership, presented by myself and Robert Armstrong, fell with 345 (69%) against and 152 (31%) for [68]. The Council motion

---

[65] An attempt can be found in *Our Place among the Churches*, pp. 96-104.
[66] *SBM*, 115.11 (November 1989), p. 8.
[67] *SBYB 1990*, Assembly 1989 Minutes, pp. 168, 180.
[68] A detailed account of the motions and debates, together with the text of my own speech are found in *Our Place among the* Churches, pp. 96-104.

*A Distinctive People*

for associate membership, presented by the General Secretary and Rev James Gordon fell with 261 (54%) against and 222 (46%) for.

Counter motion 2 for observer status, presented by Revs. Kenneth McNeish and W.G. Slack fell with 192 (40%) against and 287 (60%) for.

Counter-motion 3 for taking no part in the inter-Church bodies, submitted by Rev. Ian Cameron on behalf of the Stranraer Church fell, after some confusion, with 217 (48%) against and 234 (52%) for.

The latter two motions fell, receiving less than the required two-thirds majority. The Assembly had failed to make decisions on any of the four proposals before it. The minutes rather wanly record that 'no motion, therefore, about the Inter-Church Process was carried. It was understood that no application to enter ACTS or CCBI would be made at that time'.

## Assembly 1989 Reflections

What can be made of this grand exercise in deciding nothing? A Scottish Baptist Assembly failed to decide to take part in the new ecumenical instruments at any level – and failed to decide 'not to take part'. Two of the four proposals achieved majorities, one very slender, but the voting arrangements left the Assembly with a failure to make any decision at all. There clearly were misunderstandings and bad practice as well as regrettable attitudes. Issues that required clarification include how Baptists make decisions as a denomination and the related questions of mandating of delegates and attendance for one issue only; the requirement of a two-thirds majority resulting, contrary to a defining Baptist ideal, in the minority denying freedom to the majority; the distinction between denominationalism and separatism; the question of what is authentic Baptist practice, including the role of the Baptist Declaration of Principle and of historic Baptist principles and practice, in contemporary ecumenical contact; the issue of compromise, so regularly referred to in pre-Assembly correspondence, in the area consultations and at the Assembly itself; and, most crucially, the question whether Evangelical dispositions or convictions of belief should determine decisions over Baptist dispositions and convictions of principle in the context of a *Baptist* Assembly.[69]

All these matters in one degree or another were brought to the Scottish Baptist Community before or during the Assembly, but many acted, probably unwittingly, contrary to *Baptist* principles, believing that as primarily *Evangelicals*, they must. If Baptists believe they are called to maintain Baptist witness among the Churches in Scotland they surely need to face this issue with integrity. One result of this lack of clarity was that the freedom of Baptists in Scotland to associate with and act within the wider church was curtailed. In his

---

[69] These are all discussed in *Our Place among the Churches*, pp.105-113.

December 1989 'Scene Around' in the *SBM*, the General Secretary summed up the range of emotions following the Assembly.

> There is no doubt ... that the Assembly decision has created strong reactions within and outwith the denomination. ... Others ... feel shocked and ashamed that Scottish Baptists have taken such a negative stance. Other Church leaders have expressed their bewilderment and sadness...'[70]

Barber pleaded against unhelpful attitudes from either side of the debate and concludes by asking for prayer as the leadership try 'to honour the Assembly decision without at the same time conveying the impression that we are wholly isolationist or self-sufficient'. The Assembly outcomes required adjustments to Scottish Baptist life. Any inter-church activity that operated under ACTS was off-limits for Baptists except on a personal basis. The DICR November meeting noted correspondence from the Church of Scotland concerning a *National Mission Initiative* in Scotland. 'If this were to be sponsored under ACTS, the Union would not be able to participate'.[71] However it was thought that it was not the intention of Assembly to forbid every interdenominational activity and, at its meetings of early 1990, the Council agreed guidelines to help BUS staff members to identify where they could associate interdenominationally without compromising the Assembly outcome.[72]

At its January meeting the Council reflected on the ICP Assembly session: 'Some thought that the credibility of the Assembly had been eroded and some major Baptist Principles breached'.[73] The DICR was therefore invited to give 'urgent consideration' to the relationship between the local church, the Assembly and the Union with a view to producing discussion material for the churches and making these issues a focus of the 1990 Assembly.

The DICR at it meetings in 1990 sought clarification of possible Baptist involvement in the Mission Committee of ACTS. There was also a question on the position of Christian Aid, formerly a Department of the BCC. In fact it became a separate body. It emerged that the Union could relate to Christian Aid, but not to inter-Church mission in Scotland and specifically the proposed *National Mission Initiative* in Scotland. The possibility of a Baptist Ecumenical Fellowship, perhaps with some link to the English Union, was acknowledged following receipt of a letter from Hillhead Baptist Church. There was discussion on the process of polarisation taking place in our denomination, and it was 'felt that the nature of the Declaration of Principle as opposed to a credal Confession is inadequately understood amongst Scottish Baptists'.[74] There was a view that

---

[70] Peter Barber, 'Scene Around', *SBM*, 115.12 (December 1989), p. 18.
[71] *DICR* Minutes November 1989.
[72] For an account of the main elements of the aftermath of the non-decision, see Burrows, *'To me to Live is Christ*, pp. 175-77.
[73] 'Digest of Council Minutes', *SBYB 1991*, p. 158.
[74] *DICR* Minutes, March 1990.

Baptist principles should have enabled the denomination to cope with this issue with greater maturity, sensitivity and self-assurance. The DICR accepted an obligation to inform and educate the denomination on these matters. This led to the publication of the *'Baptist Body-Builder Workpack'*, a series of four group studies prepared by myself and Rev. Jack Quinn covering basic Baptist principles. This process of education was intended to show that Baptists were well able to hold firmly and consistently to their convictions while acknowledging the integrity of the positions of other Christians, and indeed to learn from them and work with them as *Baptists*, and that they had the principles and procedures to sustain this approach.

In the April 1990 *SBM* a letter from Dr Edgar Ferguson, Secretary of Hillhead BC, invited all churches who, like Hillhead, would like to keep in touch informally with ecumenical developments in Scotland, to a meeting in Morningside Baptist Church and this led to a two-day conference at Atholl Centre, Pitlochry, in November 1990 to consider ways of maintaining ecumenical contact for those churches and individuals that wished to do so. While such moves were encouraging to those who wanted formal relationships with other Christian communions, it remained possible for individual Baptist churches to act ecumenically in their local areas. An illustration of one such church, is Viewfield Baptist Church, Dunfermline, which continued and developed such relationships.[75]

## Moving On – The Final Ten Years

And so, somewhat winded by the 1989 Assembly and subsequent exchanges, the denomination moved cautiously ahead but with enough courage to raise some of the January 1990 Council's 'concerns' at the 1990 Assembly 'Open Forum'. Sadly, those churches that might have benefitted from *The Baptist Body-Builder Workpack* did not make use of it and in fact the take-up, the Minutes record, was 'limited'. A revision and further promotion was none-the-less agreed.

Despite our formal self-exclusion from the family of Churches in Scotland certain relationships continued as they were not under ACTS. One was the bi-lateral conversations with the Church of Scotland begun in 1984. While discussions on baptism proved to be difficult and eventually were abandoned without an agreed statement, there was 'substantial agreement between the two Churches on ministry in general and on the nature and place of the ordained ministry in particular'. A document[76] published in the Assembly papers for 1993, recommends acceptance of a 'Statement of mutual recognition of

---

[75] See *Our Place among the Churches*, pp. 118-22, for a description of the wide range of evangelistic, social and caring ministries and spiritual development activities pursued by Viewfield Baptist Church on an ecumenical basis.

[76] *SBYB 1994*, p. 179.

ministries'. This is distinct from a mutual eligibility of ministries, but includes freedom for ordained ministers of either Church to celebrate the Lord's Supper in churches of the other denomination. While each Church would require any transferring ministers to receive appropriate training, neither Church would require re-ordination. The Statement had been adopted by the May 1993 General Assembly of the Church of Scotland. However, while the Baptist Assembly of the same year accepted it as part of the DICR report, a substantial number of delegates voted against the report because of the inclusion of the Statement.

The following year brought the ACTS review. 'A request from Rev. Maxwell Craig, Secretary of ACTS, inviting the Union to be part of the review of ACTS, and also to reconsider our membership of that body, had been received.'[77] The DICR had concluded that, as the review was about structures rather than policy and vision, meaningful contributions to the review could come only from member Churches. We judged also that there had been no evidence of a change in outlook among our churches in regard to ecumenical involvement; we felt that ACTS had developed disappointingly especially in the field of mission. Using the phrase 'it is not the right time to reconsider our membership of ACTS', we recommended that we decline this invitation, and this appeared in the Assembly 1994 Handbook. This led to the submission of two written questions to the Assembly, one from Rev. Dr. William Speirs, Peebles, who asked: 'Why is it not the right time to reconsider our membership of ACTS?'[78], the other from the Hillhead Church: 'As there is clearly a lack of evangelical input to the national body that embraces the other main Christian denominations, why has the Union declined the courteous invitation from Action of Churches Together in Scotland to participate in a review of its activities and thus lost another opportunity to present an evangelical viewpoint? Could the Spirit not still guide the review to a new focus for ACTS more acceptable to our denomination and other evangelicals?[79]' In reply, I sketched the reasons for the DICR recommendation. On behalf of the Hillhead Church, Mr. Graham Little argued that the reasons given against participation were:

> not sufficient. We had not sought this invitation: it had come out of regard for individual Baptists and it deserved a grateful if cautious response. To be asked to comment without commitment was a generous offer. He proposed: "That this Assembly acknowledges the reservations expressed in the Doctrine and Inter-Church Relations Committee, the Executive and Council, but requests the Acting General Secretary to write to ACTS accepting with gratitude the renewed offer to participate in the current review of the new ecumenical bodies.[80]

---

[77] BUS Council Minutes, September 1994.
[78] *SBYB 1995*, Assembly Minutes 1994
[79] *SBYB 1995*, Assembly Minutes 1994
[80] *SBYB 1995*, Assembly Minutes 1994, pp. 189-93.

There followed the fullest debate on the ecumenical issue since the 1989 Assembly with all its accusations and hurts. New voices echoed the earlier debate, both negative and positive. On a show of hands a clear majority rejected Mr. Little's proposal.

The issue, however, would not quite go away quietly. At the following Assembly at Inverness in 1995, the usual welcome was given to ecumenical guests, a practice no-one had questioned since 1989. Among them was a young Church of Scotland minister, Rev Sheilagh Kesting who was asked to speak on behalf of other guests. The Minutes record her contribution as follows:

> Rev. Sheilagh Kesting (Secretary, Ecumenical Affairs, Church of Scotland) greeted the Assembly on behalf of the representatives of the other denominations … She referred to the conversations between the Union and the Church of Scotland in which she had taken part, which had led to better relations between the denominations and to the mutual recognition of ministers. She expressed regret that the Union had not responded positively to the invitation from ACTS for closer association: the distinctive Baptist voice would be missed. She hoped that co-operation would continue at the local level as there were grave matters to be faced together.[81]

The following day I presented the report of the DICR, my final report as Chairman, (I had been Chairman since 1992). The Minutes tell the story:

> Mr. Moyes, giving his last report, said that personally he had found Rev Sheilagh Kesting's comments on the previous day about the Union and ACTS courageous and moving. She had shown how much our 'separatedness' hurt our fellow Christians in Scotland and the United Kingdom. He hoped we might consider again a way back into the family of Churches in our land, confident in our Baptist identity and confident, too, in our evangelical convictions.'[82]

The Minutes record that the report was accepted. What they do not record was that my final sentence was greeted with spontaneous applause.[83]

The century was drawing to a close and its final years saw the Union joining the Evangelical Alliance, on the basis of its Declaration of Principle, in 1997. It had begun for Baptists with a Presidential Address on the subject of '*Christian Union and the Denominational Spirit*', which, translated into late twentieth century language might read, 'Ecumenism and Denominational Distinctives'. As providence would have it, it closed with a Presidential Address that included extensive reference to the same subject. In addressing where the Church might

---

[81] Assembly Minutes 1995, *SBYB 1996*, p. 190.
[82] Assembly Minutes 1995, *SBYB 1996*, p. 203.
[83] The actual script of this final report is recorded in *Our Place among the Churches*, pp. 126-29.

find hope as we entered the twenty-first century, I suggested that we have to look at the quality of our life together as Churches together in Scotland.

> We need to rediscover community, the common life, the shared life. The spiritual life is not a solitary, individual affair but a social experience of 'one-anotherness', both within churches and among them. We are meant to be a reconciled people - are we demonstrating this?

I then referred to Sheilagh Kesting's word to the Inverness Assembly of 1995, and the spontaneous response to my comments on her remarks and continued,

> I want to ask this Assembly whether it would be our intention as a mainstream denomination, founded in the radical wing of the Reformation, for ever to remain separate from the family of other churches in our land; and to ask whether it would be our intention to continue to co-operate, as many of our churches do, at the local and regional levels, yet never to bring influence to bear within the central structures of inter-church life?'

I then went on to put this direct question to the Assembly: '... is it not now time for us to resume our place <u>and our influence</u> in the wider family of churches in Scotland?' Finally, I asked... 'What, dear friends, are we afraid of? What are we waiting for?'[84]

Whatever it was that we were waiting for, we waited a further eight years for the issue of 'our place among the Churches' to return to the agenda of the Baptist Union of Scotland. In his report to the 2007 Assembly meeting in Glenrothes, Fife, the General Director, Rev. Bill Slack, raised as a deep concern the lack of connected-ness both within the denomination and with other Churches. As Baptists, we had been side-lined in being outside ACTS and it was time, he pled, for us to look again at the issue.[85] It was he who, in 1989, had supported Observer status in ACTS as it would give time 'to see clearly where ACTS was taking us before giving our full assent'. He went on to say that 'if it should prove to be of God we should have the grace to see this'. Clearly he envisaged a time when Scottish Baptists could give 'full assent'. Will that time come? – perhaps only when Scottish Baptists re-affirm the principle upon which they themselves are in union (a group of churches with a variety of views and traditions yet united upon a defining core), and extend that principle to other Christian streams.

---

[84] The full Address can be found in *SBYB 2000*, pp. 91-105.
[85] *Baptist Union of Scotland Assembly Papers 2007*, Glenrothes, 'General Director's Annual Report', pp. 20-23.

CHAPTER 6

# *Your Word is Truth*:
# Theological Developments among Twentieth-Century Scottish Baptists

## Kenneth B.E. Roxburgh

### Introduction

As Scottish Baptists stood on the threshold of a new century, they shared a spirit of optimism among other sections of the Christian community in the country. In 1905, J.T. Forbes, President of the Baptist Union of Scotland declared that 'the future for us is full of hope...we are on the winning side.'[1] In his report to the Baptist Union of Scotland in 1904, George Yuille[2] spoke of the previous year as being 'the best and most fruitful in the history of the Union...the Churches are full of hope and expectation. The prospects for our Baptist union brighten with our increasing opportunities of enlargement.'[3] It was a period that was generally marked by religious growth. Church attendance as a whole in Scotland continued to rise from a figure of 48 per cent of the population in 1890 to a peak of 50 per cent in 1905,[4] a period when Baptist churches in various parts of Scotland flourished.

### Higher Criticism

It was also a period of theological change within Scottish Christianity. Although the Scottish Baptist Magazine published a 'lengthy and blunt article' which condemned the work of Higher Criticism on scripture, it is clear that Baptists in Scotland were affected by these views as they impacted the lives of those who

---

[1] *Baptist Union of Scotland Year Book for 1905*, p. 29.
[2] Yuille was part-time secretary to the Union from 1880 to 1919. He served as pastor of the Stirling church from 1870 to 1913. In 1913 he became full-time secretary of the Baptist Union of Scotland.
[3] *Scottish Baptist Year Book (SBYB)*, 1904, p. 54.
[4] See Callum G. Brown, *Religion and Society in Scotland since 1707* (Edinburgh: Edinburgh University Press, 1997), p. 147.

were educated in the Scottish Universities and the Baptist Theological College.[5] Since the latter part of the nineteenth century, as a result of the 'Higher Critical' approach to the Bible and the insights of Darwinian scientific theories, new approaches towards biblical interpretation had shaken the confidence of many people in the authority of scripture. In 1881, following a protracted heresy trial in the Free Church of Scotland, William Robertson Smith, Professor of Hebrew and Old Testament exegesis at the Free Church College in Aberdeen was removed from his position.[6]

For many theological educators, however, this new approach to scripture was viewed as a positive means of communicating the Christian message in the modern world. In 1901, the Church of Scotland convened a Congress which devoted one of its sessions to 'The Bearing of Recent Old Testament Criticism on Christian Faith.' Professor A.R.S. Kennedy[7] introduced the discussion by addressing the 'spirit of anxiety and unrest' which had arisen as a result of researches into the 'origin, credibility and supreme authority of Holy Scripture as a divine revelation.'[8] Kennedy argued that the critical method would enable the Church to be 'led by the Spirit of truth to a more accurate knowledge...[of] God's ...revelation'.[9] For Professor Gilroy, Aberdeen University, the result of the critical approach had led the Christian faith to be 'purified and strengthened, because doubtful elements are removed, untenable positions are surrendered' and many of the intellectual problems associated with the study of scripture are removed, and this 'helps confirm our faith.'[10]

## George Adam Smith

George Adam Smith[11] taught Hebrew at Aberdeen University, and had, during his pastoral ministry in Aberdeen from 1882 to 1892 published several works indicating his acceptance of biblical criticism in Old Testament study.[12] In 1898 Smith traveled to American to deliver a series of lectures at Yale University on *Modern Criticism and the Old Testament*, which were published in 1901. The

---

[5] See Brian R. Talbot, 'Fellowship in the Gospel: Scottish Baptists and their relationship with other Christian churches 1900-1945' in *Evangelical Quarterly*, 78.4 (2006), p. 348. 'The "Higher Critics" and the Bible', *Scottish Baptist Magazine*, 28:8 (August 1902), pp. 135-36.
[6] See William Johnstone (ed.) *William Robertson Smith: Essays in Re-assessment* (Sheffield: Sheffield Academic Press, 1995).
[7] Kennedy was professor of Old Testament in Edinburgh University.
[8] See *World Congress: 1901* (W. Blackwell, 1901), p. 124.
[9] *World Congress*, p. 130.
[10] *World Congress*, pp. 133, 141.
[11] See Iain Campbell, *Fixing the Indemnity: the Life and World of Sir George Adam Smith (1856-1942)* (Carlisle: Paternoster Press, 2004).
[12] See 'Recent Literature on the Old Testament' in *The Expositor*, 3rd series, No. 10, pp. 386-400.

printed volume received an extensive review in the *British Weekly*[13] by P.T. Forsyth.[14] Forsyth was an enthusiastic supporter of biblical criticism, and contended that it 'need not be deadly to faith, however trying (it may be) to believers.' Forsyth agreed with Smith that 'parts of the Bible, taken as parts, cannot be said to be inspired at all; that the Bible is not there to teach us history any more than science...that its object is not history in itself, but revelation, and that the critical question is not how much history is left, but how much real revelation in the dynamic and redemptive sense.'[15] Although Smith's lectures were well received within the academic world, there were many ministers, elders and members of his denomination and among Baptists who expressed their concern over his theological perspective.[16] John Urquhart, Baptist minister in Glasgow published a pamphlet 'Case for the Higher Criticism: is there anything in it?' as a response to Smith's views.[17] When the United Free General Assembly met in May 1902 in Glasgow, however, Smith was cleared of all charges of heresy by a vote of 534 votes to 263.[18]

## James Denney

James Denney[19] was educated at Glasgow University, and then at the Free Church College in Glasgow, where he encountered 'the application of historical criticism to biblical texts' in a context where academic freedom was celebrated and its results allowed to challenge traditional theological understandings of scripture and creed.[20] Denney spent fourteen years in pastoral ministry in Broughty Ferry where he developed a reputation in preaching and biblical

---

[13] See P.T. Forsyth, 'G.A. Smith's Yale Lecture' in *British Weekly*, No. 756, April 25, 1901, pp 51, 53.

[14] P.T. Forsyth (1848–1921), Scottish Congregational minister, born and educated in Aberdeen and principal of Hackney College, London from 1901 until his death.

[15] Forsyth, 'Smith', p. 53.

[16] A number of ministers and elders within the Free Church published *The Old Bible and the New: Being a Review of Prof. G.A. Smith's 'Modern Criticism and the Preaching of the Old Testament'* and initiated a process against him in the courts of the Church.

[17] See also J. Urquhart, *The Inspiration and Accuracy of Holy Scripture* (Glasgow: Pickering & Inglis, 1895). The Scottish Baptist Magazine commended Urquhart's pamphlet. See *SBM*, 29:3 (March 1903), p. 39. John Urquhart, in an earlier work, had argued for literal historical accuracy of the Genesis account, arguing (for example) for a universal deluge, datable to 2442 BC. See *Modern Discoveries and the Bible From the Creation to Abraham* (London: Marshall Brothers, 1898), p. 185.

[18] George M. Reith, *Reminiscences of the United Free Church General Assembly 1900-1929* (Edinburgh: Moray Press, 1933), p. 31.

[19] See James M. Gordon, *James Denney (1856-1917): An Intellectual and Contextual Biography* (Carlisle: Paternoster Press, 2006).

[20] Gordon, *Denney*, pp. 70, 74.

exposition. This led to an invitation to deliver a series of lectures in Chicago Theological Seminary in 1894, later published as *Studies in Theology*.[21] Denney's ninth lecture, on Holy Scripture was one of the most controversial, one which he revised for publication.[22]

In the lecture, Denney made it crystal clear that he had abandoned a view of scripture as being verbally inspired or inerrant. He argued that scripture 'was itself human and liable to all the infirmities and errors of humanity.'[23] He criticized the Westminster Confession of Faith for placing its article on scripture at the beginning of the document, making it 'fundamental' rather than treating it, as the Scots Confession had done, under the heading of a means of grace. Denney maintained that the term 'word of God' should not be primarily assigned to scripture, but to the 'glad tidings of God's pardoning love freely offered in Christ, for the free acceptance of sinful men.'[24] This was at the heart of divine revelation, and to which scripture bears witness. Denney argued that the later attitude of Protestant Churches to scripture which spoke of the verbal inerrancy of biblical books was 'the most stupendous example on record of lying for God, of deliberately shutting of the eyes to the most palpable and obtrusive facts.'[25] For Denney, the biblical authors were not seeking to be 'chroniclers' of accurate historical facts,[26] but 'religious writers' who communicate faith in God to us, one who is 'merciful and gracious.'[27] In the last analysis, Denney stressed that 'We do not believe in the Bible, we believe in Jesus Christ'[28] and that what is of vital importance is not any 'infallibility of verbal accuracy…but an infallibility of saving power.'[29]

## Baptists in the Early Twentieth Century

During this period of time several significant ministers within the Baptist Union of Scotland were graduating from Glasgow University. Eric Roberts[30] graduated with a first class honours in Moral Philosophy. He then matriculated in 1902 for the BD, but following a year of study at Glasgow, Roberts went to Mansfield

---

[21] James Denney, *Studies in Theology* (London: Hodder & Stoughton, 1894).
[22] Gordon has transcribed the original lecture in *Denney*, pp. 237-53.
[23] Gordon, *Denney*, p. 144.
[24] The following are direct quotes from the original lecture. See Gordon, *Denney*, p. 238.
[25] Gordon, *Denney*, p. 242.
[26] Gordon, *Denney*, p. 245.
[27] Gordon, *Denney*, p. 245.
[28] Gordon, *Denney*, p. 251.
[29] Gordon, *Denney*, p. 253.
[30] For a fuller study of Roberts see Kenneth B.E. Roxburgh, 'Eric Roberts and Orthodoxy among Scottish Baptists' in *Baptist Quarterly*, 39.2 (2001), pp. 80-95.

College in Oxford to study towards a BA in Theology.[31] Once again he excelled in his studies and received prizes in Divinity and Biblical Criticism.[32] He graduated with an honours degree in 1906.

One of Roberts' fellow students at Glasgow and Oxford was W. Holms Coats who continued his study at Marburg, Germany, following his graduation from Oxford in 1906.[33] Coats traveled to Marburg, having successfully won the first Baptist Union Scholarship under the Twentieth Century Fund. Reflecting on his time in Marburg in 1907, he spoke of 'the prevailing feeling in Scotland...that in the sphere of religion Germany is the home of rationalism and a hotbed of heresy'. He spoke of his appreciation of Professor Herrmann's 'emphasis on the individual character of religious experience' along with his 'openness of mind' in theological enquiry which made his students 'indebted to him for a new view of old truth.' Herrmann was Professor of Dogmatic Theology in Marburg, a proponent of the views of Albrecht Ritschl, 'probably the most influential continental Protestant theologian between Schleiermacher and Barth...the heyday of liberal Protestantism'[34] who dismissed the concept of gospel miracles, including the resurrection, maintaining that 'redemption has *as much* to do with the life as with the death of Jesus.'[35] Coats believed that 'Higher Criticism' if 'rightly used, can only help Christianity'.[36] Coats wrote, 'We are committed by our tradition to the critical study of the Bible, which has done so much for a true understanding of the Scripture. No other method is conceivable in any modern theological college: nor is any peril of "Modernism" inherent in it.'[37]

During their time in Oxford, Coats and Roberts were undoubtedly influenced by the Principal of Mansfield College, A.M. Fairbairn.[38] Fairbairn entered the ministry of the Evangelical Union in Scotland, educated at James Morison's

---

[31] Baptist Theological College of Scotland Minute Book Number 1. Minute of 2 October 1902.

[32] Baptist Theological College Year Book for 1905.

[33] It was common practice for students who had graduated from Scottish Universities to spend a period of time studying in Germany and imbibe the fruits of German scholarship.

[34] P.N. Hillyer, 'Albert Ritschl' in *New Dictionary of Theology*, edited by Sinclair B Ferguson (Leicester, Inter Varsity Press, 1988), pp. 595-96.

[35] Alan P.F. Sell, *Defending and Declaring the Faith* (Exeter: Paternoster Press, 1987), p. 186.

[36] See 'Life at Marburg' in *Scottish Baptist Magazine*, 33.9 (September 1907), pp. 162-63.

[37] See 'The Place of the College in the Denomination' p. 8 from typewritten mss in the author's possession.

[38] See Elaine Kaye, *For the Work of Ministry: A History of Northern College and Its Predecessors* (Edinburgh: T. & T. Clark, 1999), pp 114-19. A.P.F. Sell, 'An Englishman, An Irishman and a Scotsman...' in *Scottish Journal of Theology*, 38 (1985), pp. 41-83.

Theological Academy in Glasgow.[39] He left Scotland to become a Congregationalist and from 1886 to 1909 was Principal of Mansfield College, Oxford. Fairbairn was the 'father of Liberal Evangelicalism among Congregationalists' and believed that the gospel message was encapsulated, not in the Church's creeds and traditions,[40] but in the 'Fatherhood of God,'[41] especially as understood 'through the consciousness of Christ's relationship to God as Son of the Father.'[42] Fairbairn instilled within Coats a conviction that 'theology...must engage with the thought of the age'[43] and it was this desire, to contextualize his theology that distinguished Holms Coats from the thinking of other Scottish Baptists such as John Shearer who was more content with maintaining a theological system from the halcyon days of evangelical awakenings.[44]

## John Shearer

John Shearer, although educated at Glasgow, along with Roberts and Coats, was more influenced by the revival tradition within Scottish evangelicalism than his fellow students. The revival tradition in Scotland was one which was intimately woven into the experience and expectation of many people within Scottish Christianity. During the eighteenth and nineteenth centuries, recurring periods of spiritual awakening affected the religious life of the Scottish church, often bringing surges of emotional intensity, popular interest and renewal to the life of the nation.[45] It was not, however, until 1859 that a national spiritual movement impacted the country as a whole, as Scotland shared in an awakening with truly international proportions.

During the mid-nineteenth century, one major influence on revival thinking in Scotland was that of Charles G. Finney. Finney has been described as 'one of the most compelling figures in the history of American religion.'[46] Finney's

---

[39] For Morison see Kenneth B.E. Roxburgh, 'James Morison (1816-1893)' in *Records of the Scottish Church History Society*, 32 (2002), pp. 115-41.
[40] Kaye, *Ministry*, p. 115.
[41] Sell, *An Englishman*, p. 67.
[42] Kaye, *Ministry*, p. 115.
[43] Elaine Kaye, *Mansfield College, Oxford: Its Origin, History and Significance* (Oxford: Oxford University Press, 1996), p. 95.
[44] See Kenneth B.E. Roxburgh, 'The Fundamentalist Controversy Concerning the Baptist Theological College of Scotland' in *Baptist History and Heritage*, 36.1/ 36.2 (Winter/Spring 2001), pp. 251-72.
[45] See Kenneth B.E. Roxburgh, 'Revival: An Aspect of Scottish Religious Identity' in *Religion and National Identity: Wales and Scotland c.1700-2000*, edited by Robert Pope (Cardiff: University of Wales Press, 2001), pp. 200-220.
[46] Richard Hofstadter cited in Nancy A Hardesty, *Your Daughters Shall Prophecy: Revivalism and Feminism in the Age of Finney* (New York: Carlson Publishing, 1991), p. 9.

*Lectures on Revival*, first published in 1835, marked 'the end of two centuries of Calvinism and the acceptance of pietistic evangelicalism' in America.[47] Finney launched a tirade against Calvinism and especially the Westminster Confession of Faith with its pessimistic attitude towards sinful human nature. His basic premise concerning a 'Revival' was that it 'is not a miracle or dependent on a miracle. It is a purely philosophical result of the right use of the constituted means.'[48] This view stood opposed to the older view of Jonathan Edwards, which had been influential in Scotland during the eighteenth century, that revival was a 'surprising work of the Spirit of God.' Finney argued that Christians could influence the work of the Spirit and promote a work of revival through prayer and action. Finney's influence on Scottish Christianity was seen in the life and ministry of someone like James Morison whose popular theological writings eventually led to 'the end of the Calvinist ascendancy and the beginning of an era in which evangelical Arminianism would predominate'.[49]

In the latter part of the nineteenth century, awakenings began to be associated with significant preachers such as D.L. Moody, whose appearance in the cities of Edinburgh and Glasgow in the 1870s brought many people to faith in Christ.[50] John Coffey[51] has demonstrated that Moody went out of his way to reach men and women who had little contact with the church, holding his meetings in agricultural and city halls rather than churches and chapels, thereby distancing himself from traditional, institutional religion. His simple use of language, his anti-intellectual theology characterized by 'ruin by sin, redemption by Christ and regeneration by the Holy Ghost'[52] appealed to ordinary people and drew them in their thousands to his meetings.[53] Moody's message stressed a theology of the love of God demonstrated at Calvary and was warm and moving in its appeal. Unlike many evangelists who preached on hell and judgement, Moody focused on the love of God and the joys of heaven.

---

[47] Charles Finney, *Lectures on Revivals of Religion*, Edited by William G. McLoughlin (Cambridge, Mass.: Belknap Press, 1960), p. vii.

[48] McLoughlin, *Lectures*, p. x.

[49] See Brian R. Talbot, *The Search for a Common Identity: The Origins of the Baptist Union of Scotland 1800-1870* (Carlisle: Paternoster, 2003), pp. 331 and 333.

[50] Ian Hamilton suggests that 'Moody's visits to Scotland (1873, 1881-1882 and 1891-1892) helped to transform the face of the Church in Scotland.' See I. Hamilton, 'D.L. Moody' in N.M. de S. Cameron et al (eds), *Scottish Dictionary of Church History and Theology* (Edinburgh: T. & T. Clark, 1993), pp. 605-606.

[51] John Coffey, 'Democracy and popular religion: Moody and Sankey's mission to Britain, 1873-1875' in *Citizenship and Community*, edited by Eugenio F. Biagini (Cambridge: Cambridge University Press, 1996), pp 93-119.

[52] W.S. Hudson, *Religion in America* (New York: Harper and Row, 1965), p. 223.

[53] Ken Jeffrey speaks of how Moody 'succeeded in reaching the urban masses.' *When the Lord Walked the Land: The 1858-62 Revival in the North-East of Scotland* (Carlisle: Paternoster Press, 2002), p. 18.

Moody's Arminian theology and unusual methods, especially the use of music, was favorably received in cities such as Glasgow where his mission lasted for over three months. Moody had not only demonstrated a 'successful model for evangelizing the masses 'but his 'theological inclusive gospel' converted many ministers to 'a more pragmatic theology of mission' and had an impact on the theological issues of the day.[54] His emphasis on the preaching of the gospel to all sections of society helped to stress the message of God's universal love for all humankind, in contradistinction to the message of limited atonement. This indicates a 'growing shift in Scottish Presbyterianism towards a more Arminian perception of Salvation.'[55]

Industrial development in the late nineteenth and early twentieth century brought about a change in work and the movement of population to Glasgow and Lanarkshire, as well as a challenge to the church as to how it would reach these people with the message of the gospel. J.T. Forbes, minister of the influential Hillhead Baptist Church, one of the largest in the country, addressed the Baptist World Congress in London in 1905 on 'The Attitude of the Baptists to the Working Classes'. Forbes argued that changes in society confronted Baptists with fresh opportunities and challenges, although he confessed that 'in many places we have not a great hold on the working man – the artisan and the labourer.'[56] Forbes was expressing the fear felt by many, that the institutional church was becoming alienated from the working classes. Although it was a period marked by religious growth, when church attendance in Scotland as a whole continued to rise, there was also a 'widespread feeling of despair among the British evangelical community' as they saw 'a growing disregard for religious ordinances' within society as a whole.[57]

## John Shearer: Revivals and Modernism

John Shearer entered the newly formed Baptist Theological College in 1895 and matriculated at Glasgow University where he graduated with an MA in 1900. Unlike Roberts and Coats, Shearer did not appreciate the emphasis on an arts degree and the content of his theological education in Glasgow. Later in his life, Shearer commented that 'the Arts course [at the University] displaced the Theological and we were urged [by the College] above all to secure our degree

---

[54] Gordon, *Denney*, p. 102. Gordon suggests that Denney 'looked on Moody-style evangelism with a mixture of intellectual disdain and grudging admiration.' See Gordon, *Denney* p. 96.
[55] Janice Holmes, *Religious Revivals in Britain and Ireland 1859-1905* (Dublin: Irish Academic Press, 2000), p. 72.
[56] *The Baptist World Congress, London, July 11-19, 1905* (London: Baptist Union Publications Department, 1905), p. 266.
[57] Holmes, *Revivals*, p. 167.

in Arts. It was a false preparation for the ministry and showed the growing baleful influence of Modernism.'[58]

His ministries were characterised by expository preaching and evangelistic passion, faithfully preaching 'the old gospel'.[59] When he received the call from Stirling, Shearer commented on the desire which he had 'to preach among you the grand old verities of that old yet ever fresh Theology which are the very life of our life and which were never more needed than they are today.'[60] Throughout his ministries he conducted evangelistic missions in other congregations and every year held a week of evangelistic meetings in his own congregation. One of the most formative experiences of Shearer's life was his visit to the scene of the Welsh Revival in 1905. In April 1905, he commented on his visit in the *Scottish Baptist Magazine*, speaking of the 'great waves of unseen power' which evoked 'prayer like a torrent....God is felt to be very near, and hot tears tell of deep repentance and reawakened love....strong men [are] broken down in an agony of remorse.' He returned to the Scottish Borders 'with a new heart and a new bible'[61], and 'much blessing followed' as the church held nightly meetings from 3 April to 8 July 1905, with many conversions.[62]

When the Welsh Revival occurred in 1904, it was 'totally unexpected.'[63] By January 1905 however, some 3,000 new members had been added to Baptist churches in the Rhondda Valley with similar numbers being seen in other Baptist Associations.[64] The first notice of the Welsh revival took place in an editorial within the Scottish Baptist magazine for January 1905.[65]

> An extraordinary revival of religion has visited Wales....the meetings [are] emphatically prayer meetings....Men, women and children have been taking part in the Welsh revival meetings, many of which are prolonged for hours....There are hundreds, we might without exaggeration say thousands of professed conversions....Will it visit us? Yes; if we are prepared to use the means – to pray,

---

[58] This material came from John Shearer's personal memorandum notebook in the possession of the family. Holms Coats took the opposite position when he wrote 'to present the gospel in the light of modern problems needs all the foundation in Arts studies that we can give men.' See 'The Place of the College' p. 6.

[59] Minutes of the Stirling Street Baptist Church Meetings, Galashiels for 2 September 1913. The Minutes are lodged in the Stirling District Archives, Stirling.

[60] Minutes of Stirling Baptist Church 1911-1918, for 1 July 1913.

[61] Comment in memorandum notebook.

[62] Shearer reported in the *Scottish Baptist Magazine*, 31.6 (June 1905), that 120 had been converted. Stirling Street had 37 Baptisms in 1905.

[63] T.M. Bassett, *The Welsh Baptists* (Swansea: Ilston House, 1977), p. 377.

[64] See Bassett, *Baptists*, p. 378.

[65] The *Revival Times* noted 'much blessing in connection with evangelistic services in different parts of Scotland – a new interest...a greater readiness...to respond' and particular mentioned meetings in Glasgow, Motherwell and Forfar, 15 May 1905.

not in a perfunctory and matter of custom way; but with earnestness and sincerity, that God would send us the blessing.

In his presidential address to the Baptist Union Assembly, John Mclean reflected, not only on the statistics of the revival which were impressive but on its significance for Baptists in Scotland.

> From all parts of Wales, our sister churches report abnormal progress because they received an abnormal blessing during the recent revival. The number of baptisms is far beyond anything recorded in previous years: viz. 24,651 as compared with 5,746 from the previous year, and 5,874 two years ago....If a God-sent revival were to sweep over Scotland, our churches would increase by leaps and bounds, for Baptists were born in a revival, and in revivals they have been born again down through the centuries.[66]

In March 1905, the editor of the magazine returned to the subject of revival and spoke of how 'The desire for a deep and widespread revival of religion has been growing in connection with our churches and throughout Scotland generally. Everywhere an impression prevails that a revival of no ordinary kind is coming; and this feeling has of late been much accentuated by the remarkable success that has attended the movement in Wales....We have now arrived at a stage when even worldly people look upon a revival as a thing to be expected.' He concluded his editorial by assuring his readers throughout Scotland that 'the revival has begun in many of our Churches... our own Baptist ministers are in fullest accord with the movement, and prepared to do their utmost to speed its progress.'[67]

The impact of the Welsh Revival of 1904 on Scottish Baptist Churches was limited to particular congregations, scattered through various parts of the country.[68] There is evidence to suggest that pastors who visited the scenes of the revival in Wales, or who employed Welsh evangelists in special missions, were more likely to experience of similar movement of the Spirit. Baptist churches in Scotland were already growing at the beginning of the century, although there was a particular surge of growth in 1905 when 1970 baptisms were reported, a higher than normal statistic.

The influence of the Welsh Revival, with its 'conservative evangelical ethos'[69] and the North America Baptist evangelical constituency brought

---

[66] *SBYB 1907*, p. 22.
[67] *SBM*, 31.3 (March 1905), pp. 41-42.
[68] The revival affected other Baptist churches in Scotland with John Harper, minister of Paisley Road, Glasgow (later Harper Memorial) reporting 700 conversions and over 100 added to their membership. See reports in *Scottish Baptist Magazine*, 31.4 (April), 31.5 (May) and 31.6 (June) 1905.
[69] Ian S. Rennie, 'Fundamentalism and the Varieties of North Atlantic Evangelicalism' in *Evangelicalism: Comparative Studies of Popular Protestantism in North America,*

Shearer into contact with American Fundamentalism. In his presidential address to Scottish Baptists in 1936, Shearer spoke of the 'danger [that] threatens us at the present moment. The new Rationalism that has invaded the Church has taken our feet from the firm ground of our faith and made us to flounder miserably in a quagmire of doubt'. He maintained the need to hold on to the fundamentals of Baptist faith such as belief in the Bible as 'the Word of the Living God' and 'our Lord's Deity' which will oppose the 'insidious Unitarianism that...is deep seated in the churches of our land.' Thirdly, he spoke of the 'atoning death' of Christ as a 'perfect substitution.' This he contended was 'the central truth of Christianity' and said that 'we must thank God for Karl Barth who takes his place in the noble line of the great Evangelical Theologians who has recalled the Church to the long-neglected Doctrines of Grace'. He concluded by mentioning the Lord's Resurrection, the fact of the New Birth which opposed the 'New Rationalism' with its 'system of psychology' and also the Blessed Hope of the Church which he identified as the imminent return of Christ.[70]

## Confessions of Faith

As the new century dawned, the majority of denominations in Scotland reflected on their theology, especially those Presbyterian Church which adhered to the Westminster Confession of Faith. The Church of Scotland had adopted the *Westminster Confession* subordinate standards of its constitution, and used it as a hermeneutical tool through which interpretation of scripture was judged and it therefore assumed a judicial role in the courts of the Church. During the nineteenth century the Original Secession Church used the Confession to discipline James Morison for his views on unlimited atonement and the Church of Scotland deposed John McLeod Campbell, minister of Rhu for preaching universal atonement and thereby undermining the teaching of the Confession on the doctrine of Election. By the turn of the new century, however, it was becoming clear that within the established church the 'Church no longer regarded Calvinism, although it was of the very staple of the Westminster Confession, as being in the technical sense of the sum and substance [of the faith].'[71]

Prior to any changes taking place within the established Church, other Presbyterian denominations had debated the issue and the United Presbyterian Church, along with the Free Church of Scotland had adopted *Declaratory Acts* which allowed the ministers and elders of the respective churches to give a

---

the British Isles, and Beyond 1700-1990 (Oxford, Oxford University Press, 1994) edited by Mark A. Noll, David W. Bebbington and George A. Rawlyk, p. 342.

[70] John Shearer, 'Forward: The Call to a Great Advance' in *Scottish Baptist Year Book* for 1937, pp 153-57.

[71] See G. M. Tuttle, *So Rich a Soil* (Edinburgh: The Handsel Press, 1986).

more reserved affirmation of their acceptance of the Westminster Confession, in which 'liberty of opinion' could be expressed with regard to issues that were not related to the 'substance of the faith.'

James Morison and McLeod Campbell were both deposed from their respective churches[72] for their views on the extent of the atonement. MacLeod Campbell's influence on Scottish Evangelicalism in the nineteenth century was not as significant as that of James Morison, who founded the Evangelical Union that grew to over ninety congregations by 1896.[73] In 1892, William Landels commented that Morison's 'principles have modified the beliefs of all the evangelical Churches'.[74] When Morison's own jubilee was commemorated in 1889, the Winton Place congregation in Kilmarnock congratulated him 'on the more liberal and enlightened character, which, in the course of the last generation, the theology of our country has assumed, and to which your own work, both as a preacher and as a writer, has in no small measure contributed.'[75] Oliver Flett, Paisley indicated that 'when he began his labours, the idea of the love of God for every man was all but ignored in the religious teaching of Scotland; now, it has obtained a firm footing in all the churches.'[76] Morison was not the only voice to speak of the universal nature of God's love but his influence permeated to preachers and people in various sections of the Scottish church and the *Christian News* was undoubtedly correct in saying that no one 'had done more...to mould the theological mind of Scotland of the present day and to liberalize the churches of Scotland' than James Morison.[77] By 1910, the Church of Scotland also voted to approve their own Declaratory Act, which allowed ministers and elders to declare their acceptance of the Confession and their own commitment to 'fundamental doctrines of the Christian faith contained therein', without committing themselves to accepting all of its teaching.[78]

Scottish Baptists had traditionally demurred at adopting any creed or confession as definitively prescribing their understanding of the Christian faith. In his early ministry, Shearer agreed that Baptist churches did not have any 'Creed or Confession of Faith, believing the Scriptures of the Old and New Testament to be sufficient, under the guidance of the Holy Spirit, to decide all

---

[72] The United Secession Church joined with the Relief Church in 1847, to form the United Presbyterian Church, with 518 congregations.

[73] See Kenneth B.E. Roxburgh, 'James Morison (1816-1893)' in *Records of the Scottish Church History Society* (Edinburgh, 2002).

[74] *Evangelical Union Jubilee Conference Memorial Volume* (Glasgow: T. Morison, 1892), p. 90.

[75] Morison *Jubilee*, p. 19.

[76] ibid, p. 49.

[77] *Christian News*, 5 October 1889. Cited in Morison's *Jubilee*, p. 95.

[78] Cited by A.C. Cheyne, *The Transforming of the Kirk* (Edinburgh: The Saint Andrew Press, 1983), p. 85.

questions of doctrine or government which may arise....[thereby] granting to all its members the right of private judgement with regard to doctrinal truth, subject to the Word of God'[79] Up until Eric Roberts was deposed from the Baptist ministry of Scotland in 1933, the Scottish Year Book had contained the statement that 'Baptists do not recognize Creeds and Confessions of Faith as Church institutions' and 'acknowledge no authority over the conscience but the Word of God....Against all Creeds, Confessions, Traditions whatsoever – Catholic or Protestant – Baptists place the open scriptures.'[80]

When Eric Roberts expressed his Unitarian views and denied the deity of Christ, appealing to this statement regarding creeds and confessions, Shearer expressed his opinion that 'the time has come for a clear statement of our Baptist Faith'. 'We must,' he contended, 'have a Baptist Confession of Faith for a faith that cannot be confessed is a faith not worth confessing.'[81] Shearer was convinced that Modernism which he described as *The Menace of the Evangelical Faith* was 'preached in so many of our pulpits and so craftily couched in Evangelical language that multitudes are being deceived by it.'[82] Writing shortly after the war, he made good use of the analogy of Modernism which was creeping 'stealthily into our life like a poison gas and for long we have been breathing it unconsciously'. [83] He expressed a concern that 'the Evangelical Faith is dying in our midst' and that the 'Baptist Theological College of Scotland' which was 'deeply imbued with this German Rationalism' has 'imparted it to its students'. During the 1944 debate with the Assembly, Shearer used the example of the Marshall Street congregation in Edinburgh, where Holms Coats had ministered from 1921 to 1928 and argued that a once 'flourishing church' had called a 'succession of Modernistic preachers [and] it is what it is today'[84] It was direct attack on students and lecturers of the College.

---

[79] Statement included within the Annual Report of Stirling Street Baptist Church, Galashiels in the minutes of the Church for 29 January 1913.
[80] See 'Distinctive Principles of the Baptists' in *SBYB*, 1900, p. 2.
[81] John Shearer, *The Baptist Confession of Faith* (Stirling: Jamieson & Munro, n.d. [1937]), p. 14.
[82] See Forward to John Shearer, *The Evangelical Faith*, 2nd edition (Glasgow: John Shearer, 1946), p. 5.
[83] John Shearer, *Modernism: The Enemy of the Evangelical Faith,* 1st edition (n.p.: n.d [early 1940s]), p 3.
[84] *Letter of May Hossack to George Hossack of 25 October 1944*, p 3 in author's possession. Coats succeeded Rev Thomas Stewart. The church closed in 1942, following the ministry of Thomas N. Tattershall, trained at Manchester, due to inner-city depopulation. John Barclay, 'Edinburgh and Lothian' in David W Bebbington (ed.), *The Baptists in Scotland* (Glasgow, Baptist Union of Scotland, 1988), p. 104.

From 1918 until 1936, the ministers of the church included Thomas Stewart,[85] W. Holms Coats, R.J. McCracken,[86] and Douglas Stewart.[87]

Shearer asserted his conviction that the problem with Modernism lay primarily in its belief that 'the Bible is not the Word of God' and that although 'it may contain it, it is not [in and of itself] the Word of God'.[88] He argued that a loss of conviction in the inspiration and infallible nature of scripture led 'Modernist Ministers' to find 'little pleasure in preaching from it and prefer to draw their texts from current literature, the sensational topic of the hour, or even songs that are sung in our streets'.[89] He believed that 'the doctrine of verbal inspiration…is plain common sense, inevitable truth'.[90] In June 1944, Principal Coats, James Hair[91] and A.B. Miller[92] sent out a leaflet defending the teaching of the College. It began by maintaining the 'inspiration of the Bible' without adopting any particular understanding of the nature of that inspiration.[93] This was not necessarily unusual, for even a staunch evangelical like Graham Scroggie stated that 'subscription to a particular definition of biblical inspiration was not, in his view, a test of doctrinal orthodoxy' and maintained that 'if you demand that I subscribe to your theory of inspiration, I shall decline, but I am not on that account a Modernist.'[94]

The debacle over Eric Roberts, condemned as a Unitarian and removed from the accredited list of ministers within Scotland, had not been supported by all Baptists in Scotland. According to Shearer, when the issue was debated within the Council of the Baptist Union of Scotland, the College's 'most popular lecturer plead[ed] ardently for this Unitarian…asserting that he was 'true to the heart of the Gospel'.'[95] During the Assembly of 1933, seventy-three delegates

---

[85] Stewart became General Secretary of the Baptist Union of Scotland from 1920-1930 and lectured in the College from 1918-1932 in Church History.
[86] Lecturer from 1932-1937.
[87] Douglas Stewart was a student in the College from 1924 to 1931. He moved from Marshall Street to Hampstead.
[88] Shearer, *Modernism*, p. 9. Despite his earlier positive appraisal of Karl Barth's influence, this seems to be an attack on Barth's threefold form of the Word of God.
[89] Shearer, Modernism, p. 11.
[90] Shearer, *The Evangelical Faith*, p. 8.
[91] Hair had been one of the first students at the College when it began in 1894, a fellow student of Shearer. He joined the College staff in 1936 to teach Philosophy of Religion, Christian Ethics and Comparative Religion. He acted as Convener of the Social Service Committee and was President of the Union in 1930-31.
[92] A.B. Miller was appointed Lecturer in Church History and Systematic Theology in 1938. In 1950 he became Principal of the College, retiring in 1967.
[93] *Statement by Principal and Lecturers* (Glasgow: The Baptist Theological College of Scotland, June 1944), p. 3.
[94] Cited by Ian Randall in 'Graham Scroggie and Evangelical Spirituality' in *Scottish Bulletin of Evangelical Theology*, 18.1 (2000), p. 75.
[95] Shearer, *Modernism*, p. 11.

opposed the motion to depose Roberts. Shearer believed that this was the 'blackest day in the history of Scottish Baptists'.[96] He condemned the way in which the 'whole Tutorial Staff of the College warmly supported him' implying that they had all adopted Roberts' Unitarian views, suggesting that Christ 'is Divine only in the same sense as we ourselves are Divine'.[97] It is much more likely that those who voted against his deposition were opposing the manner of his discipline rather than agreeing with his theological position. In giving his own interpretation on these events, Shearer was able to cast serious doubts on the integrity, as well as the theological orthodoxy, of the College. Without referring to the events of 1933, the College statement simply reaffirmed the fact that 'the teaching of the College regards Christ, not merely as a Good Man (as do the Unitarians) nor as a demi-god (as Arius maintained), but as the Son of God Incarnate, the Word made flesh, in whom God and man are perfectly united.'[98] Shearer refused to accept this statement and said that the College 'may issue a thousand statements: it will never remove the deep general conviction implanted that day, that it is an out and out Modernist institution.'[99]

The outcome of these events, where Shearer's desire for the denomination to sever its links with the College failed, was the formation of the Evangelical Baptist Fellowship on 27 June 1944 and the beginning of evening classes in the Christian Institute in Bothwell Street, Glasgow, in January 1945, when John Shearer and T.J. Harvey lectured. In October 1946, the E.B.F Bible College began to meet at 153 West Regents Street and moved to Queen's Drive in 1949.[100] Dr Henry Curr, a former student of the College, a Professor of McMaster University in Toronto and Principal of All Nation's Bible College became Principal.[101] After a few years, with the number of students only totaling ten, with difficulties of settlement in Scotland, and a cooling of tempers, the College closed and its former secretary and treasurer, D.S.K. Mcleay and J.D. Taylor were elected presidents of the Union, in 1959 and 1965 respectively. The concern expressed by Shearer at what he perceived to be the influence of Modernism, although widely shared by many within the denomination, did not attract the necessary support to maintain an alternative theological College. Although constitutionally the College was an independent institution, not a member body of the Baptist Union of Scotland, the

---

[96] Shearer, Modernism, p. 11.
[97] Shearer, *The Evangelical Faith*, p. 15.
[98] Shearer, *The Evangelical Faith*, p. 15.
[99] Shearer, Modernism, p. 12.
[100] Among the students were Tom Houston, Hugh Robinson, T.C. Anderson, John Johnston. Jim Findlay. Material gleaned from Shearer's Memorandum book and personal conversation with Hugh Robinson.
[101] Dr Curr and Dr Coats worshipped in Queen's Park church during this period of time.

denomination as a whole valued its ministry and appreciated the character and commitment of its tutors.[102]

## The Impact of the First and Second World Wars on Baptist Theology in Scotland

Scottish Baptist, along with other denominations were deeply involved in both of the World War conflicts in the twentieth century. In congregation after congregation the 'roll of honour' filled up as numerous young men went forward to enlist. By 1917 Baptist churches had 4,425 members involved in the fighting,[103] with twenty-eight pastors responding to the appeal for special service as Chaplains or working with the YWCA or Soldier's Christian Association.[104] This proportion of men from Baptist congregations was high coming from a denomination with only twenty-one thousand members. By the end of the war five hundred men from Scottish Baptist congregations had been killed, with the Hillhead Church in Glasgow losing fifty-five. Eighty-one men had received special honours in connection with their service, including twenty military crosses.[105]

In the early days of the war, the Church leaders eagerly anticipated a revival of religion, not only in the armed forces, but also in the churches.[106] Churches throughout the country were crowded on Sunday 9 August, and smaller denominations, such as the Baptists, reported 1,293 baptisms in 1914, an unusually high figure.[107] This intensified interest in religion was maintained through January 1915, when the King called for a 'Day of Prayer' and 'everywhere the churches were filled.'[108] Although the longed hoped for revival of religion did not occur, this did not mean that religion disappeared from the lives of either civilians or those who served at the front.

---

[102] Paradoxically, at a later session of the 1944 Assembly, following the vigorous debate initiated by Shearer, the College was offered the 'sincere congratulations' of the Assembly 'on the attaining of the Jubilee of the College, and of the growing place it now occupies in the life of the denomination. See *SBYB 1945*, pp. 52-53.

[103] *Scottish Baptist Year Book* (1917), p. 47.

[104] *Scottish Baptist Year Book* (1919), p. 42.

[105] See S.D. Henry, 'Scottish Baptists and the First World War' in *The Baptist Quarterly*, 31.2 (April 1985), p. 63.

[106] For an examination of this issue see Stewart J. Brown, 'A Solemn Purification by Fire: Responses to the Great War in the Scottish Presbyterian Churches, 1914-1919' in *Journal of Ecclesiastical History*, 45.1 (January 1994).

[107] See David Hunt, *Reflecting on Our Past: A Statistical Look at Baptists in Scotland 1892-1997* (Hamilton: Published by the Author, November 1997), Appendix 2. The next year only 727 baptisms were recorded and this figure went down even further to 619 in 1916. There were slight increases to 781 in 1917 and 868 in 1918.

[108] See 'Reflections in Time of War' in *Life and Work*, February 1915, p 52.

The awfulness of suffering, the tragic loss of the lives of over 100,000 Scotsman during the Great War, led many theologians to reconsider the particular emphasis they gave in their preaching of the gospel. Jervis Coats, in his Presidential address to the Baptist Union of Scotland in 1918, called for 'love theology' to be that which was 'wanted' more and more. He criticized a recital of orthodox theology in the creeds and confessions of faith that a church might profess, when the actions of men and women's lives expressed a different message. This, he said would be detrimental to the authenticity of the message which the Church presented to a lost and lonely world.[109] This emphasis on the love of God, as well as a concern to bring a message of comfort to thousands of parishioners who had lost husbands, sons and brothers in the trenches, led some ministers in different denominations to speak of a wider hope of salvation for those who had died, fighting for the just cause of their country. When the war concluded, churches throughout Scotland installed memorial plaques and windows in their church buildings and worked along with local communities in erected war memorials. The war memorials had, as their first objective, the commemoration of the sacrifice of those who had died as well as a means to 'help the survivors overcome their pain and allow mourning.'[110] The evidence of war memorials further exhibited the belief of salvation through honorable death in war.

One of the best known and well used scriptures, to depict the sacrifice, not only of Christ but of those who had fallen during the Great War was John 14:13 'Greater love has no man that this that a man lay down his life for his friends.' The way in which these men had died, selflessly for the sake of others, demonstrated to many people the Christ-like love that they had shown, evidence of the work of God's Spirit within their lives, whether they realized it or not. Furthermore, in a variety of images used in memorial windows installed in many church, including Baptist congregations, there is evidence of a change of theological perspective that would impact the understanding of the gospel message being proclaimed in the post-war period.[111]

When Briton declared war against Germany on 3 September 1939, although the Churches in Scotland spoke with one voice in support of Chamberlain's actions, judging the 'ideology of Nazism...as evil'[112] the statements lacked the 'jingoism' of 1914. This reflected the increased concern, not only among

---

[109] Jervis Coats, 'Vision – Atmosphere' in *Scottish Baptist Year Book* (1918), p. 35.

[110] Laurance van Ypersèle, 'Making the Great War great: 1914-18 war memorials in Wallonia' in *Memory and Memorials*, edited by William Kidd and Brian Murdoch (Aldershot: Ashgate, 2004), p. 37.

[111] See James Lachlan MacLeod, '"Greater Love Hath No Man than This": Scotland's Conflicting Religious Responses to Death in the Great War,' in *The Scottish Historical Review*, 81.211 (April, 2002), p. 91.

[112] A.J. Hoover, *God, Britain and Hitler in World War II: The View of the British Clergy 1939-1945* (Westport, Connecticut: Praeger, 1999), p. 16.

Pacifists, but within the Christian community as a whole, that war would never settle the deep seated economic, social and political problems which the world was facing, fully aware that the war would last for a long time.[113] The Assembly of the Baptist Union spoke of how the country had 'entered the struggle for spiritual value' but stressed that the church must never 'cease to love and pray for our enemies, many of whom are linked with us in the Church universal.'[114]

The Second World War continued to raise serious theologians and religious questions for Scottish churches. This was often related to the experience of war which soldiers had encountered, although, unlike the Great War, the use of bombing campaigns affected civilians who never reached the front line. Whereas the Great War had been immediately assessed by the Church as a righteous campaign, which assured the country of God's blessing and intervention on their behalf, the religious significance of the Second World War was assessed with much more caution. In August 1940, Scottish Baptists argued that if the country was willing to fight for victory then it seemed logical to pray for victory. They asked 'if we cannot pray for it, ought we to be fighting for it?' Yet they also maintained that even though the country was fighting for a just cause, this was no reason to believe that God would give them victory over Germany. Furthermore, there was a danger, in praying for victory, to assume that Britain had no share of blame in the causes that led to the outbreak of war in the first place.[115] Although the issues that churches faced in the 1940s were different to those of the Great War, theological reflection impacted the way in which churches responded to the crisis of the times.

## Karl Barth

Thomas Torrance, writing in 1955, asserted that 'Karl Barth is incontestably the greatest figure in modern theology since Schleiermacher.'[116] For Hugh

---

[113] The *Scottish Baptist Magazine* suggested that the war would be 'as awful as that of twenty-five years ago, in some respects more awful.' See Article on 'War' in *SBM*, 65.10 (October 1939).

[114] *Scottish Baptist Year Book*, 1940, pp. 159-60. Earlier, on the outbreak of war, the Council of the Baptist Union issued a statement that referred to 'Nazi ill-faith, aggression and violence' and urged the churches to support the 'cause of freedom and justice.' See Minutes of the Baptist Union of Scotland 31 May 1939 to 2 June 1942, pp. 72-73.

[115] 'Prayer for Victory' in *SBM*, 66.8 (August 1940). During the 1940 Baptist Union Assembly, Alexander Clark, the President of the Baptist Union of Scotland, spoke of 'militant atheism of Russia, the new paganism of Germany, the worship of the state in Italy, the secularism of Turkey, the self-sufficiency of America and British Humanism' which all demonstrated the sinfulness of humanity who 'disavows faith in God and has faith only in himself.' See A. Clark, 'The Church and the New Order, in *Scottish Baptist Year Book, 1941*, p. 156.

[116] Thomas F. Torrance, 'Karl Barth' in *Expository Times*, 66 (1955), p. 205.

Mackintosh, Barth's theology, as he encountered it in the late 1920s 'is the theology of a great, a volcanic soul....important and memorable.'[117] Karl Barth was born in Switzerland in 1886 and studied in Bern and Germany, serving as a pastor in Safenwil in Switzerland from 1911 to 1921. During this period of time, as Barth studied the scriptures, especially the book of Romans in the context of a world at war, he reacted against liberal theology with its anthropocentric emphasis and began to stress the transcendence of God and challenge of the 'Word of God.' Barth entered theological education in 1921, at Göttingen (1921-25), Münster (1925-30), Bonn (1930-35) and finally in Basel (1935-1962). His initial influence in Germany was later felt in Great Britain, especially in Scotland,[118] and in 1937-38 he delivered the Gifford lectures in the University of Aberdeen. Barth's theology exploded onto the theological scene through the publication of his commentary on Romans in August 1918, where he stressed 'the saving grace and compassion of God.' The book 'fell like a bomb on the playground of the theologians.'[119]

There were different reactions to Barth's theology in Scotland.[120] First of all, there were those who read his theology but were remained unchanged in their theological perspective.[121] A second group was drawn to his theology because, despite its perceived shortcomings, it was moving in an orthodox direction. D.H.C. Read considered Barth's approach as 'acting upon theology in a conservative direction.'[122] In this category, we have already noticed John Shearer's warm commendation of Barth in 1936. Thirdly, there were people who rejected Barth's theology because of its close association with Calvinism.[123] Finally, there were those who welcomed his approach with enthusiasm. Among these was R. Birch Hoyle,[124] who spent several years as

---

[117] Hugh R. Mackintosh, 'Leaders of Theological Thought: Karl Barth' in *Expository Times*, 39 (1927-28), pp. 539-40.

[118] Richard H. Roberts, 'The Reception of the theology of Karl Barth, in the Anglo-Saxon world: history, typology and prospect' in S.W. Sykes (ed.), *Karl Barth: Centenary Essays* (Cambridge: Cambridge University Press, 1989), p. 124.

[119] Comment by Karl Adam, cited by John McConnachie, 'The Teaching of Karl Barth' in *Hibbert Journal*, 25 (1926-27), p. 386.

[120] See Alec Cheyne identifies four responses. See A.C. Cheyne, *Transformation*, pp. 207-208.

[121] Among this group was David S. Cairns (1862-1946), Professor of Apologetics at Aberdeen University.

[122] D.H.C. Read, 'Forward with Calvin: A Glance at the New Orthodoxy' in *British Weekly*, No. 2666, 2 December 1937, p. 171.

[123] See John McIntyre, 'Karl Barth's Predestination' in *British Weekly*, No. 2917, 24 September 1942, p. 294.

[124] Hoyle (1875-1939) was educated at Regent's Park College in London from 1895 to 1900 and served as a Baptist minister, in Scotland and England for 26 years. He published *The Teaching of Karl Barth: An Exposition* (London: Student Christian Movement Press, 1930) and translated Barth's *Theological Existence*, in 1933.

Baptist minister in Aberdeen prior to the Great War. Robert James McCracken, who moved from Scotland, following two ministries in Edinburgh and Glasgow, along with lecturing in the Baptist Theological College, encountered Barth in Scotland and Germany. During a visit to Germany in 1937, McCracken met German students avidly reading Karl Barth's second volume of *Dogmatics*.[125] This early contact with Barth's theology became a major influence on McCracken[126] in three specific areas of his intellectual development and pastoral ministry. Barth's stress on the 'sovereignty' and 'wonder of God' led McCracken to question the earlier emphasis of Schleiermacher on religious experience 'as a source both for theology and preaching.'[127] Secondly, he became acutely aware of the 'uniqueness of the Biblical revelation' especially in Barth's interpretation of revelation 'in terms of concrete events and personal encounters' and the way in which God speaks directly through the Bible. This led, finally, to a profound change of thinking with regard to McCracken's preaching. Although he deeply appreciated the liturgical reform movement, he became more and more convinced that 'there can be no substitute for the sermon since it is the very act which forms the crux of the service.'[128] As the preacher recognizes that there is nothing more relevant 'than the speaking and the hearing of the Word of God', he stands in the pulpit 'not so much to offer a message of insight from man to man, but a revelation from God to man.'[129] Barth's influence on Scottish Baptists was particularly significant among those student who studied with Thomas F. Torrance in New College and included Peter Barber, Andrew MacRae and Gordon Martin.[130]

## Theological Reflection among Scottish (Edinburgh) Baptists

An examination of the minutes of the Edinburgh and Lothian Baptist Minister's Fraternal (ELBA) indicates a strong interest in discussing theological themes, especially up until the 1970s.[131] Theological papers, on a variety of subjects, normally occupied the fraternal on a monthly basis. There were occasions, such as May 1973, when Bruce Milne spoke on 'Recent Theology' when many

---

[125] See letter to Chancellor Whitton, dated 28:7:38 in McMaster Archives, Box 121, File 106.

[126] See Robert J. McCracken, 'How Barth has influenced Me' in *Theology Today*, 13 (October 1956), pp. 361-63

[127] McCracken 'How Barth Influenced me', p. 362.

[128] Robert J. McCracken, 'Let the Preacher Preach the Word' in *Theology Today*, 2.1 (April 1945), p. 80.

[129] McCracken, 'How Barth Influenced me,' p. 363.

[130] Peter Barber and Andrew MacRae both served as general Secretary of the Baptist Union of Scotland Gordon Martin was Principal of the Scottish Baptist College.

[131] See Kenneth B.E. Roxburgh, 'Edinburgh behind closed doors: The Edinburgh and Lothian Baptist Association Fraternal 1947-1987' in *Baptist Quarterly*, 38.1 (1999), pp. 33-45.

members of the fraternal 'felt that we were swimming in very deep waters' although 'we nevertheless enjoyed and benefited by sharing in the scholarly presentation of the subject.' [132] At the conclusion of the fraternal in September 1962, 'there was a sudden and complete disappearance of all members of the fraternal' to attend the Gifford lectures.[133] Controversial subjects, such as Election raised their heads every so often.[134] In October 1963, the fraternal secretary wondered if a paper by R.E. Clements on the 'Evangelical understanding of the Old Testament' would raise divisive issues but when the speaker commented that 'the bible is more than history, the bible is God breathed scripture, the bible is the word of God' the comment was made that 'the modest doctor came perilously close to receiving a cheer.'[135] In November 1981, David Wright, lecturer in Church History at New College spoke on 'The Doctrine of Scripture and Evangelicalism', a paper given as the Tyndale Historical Theology lecture in 1978. Eventually the chair 'brought the discussion to a close just as it was about to explode'.[136]

Despite the ambivalent attitude of some members of the fraternal towards theological discussion, a paper presented in 1962 by Fred Cawley on Jesus and Paul led to the comment that 'there was an eloquent stillness as the Doctor brought his disquisition to its climax. There was a presence in the midst.'[137] Theological reflection had made its impact on the spiritual formation of those who were present.

## The Theology of Baptism

The 1950s and 1960s witnessed an extensive investigation by the Church of Scotland into the subject of baptism and a Commission was set up in 1953 under the convenorship of T.F. Torrance. The Commission published a series of reports in the Church of Scotland General Assembly papers from 1956 to 1963, including an assessment of Baptist teaching in 1959.[138] The ELBA fraternal entered into an extended discussion on the subject which began into April 1956 and continued for ten consecutive meetings of the fraternal, coming to a conclusion in September 1957. The fraternal obviously felt that their position as Baptists was coming under threat in the context of Presbyterian Scotland. The initial discussion centred on the report on New Testament doctrine which

---

[132] Vol. 4.42
[133] Vol. 2.205
[134] Vol. 1.126.
[135] Vol. 3.14.
[136] Vol. 5, 155.
[137] Vol. 2.186.
[138] *Report to the General Assembly of the Church of Scotland in 1959* (Edinburgh, 1959), pp. 629-62.

appeared in the General Assembly of 1955.[139] The fraternal took the opportunity of meeting with Professor Torrance and felt that the main issue which divided Baptists from the Church of Scotland was 'the definition and description of the nature of the Church' and that the 'idea of the 'gathered church' was the solution.'[140] The fraternal remained convinced throughout their discussions that 'the Report had not challenged our position seriously, and could be countered very effectively, by sound Biblical exegesis.'[141] William Whyte, Minister of Portobello led the discussion on seven occasions, engaging in a detailed analysis of the report which he referred to in his Presidential address in October 1960, concluding that 'Infant baptism is a gross denial of all evangelistic activity...it is a denial of the Gospel of the Grace of God. We believe that infant baptism has no place whatsoever in the New Testament.'[142] This debate was widespread within the denomination and between May 1960 and January 1961 seven articles on the subject of Baptism appeared in the *Scottish Baptist Magazine*.[143]

One of the most significant contributions to this discussion was that of R.E.O. White. White was minister of Rutherglen Baptist Church in Glasgow from 1950 to 1954. From 1951 he also acted as New Testament tutor in the Baptist Theological College of Scotland.[144] White contributed a brief response to the Church of Scotland Report in 1956.[145] In 1960 White published *A Biblical Doctrine of Initiation*, which was a detailed biblical and theological investigation of the subject of Baptism, one which saw baptism as a sacrament, closely related to membership of the Christian Church. White argued that 'baptism was a rite of spiritual enduement, eschatologically effective, conferring remission...in the assurance that God as well as man was at work in each administration.'[146] He contended that while this sacramental understanding should not be confused with 'magico-ritualist notions of infused grace' Baptists needed to reject the view that baptism was 'an idle form or traditional symbol performed without spiritual profit.'[147] White maintained that 'believer's baptism loses much of its scriptural significance...when baptism and church

---

[139] *Report to the General Assembly of the Church of Scotland in 1955* (Edinburgh, 1955), pp. 609-62. This was followed by a report on the Fathers in 1956 (pp. 605-46).

[140] Vol. 2.50-51.

[141] Vol. 2.53.

[142] *Scottish Baptist Year Book for 1961*, pp. 9-10.

[143] The articles were written by A.B. Miller (two), Peter Barbour, A.W. Argyle, H Cook, R.E.O White and Jim Taylor.

[144] In 1966 he became full-time tutor in New Testament and then Principal in 1968.

[145] R.E.O. White, 'Theology and Logic' in *Baptist Quarterly*, 16.8 (October, 1956), pp. 356-64.

[146] R.E.O. White, *The Biblical Doctrine of Initiation* (Grand Rapids: Eerdmans, 1960), p. 305.

[147] White, *Initiation*, pp. 308-309.

membership are treated as two questions, and baptism into the church, into the body of Christ, is allowed to disappear from baptismal theology and practice.'[148] When the ELBA fraternal met in October 1960, a debate took place on White's book which led to a 'vigorous discussion which made it clear that to some, a simpler and less elaborate view of baptism was more congenial'[149] an indication that within the fraternal there were signs of contrasting churchmanship, both high and low.

## Conclusion

Throughout the twentieth century Scottish Baptists were deeply involved in theological developments in Scotland. The debates on biblical and creedal authority impacted the thinking of Scottish Baptists of various theological perspectives. Although Scottish Baptists maintained a fairly conservative and evangelical viewpoint, this was by no means a uniform opinion. As those who lived within the heritage of the reformed faith, Scottish Baptists maintained a love for the scriptures and a commitment to liberty of interpretation of biblical truth, accepting that insight into biblical interpretation could be enhanced by the fruit of modern scholarship. Openness to theological discovery, learning from various streams of theological thought, continued to enliven the denomination through the vagaries of twentieth century life.

---

[148] White, *Initiation*, pp. 315.
[149] Vol. 2.132.

CHAPTER 7

# *Pour out your Spirit*: Experiences of the Holy Spirit amongst Scottish Baptists in the Twentieth Century

## Alasdair Black

### Introduction

In 1965 a young Scottish Baptist minister, the Revd. David Black, had an overwhelming experience of the Spirit of God. He had invited a fellow Baptist minister, Revd. Douglas McBain of Wishaw Baptist, and the Revd.Tom Smail, a Church of Scotland minister from Motherwell, to the manse of Springburn Baptist Church at Bishopbriggs. He wanted them to pray for him to receive the gift of tongues. But after laying their hands on him and praying for a period of time very little had happened. Black was disappointed not to have received the anticipated experience of the Spirit. Yet after saying goodbye to McBain and Smail, 'he felt what he described as the hand of God resting on him and a great weight coming upon him, forcing him to the floor. He was overcome with a powerful sense of the glory of God, "the shekinah"'. Unable to walk he lay prostrate on the stairs for a while, before crawling to the landing where he found he was praising God in an unknown and unlearned language, he had received the gift of tongues. After this experience of what was described as 'fullness or baptism in the Spirit', Black went on to become one of the key leaders and pioneers of charismatic renewal in Scotland.

Born in Glasgow in 1937 as the only child of William and Margaret Black, Black's first encounter with Baptist church life was in Hillhead Baptist, where his father had served as the treasurer for almost twenty years. Deeply influenced by the ministry of Guy Ramsay, Black felt called to the Baptist ministry, but in the course of his training experienced a deep spiritual dissatisfaction. He perceived the roots of this dissatisfaction in the stories of the Lewis Revival and Mission Scotland which had brought Billy Graham to the Kelvin Hall in Glasgow. As he noted:

> Billy Graham, Tom Allan and D.P. Thomson founder of the Crieff Centre made a tremendous impact through the 1953 and 1955 Tell Scotland campaigns. Although they were Scotland wide the central belt gained the most. As a young Christian I remember the impact of huge numbers of people travelling by the

subway to the Kelvin Hall and singing all the way 'This is my story, this is my song, praising my Saviour all the day long'. Fellow students at school were terrified to go anywhere near the meeting place in case they were converted!

There is no doubt all these things created a spiritual hunger in many who tragically did not find the reality they were seeking in the normal expression of Sunday Church. So much work and faith went into the organisation of these events that most were happy to let things lie after they finished, but they had given us a taste of the way things could be.[1]

The Lewis Revival in 1949 was also an important influence. Although revivals were very much part of the landscape of Hebredian Presbyterianism the involvement of an outsider, Duncan Campbell from the Faith Mission in Glasgow, made this different. Campbell's involvement meant that the stories of the Revival were widely recounted in evangelical circles throughout Scotland in the 1950s. This recounting awakened in some Scottish Baptists an interest in the work of the Spirit that was ultimately to find expression in what came to be called the Charismatic movement.

This movement had a profound effect on many Baptist churches in Scotland towards the end of the twentieth century as they either embraced or resisted its influence. Yet the impact of this movement amongst Scottish Baptists cannot be understood in isolation from a number of diverse theological and ecclesiological antecedents that reach as far back as the nineteenth century. This movement was part of a historical continuum that was deeply rooted in earlier moves of the Spirit and certain aspects of Scottish Presbyterianism and the Holiness movement. These historical antecedents were important factors in determining how Scottish Baptists perceived the work of the Spirit and their reactions to the arrival of the Charismatic movement.

### The Rise of Dispensationalism

Although various points of departure can be chosen for understanding the Charismatic movement globally and in Scotland, it cannot be truly understood without some consideration of the rise of the Holiness movement and dispensationalism. These are movements that came to the fore in the second half of the nineteenth century and set the scene for the subsequent experiences and understanding of the Spirit amongst Scottish Baptist in the twentieth century. One of the most important figures in this regard was an early nineteenth century Presbyterian minister, called Edward Irving. Irving's theology of the Spirit was the focus for the doctorate studies of one of the pioneers of charismatic renewal in Scotland, Gordon Strachan. Strachan's thesis was published in 1973 under the title *The Pentecostal Theology of Edward Irving*, although many of the same

---

[1] D. Black, Autobiographical Memoir (2003), unfinished manuscript in author's possession.

ideas appeared in an earlier article 'Edward Irving and Regent Square; a Presbyterian Pentecost'.[2] This thesis proved highly influential in the early days of Scottish Charismatic renewal.

Irving's theology was rooted in what is known as Christian millennialism. The term millennialism is derived from a reference in the book of Revelation were Jesus is seen to reign on earth for a thousand years prior to the last judgement (Rev.20:2-6). Before the Reformation this thousand year period was generally understood to be a metaphor. It did not represent a future period or era in the history of the world, but symbolised the time between Jesus' first and second coming. It expressed the reign of Christ that was to be found within his Church in the world (a view known as 'amillennialism'). But after the Reformation this view began to change, so that by the beginning of the nineteenth century most evangelical Christians believed the millennium was an actual future reality. Eschatological timetables began to appear that detailed the events leading up to the return of Christ that linked the vision of the book of Revelation with the Pauline teaching in Romans 9-11 concerning the conversion of the Jews and the 'ingathering' of the Gentiles. In the wake of these timetables the millennium became an imminent actuality rather than a symbolic representation. Although views continued to differ over its precise nature (was it a literal thousand year period or simply an unspecified time of future blessing), it was now something towards which the church was moving.

This sense of human history moving towards a new dawn was also being generated by the dramatic changes taking place in society at large. The industrial revolution and the political and social tumult of the French and American revolutions had also added to this sense of historical momentum. The millennialism of the nineteen century, therefore, was providing Christians with a way to relate contemporary affairs to a biblical prophetic matrix. It was giving a framework for the understanding and interpretation of God's work in human history. Many Scottish Presbyterians, given their Calvinist theology and reading of the book of Romans, maintained the Jews would be saved and then there would be an ingathering of the Gentiles (a world revival) as a precursor to the return of Christ. This idea of a great revival before the second coming came to be known as post-millennialism. The thousand year reign of Christ would come after (post) the great world revival. Thus the expectation was that the Christian church was on the precipice of a great and unprecedented wave of revival.

This postmillennial hope acted as the impetus for a new emphasis on the evangelization of the Jews spearhead by men like Robert Johnston and wider Christian mission involving famous Scots like David Livingston and Alexander Duff. In Scottish Baptist circles a postmillennial vision of the future fuelled the mission endeavours and revivals led throughout Scotland by the Haldane

---

[2] G. Strachan, *The Pentecostal Theology of Edward Irving* (London: Darton, Longman & Todd, 1973); G. Strachan, 'Edward Irving and Regent Square: A Presbyterian Pentecost', *Journal of the Presbyterian Historical Society*, 14 (1968-72), pp. 186-95.

brothers. But it was primarily through the writings and work of the great Scottish divines like Thomas Chalmers, 'Rabbi' John Duncan and Robert Murray McCheyne that this postmillennial reading of world history and scripture found expression. Irving was born into this postmillennial hope and served as Thomas Chalmers assistant at St John's, Glasgow when he was first ordained into the Church of Scotland. But his significance is found in that he challenged this postmillennial worldview and introduced the idea of the work of the Spirit into his reading of history.

Irving moved to London in 1822 to pastor what became the largest Scottish Presbyterian church in the capital. His preoccupation with what he believed was the imminent return of Christ and the biblical prophecies which spoke of this event provided a powerful impetus to his thinking. Yet Irvine found that he could not reconcile the optimistic aspirations of the Scottish postmillennialists with what he read in scripture. In a provocatively entitled address to the London Missionary Society in 1824, 'Babylon and Infidelity Foredoomed',

> Irving advanced the assertion that the Church, far from being on the threshold of a new era of blessing, was about to enter a 'series of thick-coming judgments and fearful perplexities' preparatory to Christ's advent and reign.

Irving began to teach that rather than a period of revival the prelude to Christ's return would be marked by apostasy and a general resistance to the ways of God. Christ would then remove the church from the world and there would then be a period of time which would see the restoration of Israel and her witness to the rest of the world. As he observes, 'When the Lord shall have finished the taking of witness against the Gentiles... he will begin to prepare another ark of testimony... and to that end will turn his Holy Spirit unto his ancient people, the Jews, and bring them unto those days of refreshing... This outpouring of the Spirit is known in Scripture by 'the latter rain'.[3] Thus the promised restoration of the Jews and the ingathering of the Gentiles would occur after Jesus' had taken his church out of the world and prior to the promised millennium.[4]

---

[3] Edward Irving, preliminary discourse, 'on Ben Ezra', *The Coming of Messiah in Glory and Majesty, by Juan Josafat Ben-Ezra a converted Jew, Translated from the Spanish, with a Preliminary Discourse* (London: L.B. Seeley & Sons, 1827), pp. 5-6.

[4] This conviction is believed to have been inspired by a prophetic vision given in 1830 to one of Irving's associates, Margaret MacDonald from Port Glasgow. MacDonald claimed:

> The awful state of the land that was pressed upon me. I saw the blindness and infatuation of the people to be very great. I felt the cry of Liberty just to be the hiss of the serpent, to drown them in perdition. It was just 'no God.' I repeated the words: Now there is distress of nations, with perplexity, the seas and the waves roaring, men's hearts failing them for fear. Now look out for the sign of the Son of Man. Here I was made to stop and cry out, O it is not known what the sign of the Son of Man is; the people of God think they are waiting, but

This view came to be known as premillenialism. It implies a radically different view of God's work in the world and the church from that of the postmillennialists. The Christian church rather than participating in the transformation of society prior to Christ's return has to retreat from it and keep itself safe from the looming apostasy and moral disintegration. Irving came to believe that in view of the imminent threat that the forces of apostasy represented to the life of the church, it was essential that a Christian be 'baptised in the Spirit'. Only those who had had an experience of the Spirit would be able to prevail amidst the moral decay that would exist in society prior to the return of Christ.

This conviction led Irving in 1830 to endorse a woman from Glasgow and two men from Greenock who had experienced glossolalia (speaking in tongues), prophecies, and miraculous healings. 'Linking these phenomena with baptism in the Spirit, as a distinct post-conversion experience, Irving welcomed their manifestation in his own church in 1831'.[5] His endorsement of these spiritual gifts and a heretical Christology inevitably led to a breach with the Church of Scotland and the birth of a new church movement known as the Catholic Apostolic Church. This movement emphasised New Testament patterns of church government appointing Apostles, Prophets, Evangelists and Pastors [also known as Angels], as well as encouraging the manifestation of glossolalia and other related gifts of the Spirit. However, the influence of this movement on the wider church was negligible and by the beginning of the twentieth century it had virtually ceased to exist in a British context. Yet Irving had left a much more

---

> they know not what it is. I felt this needed to be revealed, and that there was great darkness and error about it; but suddenly what it was burst upon me with a glorious light. I saw it was just the Lord himself descending from Heaven with a shout, just the glorified man, even Jesus; but that all must, as Stephen was, be filled with the Holy Ghost, that they might look up, and see the brightness of the Father's glory. I saw the error to be, that men think that it will be something seen by the natural eye; but 'tis spiritual discernment that is needed, the eye of God in his people... Only those who have the light of God within them will see the sign of his appearance. No need to follow them who say, see here, or see there, for his day shall be as the lightening to those in whom the living Christ is. 'Tis Christ in us that will lift us up- he is the light – 'tis only those that are alive in him that will be caught up to meet him in the air...
>
> A Huebner, *The Truth of the Pre-Tribulation Rapture Recovered* (Millington, N.J.: Present Truth Publishers, 1976), pp 67-69.
>
> In the light of this vision, the idea of the rapture began to gain currency amongst Irving and his followers. The second coming would occur in a series of stages. Jesus would initially return and gather the church as a prelude to a series of other events that would happen prior to the final judgement.

[5] N.M. de S. Cameron et al (eds), *Dictionary of Scottish Church History & Theology* (Edinburgh: T. &T. Clark, 1993), p. 436.

enduring legacy. His apocalyptic vision of the end of the world and his re-assessment of the postmillennial aspirations of Scottish Presbyterianism had influenced a number of others. Foremost amongst these individuals was a young man called John Nelson Darby, who is attributed with being the founder of the Plymouth brethren.[6]

Yet the pre-millennialism of Darby entirely rejected Irving's notion of Baptism in the Spirit and the manifestation of spiritual gifts. As a contemporary of Darby reflects,

> The favourite, the inexhaustible subject of talk among serious people was unfulfilled prophecy. The Irvingite movement, (as people would call it) had popularized Millenarian speculations among many who resisted steadily all belief in the new 'Miracles' and 'Tongues'. Names now utterly forgotten of writers on prophecy formed the staple reading, I am afraid, for a good many of the religious folk among whom I lived; and their speculations turned chiefly on the chronology of the future – in what year the Jews were to be restored, Popery to be destroyed, and the Millennium to begin.[7]

Darby's premillennialism evolved into what is known as 'dispensationalism'. Adopting a maxim of Irving that 'the second coming of the Lord is the 'point de vue', the vantage ground...from which, and from which alone, the whole purpose of God can be contemplated and understood', Darby advanced the idea that the bible and history of the church can be divided into distinctive periods or dispensations.[8] These dispensations showed God's future intent in the last days and the ways that he had worked throughout biblical history. Through his use of dispensations Darby could draw a sharp distinction between the work of the Spirit as found in the New Testament and the contemporary church's experience of the Spirit. Gossolalia (speaking in tongues), prophecies, and miraculous healings all belonged to a different epoch or dispensation.

---

[6] Through 1826-30 Irving had held a series of prophetic conferences at Albury Manson in Surrey, the home of Henry Drummond a London banker. In 1831 a similar conference occurred in Ireland at Powerscourt. Darby was present at this conference and was very influenced by the premillennial vision of the Irvinites that saw apostasy rather than revival as the prelude to the return of Christ. Breaking with the Church of Ireland in 1832, 'the apostate church', the Brethren movement of which Darby was a part 'became the single most potent channel through which premillennialism spread among British Evangelicals in the middle decades of the nineteenth century, undermining the old postmillennial consensus'—Cameron et al (eds), *Scottish Church History and Theology*, p. 563.

[7] Henry Houseman, *John Ellerton, A Sketch of His Life and Works* (London: S.P.C.K., 1896), p. 19.

[8] M.O.W. Oliphant, *The Life of Edward Irving* (London: Harper & Brothers, 1862), p. 255.

## The Holiness Movement and the Welsh Revival

Nevertheless, Irving's understanding of the work of the Spirit independently found fresh expression in the North American Wesleyan teaching on Christian sanctification and perfectionism. The Holiness movement, as it came to be called, taught that apart from an initial conversion experience a Christian needed to experience a second work of God in their life, sometimes called 'the second touch,' or 'being filled with the Holy Spirit'. This post-conversion experience of the Holy Spirit was necessary to bring about 'entire sanctification' and suppress the inclination to sin. Like Irving, the Holiness movement came to teach that if the church was to prevail in the trails and temptations of the last days an experience of the Spirit's sanctifying power was essential. Although this movement resisted the Irivinites emphasis on spiritual gifts, it encouraged the perception of the church as a Spirit-filled and separate counter culture in an increasingly hostile and reprobate world.

In Britain this movement was popularised by the visits of the American evangelist Dwight L. Moody and the birth of the Keswick convention in. Through their influence the idea of a second blessing was increasingly combined with the emerging premillennial convictions that were rooted in evangelical thinking. Thus by the beginning of the twentieth century the premillennialism that Irving had authored was moving in two very different directions in relation to the work of the Spirit. The dispensationalists were discouraging any emphasis on a New Testament pattern or expression of the Spirit. They subscribed to what is called 'cessationism', the idea that the gifts of the Holy Spirit were given only for the foundation of the church and ceased after the death of the Apostles. Glossolalia (speaking in tongues), prophecies, and miraculous healings were all to be consigned to the past. On the other hand, the Holiness movement, although sharing the dispensationalist's suspicion in relation to the gifts of the Spirit, emphasized the New Testament notion of 'baptism of the Spirit'. The church needed to know the sanctifying and empowering presence of the Spirit of God if it was to remain faithful in the hostile and reprobate world that would exist prior to Christ's return. Only through the outpouring of the Holy Spirit would the church be able to usher in a period of revival that would see people saved and delivered from the corrupting influences of modernity.

Scottish Baptists were affected by both these attitudes to the work of the Holy Spirit throughout the first half of the twentieth century, although it was the Holiness movement that initially proved the more significant influence. This was largely due to the impact that the Welsh Revival (1904-05). Born out of the growing influence of the Holiness movement in Britain, the Welsh Revival promoted an active pursuing of 'the baptism of the Spirit' as a necessary condition for evangelism and Christian ministry. Evan Roberts, the leader of the Revival, believed that what they were experiencing was a prelude to a worldwide awakening that would resemble the day of Pentecost. As he insists: 'The world will be swept by His Spirit as by a rushing, mighty wind.'[9]

Thus the 'Baptism of the Spirit' was seen to be the key to all that was occurring. As Jessie Penn-Lewis, a contemporary chronicler of the Welsh Revival, observes:

> The Baptism of the Holy Spirit is the essence of Revival, for Revival comes from a knowledge of the Holy Spirit, and the way of co-working with Him which enables Him to work in Revival power. The primary condition for Revival is, therefore, that believers should individually know the Baptism of the Holy Ghost. This term being used as a convenient expression for describing a definite influx of the Holy Spirit which thousands of believers throughout the Church of Christ have received as a definite experience. Such an infilling of the Spirit was the cause not only of the Revival in Wales in 1904, but of all other Revivals in the history of the world.[10]

She continues:

> The Baptism of the Holy Spirit may be described as an influx, sudden or gradual, of the Spirit of God into a man's spirit, which liberates it from the vessel of the soul, and raises it into a place of dominance over soul and body. The freed spirit then becomes an open channel for the Spirit of God to pour through it an outflow of Divine power. The mind receives, at the same time, a clarifying quickening, and the 'eye of the understanding' is filled with light (Eph. 1:18). The body becomes entirely under the man's complete control, as the result of the dominance of the spirit, and often receives a quickening in strength for endurance in the warfare service he finds he has emerged into.[11]

Certain Scottish Baptists were becoming increasingly aware of this emphasis on the work of the Holy Spirit through the influence of the Holiness movement, as well as the evangelistic crusades of men like D.L. Moody and Ruben A. Torrey, the first President of the Bible Institute of the Chicago Evangelization Society (now known as the Moody Bible Institute). In February 1903 Torrey conducted a four-week mission in Edinburgh. He maintained that the church could experience an out pouring of the Spirit of God which would act as a prelude to revival if it diligently sought the empowering of God through prayer. [12] Thus through Torrey a number of Scottish Baptists had become increasing convinced of the need for an outpouring of the Spirit on the church. An outpouring that would usher in an age of revival that would see the lost saved before the imminent return of Christ. Therefore, at the turn of the century there was in

---

[9] W.T. Stead, *The Story of the Welsh Revival* (New York: Fleming H. Revell, 1905), p. 8.

[10] Jessie Penn Lewis, *War on the Saints* (Thomas E. Lowe Ltd., 1994), pp. 286-87.

[11] Ibid, p. 288.

[12] Cameron et al (eds), *Scottish Church History & Theology*, p. 715.

some Baptist churches, especially in Edinburgh, a growing sense of urgency and desire for spiritual empowerment.

When reports of the Welsh revival started to reach Scotland some Scottish Baptists were very receptive to the idea of an outpouring of the Holy Spirit. Several Scottish Baptist ministers made pilgrimages to the Revival, although possibly more out of curiosity or even concern, than an actual desire for baptism in the Holy Spirit. The *Scottish Baptist Magazine* in April 1905 carries the report of one such visit by John Shearer, the minister of Galashiels Baptist Church. He recounts the 'great waves of unseen power' which evoked 'prayer like a torrent.... God is felt to be very near, and hot tears tell of deep repentance and reawakened love.... Strong men [are] broken down in an agony of remorse.' The result of Shearer visit was a series of revival meetings in Galashiels which ran from 3 April to 8 July 1905, and he speaks of ministering 'with a new heart and a new bible'.[13]

Yet Shearer was not the only Scottish Baptist to experience the effects of the Welsh Revival. In 1905 the Baptist Union of Scotland sent out postcards to 50 of its ministers asking them if they had 'anything special to communicate'.

> Replies came immediately from all over Scotland – from Arbroath, Bellshill, Bowhill (Fife), Bridgeton (Glasgow), Bristo Place (Edinburgh), Clydebank, Cowdenbeath, Denny, Elgin, Forfar, Galashields, George Street (Paisley), Gilcomston Park (Aberdeen), Hawick, Inverkeithing, Kelvinside (Glasgow), Maxwelltown (Dundee), Maybole, Motherwell, Orangefield (Greenock), Paisley Road (Glasgow), Partick (Glasgow), Port Ellen (Islay), South Leith, Victoria Place (Glasgow), Stirling and Wishaw.

However, the revival had its greatest impact in Charlotte Baptist Chapel, Edinburgh. In 1902 this church called Joseph Kemp. Kemp was a premillennialist who had been influenced by the Holiness movement and so was not typical of Scottish Baptists at the time who were still predominately postmillennial. He was convinced the church was in the last days. Before the day of judgement the church needed to save as many lost souls as possible from the reprobate world around it. But in order to do this the church would require the supernatural unction of the Holy Spirit which would only come through diligent and persistent prayer.

In January 1905 Kemp visited the Welsh Revival and was deeply taken by the move of God. As he writes,

> I spent two weeks watching, experiencing, drinking in, having my heart searched, comparing my methods with those of the Holy Ghost; and then I returned to my people in Edinburgh to tell what I had seen. In Wales I saw the people had learned to sing in a way which was new to me. I never heard such singing as theirs...The Holy Ghost was in their singing as much as in any other exercise.

---

[13] See Chapter 6 n.61 on page 136 for details.

They had the New song....The world knows nothing of it. Do not tell me that the sporting clubs, the dance halls, the movies, and operas can give you joy. They can for the moment give you some fun, but that is not joy. Joy is the gift of God. When a revival from God visits a congregation it brings with it joy.[14]

Returning to Edinburgh with a Welsh evangelist on Saturday 22 January 1905 Charlotte Chapel experienced something of the Revival, 'the fire of God fell - the prayers of many months were answered'. This meeting in January was the start of a continuous succession of prayer meetings and evangelistic gatherings. In March 1906 Kemp wrote: 'the Chapel has been open every night, for 455 nights [that is since January 1905] without one solitary break, and during the whole of that period, there have been but few nights when there have not been anxious souls seeking the way of life'.[15] It is claimed that during this period there was well over a thousand conversions.[16]

The work of the Spirit was central to all that was going on. In one particular Sunday morning service in January 1907 Kemp stood up and announced 'I cannot preach this morning; the Holy Spirit has said I am not to preach this morning.'[17] At this the church spontaneously began to pray and by the end of the morning service over thirty people had made a profession of faith. This spontaneity and sense of the Spirit's directing was a fundamental characteristic of the revival. As Kemp again observes:

> To the curious the meetings appear disorderly; but to those who are in them and of them, there is order in the midst of disorder. The confusion never gets confused; the meetings are held by invisible hands. Believers have been awakened to a sense of having lived defeated lives...Over all these things victory has been claimed. Brethren have been reconciled to one another; differences which kept sisters apart have been destroyed....While the work has been chiefly confined to the saints of God, purifying, humbling, purging, cleansing, there have been numerous conversions.[18]

---

[14] Ian Balfour, *Revival in Rose Street* (Edinburgh: Rutherford House, 2007), p. 99.
[15] ibid, p. 100.
[16] As Kemp observed, 'I have yet to witness a movement that has produced more permanent results in the lives of men, women and children. There were irregularities no doubt; even some commotion...The people poured out their hearts in importunate prayer. Such a movement with all its irregularities is to be preferred far above the dull, dreary, monotonous decorum of many churches. Under these influences the crowds thronged the Chapel, which only three years before maintained a 'sombre vacuum'. After the first year of this work we had personally dealt with no fewer than one thousand souls. Who had brought it? God, during the prayer meetings. Ibid, p. 101.
[17] ibid, p.108
[18] ibid.

The Holy Spirit was purifying His church so that it would be unpolluted by the ways of the world. Believers were being delivered from the apostate state that would characterise so much of the Christian religion at the end. Yet this process of sanctification was also empowering the church to reach out to the lost so that as many as possible could escape the ensuing wrath of God. The congregation's chaotic encounter with the Spirit of God was bringing about their sanctification, and empowering the church to reach out to the lost prior to the second coming.

However, this emphasis on the work of the Spirit did not persist in Scottish Baptists circles. Although the basic premillennial paradigm of a church surrounded by apostate tendencies became pervasive, the emphasis on the role of the Spirit in delivering the church and saving the lost rapidly diminished. The reason for this loss of emphasis was largely due to the rise of Pentecostalism. Heavily influenced by the American Holiness movement Pentecostalism emphasised the need of the believer to receive the 'baptism of the Holy Spirit'. Yet unlike the Holiness movement Pentecostalism insisted that the evidence of this baptism of the Holy Spirit was not only an experience of sanctification, but the presence of speaking in tongues (glossolalia). Pentecostalism after the Azusa Street revival (1906-11) in Los Angeles taught that the church was in the last days and the Spirit of God was to be poured on his people. Only through this out-pouring of the Spirit would the true church be able to resist the apostate tendencies of the end and truly reach the lost. The evidence of this out-pouring was the expression of glossolalia.

Such an emphasis on speaking in tongues and spiritual gifts was seen by many Scottish Baptists who were sympathetic to the Holiness movement and the Welsh revival to be a misappropriation of the work of the Spirit. Yet the tendencies engendered by the Welsh revival did seem to invite such a Pentecostal progression. Evidence of this fact was seen in Charlotte Chapel. In 1908 one of their elders, Eilif Beruldsen, who had been deeply influenced by their experience of revival left with a number of others to form the first Pentecostal Assembly in Leith, Edinburgh.[19] The defection of men like Beruldsen from the Baptist cause only heightened concerns. Thus the emphasis on the work of the Spirit that the Welsh revival had encouraged was increasingly seen in Scottish Baptist circles as something of a Pandora's box that needed to be kept shut.

Evidence of such a feeling can be seen in the experience of Stirling Baptist Church. Stirling had become aware of the Welsh revival in March 1905 through reports from Bristo Baptist Church, Edinburgh. George Yuille, the minister of the church visited the revival and was profoundly touched. As William Ashby one of his close friends commented in 1936 after Yuille's death, 'His visit to Wales during the Revival made an abiding impression on him: he then entered

---

[19] Cameron et al (eds), *Scottish Church History & Theology*, p. 652.

into a deeper experience of the Spirit'.[20] Yuille's experience of the Spirit and endorsement of the Revival was very important for the acceptance of this movement among Scottish Baptist. Yuille's voice was the most influential and respected within the Scottish Baptist Union and so his sanctioning of what was going on was critical. It also profoundly affected Stirling Baptist Church. In January 1906, the year 1905 was described as 'the most prosperous in the history of the church', as the church experienced something of the power of the Revival.[21]

Yet this experience of the Welsh revival meant that elements within the congregation at Stirling were very receptive to the work of the Spirit. Therefore it is not surprising to find that Pentecostal meetings had commenced in the church hall in the wake of the Azusa Street Revival. In May 1908 these meetings attracted the attention of the deacons and the following minute was recorded:

> Some discussion arose about certain manifestations in meetings [margin note 'gift of tongues'] in the church hall by a company of Christians who were waiting on God for the Baptism of the Holy Ghost and Fire, the suggestion being that they were a hindrance to the work of the church....On the motion of Mr Taylor it was agreed that none of these meetings be held under the auspices of the church.[22]

Interestingly they didn't stop the meetings, but the minute shows the way in which those Scottish Baptist churches that had been touched by the Welsh revival were now distancing themselves from a new move of the Spirit. The 'Baptism of the Holy Ghost' was something that was to be associated with Pentecostals and not Scottish Baptists.

This distancing of Scottish Baptists from experiences of the Holy Spirit was further reinforced in 1907 by the publication of the Scofield Reference Bible which helped popularise the notion of dispensationalism. Published in 1907, this annotated study Bible provided what amounted to an innovative commentary on the text of the King James Bible. Yet the commentary was heavily influenced by a premillennial dispensationalism. Its system of cross referencing tied together related verses of Scripture and allowed a reader to follow biblical themes and dispensations from one chapter and book to another. Through its publication Darby's premillennial dispensationalism began to exercise an influence over evangelical thinking well beyond the confines of Brethren assemblies. Reinforcing the notion of the apostate church prior to the return of Christ, speaking in tongues and certain experiences of the Spirit were all redefined along with alcohol, dance halls, cinemas and theological liberalism

---

[20] Cited in Brian R. Talbot, *Standing on the Rock: A History of Stirling Baptist Church 1805-2005* (Stirling: Stirling Baptist Church, 2005), p. 57.

[21] Ibid, p. 60.

[22] Ibid, pp.60-61

as those things that would deceive and lead astray even God's elect in the last days.

Nevertheless, aspects of the work of the Spirit continued to persist in the consciousness of certain Scottish Baptists, although a subtle shift occurred. This shift is typified and may even have been precipitated by Kemp's successor at the Chapel, Graham Scroggie. Scroggie was one of the most influential Scottish Baptists in the first half of the twentieth century. He was heavily influenced by the Holiness movement and spoke regularly at Keswick, although he was brought up in the Christian Brethren. True to his background he taught a form of premillennial dispensationalism, but he combined this in a very unique and distinctive way with influences from the Holiness movement. Unlike other dispensationalists Scroggie leaves open the question of the gifts of the Spirit, although he would not have invited their manifestation in the Chapel. He also affirms an experience of the Spirit in the life of the believer. Yet he distinguishes between the 'baptism' of the Spirit and the 'in filling' of the Spirit. 'Baptism is once for all, the Filling is oft repeated (cf. Acts 4:31; Eph. 5:18)...We are made Christians and members of Christ's Body by the Baptism; but we are made Christ-like by the Filling'.[23] Thus he affirms a continuing experience of the Spirit in the life of the believer, while distancing himself from the Pentecostal notion of 'Baptism in the Spirit' (a model that was subsequently adopted by some 'charismatics').

However, if one studies closely Scroggie's emphasis on the work of the Spirit it can be seen to be very cleverly redefining the experience of the Spirit in terms of the interpretation and application of biblical truth. Although references to the Spirit are relatively infrequent in his work, when they do occur the work of the Spirit is invariably synonymous with the work of the scriptures. It is the Spirit who leads into all truth through enabling the interpretation and application of the Bible to the life of the believer. The work of the Spirit occurs not in a way that is distinct from the Bible, but through the Bible. For Scroggie Christian sanctification is wrought not through some distinct spiritual experience, but by means of an encounter with God through His word. One experiences the Spirit through the written Word. Thus the work of the Spirit is synonymous with the work of the scriptures.

The Baptist orthodoxy that Scroggie fostered throughout the nineteen twenties and thirties did not deny the work of the Spirit, but rather redefined it. According to Scroggie's premillennial convictions which had found added impetus in the First World War and the Great Depression, apostasy and social decline were the prelude to the return of Christ. The church would only prevail and avoid the coming judgement if it remained pure and unpopulated from 'the ways of the world' (generally defined by drinking, dance halls and picture houses). However, this was only possible through the sanctifying power of the

---

[23] G. Scroggie, *The Unfolding Drama of Redemption* (Glasgow: Pickering & Inglis, 1957), vol. 2, pp. 205-206.

Spirit that was to be encountered through God's word. It was the Word of God and the believer's devotion to it that would enable one to stand in the face of the moral and spiritual apostasy that was to envelop the world prior to the second coming.

Thus as a premillennial outlook increasing took hold of Scottish Baptist thinking the focus fell on the Bible and not the work of the Spirit. By the time of the Second World War the notion of a distinctive work or experience of the Spirit apart from the Bible was increasing alien to Baptists in Scotland. Still open to an experiential dimension of faith, this experience was seen to be grounded and mediated through the Bible. If Christians were to resist the forces of apostasy that surrounded the church and prevail until the return of Christ they required not a distinctive experience of God and His Spirit, but a biblically based faith. Yet the memory of the Welsh Revival and the encounter of the Spirit that it precipitated persisted, even if only in folklore. It was this memory which was to act as the catalyst for the charismatic experience of many Scottish Baptists in the second half of the twentieth century, especially in the wake of the Lewis revival.

## Charismatic Renewal

The Lewis revival represents a highly significant moment for the birth of the Scottish Charismatic movement. Although the Scottish charismatic movement was clearly born out of transatlantic antecedents in the nineteen sixties, Lewis exposed Scottish evangelicals to a largely forgotten post-millennial mind set. As we have already seen, Campbell who led the revival was a representative of the Holiness tradition of the Faith Mission and Keswick which emphasised the role of the Holy Spirit in personal sanctification. This meant that as the stories of the Lewis Revival were retold the writings of men like Torrey, Evans and F.B. Meyers were brought to the fore and the notion of a 'second blessing' or 'baptism of the Spirit' began to reappear in the Baptist psyche. As Black observes in his experience while a student at the Bible Training Institute, Glasgow in 1960:

> I began to realise God wanted to release the power of His Spirit in my life and bring me into a wider experience of His grace and love. I found I only wanted to know the answers to theological questions that arose regarding the person and ministry of the Holy Spirit! I sought spiritual advice from the Revd. Andrew MacBeath the principal and since he could not find the book he felt would be helpful instead he handed me, *The Way to Pentecost* by Samuel Chadwick. It introduced me to a new way of thinking. He taught that the Gifts of the Holy Spirit were for today. 'The Baptism of the Holy Spirit is a definite and distinct experience assured and verified by the witness of the Spirit.' 'It is distinct from that of Regeneration.' To say the least for a traditional Baptist it was a revolutionary thought! However, my conclusion was that although there was a

further experience of God the Spirit, He would give me this when I needed it and possibly only when my back was to the wall. There was nothing else I could do! [24]

In 1962 this fresh interest in the work of the Spirit resulted in what was called a 'revival' at Hermon Baptist Church, Glasgow. As Black again recounts:

> While at the Baptist Theological College of Scotland you can imagine the talk of the common room when stories began to emerge of strange happenings in Hermon Baptist Church. They were talking in tongues, frothing at the mouth, swinging on the chandeliers. The challenge was for a student representative to go and attend some of the meetings. From all the erudite theological students nobody was brave enough to go!
> The happenings at Hermon Baptist were not akin to the later 'charismatic movement'. They were still part of the traditional Pentecostal movement with a strong emphasis on holiness. Jim Handyside, Hugh Black and Jack Kelly played an influential part in that move. Jim formed the Scottish Gospel Outreach in Clydebank. Hugh became a noted independent Pentecostal holiness leader and founder of the Struthers Memorial Churches which made an initial impact amongst university students and developed into a denomination in its own right. While Dr Jack Kelly established a church and conference centre at Auchenheath in Lanarkshire which brought significant leaders like Campbell McAlpine to Scotland. [25]

According to Black, the essence of this revival was 'old-time Wesleyanism' which pursued sanctification through the outpouring of the Spirit, yet also embraced glossolalia. The revival had largely come about due to the influence of G.W. [Wally] North, who along with the South Chard Fellowship in England, represented an independent stream of neo-Pentecostalism that pre-dated charismatic renewal.

Other Scottish Baptists were also introduced to an experience of the Spirit through these neo-Pentecostal Holiness groups. Jim Graham of Viewfield Baptist Church in Dunfermline was deeply influenced by the work of Roy Hession of the Worldwide Evangelization Crusade [WEC]. In the early 1950s, Dr. Hession had encountered revival teaching among people on the WEC mission field in Rwanda. This teaching maintained that one is filled with the Spirit through a process of brokenness and confession. In order to be filled with the Spirit, the believer is to let self be broken as Jesus was broken for him on the cross, and through cleansing oneself of all sin, experience the fullness of the Spirit in one's life. Graham had entered into an experience of such fullness in the early nineteen sixties before charismatic renewal had begun to take hold, but went on to become an important influence on the movement as it grew in a British context.

---

[24] Black, *Memoir*, (2003).
[25] Ibid.

This resurgence of the Holiness movement and its emphasis on a neo-Pentecostal experience of the Spirit continued to have an influence on some Scottish Baptist ministers throughout the early sixties. But Black and others drew a sharp distinction between this neo-Pentecostalism born out of the Holiness movement and what was to become Charismatic renewal. This distinction was more than superficial. Despite the fact that the Lewis revival mimicked many aspects of the earlier Welsh revival and was led by a member of the Holiness tradition, it was grounded in the post-millennial Presbyterianism of an earlier century. Yet this postmillennial vision had largely been forgotten in the land of its birth and was invariably only to be found in isolated communities like the Western Isles. But the Lewis revival was again to bring it into sharp focus. For young theological students like Black, Mission Scotland and the Lewis revival again raised the question of a postmillennial hope. Could we be on the verge of a world revival as a prelude to Christ's imminent return? This together with the inherently optimistic mentality of a post war Britain now seemed to be challenging the premillennial mindset of Scottish Baptists which rather than seeking the transformation and renewal of the social order, apparently sought to retreat from society and await the second coming.[26]

It was this increasing dissatisfaction with the existing premillennial vision and mentality of traditional Baptist church life that for men like Black drew them towards their experience of Charismatic renewal. Their encounter with the Spirit was to be shaped by a postmillennial rather than a premillennial vision of the church and revival. It was driven by a vision which ultimately sought to see the social order transformed and renewed by the power of the Spirit (revival) as a prelude to the second coming. Charismatics sought an experience of the Spirit not as some safeguard against the reprobate and disintegrating nature of society that would exist prior to Christ's return, but as a prelude to world revival. Thus although in the initial phases of Charismatic renewal the emphasis on 'the Baptism of the Spirit' and glossolalia largely mimicked and was deeply influenced by the neo-Pentecostalism of the Holiness movement, it nevertheless was quite distinctive. The Charismatic movement was being birthed out a new postmillennial vision of the church and the world, whereas Pentecostalism and the Holiness movement largely continued to cling to the old premillennial paradigms.

---

[26] One of Wallis' early associates in renewal, David Lillie addresses this theme in his book *Beyond Charisma*. He observes:...it is believed [by dispensationalists and others] that we have now reached the final 'Laodicean' period when the churches are marked by indifference (neither hot nor cold)... this depressing interpretation which is used by devotees of the failure syndrome has nothing really to commend it exegetically...there is nothing inevitable about apostasy...we are not shut in to a bleak prospect of universal apostasy, or even of 'laodicean lukewarmness' simply because these conditions were found among some of the churches mentioned in Revelation 2 & 3. D. Lillie, *Beyond Charisma* (Exeter: Paternoster, 1981), p. 5.

It was the Lewis revival that very much shaped this new postmillennial charismatic vision. In 1951, Arthur Wallis, one of the principal architects and influences in the early charismatic movement throughout the world, spent some time on Lewis. In the wake of his experience on the island, he published in 1956 a seminal work on revival entitled, *In the Day of Thy Power*.[27] As the title suggests this was more than a history of revival, but a blue-print for the subsequent rise of the Charismatic and Restorationist movements in the UK and New Zealand. In the book Wallis maintains, 'God has a grander and greater purpose for this age than simply saving souls from hell; he is bringing "sons unto glory"...He is forging an instrument, glorious and holy, that shall rule and administer the world in the coming age...'[28] Turning to the prophecy of Joel found in the book of Acts Wallis links the national restoration of Israel with a final outpouring of the Spirit prior to Christ's return. He notes, 'Joel predicts for Israel, at the time of her national restoration, the return of the former and latter rain in Palestine...to be followed by a glorious "latter rain" of the Spirit.'[29]

In the rest of the book Wallis works through Acts 2 and describes what will constitute this 'latter rain of the Spirit', affirming both the miraculous and glossolalia.[30] In view of this, he insists,

> We may look on Pentecost as the commencement of the former rain, for it was during those first and powerful effusions of the Spirit that the gospel was spread throughout the civilised world, and the ground prepared for harvest. Before the age concludes with the personal return of Christ at harvest time we must expect the latter rain of promise, or the rain of ingathering....we should expect before the Coming of Christ a season of mighty outpourings, eclipsing all that the Church

---

[27] In the forward of this book Duncan Campbell who first met Wallis on the Isle of Lewis in 1951, states 'What I saw of the movings of God in the Hebrides during the past few years is in keeping with the revival called for in this book' A. Wallis, *In The Day of Thy Power* (London: CLC, 1956) p. ix.

[28] Wallis, *Day of Thy Power*, p. 10.

[29] Wallis, *Day of Thy Power*, p. 38. The fate of the Jewish people in God's eschatological timetable that had so exercised men like Chalmers and McCheyne again appears in early charismatic teaching. David Pawson in 1967 at one of the first leaders gatherings hosted by Fountain Trust at High Leigh, Hoddesdon, taught on Romans 9-11, alongside the teaching on 1 Cor.12. This theme was further developed in the following decade by Lance Lambert, one of the forerunners of charismatic renewal in the UK and Derek Prince, a highly influential English Bible teacher based out of the United States and Israel.

[30] Noting the change that Peter made on the day of Pentecost to Joel's prophecy (Joel 2:28) from 'it shall come to pass afterward' to 'it shall be in the last days', he claims: This wonderful promise relates then to a period of time, 'in the last days', not just to a moment of time, such as the day of Pentecost. It is equally clear from the words that Peter quotes that the prophecy had but a partial fulfilment on that day. There was evidently more to come.

has experienced since the Reformation, and only comparable in character and in power with the former rain of the early church.[31]

Wallis was joined in propagating these postmillennial convictions in New Zealand and at a series of three English conferences by a Scottish bible teacher, Campbell McAlpine.[32] McAlpine traced his early Christian experience back to the ultra-conservative and post-millennial Reformed teaching of Willie Still, a Presbyterian Church of Scotland minister in Aberdeen. After an experience of the Spirit, McAlpine went on to be a highly influential figure in the Charismatic movement on both sides of the Atlantic. In 1964 he deputised for Wallis as the inaugural speaker of Fountain Trust, an organisation that had been set up by Michael Harper a former curate of John Stott at All Souls, Langham Place, to promote Charismatic renewal. Thus we find at the birth of Charismatic renewal in Britain those who had been significantly influenced by a postmillennial vision of revival in a Scottish context.[33]

Scottish Baptists like Black were first exposed to this new charismatic vision of the church in meetings at Adelaide Baptist Church, Glasgow, hosted by Dr Kelly of Hermon. In the early sixties Kelly regularly invited speakers like Wallis and McAlpine to address a Scottish audience.[34] Yet these visits made their greatest impact on Scottish Presbyterians. These men were Presbyterians who had little or no exposure to the Holiness movement, who were now entering into a whole new experience of the Spirit. These Presbyterians were

---

[31] Wallis, *Day of Thy Power*, p. 41.

[32] Max Turner claims, 'The roots of the apostolic, restorationist house church movement can be traced back to meetings arranged (for Brethren and Pentecostalist leaders) by the independent ex-Brethren charismatics Arthur Wallis and David Lillie in 1958 (Countess Wear, Devon), 1961 (Okehampton) and 1962 (Mamhead Park) –it was from these meetings that the Charismatic Movement arose, and Restorationism is to be seen as a radical form of that movement which refused to see the charismatic emphases diluted in denominational and ecclesiastical traditions'—'Ecclesiology In The Major 'Apostolic' Restorationist Churches In The United Kingdom', *Vox Evangelica* 19 (1989), p. 84. See also P. Hocken, *Streams of Renewal: Origins and Early Development of the Charismatic Movement in Great Britain* (Exeter: Paternoster, 1986), chs 2-7, 21.

[33] In 1967 in *Renewal Magazine*, Harper describes the progress of renewal in the UK in terms of this postmillennial vision of world revival. As he states:

> The overwhelming evidence of the last few years points to the fact that the day of world revival has dawned. In spite of the persistent opposition of some, and the excesses of others, there are ample grounds for much rejoicing. God is pouring out His spirit on the world wide Church on a scale hitherto unknown. Careful though we must be concerning the dangers of counterfeit, and sensitive to the guidance of the Spirit, we would be grieving God if we suggested that what is happening is anything less than the first fruits of world revival. *Renewal Magazine*, 9 (June/July 1967).

[34] Black, *Memoir* (2003).

largely the inheritors of the Scottish Postmillennialism of Chalmers and McCheyne. Although brought up within a Reformed tradition they were very receptive to the notion of an outpouring of the Spirit of God as a prelude to a postmillennial hope. They also empathised with the sharp division that charismatics like Wallis where making between human and divine institutions. The outpouring of the Spirit meant denominational barriers where to come down, traditional forms of worship had to change and new structures needed to appear which reflected the work of God and not man. This contrast between what was the work of God and human invention had an inherent appeal to New College (Edinburgh University) students heavily influenced by Barth.

These meetings in Glasgow also coincided with another event taking place in America. Dennis Bennett, an Episcopalian minister, after being 'baptised in the spirit' and speaking in tongues had been forced to resign from his church in Van Nuys, California. The resignation generated such a furrower it was reported by all the national papers and TV networks in the USA, as well as being highlighted by *Time* and *Newsweek* Magazine. In the UK the story was carried in *Trinity* magazine and *The Churchman* and stirred up considerable debate and interest. The book that Bennett subsequently wrote called *Nine O'clock in the Morning* became the definitive text in charismatic experience and provided the blueprint for the renewal movement for the next twenty years. In May 1962 Brian Casebow, minister of St Margaret's Church of Scotland congregation in Motherwell, who was reading the book found himself seeking a similar outpouring of the Spirit in his life. After an experience of glossolalia Casebow led his church, (St Margaret, Motherwell) into what the Scottish Daily Express described as 'a mysterious new form of worship bordering on the supernatural'.[35] In 1965 Casebow then arranged for Dennis Bennett to come to Glasson Church of Scotland, Motherwell. Several Scottish Baptist ministers were present at this gathering including David Black of Springburn Baptist, Douglas Ross of Motherwell Baptist and Douglas McBain of Wishaw Baptist.

The Motherwell conference for Black represented the start of the Charismatic renewal movement in Scotland.[36] A few months after Bennett's visit, Casebow organised another conference of about twenty ministers at Scottish Churches House, Dunblane. The subject for the conference was the 'Spirit Thing' and although predominantly Presbyterian, Black was present. Most of the ministers who attended received pray for 'the baptism of the Holy Spirit', yet already there was a recognition that this new movement was concerned with much more than simply an experience of the Spirit. Ultimately it was a vision of a renewed church that could usher in revival that drove the movement. From 1965 onwards this new vision of the church was sustained by a small group of ministers who meet in central Scotland. Black again recounts:

---

[35] Cited in Douglas McBain, *Fire over the Water* (London: Darton, Longman Todd, 1997), p. 37.
[36] *Memoir*, 2003.

> I joined this group that met in various manses in the Lanarkshire area over a number of years. It was all so foreign and rather frightening to my Baptist background. It was there that I met a number of ministers, Church of Scotland men like Brian Casebow, Gordon Strachan, Tom Smail and Bill Brown. Along side them there was Ken McDougall (Methodist St Johns Glasgow) Douglas McBain (Wishaw Baptist), and Douglas Ross (Motherwell Baptist).
>
> There was no theological way to describe what was happening other than renewal although for a short period the phase 'Spirit thing' was used. They had been brought into a new way of worship, freedom of prayer and the beginning use of the gifts of the Holy Spirit. [37]

This group went on to develop strong links with Fountain Trust in England. Scottish delegations were sent to large renewal gatherings that were being held in various English cathedrals. Scotland was seen to have an important role in the ensuing revival as is shown by a celebrated prophecy by Jean Darnell, an American Pentecostal. In this prophecy Darnell prophesised revival would begin in Scotland and sweep through Europe.[38] Yet despite the poignancy of this prophecy by the end of the nineteen sixties the 'spirit thing' had made little or no impact on the life of Scottish Baptists or any other Scottish churches for that matter. A number of ordained ministers had begun to take an interest in 'things of the spirit', but this had not translated into church life.

In 1968 Douglas McBain of Wishaw Baptist Church went south to Streatham, London, and in 1972 set up Manna ministries, one of the principal renewal vehicles for the Baptist Union of Great Britain and Ireland (BUGBI) in the following decade. In the same year, Jim Graham of Viewfield, Dunfermline, became David Pawson's successor at Goldhill Baptist Church and went on to become a widely recognised renewal speaker. The following year, Tom Smail went to Northern Ireland before becoming the assistant director of Fountain

---

[37] Ibid. In the same paper Black goes on, 'The term charismatic was to come later. I always thought it was an unfortunate phrase to give to a movement of the Spirit. I felt it was inadequate, as it did not do justice to what it was all about. It tended to divide and forgot that the church by its very nature is charismatic and to call a movement by an experience which was at the heart of the church could only lead to misunderstanding and theological suspicion. It seemed separate to the work the church has always been active in and isolated the work of the Holy Spirit into have and have nots. All Christians by spiritual birth are charismatic.'

[38] Phase 1: Jean saw, from a bird's eye perspective, a map of the British Isles with haze over it. She then saw little pin-pricks of light appearing from Scotland to Land's End. These were fires burning. When she sought the Lord about this, he said that this first phase represents 'Awakening in the Churches'. Each pin-prick of light symbolizes a group of people that are intensely hungry for New Testament Christianity, who are very hungry for the Holy Spirit, and who would be filled with power. In these groups, the whole concept of the Body of Christ would come alive, and denominational barriers would come crashing down. These groups would also be tested through a season of waiting.

Trust in 1972 and then director in 1975. Mention could also be made of Bob Gordon, a Congregationalist who also moved to England to become one of the leading apologists and figures in the emerging Charismatic movement. Black also left to go to South Korea to work with a Christian relief agency. This effectively left at the forefront of renewal in Scotland Gordon Strachan of the Church of Scotland and Ken McDougal who had left the Methodists in 1969 to become the minister of New Prestwick Baptist Church.

In 1971 when Black returned from South Korea to become the minister of Dennistoun Baptist Church he felt Scotland had been left behind in what he believed was a global move of the Spirit. 'Scotland either through its geographic isolation, distinct Calvinist Christian culture, or suspicion of those things birthed out with the Nation was slow to respond'.[39] Many of the Church of Scotland ministers that had shown such interest in the nineteen sixties had failed to sustain their commitment to renewal. Black speculating at a later time as to why this was saw its causes in an institutional structure that was resistant to change, disillusionment, family and peer pressures, and a basic insecurity and fear about what renewal might mean. Yet undeterred Black and his fellow Baptist minister Ken McDougall began to organise renewal meetings in Glasgow and Edinburgh under the auspices of Fountain Trust.[40]

However, by 1974 Black's involvement with Charismatic renewal was encountering considerable opposition within his own church, Dennistoun Baptist. Contact with The Full Gospel Business Men's Fellowship International (F.G.B.M.F.I), a neo-Pentecostal American group that encouraged renewal amongst business men, had brought an emphasis in Black's ministry on 'signs and wonders' and deliverance that was ultimately irreconcilable with a traditional Baptist pastorate.[41] This tension with Dennistoun coincided with a recognition that if Charismatic renewal was to take hold in Scotland there was a

---

[39] Black, *Memoir* (2003)

[40] The first took place on 30 September, 1972, in Renfield Church of Scotland, Glasgow, with Ken McDougal and Tom Smail as the keynote speakers. The next was in Scottish Churches House, Dunblane, on 9 October, 1972. Several others then followed the next year, with day conferences in Glasgow and Edinburgh on 24 March and 12 October respectively. There was also a meeting in Stirling on 18 August organised by Margaret Lovett, a member of Stirling Baptist Church.

[41] Black's Christmas News Letter of 1972 vividly illustrates the tension as he speaks of the church 'afflicted by the spirit that so often prevails in the city, apathy, formality, traditionalism', in contrast with the 'many indications of renewal' he was seeing throughout the country.

> The winter of the church, with its apparent deadness, is passing and the spring of new life is surging up. One manifestation of the Spirit has been the gift of miracles and healings. The deaf have received hearing, hearts that were medically incurable have been touched and completely restored, limbs have been extended as discs have slipped into place! This is exactly the same experiences so many of you have shared with us.

need for a national body to be dedicated wholly to this end. Although in 1973 there was considerable debate within a newly established advisory committee as to the appropriateness of a Baptist as opposed to a Presbyterian leading this body, Black was invited to become the first general secretary of Scottish Churches Renewal [SCR].[42] The induction to this new post took place in Hillhead Baptist Church in September, 1974. Present along with Michael Harper, Director of Fountain Trust and Tom Smail, Assistant Director, were Kerr Spiers, the minister of Hillhead, and Andrew MacRae, the General Secretary of the Baptist Union of Scotland.

This Baptist setting for the inauguration of SCR is significant. Although renewal in Scotland had Holiness and Pentecostal antecedents, its aims and expression clearly resonated with a Baptist ecclesiology. SCR set out four specific aims:

> 1] The Renewal of the life of the Christian Church in Scotland by the recovery of the full ministry of the Holy Spirit in the Body of Christ.
> 2] To encourage Christians to know the release of the power of the Holy Spirit in their lives and to glorify the Lord Jesus Christ by manifesting the fruit and gifts of the Spirit so that, by a balanced faith which seeks to avoid the dangers of fanaticism and division, they may enrich their worship, strengthen their witness and deepen their walk with God.
> 3] To endeavour by all means to serve the local churches, recognising that spiritual renewal must operate at the local level.
> 4] To encourage Christians to pray and prepare for revival in Scotland.

Charismatic renewal emphasised the local church and its importance and sought as a movement to strengthen and develop this institution. It promoted the notion of the gathered community of God's people, a community which when it came together was directed and guided by the Spirit of God, not some ecclesiastical hierarchy. It encouraged the breaking down of the distinction between laity and clergy and promoted the idea of every member ministry. Thus for men like Black there was ultimately no conflict between their Baptist convictions and the work of renewal. Yet in many ways the nature of charismatic renewal could not be further removed from Scottish Baptist Church life in the early seventies. At this time the majority of Scottish Baptists held to a pre-millennial mind set which neither shared the post-millennial vision of the church or revival that was implicit within the Charismatic movement. Scottish Baptists, therefore, initially

---

[42] On this committee there were a number of Church of Scotland ministers: Alex Allan, Brian Casebow, Denis Sutherland, Gordon Strachan and Geoff Underwood; a Roman Catholic, Fr Mark Dilworth; a Pentecostal, Jim McClure and four Baptists: Douglas Kynoch, a national news reader from Hillhead, Raymond Wylie, a music teacher and professional opera singer from Dennistoun, David Black from Dennistoun and Ken McDougal, New Prestwick.

proved highly resistant, if not hostile to renewal, while some Presbyterians who resonated with this vision were much more responsive.

However, this began to change in the wake of Scotland's exposure to the Jesus movement. The Jesus movement was a young people's movement from California that had swept through the hippie counter-culture in the States. Introduced to Scotland by the visits of Arthur Blessitt in 1972 and 1973 it shared with charismatic renewal an emphasis on community and the breaking down of boundaries, informality in prayer and a new expressiveness in worship through hand raising and even dancing. Although such things were not new in terms of renewal, as a series of rallies took place in Glasgow and Edinburgh this was the first time that the evangelical churches in Scotland had been exposed to them en masse. The converts of these rallies represented a new type of Christian that did not sit easily with the formalism and traditions of the existing churches. As these young converts become part of Baptist churches it introduced into the denomination a new element that was open to renewal. In Queen's Park Baptist Church a bikers group was formed which laid the foundation for the subsequent renewal in the church under Edwin Gunn. In Charlotte Chapel the Fire YF run by the Gunn-Russells provided the impetus for the Hazeliburn Renewal Centre, while a new Baptist fellowship came into being in Craigmillar, Edinburgh, as a group of Baptists students took over a failing United Reformed Church.

Yet the most dramatic example of this new generation of Christians was seen in the birth of Bishopbriggs Baptist Church [which came to be known as Bishopbriggs Christian Centre]. Very much influenced by the values of the Jesus Movement, a small group of fourteen young people who had been converted through a Youth With A Mission [YWAM] outreach started to meet in Bishopbriggs, Glasgow. In 1974 they invited David Black who had just left Dennistoun to lead the work of SCR to be their pastor. The group grew from fourteen to just over seventy people in the course of the next year and made application to the Baptist Union of Scotland for membership. This application caused some considerable consternation within the Union. The minister of the neighbouring Baptist Church had recently written an article for the local press denouncing the Bishopbriggs group as a sect. However, in 1976 Andrew Macrae, the General Secretary, and Black exchanged a knowing smile, as this same minister in his presidential year gave Bishopbriggs the right hand of fellowship and admitted them into the Union.

The fact that Bishopbriggs had persisted in becoming a Baptist church despite opposition is significant. The vision of renewal was to revitalise the denominational life of the country and not displace it. Black described SCR as 'an arm of the established churches'. Bishopbriggs as one of the first overtly charismatic church in the Union and possibly of any mainstream denomination in Scotland was to be a model. It was to provide an example of what a renewed church would look like, with its freedom and informality in worship, its exercise of spiritual gifts and its relational values. [These relational values ultimately led to a Christian neighbourhood where a number of houses were built around a church centre]. Bishopbriggs was also uniquely positioned to influence other Baptist churches. Strong links were built with several churches in Glasgow, including Queens Park (vacant), Govan (Sandy McKeith), Alexandria (Alex Russell), Shettleston (John Greenshields) and later Easterhouse (Sandy Weddell). Links were also made with Craigmillar in Edinburgh [Harry Sprange and Alistair Brown –a student]. Through these links a renewal group was started within the Union, the purpose of which was to meet for livelier prayer and worship during assembly.

In July 1976 the first week long renewal conference was held at St Andrews. It saw the return of Dennis and Rita Bennett to Scotland, as well as Jim Graham from Goldhill Baptist Church. In the following years a number of speaker were brought to Scotland including Cecil Cousins, Campbell McAlpine, David Pawson, Colin Urquhart, Trevor Dearing, Graham Pulkingham, Frances McNutt, Juan Carlos Ortis, Larry Christenson, Brian Miles, Michael Harper and Tom Smail. Individual Baptists from throughout Scotland were present at the various renewal events, although the Baptist churches in general were relatively untouched. Many Baptists were alienated from the Charismatic movement through its involvement with Roman Catholicism. The visit of Cardinal Suenens in 1977, organised jointly by Black and Catholic Charismatic Renewal intensified this opposition. Cardinal Suenens had been the principal architect of the second Vatican Council, sharing with Pope John XXIII the belief in the need of the Catholic Church for renewal. As one commentator wrote: 'If Pope John opened the windows, it was Suenens who pulled back the curtains so that fresh air could circulate.'[43] In 1976 David Black had gone to stay at the Cardinal's palace at Mialines near Brussells and this had led to an invitation to visit Scotland. In a highly sectarian age the thought of a Baptist bringing a Catholic cardinal to this country was more than most Scottish Baptists could bear. It confirmed to many what they had always suspected, that the charismatic renewal movement was simply a vehicle for the subversion of the Protestant churches by Rome, a tool which would bring apostasy.

## Restorationism

Yet it was not Charismatic renewal's involvement with Rome that was to represent the greatest threat to the established churches. Latent within renewal there was always the possibility of a more radical postmillennial vision of the church. This vision sought not only to renew existing structures and forms, but to completely replace them. It wanted to do away with the 'doom-and-gloom' theology of pre-millennialism and create a new movement to oversee the coming of the kingdom, and the restoration of the glorious endtime church. From 1975 onwards the principle conduit by which this new teaching and vision

---

[43] *Time* Magazine, 'The Pentecostal Tide', 18 June 1973.

of renewal was communicated to the wider church was the Dales Bible week held at the Great Yorkshire Showground near Harrogate.

The five principal speakers of this week were Don Basham, Charles Simpson, Bob Mumford, Derek Prince, and Ern Baxter. These men were all gifted Bible teachers from the USA who were connected with Christian Growth Ministries, Fort Lauderdale, in Florida. In a highly persuasive and compelling way they popularised the postmillennial restorationist vision in Britain, a vision that was first expressed in the UK by Wallis.[44] They taught renewal was the first step in a threefold progression. It would give way to restoration. In this restoration the church would ride itself of all its impurities and man-made structures and practices. It would re-constitute itself with a biblical structure of church government based on the Ephesians chapter four ministries. Only when one came under this type of spiritual authority could God and his Spirit work in the life of the believer, the church and the community in the way that he intended. Thus restoration would give way to revival and a great spiritual harvest that would be a prelude to the return of Christ.[45]

As groups from Scotland began to go down to the Dales, they came under the influence of this vision that ultimately rejected the premillennialism that shaped so many aspects of Baptist, Brethren and Pentecostal churches. After returning from the Dales in 1978 the Youth Fellowship of Alexandria Baptist Church broke away with a United Free Church minister from Drumchapel, Alex Gillies, to form Glasgow Christian Fellowship. The following year, Brian Hayes of Edinburgh and Hugh Clark of Coatbridge were expelled by the Elim Pentecostal Church for adopting a restorationist ecclesiology. Taking most of their congregations with them, Edinburgh Christian Fellowship and King's Church Motherwell were born. These were soon followed by a number of Presbyterian defections in the North East. Stewart Brunton founded the Gate fellowship in Dundee and Jim Kincaid started the Abbey Fellowship in Aberdeen. Thus by the early eighties 'House churches', as they were called, could be found in all the principal cities of Scotland. And by the time the Scottish Baptist Viewpoint leaflet on renewal was written in 1986, it could speak of over seventy new fellowships throughout Scotland.

Yet the founding of these churches had profound implications for the work of Charismatic renewal. Behind charismatic renewal there had always been this

---

[44] Denominations were seen to be human institutions and not part of the divine plan. In 1974 Wallis observed: 'I see no future for denominations, but a glorious future for the Body of Christ.'

[45] 'Restorationism' or what was initially known as the 'House Church movement' was rooted in the postmillennialism of the Canadian Latter Rain Revival of the nineteen forties. The Latter Rain movement proclaimed: 'we should expect before the coming of Christ a season of mighty outpourings, eclipsing all that the Church has experienced since the Reformation, and only comparable in character and in power with the former rain of the Early Church'.

notion of a postmillennial out-pouring of God's Spirit and a period of revival. But this engine which had driven the movement and created a sense of the work of God's Spirit in the world now appeared to be taking the movement in a very different direction. If there was to be an eschatological golden age in which believers were empowered and united, and millions were to be harvested into the Church, then this seemed to go far beyond the renewal of the current church structures. Thus restorationism shook the vision of renewal to its core and in its wake the renewal agenda had very much changed. The question was no longer whether dry bones could live, but could new wine go into old wineskins?

Black struggled with this question for a while, but recognised that even if one was not convinced of the restorationist position, the reality was that renewal now threatened the unity of the life of the local church. Charismatic renewal would follow the path of least resistance and it was unlikely those who had had an experience of the Spirit would struggle with resistant and hostile institutional forms, now that there was such momentum in the new churches. To persist with renewal was simply to fuel schism. Therefore, in a move that surprised a number of people, Black withdrew from Scottish Church Renewal in 1980, sensing that its time was over. The vision of a renewed church was left unrealised, but every community in Scotland now had a charismatic witness that embodied the values of renewal. It was at the local level in the diversity of charismatic fellowships that the work would continue.

In the Baptist Union the seeds of renewal that Black and others had planted and nurtured where just coming to fruition. Scottish Baptists were reluctant to become part of the restorationist movement. Although there is probably a number of reasons for this, the hierarchical and authoritarian structures of its ecclesiology did not sit easily with them. Thus the original vision of renewal continued to persist in the denomination increasingly fuelled by the changes in the wider evangelical world which were reflected in events like Spring Harvest. By the early eighties no other mainline denomination in Scotland had anything like the number or the sort of distribution of charismatic fellowships as did Scottish Baptists.

There were a number of large rapidly growing churches like Queen's Park, Glasgow (Edwin Gunn), Falkirk (Ian Reid) and Maderia Street (Bill Cowie), while many other churches were experiencing some type of renewal. In the North there was Stromness in Orkney (Francis Gordon), and Gerrard Street (Alistair Brown) in Aberdeen while in the borders at Selkirk [Ron Robertson]. In Fife, Buckhaven (Alex Russel), Leslie (John Greenshields), Leven (Jim McGillivray) and Inverkeithing (Ian Paterson) and along the Clyde coast at Erskine (Fergus Stokes) and Gourock (Alistair Airdie). Glasgow apart from Bishopbriggs and Queen's Park also had Govan (Sandy Mckeith) and Easterhouse (Sandy Weddell), while Edinburgh along with Maderia Street could number Craigmillar (Harry Sprange) and Granton (Andy Scarcliff).

Yet apart from all these churches moving in some type of renewal there was also a number of ministers who were either charismatic or very open to the work of the Spirit. For instance, Graham Bridley Main (Uddingston), Keith Crozier (Peebles / Bearsden), Nigel Heath (Abbey Hill), Alan Berry (South Leith / Bethany Trust) and Charlie Geliatry (Portobello). One estimate suggested that almost 45% of those involved in Scottish Baptist ministry had been in some way touched by the charismatic movement. Although this figure is somewhat speculative, it illustrates the pervasiveness of renewal in the Baptist Union of Scotland at this time. It is hardly surprising, therefore, to find that Inter-Church Relations and Doctrine core group in 1986 suggested that 'a cautious not uncritical acceptance of the [charismatic] movement would, in all circumstances, commend itself as the proper course of action'.

However, the wave of renewal and growth in the early and mid eighties did not sustain itself and gave way to disillusionment and discouragement in subsequent years. Various schisms occurred and the Union as a whole was basically divided on the issue of renewal. As Peter Barber, the then General Secretary of the Union noted in reply to a concerned questioner in the *Scottish Baptist Magazine* in March 1987:

> Moving among the church as I do, I find a variety of views on this subject. Some regard the movement as a satanic distraction, other as a temporary irrelevance, others as a divisive threat, and others as the supreme answer to the church's contemporary needs.[46]

The aims of renewal as set out by SCR in 1974 clearly had not been fulfilled. Yet the postmillennial vision of the church and the work of the Spirit had by the end of the century exercised a considerable influence over Scottish Baptist church life. Although vestiges of the premillennialism of the dispensationalists and Holiness movement could still be found amongst Baptists, this was generally being superseded by a new paradigm. This paradigm was open to the experiential dimensions of faith and comfortable with the ongoing need of fresh encounters with the Spirit and even spiritual gifts. It was embracing forms of worship, styles of prayer and an understanding of ministry that were largely pioneered in renewal. The vision and understanding of the church was also undergoing a serious revision. Increasingly the church was no longer being perceived as a besieged band waiting for the return of Christ, but as a radical community that was called to transform the world around it through social action and justice. The Charismatic renewal of the 1970s can be seen to be the forerunner of much of what constituted a large part of contemporary evangelical spirituality in Scotland at the end of the twentieth century. Like so many other movements of the past, although the initial experience of the Spirit has not persisted the underlying philosophy and ideals which this experience carried have very much taken root, even amongst Scottish Baptists.

---

[46] P. Barber, 'Charismatic Movement', *SBM*, 113.3 (March 1987), p. 2.

CHAPTER 8

# *Fighting the Good Fight*: Changing Attitudes to War in the Twentieth Century

## Neil Allison

The Free Churches in Great Britain generally supported the South African war (1899–1902), as did 'most of the clergy of the non-Afrikaner churches in the Cape Colony, Natal and the occupied territories.'[1] There were also a number of prominent Free Church voices opposed to it such as John Clifford, Alexander Maclaren, F.B. Meyer and J.C. Carlile.[2] John Clifford was president of the 'Stop the War Committee' which was formed in 1900 as an instrument of passive resistance to the war effort. He believed it was not necessary for these two Christian countries to go to war but rather the problems could and should be solved by careful and sympathetic negotiation. In a letter Clifford expressed his own views and the aims of this committee:

> The Boer is a 'new creature' in the British imagination already and the full revelation of his character has not yet been given. The theory of a Boer conspiracy preceding the Jameson Raid[3] is dead as a nail and will be flung aside soon. The cry of help for the 'native' is felt to be as hypocritical and hollow as any that ever led to mischief. John Bull will annex – i.e. he will steal again, and the Churches will bless his theft! He will begin to talk about justly administering what he has unjustly taken. And no attempt to atone for what he has so unjustly done.[4]

Some of these concerns were also reflected amongst some Scottish Baptists. Robert Somerville, a member of Galashiels Baptist Church, was elected President of the Baptist Union of Scotland in 1900. In his Presidential address for that year he stated that the war was 'evil' but did not define clearly whether

---

[1] Frederick Hale, 'Captives of British Imperialism?,' *Baptist Quarterly*, 39.1 (January 2001), p. 15.
[2] Ian M. Randall, *The English Baptists of the 20th Century*, (Didcot: The Baptist Historical Society, 2005), p. 41.
[3] The Jameson Raid took place on the 30th December 1895.
[4] James Marchant, *Dr John Clifford* (London: Cassell and Company Ltd, 1924), p. 147.

it was British government policy that was evil.[5] Even though there was some opposition, mainstream Nonconformity generally believed that this African War, commonly referred to as the 'Boer War,' was 'honourable but lamentable' according to Bebbington.[6] This would also be a fair description of Scottish Baptist thinking in general. Greg Cuthbertson explains how this thinking developed amongst nonconformists:

> Nonconformists had until the 1880s been opposed to Britain's expansion overseas, but by the late 1890s they had become keen imperialists... The empire was regarded as a providential gift of God for the spread of Christianity and civilisation which meant that there was no clear distinction between religious and secular motives in this period.[7]

Even Missionary societies believed that the beneficent British imperialism enabled the gospel to be preached, and races in their 'childhood' would be given the opportunity to mature under the benefits of Christian civilisation.[8] Therefore Scottish Baptists who were principally committed to evangelism and missionary endeavour tended to support the defence of the British Empire and therefore were also supportive of the 'Boer War.' This attitude continued to be dominant until the outbreak of World War One.

In January 1913 the editor of the *Scottish Baptist Magazine* suggested that 1912 would be chiefly memorable for the uprising of the Balkan people against the 'Unspeakable Turk,' but was chiefly concerned that the threat of a widespread European war was becoming a strong possibility. He reflected that:

> Thankfully peace was being negotiated, but much prayer for this was needed and should surely be followed up by eager and persistent efforts to combat on the one hand the militarism and on the other the jealousy and panic fear of other nations and their activities, which are at work like fevers in the blood of the European peoples.[9]

The feared European war could not be avoided and the German invasion of neutral Belgium had aroused righteous indignation amongst the most moderate of British people, providing them with a just cause for going to war with

---

[5] *Scottish Baptist Yearbook 1900* (*SBY*), p. 134.

[6] D.W. Bebbington, *The Nonconformist Conscience: Chapel and Politics 1870-1914* (London: Allen & Unwin, 1982), p. 121.

[7] Greg Cuthbertson, 'Pricking the "nonconformist conscience': Religion against the South African War' in Donal Lowry (ed.), *The South African War Reappraised* (Manchester: Manchester University Press, 2000), p. 183.

[8] Alan Wilkinson, *Dissent or Conform? War, Peace and the English Churches 1900-1945* (London: SCM, 1986), p. 18.

[9] Cited in S.D. Henry, 'Scottish Baptists and the First World War', *Baptist Quarterly*, 31.2 (April 1985), p. 52.

Germany.[10] Walter Mursell, pastor of Coats Memorial Church, Paisley, wrote a book emotively entitled *The Bruising of Belgium and other Sermons*. This book demonstrated that the Baptists in Scotland shared the same sentiments as those south of the border. Mursell preached the title sermon on 15 November 1914 and declared "That one word – 'Belgium' – is enough to justify our entry into this war, enough to rouse the chivalry of our people, enough to determine us to fight to such a finish that tyranny will never be able to create or to grasp such an opportunity again."[11] It was, therefore, not surprising that when Britain declared war on Germany on 4 August 1914 that there was a keen response from Scottish Baptists. Even after two years of fighting and heavy casualties, while deploring the evils of war, Scottish Baptists had no doubt about the rightness of the cause. W.T. Oldrieve, in his 1916 presidential address declared:

> We feel as a Nation that if we do not put forth our best efforts we are likely to go under the heel of an unscrupulous foe... Most of us detest war, but now feel that we would count it an honour to make any sacrifice we can to aid the overthrow of powers which have oppressed weaker nations with brute force on a subverted principle so opposed to the Christian ideal. Thank God our Baptists in Scotland have not been backward in taking their part.[12]

It was not just civilians at home who pushed this view of honour and heroic sacrifice above all else. Indeed Oldrieve may have been influenced by the writings of Scottish Baptist Chaplains serving at the Front. One prominent and influential army chaplain was the highly respected William Cramb Charteris[13] pastor at Ayr Baptist Church. He had previously served and been wounded in the South African war of 1899 while serving as an Army Scripture Reader and acting chaplain to the British forces. Reporting from 'the Front' he wrote:

> A number of ambulances go forward after dark to bring in the sick and wounded, and we are there to comfort and cheer them. How brave the men are – 'Heroes all'— and optimistic. Those who have been permanently injured are so glad that they have done their bit; the others willing, if need be, to go back and 'see this thing through.' Our great Empire is secure while she can produce such sons.

---

[10] J.H. Thompson, 'The Nonconformist Chaplain in the First World War,' Ed: Michael Snape & Edward Madigan, *The Clergy in Khaki: New Perspectives on the British Army Chaplaincy in the First World War* (Ashgate: Surrey, 2013), p .21.

[11] Henry 'Scottish Baptists and the First World War, p. 52.

[12] *SBY 1916*, p. 25.

[13] See Neil E. Allison, 'Shakespeare's Man at the Front. The Rev. W.C. Charteris O.B.E. M.C.', *Baptist Quarterly*, 41.4 (October 2005), pp. 224-35. See also David Stowe, 'Re-thinking 10 /West Yorks at Fricourt', *Standto! The Journal of the Western Front Association* (August / September 2008), pp. 39-47. This paper presents the context in which Charteris served. He is mentioned on p. 40.

Christianity has not failed while it can inspire men to suffer and die for divine ideals and principles."[14]

A few months later Charteris recorded the genuine sentiments of those he worked with, the men in the trenches. He also used it for recruiting purposes. He wrote that 'The only thing they cannot understand is "Why the men at home are so loathe to come and help." No man could look at the white pinched faces of the widows and orphans and the devastated homes of Belgium without having his soul inflamed...'[15] Towards the end of the war the passion amongst many Scottish Baptists had mellowed, recognising the sheer bloody cost, although the support for the war remained no less strong. Principal Jervis Coats, in his presidential address in 1918 acknowledged that:

> War may be regarded from one point of view as the unpardonable sin; but looked at in another way it may be described as a moral and even sacred necessity... War is a thing of horror, but there may be worse things than war. It is worse to lose one's soul, and the soul of Britain would have been lost, if we had not come to the rescue of those principles of good faith and humanity which make life worth living.

The First World War caused Arthur J. Westlake, pastor of Springburn Baptist Church, to think through his Christian position and offers theological justification in support of such a war. In an article for the *Scottish Baptist Magazine* he distinguished between 'retaliation,' which the Lord forbids, and 'resistance.' concluding:

> When human bodies and souls are threatened with violence and outrage there arises not a desire to avenge wrong done to us, but a strong Christian passion to relieve the downtrodden and resist the oppressor. Force, which cannot be a neutral element, is allied to a spiritual ideal. We resist at such times with a sound conscience, but also with the confident hope that the day will dawn when spiritual ideals will find a worthy medium of expression and when implements of barbarism shall drop for ever from our hands.[16]

Scottish Baptists clearly saw the war as just in defence of an innocent or weaker nation such as 'little Belgium.' This support was echoed by John Wishart, in his presidential address soon after the war was over and the nation was coming to terms with the huge attrition of war. He movingly described Germany's 'deserved' situation giving God the glory for final victory:

---

[14] *Scottish Baptist Magazine* (*SBM*), 41.10 (October 1915), p. 156.
[15] *SBM*, 42.4 (April 1916), p. 58.
[16] Edward Burrows, *Change at Springburn: A Centenary History of Springburn Baptist Church* (Glasgow: Springburn Baptist Church, 1992), pp. 36-37.

In the dust-prostrate; her armies broken; her submarines surrendered; her battleships and cruisers – scuttled by her own sons – in the depths of Scapa Flow. Could retribution have been swifter or more complete? It was the Lord's doing, and marvellous in our eyes ... No doubt this country had no other alternative but to fight in defence of the sacredness of international treaties, and on behalf of the weak who appealed to us for help. We were morally forced in to war. Not only did we not choose it, we did everything in our power to prevent it.[17]

The general support for the war amongst Nonconformists also gave opportunities for new denominational and inter-church initiatives. On 14 January 1915 a Free Church initiative, the United Navy and Army Board,[18] was constituted and initially represented the interests of Baptist, Congregationalist, United and Primitive Methodists. This United Board was a development of the United Congress which had been launched through the vision of J.H. Shakespeare.[19] It is interesting to note that out of the first four Baptist chaplains commissioned into the army two were Scottish Baptists, W.C. Charteris and Thomas Jones, pastor of George Street Baptist Church in Paisley. The first United Board commissioned Royal Navy chaplain was Merrick Walker[20], another Scottish Baptist. Certainly, the opportunity for military service was enthusiastically taken up, not only for the defence of the realm but also as a denominational opportunity. Charteris gave a report to the deacons' court of Ayr Baptist Church which was recorded: "He stated that he would like to be back amongst us but he felt that the work he was doing at the Front was pioneer work for the Denomination at large and it would be a pity to loose [sic] the opportunity which would like [sic] to never occur again."[21] Naturally a key concern of the United Board was that Free Churchmen were being attested to a wrong denomination when they joined up. They were often put down as Church of England, Wesleyan, or in Scotland as Church of Scotland rather than one of the recognised Nonconformist denominations. This was a significant issue as the percentage of chaplaincy places allocated by the Ministry of War was solely based upon the numbers of their denomination joining up. Wrong attestation meant less chaplains and this would later cause difficulties for the Scottish Baptists who wanted, through the United Board, to gain chaplains for Scottish Divisions. They needed five hundred attestations if they were to get any

---

[17] John Wishart, 'The Present Situation and how to meet it', *SBYB 1920*, p. 26.

[18] See Neil E. Allison, *The Official History of the United Board Volume One: The Clash of Empires 1914-1939* (Great Bookham, Suffolk: United Army, Navy and Air Force Board, 2008), p. 22.

[19] See Peter Shepherd, *The Making of a Modern Denomination: John Howard Shakespeare and the English Baptists 1898 – 1924* (Cumbria: Paternoster Press, 2001), pp. 96-103.

[20] John S. Fisher, *Impelled by Faith: A Short History of the Baptists in Scotland* (Stirling: Scottish Baptist History Project, 1996), p. 39.

[21] Ayr Baptist Church, Deacons' Meeting Minutes, 6 October 1916, n.p.

chaplains,[22] but despite the large numbers of Scottish Baptists who were enlisting into Scottish Battalions, there were no chaplains to serve their denominational needs. Thomas Jones, Senior Chaplain, was seeking to gain two U.B. chaplains to be able to serve with the Scottish Divisions. The Scottish Baptist Church Council was looking into this matter.[23] However, despite all their efforts the Scottish Regiments remained in the hands of the Scottish Presbyterians for the duration of the Great War.

There were plenty of other chaplaincy initiatives that were independent of the State mechanisms such as Young Men's Christian Association (Y.M.C.A.) chaplaincy.[24] A number of Scottish Baptist ministers saw this as a way to serve the soldiers at the front. They took it in turns to serve for four months at a time. In 1918 it was reported that Alexander Clark of Alloa, R.H. Martin, Alva, and William Wyse, Larbert, had returned from France with David Hoyle from Tillicoultry engaged to serve for four months from January 1919. John Shearer from Stirling was the one Stirling and Clackmannanshire Baptist Association minister in France in the autumn of 1918.[25] In May 1917 Arthur Westlake spent twenty-five days in Richmond (Yorkshire) ministering to the soldiers in the 'Baptist Hut' there. Later in the year he received an invitation to undertake Y.M.C.A. work in France with the army and the Church agreed to release him for four months from 1 December 1917. This had to be postponed on medical advice.[26]

When compulsory conscription was introduced by the British government in June 1916 this placed the minority who opposed the war in a difficult position. 18 to 41 year olds were now compulsory called up for military service in order to get enough manpower to continue the prosecution of the war with only a few exceptions being allowed. Hobhouse, a pacifist writing at the time explained:

> The exemptions were planned by Parliament on a generous scale, and were to be administered by Local Tribunals. There was a total exemption for those whose conscience insisted; but, since it was known that almost everyone in the country was eager to help his country as best he could, there were also the possibilities of exemption conditional on the applicant being engaged in work of national importance of a non-military kind, and also non-combatant service in the army itself.[27]

---

[22] *SBM*, 42.10 (October 1916), p. 162.
[23] 'UB Minutes', 9 May 1917, p. 271.
[24] See Michael Snape (ed.), *The Back Parts of War: The YMCA Memoirs and Letters of Barclay Baron, 1915-1919*, (Woodbridge, Suffolk: The Boydell Press, 2009).
[25] Brian R. Talbot, *A Brief History of Central Baptist Association 1909-2002* (Glasgow: Baptist Union of Scotland, 2002), p. 10.
[26] Burrows, *Change at Springburn*, p. 39.
[27] Mrs Henry Hobhouse, *I Appeal unto Caesar* (London: George Allen & Unwin Ltd, 1917), p. vii.

Talbot recorded in his history of Stirling Baptist Church that this ideal was not always realised: 'After compulsory conscription in 1916, there were increasing complaints against military tribunals, as butchers, plumbers and even two of the eight doctors in Stirling, for example, were sent to war in 1917.'[28] The Tribunals were not well respected by those who simply wanted them to honour their own policy. Hobhouse was one of those:

> The first and most obvious fault about many of them [on the Tribunal Board] was their lack of the necessary qualifications for dealing with questions of conscience, or for at all understanding the mind of an intellectual or religious man, not to speak of an eccentric or an enthusiast. Besides this, they were anxious to please the War Office, to satisfy the more turbulent newspapers, and to display their own patriotism by sending other people to the trenches. They were very reluctant indeed to grant total exemption.[29]

Those who steadfastly refused military service had to stand before such a 'Tribunal' to seek exception. These Tribunals became platforms for presenting their arguments because conscientious objectors usually were articulate and eager to discuss and debate. This reflected, in many cases, their previous involvement in Nonconformist chapel life or in the I.L.P.[30] politics.[31] Most Conscientious Objectors (C.O.s) were content to accept alternative non-combatant service[32] but about 1,500 were considered to be 'absolutist' and a number of these were 'subjected to brutal punishment.'[33] Up to thirty-four Conscientious Objectors, for example, were forcibly deployed on military service in France and were 'sentenced to death for refusing to obey military orders.'[34] It has been estimated that by July 1917 between 800 and 1,000 conscientious objectors were in prison and committed to hard labour. However the flawed law was not applied consistently. For example, in Scotland the regulations were far more severe. Conscientious Objector prisoners were forced

---

[28] Talbot, *Standing on the Rock: A History of Stirling Baptist Church* (Stirling: Stirling Baptist Church, 2005), p. 78.
[29] Hobhouse, *I Appeal unto Caesar*, p. vii.
[30] I.L.P. is most likely referring to the Independent Labour Party.
[31] Keith Robbins, 'The British Experience of Conscientious Objection' in Hugh Cecil & Peter Liddle (eds), *Facing Armageddon: The First World War Experience* (Barnsley: Pen & Sword, 2003), p. 696.
[32] Even Quakers were willing to serve at the Front as non-combatants. See Meaburn Tatham & James E. Miles (eds), *The Friends Ambulance Unit 1914–1919. A Record* (London: The Swarthmore Press Ltd, 1919).
[33] Ian M. Randall, 'The Role of Conscientious Objectors: British Evangelicals and the First World War', *Anabaptism Today* (February 1996), p. 14.
[34] Randall, 'Role of Conscientious Objectors', p. 15.

to sleep without a mattress for up to fourteen days compared to seven in England.[35]

The Baptist Unions did tend to support the rights of Conscientious Objectors, even if a little reluctantly. They could in general not comprehend the C.O.'s perspective. Often this lack of understanding was expressed in questions. The kind of statement was how could people object to fighting, or at least supporting those who were fighting, in such a 'righteous' cause? How could C.O.s simply stand by and let German aggression and injustice succeed because they would not fight? However, the Baptist Union of Great Britain did seek to defend the Conscientious Objector's rights. The law now placed those who had conscientious objections to the war in direct conflict with the British State. They could no longer simply 'not volunteer', but had to argue against being called up. Many set themselves against 'experiencing war' absolutely.[36] It was F.B. Meyer who was eloquently to highlight Conscientious Objectors' religious convictions in his pamphlet *The Majesty of Conscience* which would become a major piece of work on their behalf. Randall in his significant study of Meyer summarises his argument in their defence and writes that the C.O. 'had fought a spiritual war for men whose conscience would not allow them to fight a worldly one.'[37] W.T. Whitley[38], a supporter of the war effort, wrote a thoughtful and well balanced article in the *Baptist Times and Freeman* entitled simply 'Conscientious Objections.' Whitley explained that 'In Christian circles, for a man to assert a conscientious objection is tantamount to saying that he believes the course enjoined upon him would involve his sinning against God.'[39] This sets out the difficult position of the Conscientious Objectors' arguments, the sincerity of which is not questioned by Whitley. He suggests that before the objector sets out on his course of action he should question himself concerning the legitimacy of his position. Whitley advised that 'when a man has qualms of conscience, his first duty is not to disobey, but to educate his conscience till he sees clearly.'[40] It is only 'after such a prayerful consideration' that he has the right to act on a conscientious objection. 'But when he has cleared matters up to his own satisfaction, he has not only a right, but a duty to act. To him that knows to do good and does it not, to him it is sin.'[41] Yet a more common view expressed in Scotland can be illustrated in the words of Charteris. He declared: 'Whilst not wishing to judge any man, we believe it is a tender conscience and a

---

[35] Hobhouse, *I appeal to Caesar*, p. 47.
[36] Robbins, 'British Experience', p. 691.
[37] Ian M. Randall, *Spirituality and Social Change* (Carlisle: Paternoster Press, 2003), p.127.
[38] William Thomas Whitley M.A, L.L.M, L.L.D, F.T.S, F.R.Hist.S, Pastor of Fishergate Baptist Church, Preston, 1902-1917.
[39] *Baptist Times* (*B.T*) (4 February 1916), p. 68.
[40] *B.T.* (4 February 1916), p. 68.
[41] *B.T.* (4 February 1916), p. 68.

love of righteousness and liberty which have driven the choicest of our sons and brothers to take their place in the Kingdom's forces.'[42] J.T. Forbes of Hillhead Baptist Church is even more forceful and objects that: 'The extreme pacifist believes not only in martyrdom for himself but is prepared to stand by and let others be martyred.'[43] The Liberal government's approach to contentious objection, supported by most Baptists during this period, can be understood from the words of Prime Minister David Lloyd George who stated: 'I do not think they deserve the slightest consideration. With those who object to the shedding of blood it is the traditional policy of this country to respect that view, and we do not propose to depart from it: but in the other case I shall only consider the best means of making the lot of that class a very hard one.'[44] It was within the context of this intense patriotic fervour, where the small but vocal group of Conscientious Objectors and pacifists were effectively sidelined by the denomination and by society, although their rights were reluctantly represented within the Scottish Baptist Union.

As much as the war was a terrible experience many hoped that the spartan life and hardship might eventually lead to a religious revival.[45] John Wishart in 1920 expressed this desired hope publicly, although he concluded this hope had not been realized. He recorded that 'It seemed as if we were on the eve of the great spiritual awakening for which we had waited long; but our hopes were not to be fulfilled.'[46] This comment is telling as there was a common belief amongst Baptists generally and Scottish Baptists in particular, influenced by the 1905 Welsh Revival, that the war would be a catalyst for a revival. The evidence for such a hope was reported from the Front which Charteris amongst others[47] was eager to record.[48]

Having looked at the evidence Allison concluded that there was indeed evidence that a 'revival' at some level[49] did take place and that: 'Many believed there was evidence of a genuine revival but its influence on the churches or society was not felt because so many were killed in the war or died from the

---

[42] *SBM*, 42.4 (April 1916), p. 51.
[43] *SBM*, 41.12 (December 1915), p. 186.
[44] Alan Wilkinson, *The Church of England and the First World War* (London: S.P.C.K., 1978), p. 49.
[45] See Neil E. Allison, 'Free Church Revivalism in the British Army during the First World War' in Michael Snape & Edward Madigan (eds), *The Clergy in Khaki: New Perspectives on the British Army Chaplaincy in the First World War* (Farnham: Ashgate, 2013), pp. 40-55.
[46] *SBY 1920*, p. 26.
[47] Frederic C. Spurr, *Some Chaplains in Khaki* (London: The Kingsgate Press, 1916), p.76-113
[48] *SBM*, 42.6 (June 1916), p. 91.
[49] Richard Schweitzer, *The Cross and the Trenches. Religious Faith and Doubt among British and American Great War Soldiers* (Westport C.T: Praeger, 2003), pp.185-95.

influenza pandemic.'[50] Snape explains in God and the British Soldier that the 'casualty levels at Ypres, Gallipoli, Loos and the Somme were such that many of the men who experienced either a religious conversion or a deepening of their faith in 1914-15 simply did not survive...'[51] After the war Scottish Baptists were trying to find some meaning to a war which did not lead to a great and general revival.

During the war Scottish Baptist churches worked hard in the Home Front to offer practical support to those who were serving in uniform and the families left behind. Joseph Burns of Kirkintilloch Baptist Church described some of his duties on the Home Front. He wrote that his: 'Duty was to bring comfort and help to the families of those who were serving in the armed forces and particularly to those with casualties.' Thirty people from the church joined the military and ten had died.[52] As early as 1914 an appeal was launched by Jessie Yuille, wife of the Secretary of the Baptist Union of Scotland, for £500 to be raised by women of the denomination. The aim of this appeal was 'to purchase a motor ambulance, to be given to the war office' to help the wounded. The response was so swift that in only one month after the appeal enough money was raised for two Motor Ambulances. These ambulances would help those at the front who were giving themselves to 'Preserve the liberty and the very existence of our country'.[53] In November an appeal was received for help in the supply of Christmas puddings to soldiers and sailors.[54] The United Board also encouraged the women of the free churches it represented, to make and collect 'comforts' for the troops on the front line. The Baptist women of Scotland responded enthusiastically to this war effort. The Women's Auxiliary was also mandated by the Baptist Union of Scotland to provide 'a liberal and continuous supply of comforts for our soldiers and sailors.'[55] At a dedication service, held at Adelaide Place Baptist Church, Glasgow, on Thursday 19 November 1914, George Yuille prayed in a 'devout and patriotic tone'[56] and dedicated these gifts to 'the service of God and humanity.'[57] Springburn Baptist Church used the 'Harvest Festival' in 1915 to collect food which was taken to the wounded soldiers in Springburn Hospital. Christmas gifts of soldiers' wallets were also sent to members and friends on war service.[58] D. Merrick Walker, while

---

[50] Allison, *The Clash of Empires 1914-1939*, p.69.
[51] Michael Snape, *God and the British Soldier: Religion and the British Army in the First and Second World Wars* (London: Routledge, 2005), p. 167.
[52] Edward Burrows, *From Faith to Faith: Kirkintilloch Baptist Church 1887-1987* (Kirkintilloch: Kirkintilloch Baptist Church, 1987), p. 35.
[53] *SBM*, 40.12 (December 1914), p. 205.
[54] Burrows, *From Faith to Faith*, p. 31.
[55] *SBM*, 40.12 (December 1914), p. 205.
[56] *SBM*, 40.12 (December 1914), p. 205.
[57] *SBM*, 40.12 (December 1914), pp. 205-206.
[58] Burrows, *Change at Springburn*, p. 38.

working as an Officiating Chaplain, described how he used such small comforts. He spoke of collecting and distributing 'little comforts' at military centres and on Warships which were 'the keys with which hearts and ears were opened to the gospel.'[59] These comforts were primarily distributed through the chaplains and other Christian workers. The various Christian institutes also became well resourced with 'Daily papers, magazines, books, tracts, Gospels, and New Testaments. And the New Testaments [were] received more gladly than the rest.'[60] Walker tells numerous stories of the spiritual interest of those serving within the forces, the tender joy of being able to share Holy Communion, and how he was able to distribute 700 tracts on an army transport train. The urgency of this spiritual work is made very clear leaving no doubt in the readers' minds. He informs them: 'Many of them have fallen since in the Dardenelles fighting. If the Saviour has gathered them to Himself our reward is complete.'[61]

The war which many hoped would be over by Christmas[62] had a devastating effect on the churches though the 'impact of the First World War on the spiritual life of the churches is a complex issue...'[63] Between 1914 and 1918 'almost 5,000 members of Scottish Baptist churches served in the forces and about one-fifth never returned....'[64] Ayr Baptist Church reported that a third of the congregation were serving in the forces and seven of these had been killed.[65] Even as early as 1914 the churches were already preparing for the reality of loss though they could not have known how great the loss would be. At the annual meeting of Springburn Baptist Church on 9 September 1914 the following resolution was adopted:

> We, the Members of Springburn Baptist Church, recall in affectionate remembrance the members of the Church and congregation who have relatives on active service in the Army, Navy and Territorial Forces. We are united as a country; we desire a closer unity with these friends in Christian Fellowship, sharing their gratification at the response of sturdy sons and their anxiety respecting the future.[66]

---

[59] *SBM*, 41.8 (August 1915), p. 118.
[60] *SBM*, 41.8 (August 1915), p. 118.
[61] *SBM*, 41.8 (August 1915), p. 119.
[62] Martin Middlebrook, *The First Day of the Somme* (Barnsley: Pen & Sword, 2006), p. xv.
[63] Brian R. Talbot, *Standing on the Rock: A History of Stirling Baptist Church 1805-2005* (Stirling: Stirling Baptist Church, 2005), p. 79.
[64] Fisher, *Impelled by Faith*, p. 40.
[65] George Hossack, *Ayr: Our Baptist Story* (Ayr: Ayr Baptist Church, 1986), p. 14.
[66] Burrows, *Change at Springburn*, pp. 35-36.

For 'In the shadow of war that courage was often drawn from prayer.'[67] One significant cultural change, because of the number of men being killed, was the employment of women in occupations traditionally employing men:

> The loss of young men from Stirling, as in other communities in Britain, would have had a major impact on all aspects of community life. Women rose to prominence taking over the jobs vacated by volunteers. In May 1915 the first two post-women began work at Stirling Post Office and by 1918 there were women bus conductresses, teachers in Stirling High School and even women working in the mines...[68]

Charlotte Chapel recorded that 173 young men from the Chapel had served in the war. Of these 30 were killed, 29 in the army and 1 in the Royal Flying Corps.[69] Stirling had lost 17 young men and the same sad list of losses extended throughout the Scottish Baptist Churches. The reality of war had taken its toll on those who were serving at the front and they would never be the same again and the churches needed to recognise that the traditional approach to life and society would no longer be appropriate. Charteris challenged forcibly his own congregation in a sermon preached shortly after the first Somme Offensive in 1916. He warned that these:

> men have been in the mouth of hell, and lived in the presence of life and death. There they met and touched God. In these awful circumstances they have scaled heights and touched depths, and found a wideness in God's mercy that you at home will have never dreamed of... Should they refuse to subscribe to the shibboleths that have served a past generation, don't conclude that they have not the truth. The truth is eternal, but demands new expression to meet the ever changing needs of experience. These men have lived intense lives; they are men of action, and have neither time nor patience for a lot of the embroidery of modern religion. They will demand the right to live a manly and robust Christian life.[70]

After such personal and national losses the nations mind turned to honouring the 'GLORIOUS DEAD' and 'Remembrance.' One way of celebrating a person's life lost in the war was to locally publish a private memoir or biographical sketch by the local newspaper. One such book was published to celebrate the life and work of Pte. Lockhart L. Ireland (1887-1916) who served with the 7th Battalion Gordon Highlanders, and was a Scottish Baptist with a long family heritage connected with the Whyte's Causeway, Regent's Park

---

[67] Burrows, *Change at Springburn*, p. 37.
[68] C. Mair, *Stirling: The Royal Burgh* (Edinburgh: John Donald, 1990), pp. 212-13.
[69] I.L.S. Balfour, *Revival in Rose Street Charlotte Baptist Chapel Edinburgh 1808-2008* (Edinburgh: Rutherford House 2007), p. 209.
[70] *SBM*, 42.12 (December 1916), p. 187.

Chapel and Dublin Street, Baptist Church, Edinburgh.[71] The book began with a quote from his 'Last Will and Testament' informing the reader which well described the churches mindset during and immediately following the war:

> never allow anyone to say (if I am killed in this war) that it is sad. It is not sad at all; it is glorious. I do not look forward to it with fear or foreboding. Christ has brought me round a few hard corners and death does not seem to me even a hard corner. It is only a wee loup in the dark, with a strong hand holding mine...[72]

This man of faith and 'uncommon' literary talent was killed in action on 25 July 1916, dying a 'noble death' during the first Somme Offensive. There was 'a desire on the part of friends to possess a selection of these stories and articles in some more permanent form...'[73] Remembrance would become a key theme at the end of the war.[74]

The great post-war hope was that this war, supported by the national churches, would end all wars. Therefore a key concern amongst the British population, including Scottish Baptists, was for the establishment of systems of government that would help prevent war rather than force the nation into it in future. In 1920 the Union President stated his hope that such an institution could exist. He wrote:

> New generations may arise that perceive only the glamour of martial deeds, and know nothing of the heart-aches and unspeakable miseries which follow in their train. It is, therefore, incumbent on all right-thinking persons to do what they can now to render future wars impossible. Distinguished statesmen in allied and other countries are alive to the need for such action. They have made a good beginning towards the establishment of a universal League of Nations.[75]

Like many of his generation, Sidlow Baxter had high hopes that the League of Nations, set up after the First World War, would mediate in international disputes and so avoid another armed conflict. However, by the time he came to Edinburgh he despaired of it as little more than a talking shop: 'The League, like all other human methods, tries to work from the outside and fails. God's method is to begin with the heart of man himself. When that is right all is right. Not international co-ordination, but individual regeneration, is the solution.'[76]

---

[71] Lockhart Landels Ireland, *Pte. John Maclean. The Black Watch* (Kirkaldy: The Fifeshire Advertiser Ltd, 1917), p. 11. Irelands's memoirs were recorded under the title of Pte. John MacLean, a character created by Ireland for some of his fictional stories. He was the grandson of Dr William Landels.

[72] Ireland, *Pte. John Maclean*, p. i.

[73] Ireland, *Pte. John Maclean*, Prefatory Note.

[74] Ireland, *Pte. John Maclean*, Prefatory Note.

[75] *SBY 1920*, p. 26.

[76] Cited in Balfour, *Revival in Rose Street*, p. 247.

International peace was the great desire of the inter-war period but tragically this was a forlorn hope and another great war was soon on the horizon.

The Second World War began for the British Empire on 3 September 1939 when the British Government was forced to declare war on National Socialist Germany. All over Scotland people came out of morning services to be told the content of Prime Minister Neville Chamberlain's radio broadcast at 11.15 a.m. German troops had invaded Poland on 1 September and unless the German forces withdrew from Poland a state of war would exist between Britain and Germany. No assurance was received, so Chamberlain told the nation that Britain was once again at war. The majority of Scottish Baptists would once again support British participation in a world war but without much of the jingoism of the past. Sidlow Baxter, pastor of Charlotte Chapel, Edinburgh, commented:

> We ourselves deplore war even as the extreme resort, but we are at one with all our fellow-Britishers in believing that our cause is righteous. The war was thrust upon us… ample facts have accumulated before us to expose Hitler's hypocrisy and his blame for the newly broken out conflict. The fact remains therefore that this war we are without doubt championing right and truth against a brutal system of oppression which threatens our very civilisation.[77]

In the Baptist Union of Scotland Council Minutes of 20 September 1939 it is simply and thoughtfully recorded that: 'We remember in prayer our allies, and shall not cease to love and pray for our enemies, many of whom are linked in the church universal. We desire supremely that the God and father of our Lord Jesus Christ will over-rule the dread happenings of our time that his will may be done in earth as it is in heaven.'[78] James Craig, pastor of Springburn Baptist Church, wrote in his article for the January 1939 issue of the *Scottish Baptist Magazine* the following words:

> In the experiences that lie ahead of us we need the presence of God more than His power. Will He be in the thunder, the earthquake, the fire? That is what we want to know. God may hide His mysteries in the great deep, bury his purposes in the vast silence, conceal the meaning of life's tears and tragedies, but our cry will be 'Show us the Father and it sufficeth us.' The furnace will not affright us, if we can see the One like unto the Son of Man. We shall then know that amid the lightening of Mount Sinai sits the form of the Law-Giver, that the burning bush of Horeb is lit by the torch of love. Seeing Him who is invisible, we shall endure.[79]

There had already been a growing anxiety concerning the activities of Adolf Hitler, who had come to power in 1933, and soon after the persecution of the

---

[77] Balfour, *Revival in Rose Street*, p. 251.
[78] Baptist Union of Scotland Council Minutes, 20 September 1939, p. 73.
[79] Cited in Burrows, *Change at Springburn*, p. 69.

Jewish people had begun. The British Evangelical Alliance Council had already expressed its outrage in a resolution on 27 April 1932. This resolution recognised how the Jews were suffering 'at the hands of those who profess and represent the Christian faith'.[80] In the *Baptist Times* a book review on Six Years of Hitler, stated that:

> It is almost impossible to believe this record of studied brutality; there is nothing like it in modern history, or indeed in the history of any period. It is not the outburst of fury but a carefully planned, elaborately-worked-out scheme for the annihilation of a race... the attacks on religion are disgusting and blasphemous; not only the Jews but the Christians are concerned with the disgraceful way in which reference is made to 'Jehova the criminal'. The Jews are outlawed in every respect.[81]

However, 'Nonconformist churches distanced themselves from the pacifist movement at the outbreak of war'[82] especially because of the utter failure of appeasement to keep the peace with such an unreasonable dictator. There was a firm ideological conviction that Nazi tyranny would not be allowed to triumph over 'Christian democracy.' This was ably expressed in the minutes of the Baptist Union of Scotland's dated 20 September 1939. In view of the outbreak of war on the Continent the Council felt that a statement on the situation should be made before dealing with any item of business. The Rev. Alexander Clark, on behalf of the Social Service Committee, submitted the following statement:

> The Baptist Union of Scotland desires to express its profound sorrow at the outbreak of war between this country, Poland and France on the one hand and Germany on the other. It recognizes and is deeply grateful for sustained efforts directed by the Allies, and particularly by our national leaders, during the past year towards peace. It expresses deep sympathy with the Polish nation in its heroic stand against Nazi ill-faith, aggression and violence. It marks with thanksgiving the unity, solemnity and self-dedication with which the British Commonwealth of nations has entered the struggle for spiritual values, without which civilisation must perish. It offers unceasing prayer that these values may not be lost sight of during war or in the making of peace, but that righteousness, mercy and faith may characterise the nation in all its actions. We commend to the grace of God our king and his ministers, and all at home and abroad serving the cause of freedom and justice. We remember in prayer our Allies, and shall not cease to love and pray for our enemies; many of whom are linked with us in the Church universal.[83]

---

[80] Wilkinson, *Dissent or Conform*, p. 197.
[81] *Baptist Times* (*B.T.*), 31 August 1939, p. 670.
[82] Alan C. Robinson, 'The Role of British Army Chaplains during World War Two' (Ph.D. thesis, University of Liverpool, 1999), p. 84.
[83] Baptist Union of Scotland Committee Minutes, 20 September 1939, pp. 85-87.

This time in contrast 'with the belligerent outlook which characterized much mainstream British Christianity during the First World War, the predominant mood at the beginning of the Second World War, was one of restraint.'[84] Sidlow Baxter, minister of Charlotte Baptist Chapel, Edinburgh, declared:

> We ourselves deplore war, even as the extreme resort, but we are at one with all our fellow-Britishers in believing that our cause is righteous. The war was thrust upon us... ample facts have accumulated before us to expose Hitler's hypocrisy and his blame for the newly broken out conflict. The fact remains, therefore, that in this war we are without doubt championing right and truth against a brutal system of oppression which threatens our very civilisation.[85]

John Macbeath sums up a common feeling that the war was just. He wrote that: '... If the future of the war is to be mainly a British effort, if the freedom of the peoples of the world is to be our care, if God has matched us with this great task, let us gird up our loins to a trust so great and a call so holy, and by the grace of God we shall not fail.'[86] The declaration of war came as no surprise since the country had been on a war footing since early 1938 and many citizens had already volunteered for National defence training. During this period the nation was still 'self-consciously Christian. Besides the existence of established or national churches in England and Scotland, the monarchy provided the focus for a British civil religion which was expressed in the development of a national cult of remembrance in the aftermath of the First World War.'[87] However the peace movement had made great gains during the inter-war period and was particularly influential within Free Church circles.[88] David Hicks, like many others of his generation were deeply sympathetic to that cause. He recorded:

> I grew up in the aftermath of the First World War and the memory of that awful slaughter cast a long dark shadow... It seemed obvious to me and to many others that if only everyone refused to fight then wars would cease; and this surely was what the teaching of Jesus required?... The Revd Dick Shepherd of St Martins-in-the-Field had founded the Peace Pledge Union in the thirties and I was one of the many who signed it. The rise of Hitler could surely best be met – so it rather naively seemed to me at the time – by spreading the Gospel of Pacifism in Germany.[89]

---

[84] Robinson, 'Role of British Army Chaplains', p. 200.
[85] Cited by Balfour, *Revival in Rose Street*, p. 251.
[86] *SBM*, 66.7 (July 1940), p. 11.
[87] Snape, *God and the British Soldier*, p. 20.
[88] Snape, *God and the British Soldier*, p. 85.
[89] David Hicks, 'Memoirs of World War Two', unpublished document, 2008, Author's Collection.

However, as the Second World War developed even committed pacifists were joining the armed forces. One example of this trend was William Speirs,[90] who joined up in 1942 as a Baptist Chaplain straight from New College, Edinburgh, with only limited pastoral experience.[91] In his correspondence he stated that even: 'At school I was a pacifist – a Scout not a Cadet.'[92] Speirs registered as a C.O. while at university and describes himself as a 'raucous pacifist' serving with an 'all-theological ambulance team.'[93] He spoke later of suffering 'a conflict of conscience as if in a sense [he] was denying Christ'[94] and volunteered after he had heard about the bombing of Rotterdam, even though it had declared itself an open city.[95] Speirs concluded that: 'My "call" to chaplaincy was as strong as my call to ministry, and might have been seen by the denomination as compelling as a call to missionary service.'[96] Douglas Robb, a Scottish Baptist Naval chaplain, also used such earnest language. He confessed in an interview that: 'At the time war broke out, he felt an "urge" to enter the Armed forces to serve in the capacity of chaplain. He and his fiancee felt this was the right thing to do at the time.'[97] He then informed the deaconate of the Granton on Spey Baptist Church at the time and they appeared to be happy for him to do this, despite the shortness of his service with them. However, when the papers came from the War Office, the deaconate had changed their mind and opposed his move. Douglas took the matter up with Church House, but found that they backed the deaconate... two years later... he was accepted by the War Office. This time the church did not stand in his way and he was posted to Tidworth on 18 November 1943.[98]

Scottish Baptists as in World War One had helped to recruit chaplains from amongst their own ministers to serve within the three services although the Baptist Union of Scotland Chaplaincy Committee had concluded its work on 1 February 1927.[99] A *Scottish Baptist Magazine* editorial at the end of World War Two could declare that: 'I believe they have had a better opportunity and seized it more successfully than in the war of 1914-18.'[100] W. Holmes Coats, in another editorial written earlier in 1942 stated:

---

[90] See Neil E. Allison, *The Official History of the United Board Volume Two: The Clash of Ideologies 1939–1945* (Great Bookham: The United Navy, Army and Air Force Board, 2012), pp. 59–62.
[91] Neil E. Allison, *The Scottish Thistle: Rev. Dr William 'Bill' Speirs, 10 June 1917 to 13 June 2013* (Norfolk: Privately published, 2013), p. 10.
[92] Letter: William Speirs to N.E. Allison, 18 March 1997, held in author's collection.
[93] William Speirs, 'Their Name Liveth', *R.A.Ch.D Journal*, 19.97 (June 1964).
[94] Letter: William Speirs to N.E. Allison, 18 March 1997.
[95] Letter: William Speirs to N.E. Allison, 18 March 1997, Author's Collection.
[96] Letter: William Speirs to N.E. Allison, 6 April 1997, Author's Collection.
[97] Interview Notes: Douglas Robb, 2 February 1988.
[98] Interview Notes: Douglas Robb, 2 February 1998.
[99] Baptist Union of Scotland Council Minutes, 1 February 1927, p. 69.
[100] *SBM*, 72.8 (August 1946), p. 1.

> The padre was popular; most of them were. I found them of a far higher average than those of the last war: they had been carefully chosen, and there were few misfits. It was interesting to note that the men liked their padre to be a padre; they had no time for the man who aped cheap popularity by swearing, boozing, or retailing lewd yarns... No body of men did more to combat the demoralising influence of boredom, or did it more energetically or successfully.[101]

Military chaplains were well respected within Scottish Baptist Church circles. The modern approach of bombing of cities to promote war aims would become a sad and repeated theme throughout this war. In 1941 the Union Secretary reported to the Council: 'that the following churches had suffered major damage through enemy action, Harper Memorial and Whitechurch, Glasgow; Madeira St Leith; George Square and Orangefield, Greenock and the manse at Clydebank. Two churches had suffered financial loss through the evacuation of their members, Whitechurch and Clydebank, and 14 members and adherents belong to eight churches had been killed.'[102] In the light of this it would be important for the Council to formulate plans to help cover the costs of war damage to Church property. It was documented that:

> a war bonus fund, the *sustentation* and finance committees received a report regarding several churches which had suffered through enemy air-raids, and [they] decided that the plight of those churches must have a place in their deliberations. It was therefore agreed to include in the war bonus scheme a provision for ministers of churches which had suffered distress through enemy actions. The joint committees recommended that the sum of £7500 be raised for the dual purpose, to be spent over a period of 4 years.[103]

However, the plight of the Scottish had registered abroad. An example of this concern is seen in a letter from Rev. W. Morrow Cook M.A. Durban South Africa 'enclosing a bank draft for £56 from his church and Sunday school for the relief of Baptist families on Clydeside who had suffered through enemy air-raids, and intimating the dispatch of several cases of new and second-hand clothing to be distributed to distressed Baptist families in Clydeside area.'[104] War was increasingly brutal both for civilians and those serving in the military which T.N. Tattersall[105] reflected in the *Scottish Baptist Magazine* in 1940 about the cause of the war, responding to a commonly held view that the war was a judgment of God and worth quoting substantially. He wrote:

---

[101] *SBM*, 68.9 (September 1942), p. 2.
[102] Baptist Union of Scotland Council Minutes, 28 May 1941, p. 492.
[103] Baptist Union of Scotland Council Minutes, 28 May 1941, p. 488.
[104] Baptist Union of Scotland Council Minutes, 27 October 1941, p. 586.
[105] See Neil E Allison, 'T.N. Tattersall D.S.O: His War Experience and Medals,' *The RAChD Journal* Vol. 45, 2006, pp. 31–34.

Why He has permitted it is not a problem for those who believe in a moral order affecting all things...But God has not delivered that judgment from a throne of doom; upon Him lies no responsibility for this dreadful scourge; it is man's doing... No reasonable faith, that is, no faith based upon reason, will be shattered by the calamity, though, just because we are bound up together in the bundle of life, the calamity falls upon just and unjust alike... These overbold spirits declare that the ravaging of fair lands, the slaughter of men, the torture of prisoners, the burning of cities, the bombing of the defenceless - all these things are God's judgement upon iniquity, and His vindication of righteousness. They hear the lamentation of Rachel for her children, they see the long trail of sorrow to the concentration camp, the wounded and the blinded passing on their weary way, and they believe that they are seeing God's open judgment upon a rebellious world. But so saying they do our faith a great disservice. If it were God's doing it would be hateful in our eyes. The world's conscience would be revolted by it....God's judgment upon iniquity is a cross whereon the Prince of Glory died... The God of Love our Lord revealed bears our sorrows, even our self-inflicted sorrows, upon His tender heart,... for Him to do right is for Him to love mercy and abundantly pardon...[106] But if any seeds of prosperity were the germs of the last war that cannot be said this time. The last twenty years have been long drawn-out years of hardship, unemployment, depression... Is it then the world's poverty that has brought this evil; upon us? No more than the world's prosperity brought on the last war.[107]

The war in Europe was over in 1945, but it would be the ending of the war in the East that would give new impetus to the peace movement with the dropping of an atomic bomb on Hiroshima on 6 August 1945 which cost the lives of at least 75,000 in the first few hours, reaching 200,000 by the 1950's. Nagasaki was bombed on 9 August 1945 killing around 40,000 people. The total number of deaths was approximately 140,000 by the end of 1950. It must be remembered that these bombs were dropped on centres of Japanese population and considered by many at the time as a necessary action to bring such an unbelievably costly war waged by fanatics to a conclusion. Modern commentators are more likely to view it as a war crime. Certainly, many feared the cost of an all out nuclear war in the light of the proven destructive power of nuclear armaments and the peace movement gained impetus and strength.

One of these new peace groups was called the Campaign for Nuclear Disarmament (C.N.D).[108] It was founded in the 1950s. This movement was a significant and continuing influence on Christian opinion, especially in Scotland whose population tended to support left wing policies and who identified closely with the Nuclear Disarmament lobby. International peace was the aim and was believed to be the only real alternative, because if a nuclear war was

---

[106] *SBM*, 66.1 (January 1940), p. 4.

[107] *SBM.*, 66.1 (January 1940), p. 5.

[108] See Kate Hudson, *CND Now More than Ever: The Story of a Peace Movement* (London: Vision Paperbacks, 2005).

entered into with the Soviet Union, it was believed it could wipe out the human race. Christians began to identify and emphasize their role as peace makers in a world of conflict. This concept became a defining characteristic of the follower of Jesus at the end of the twentieth century. It would explain the lack of comment on war and conflict within the pages of the *Scottish Baptist Magazine*, except to remind its readers now and again that the cost of war in human lives is always horrific and that war is a sinful activity. This helps explain S.D. Henry's comments regarding the Falkland Conflict (1982). In his excellent article published in the *Baptist Quarterly*, relating to the First World War, he shared his deep concern regarding the return of 'jingoism' with regards to the Falkland Conflict. He wrote that:

> The mass jingoism that apparently swept the country in August 1914 was impossible today. Yet the 1982 South Atlantic War, whether a necessary and bold success for British military skill or the last squalid colonial war, showed to those of us the idea of a nation in arms meant little, just how quickly war develops and how 'public opinion,' both Christian and Secular, can move easily and quickly from relative pacifism to bellicosity.[109]

There was no sign that Scottish Baptists had joined into this 'bellicosity.' Certainly, there was less bellicosity during the first Gulf War in 1991, but there was a general humanitarian concern for the Kurds and the Marsh Arabs in Iraq. When the ground war, Operation Desert Storm, began it was the hope that it would not be protracted and human suffering would be limited[110] and the fear 'that when hostilities have ceased in the Gulf area a kind of guerilla war of terrorist attacks will continue in other parts of the world'[111] would not be realized. At the time, Ian Livingstone, a former pastor of Orangefield Baptist Church, Greenock, was serving in the Royal Navy and would serve in the Gulf. However, it was not until the wars in the Balkans that Scottish Baptist opinion was galvanized into significant and unified action outside of supporting peace initiatives. The Bosnia Conflict (1991-1995) and the Kosovo Conflict (1998-1999) horrified public opinion with the daily horror stories of ethnic cleansing and the attendant refugee crisis. In January 1993 this concern was individualized when it was reported that pastor Boris Karceravic and his family had escaped from Sarajavo into Croatia. This escape was organized by pastor Stevo Dereta of Rijeka, Croatia and reported by Bill Steele, Baptist Missionary in Belgrade, Serbia.[112] This would be the beginning of a long term relationship with the Scottish Baptist Union the Croatian Baptist Union and Rijeka Baptist Church in particular. Even the sanctified day of National Remembrance was

---

[109] S.D. Henry, 'Scottish Baptists and the First World War', *Baptist Quarterly*, 31.2 (April 1985), p. 52.

[110] *SBM*, 117.3 (March 1991), p. 1.

[111] *SBM*, 117.3 (March 1991), p. 1.

[112] *SBM*, 119.1 (January 1993), p. 9.

high-jacked for the Bosnia cause. A person named simply as 'Olive,' writing in the Scottish Baptist letters page, suggested that people in Britain 'who wished to express their concern at the plight of Bosnia join in solidarity at exactly the same moment?... At 11.11.11 [readers were asked] to pause for one minute in order to pray: "Dear God, please stop the war in Bosnia, and help the people to forgive one another and rebuild their land."'[113] Robert Armstrong would provide the leadership and focus for a Christian response to the Balkan conflicts. In 1992 he wrote in the editorial of the *Scottish Baptist Magazine* that:

> what was once Yugoslavia' has become increasingly doom-laden with every news bulletin. Images of physical destruction as towns and cities are laid waste by mortar and artillery attacks together with those of personal dejection as people have fled from the battle zones either in refugee convoys or are seen scurrying around streets avoiding sniper fire, have become unfortunately familiar but are nonetheless harrowing. It is profoundly saddening to see what fellow human beings are dong to one another, their community and the country in which they have lived in comparative harmony for many generations... A Christian response to these and other similar situations is obviously to support wherever it is possible efforts to relieve human suffering and to encourage by our prayers all efforts to bring peace and reconciliation.[114]

The media 'carried graphic colour photographs of the mutilated victims of the shelling of Sarajevo's Markale marketplace – dead and living.'[115] This attack happened on 28 August 1995 and caused the wounding of ninety people and the killing of thirty-seven. Shawcross commented that 'These were the deaths which, in effect, ended the war in Bosnia'[116] and allowed the intervention of NATO forces with a more robust mandate than that of the UN.[117] Stephen Younger expressed his doubts about military intervention as early as 1994 and this was representative of Scottish Baptist opinion at the time. He wrote:

> NATO's commitment to its first ever 'official' military offensive around Sarajevo was an enormous risk: casting 'peacemakers' as 'widow makers' and combatants. Clearly to do nothing was to risk an escalation of the horror and equally to do something was to risk the same. This is a cruel no-win situation where no-one has impeccable motives for intervention either.'[118]

---

[113] *SBM*, 119.12 (December 1993), p. 2.
[114] *SBM*, 118.9 (September 1992), Editorial.
[115] *SBM*, 120.7 (July/August 1994), Editorial.
[116] William Shawcross, *Deliver us from Evil: Warlords and Peacekeepers in a World of Endless Conflict* (London: Bloomsbury, 2000), p. 125.
[117] Laura Silber and Allan Little, *The Death of Yugoslavia* (London: BBC /Penguin, 1995), p. 345.
[118] *SBM*, 120.3 (March 1994), p. 1.

Although there was a real concern about military intervention there was also a growing feeling that the humanitarian problem had to be addressed with commitment. Cath Chisholm wrote a letter to the editor of the *Scottish Baptist Magazine* expressing what many other readers felt. She wrote:

> As we go about our ordinary everyday lives, free to go where we will, it is horrifying to think of what is happening now in Bosnia...But what can we do? We give financially and send material goods, but surely we can do something more constructive? To whom can we write to express our concern and horror?[119]

Lowell Shepperd representing Spring Harvest visited Croatia and made a very telling remark. 'The refugee crisis is evidence not only of professional armies at war, but of a tide of ethnic hatred that finds ordinary people acting with unprecedented inhumanity.'[120] In February 1993 it was reported that the Croatian cities of Rijeka and Karlovac had received 57,000 refugees from the estimated two million people displaced so far by the conflict.[121] A committee was formed adopting the name 'Borders for Bosnia.' This organization would galvinise Scottish Baptists into action and would significantly affect church opinion. The Selkirk Baptist Church Team contacted all the churches in the central Borders area and some schools. The result was that: 'a half ton of foodstuffs was gathered and was added to two lorries [One from the International Baptist Church, Aberdeen and one from Viewfield Baptist Church] which left Viewfield, Dunfermline in February. Baptists there hired a seven and a half ton lorry[122] every two months and drove it to Rijeka in Croatia. The Christians of Rijeka Baptist Church then distributed the aid in fuel, ferry and stops.'[123] These supportive activities were also to encourage the Croatian Christians to continue to behave in a Christian manner in spite of all the pressure to let bitterness rule their actions. The *Scottish Baptist Magazine* reported that: 'The Croatian churches are at a crossroads. Where Christians are responding with the words and works of Jesus we want to offer our support.'[124] The key areas that received Scottish Baptist support was 'Borders for Bosnia', 'The Life & Peace Centre' and 'My Neighbour Organisation' all administered through the Eurosave charity. The 'My Neighbour' initiative was founded by Rijeka Baptist Church and 'became, after the UNCHR and the Red Cross, one of the largest voluntary aid organizations in the former Yugoslavia.'[125] Rijeka

---

[119] *SBM*, 119.10 (October 1993), p. 2.
[120] *SBM*, 119.2 (February 1993), p. 12.
[121] *SBM*, 119.2 (February 1993), p. 12.
[122] Drivers came from a number of Baptist Churches. I have confirmed volunteer drivers from Viewfield, Dunfermline; International, Aberdeen; Saltcoats; Cumbernauld; Selkirk and Hillhead, Glasgow.
[123] *SBM*, 119.4 (April 1993), p. 11.
[124] *SBM*, 119.2 (February 1993), p. 12.
[125] *SBM*, 122.3 (March 1996), p. 10.

Baptist Church, now twinned with Viewfield Baptist Church, Dunfermline, had written to the Viewfield congregation: 'Thank you for all the help... The deliveries of food are especially important. We really need as much food as we can obtain in order to get it to the people of Bosnia. People are beginning to starve to death and we need to do all we can.'[126] The article then challenged readers to action with the guilt intensive phrase 'What are you doing?', but the clear emphasis was on humanitarian aid and not war service. The 'Life and Peace Centre' situated near Rijeka which was primarily responsible for caring for traumatised families from the different religious and ethnic groups in the region, also sought to develop some kind of humanitarian work 'among returning soldiers with terrible memories of what they have seen or done.'[127] At least one Scottish Baptist did serve in the military, although firmly as a noncombatant. Neil Allison, pastor of Glenrothes Baptist Church, joined the military as a chaplain and would serve during the Balkans conflict in Kosovo. Previously, while serving as a Territorial chaplain he had been moved to volunteer to serve in Bosnia in 1995.

The aggressive bombing of Serbian military targets and infrastructure by NATO planes began on 24 March 1999 in response to Serbian ethnic cleansing of the Albanian Muslim majority in Kosovo[128] and in particular the murder of Albanian villagers at Racak.[129] Eventually NATO ground forces intervened. Allison, described his experience of the 'entry' into Kosovo and ministry opportunities that arose. He explained that as:

> we lined up waiting for our entry into Kosovo it was a nervous time. We were hoping for the best, but expecting the worst. Soldiers had plenty of time to think about life and death issues and many were desperate to talk and pray. I spent time with Recce Troop who would be first to enter after the Paras and Ghurkhas had secured the entry route through the narrow pass known commonly as the 'Death File.' At the soldiers request I prayed with a number of crews in their armoured vehicles. I also collected a number of 'last letters' and personal effects if anything should happen.[130]

Once they had crossed the line from Macedonia into Kosovo Allison recorded: 'We were treated as liberators rather than peace keepers. They [Albanians] threw flowers all over our vehicles and at times we had to stop to remove this

---

[126] *SBM*, 119.4 (April 1993), p. 11.

[127] *SBM*, 122.3 (March 1996), p. 10.

[128] Shawcross, *Deliver us from Evil*, p. 324.

[129] Shawcross, *Deliver us from Evil*, p. 329.

[130] Neil E. Allison, 'Operation Agricola: Our Entry into Kosovo', *RAChD Journal*, 39.1 (January 2000), p. 13. See also Ines-Jacqueline Werkner & Christine R. Barker, *Der Militarpfarrer im Auslandsein: Gestig-religioser Beistand oder nur Sozialarbeiter? Zur Funktion von Religion in einer zunehmend sakularen Welt, in Diener zweir Herren* (Berlin: Sonderdruckk, 2005), p. 181.

debris of joy...'[131] Yet deep concerns remained. Ruth Allison wrote about these issues in a periodical for the wives of Scottish Baptist ministers. She reflected: 'Like most of the wives I spoke to, I wasn't too keen for my husband to be involved in a conflict when there had been quite a bit of concern voiced in the media about the rightness of the NATO bombing.'[132] Scottish Baptists at the end of the twentieth century were deeply concerned about the ethics of war and the manner in which warfare was conducted. The increased flow of information out from a war zone at the end of the twentieth century had a major influence both on participants and their families together with a growing proportion of the general public.

At the beginning of the twentieth century Scottish Baptist Churches and its ministers had been supportive of the British Empire identifying it with missionary opportunity and enterprise. When war broke out in 1914 in Europe Scottish Baptists flocked to the colours to fight for God, King and Country without a hint of cynicism. The attrition rate during World War One was greater than anyone at the time could have possibly imagined. Therefore the post war period was dominated by an overwhelming desire for peace almost at any cost and the idea of the League of Nations gained currency with the general population. However, when the next European war began in 1939 there was a committed desire to support the national war effort on ideological grounds with many citizens reconsidering a former pacifist stance. Adolf Hitler had proven that he could not be reasoned with and therefore war was considered the only option. This was reluctantly recognized after many peace initiatives had failed most famously Chamberlain's 'white paper' which had declared 'peace in our time.' Once the threat of Fascism had been defeated the key post war concern became the aggressive extension and influence of Communism. Of particular concern was the development of the Soviet Union state and the threat of imminent nuclear war with the democratic west. It was commonly believed that there could be no winners in such a war and that everything should be done to prevent this, though Scottish Baptists had not been a part 'of the so-called "historic peace churches"...'[133] In general they began to be less supportive of military force and concentrated on the provision of humanitarian help for those caught up in conflict particularly after the horrors of the Balkans conflicts. Scottish Baptists had become truly peace loving, supporting humanitarian aid and reconciliation projects with the prayerful hope that they could make a significant difference. Stephen Younger eloquently summed up this feeling: 'We pray for our world – we must pray for our world – but we certainly do not do so as those who are fleeing to a last and desperate resort. We belong to and

---

[131] Allison, 'Operation Agricola: Our Entry into Kosovo', p. 13.
[132] Ruth Allison, 'A Wife's View of Ministry', *Caring and Sharing* The Magazine of the Scottish Baptist Ministers' Wives' Fellowship (Spring 2001), p. 4.
[133] See Paul R. Dekur, *For the Healing of the Nations: Baptist Peacemakers* (Georgia: Smyth & Helwys Publishing, 1993).

speak to a God who makes enemies into friends and turns bad news into good news.'[134]

---

[134] *SBM*, 120.7 (July / August 1994), p. 1.

CHAPTER 9

## *First in Jerusalem*: Scottish Baptist Home Mission Work in Twentieth-Century Scotland

### Brian Talbot

#### Introduction

The desire to engage in home evangelisation has been at the heart of Baptist identity since the inception of the movement in Scotland. Organised efforts to co-ordinate mission strategy began in a small way in the late 1790s and a number of agencies were founded to carry out this work in the next couple of decades. However the earliest united effort by Scottish Baptists to combine their home mission agencies began with the founding of the Baptist Home Missionary Society (BHMS) in August 1827. As a result of pooling their resources Scottish Baptists were able to employ more pastor-evangelists, in excess of twenty men each year, in the remainder of the nineteenth century. They were also the beneficiaries of greater financial resources, both from churches in England and Scotland, and provided Christian ministry at around seventy churches and preaching stations in some of the more remote areas of Scotland both on the mainland and on the islands, together with a limited number of initiatives in urban areas of central Scotland.[1] When the current Baptist Union of Scotland was founded in 1869 the first of its four objects was: 'to strengthen and extend our Missionary operations, especially those of our Home Missionary Society, for the dissemination of the Gospel of Christ in Scotland.' Part of its second object was: 'and to encourage movements designed to originate new Churches in the larger towns'.[2] This point signalled that the evangelistic work of the Baptist Union would not be confined to the activities of the home missionary society. This chapter will focus not only on the work of the BHMS but also on the other outreach initiatives of the Union, including the

---

[1] Details of this work is found in 'The Baptist Home Missionary Society: A Substitute Union, 1827-1868?' in B.R. Talbot, *Search for a Common Identity: The Origins of the Baptist Union of Scotland, 1800-1870* (Carlisle: Paternoster, 2003), pp. 153-90, 346-53.

[2] *First Report of the Baptist Union of Scotland* (Edinburgh: John Lindsay, 1869), p. 4.

Evangelism Committee set up on 19 November 1889[3] and the much more recent Church Extension Committee founded in 1948,[4] that was to absorb the work of the home mission committee into its remit in 1971.[5]

## Home Mission Work Vision in the BUS post 1869

The work of the BHMS was kept separate from other outreach activities of the Baptist Union though not all Scottish Baptists were happy with this development. William Tulloch, President of the Baptist Union in 1882, declared in his presidential address: 'if however the Society [BHMS] and the Union had combined in this work...and [if they] had the sympathy and hearty co-operation of the pastors and churches, who can calculate the amount of good that might have been accomplished?'[6] Prior to this statement Tulloch had drawn attention to the outreach work of the Baptist Union carried out, in addition to the BHMS activities, between 1869 and 1882.

> There is no part of Union work on which I look back with greater satisfaction than the evangelistic and church extension work. Nor any I think in which the Union has been so successful. Not to speak of my own labours and the labours of our summer evangelistic deputies, I regard the formation of the Govan, Wishaw, Irvine, Broughty Ferry, and [Ward Road] Dundee Churches and the fostering into self-sustentation of these and the Arbroath, Rothesay, Elgin, St Andrews and Leith Churches as the best thing the Union has done.'[7]

These initiatives had happened informally under the general auspices of the Baptist Union but it was not until November 1889 that a group of leading Scottish Baptists met to form the Evangelistic Committee of the Baptist Union of Scotland. The remit given by the Baptist Union Council was to: 'arrange evangelistic meetings in suitable centres of population and to assist Baptist Churches in evangelistic efforts. That the committee have power to nominate for election by the Council one or more evangelists, should funds be subscribed

---

[3] *The Twenty-Second Annual Report of the Baptist Union of Scotland 1889-1890* (Glasgow: Baptist Union of Scotland, 1890), pp. 42-47.

[4] 'Reports – Church Extension', *Scottish Baptist Yearbook* (*SBY*) (Glasgow: Baptist Union of Scotland, 1950), p. 137.

[5] 'Home Mission Committee Report', *SBY 1972* (Glasgow: Baptist Union of Scotland, 1972), p. 35. A good summary of the changes in home mission work for the major Scottish denominations, including Baptists, is found in: D.E. Meek, 'Religious Life 8: Highlands since the Reformation', in M. Lynch (ed.), *Oxford Companion to Scottish History* (Oxford: Oxford University Press, 2007) pp. 515-22.

[6] William Tulloch, 'President's Address', *The Fourteenth Annual Report of the Baptist Union of Scotland* (Glasgow; Baptist Union of Scotland, 1882), pp. 47-48.

[7] Tulloch, 'President's Address', 1882, p. 47.

for that purpose...'[8] Even at its inception there was a significant overlap in membership between the Home Mission and the Evangelism committees. Regrettably no copies of home mission annual reports have survived between 1869 and 1898, however a comparison between the names listed on the 1898 BHMS committee and that of the earlier 1889 Evangelism committee reveals that ten of the thirteen members of the later agency were also identified with the home mission, including prominent Edinburgh Civil servant Percival Waugh, the secretary of the Home Mission and an elder at Bristo Place Baptist Church in Edinburgh.[9] At this early stage in the life of the Baptist Union it was the first step to the institutional control of Baptist home mission work under the Union's auspices.

It is clear that the focus of the work under the direction of the Evangelism Committee was primarily in locations not featured in the work of the home mission. Of the two conducted in the first year in Peterhead and Glasgow the most successful mission, in numerical terms, was conducted by Kelso Baptist minister Edward Last in Cambridge Street Baptist Church, Glasgow, between 13 and 24 January 1890. Here there were twenty-six professions of faith of which seven individuals from this group were baptised and added to the church membership roll.[10] From this small beginning in 1890 the work steadily grew. In 1897 a full-time Evangelist William Fotheringham was appointed to work with a small group of believers to plant a church in Port-Glasgow, following the completion of his studies at the Bible Training Institute in Glasgow. Within a couple of years a church was constituted with seven deacons and forty-seven members. Six other missions took place with particular encouragements experienced by the Oban Church. There a two week mission conducted by Peter Macleod, minister of Dumbarton Baptist Church was extended to a third week. The Masonic Hall which the Baptists normally used for meetings was too small for the crowds that wished to attend. The Argyle Square Free Church, Oban, offered the use of its premises and its minister D.J. Martin and church members supported the mission as did many local Congregationalists and the local branch of the Faith Mission. The style of missions reflected the theological views of participants. At Oban and Hamilton, a home mission station, where more Reformed views were held more cautious comments were made regarding possible outcomes of the meetings. J.R. Chrystal, minister of the Hamilton Church, made it plain that Evangelist Mr Richard Hill 'keeps to the old paths'. At Burray in Orkney minister Samuel Lindsay tried to use new measures to produce more professions of faith amongst adult hearers. He stated: 'We tried to introduce after-meetings, with the hope of getting at the people personally, but our efforts were unsuccessful.' By contrast the new measures were introduced at

---

[8] *The Twenty-Second Annual Report of the Baptist Union of Scotland 1889-90* (Glasgow: Baptist Union of Scotland, 1890), p. 42.
[9] *Twenty-Second Annual Report*, 1890, p. 42.
[10] *Twenty-Second Annual Report*, 1890, p. 43.

Largo Baptist Church during the mission led by T.W. Lister, minister of Rattray Street Baptist Church, Dundee, but significantly this mission was aimed at children most of whom were enthusiastic about staying on for an 'after meeting'. The vision for evangelistic missions on the threshold of the twentieth century was growing with an amazing forty-one pastors of Baptist Union churches offering to conduct them in the following year.[11]

At the end of the nineteenth century the BHMS had twelve districts comprising of twenty mission stations, of which seven were on islands namely Mull, Skye, Tiree, Islay and Colonsay, together with the Orkney and Shetland Isles. There were two in the north of Scotland; one was in Caithness located at Keiss and Scarfskerry, and the other in Perthshire was based at Tullymet, near Pitlochry. One station was retained in Argyllshire at Lochgilphead with two others based in central Scotland. In Fife home missionaries were based at Largo and Cowdenbeath and in Lanarkshire at Hamilton. In total eighteen BHMS Evangelists were employed at the end of the nineteenth century. This total had declined slightly from the last surviving statistics from 1868. In that year there were thirteen designated districts and twenty-four mission stations in which twenty-five men were employed to work for that society. In 1898 gross total income for BHMS work was £2,490 12s 10d up from £1543 6s 5d in 1868.[12] Although a 28% decline in staffing levels was an indication of a significant reduction in the work being done by the BHMS by the end of the nineteenth century, a 62% increase in income over that period did suggest at least an indication of the confidence of its supporters in the work being done and high expectations for the new century. This impression was correct but increasingly the more creative and innovative outreach initiatives would come from the Evangelism Committee rather than the Home Mission, however both entered the twentieth century full of confidence for the work that lay ahead.

## Home Mission Work 1900-1931

At the annual meeting of the BHMS held in Bristo Place Baptist Church in October 1899 chairman Alexander Young of Glasgow offered some general reflections on the work of home and overseas missions. He rejoiced in 'the deep and growing interest in Foreign Missionary work, an interest happily extending to all our churches...After drawing attention to the rapid growth of the large towns and cities of Scotland, he nevertheless appealed to his hearers not to neglect the rapidly declining population in rural areas of Scotland.

---

[11] All unidentified references from this paragraph are from *The Thirtieth Annual Report of the Baptist Union of Scotland for 1897-98,* printed in the *SBY* (Glasgow: Baptist Union of Scotland, 1899), pp. 96-99.

[12] *Report on the Baptist Home Missionary Society for Scotland* (Edinburgh: D.R. Collie & Son, 1868), pp. 22-36.

> The work is needed because of the isolation of the people...In some parts of the Mission districts the face of the stranger is rarely seen and the nearest neighbour is miles away. The poverty of the people grounds another claim....They are unable to maintain gospel ordinances without our help. Their natural workers, the young, the strong, have come to us and are workers in our city churches.[13]

Here were underlying fears that the Highlands and Islands would be neglected by Scottish Baptists as greater attention was naturally given to the growing numbers of unchurched people living in more central areas of Scotland. These concerns, though, must be placed in a context of general optimism in the denomination for the new century. George Yuille, in a review of the first thirty years of the Baptist Union from 1869 to 1899, described a picture of steady growth from fifty-one to 108 churches and from 3,700 to 15,236 members.

> This must be regarded as a complete justification of union; though it will not be regarded with any feeling of complacency when we keep in view the natural increase of the population, the urgent spiritual need of our great cities and the parts of the country where Baptists are as yet unrepresented...These figures indicate the need there is for church extension and may suggest that a Union church-extension scheme might very fittingly introduce the new century.[14]

The growth in Baptist numbers continued until 1935 when there were a total of 23,310 members indicating growth of around 35% since 1898 in 152 churches up from 108 an increase of 29%.[15] Scottish Baptists had made good progress in their home mission activities in the first three decades of the twentieth century. It is appropriate to look briefly at some of the outreach activities that led to this growth.

In accordance with the wishes of George Yuille the remit of the Evangelism Committee was changed in 1901 to 'Church Extension and Evangelism Committee'. It provided assistance that year to five causes that had begun in the previous decade at Shettleston, Glasgow, Renfrew, Bellshill, Dunblane and Gorgie, Edinburgh. In the case of the first three congregations there were significant encouragements. Shettleston had a net increase in new members of thirty-one, raising its total membership to sixty-three with an increase in the Sunday School from forty to sixty-five pupils. Renfrew Baptists had a difficult year with many people choosing to leave, yet they had a net increase of ten people to forty-four on the membership roll and up to ninety in the Sabbath School. Bellshill under the inspirational leadership of George Harper, formerly

---

[13] 'Report of the Baptist Home Missionary Society for Scotland for 1899', *SBY* (Glasgow: William Asher, 1900), pp. 6-7.

[14] George Yuille, 'Baptist Union of Scotland', *SBY* (Glasgow; William Asher, 1899), p. 9.

[15] D. Hunt, *Reflecting On Our Past* (Hamilton: Hamilton Baptist Church, 1997), p. 6 and Appendix 2: Table of Annual Statistics, n.p.

a Baptist minister in Bradford, made rapid progress from a membership of twenty in 1900 to seventy-eight in 1902 as a result it no longer needed support from this Union committee. However despite assistance the Dunblane and Gorgie causes closed in 1902.[16] More traditional missions were held under the auspices of this committee during the session 1901-1902 in the churches at Peebles, Oban, Alloa, Dumfries, Irvine, Lerwick, Shettleston, Anstruther and in the area of Hawkhill, Dundee where the mission was planned to support the first steps of a proposed church-plant. Different approaches to outreach were in evidence in the different locations. In Peebles a high profile literature campaign throughout the whole town preceded the two weeks of meetings comprising each day a Bible Study for Christians, a prayer meeting, children's meeting and at 8pm the evangelistic meeting for adults. Oban Baptist Church had a different strategy. They drew up a large list of people they wished to attend the meetings and sent 'printed letters to them through the post; and in this way several hundreds received individually a personal invitation.'[17] In Dumfries the guest preacher brought a 'large and beautiful model of the 'Tabernacle' from the Old Testament. Apparently 'his clear elucidation of the symbolic meaning of all that pertained to it and its ceremonies was most instructive and inspiring' with attendances increasing each night to hear his messages. At Irvine the twelve day outreach was preceded by a conference on 'Spiritual Revival' for Christians with a view to encouraging their efforts during the mission, but it failed as very limited numbers attended due to seriously inclement weather. At Lerwick there were twin strategies to reach people. First of all there was a focus on small cottage meetings together with the Evangelist choosing to go to places where local men could be engaged in conversation during the day and where appropriate be invited to evening meetings where the Evangelist's preaching: 'was not only earnest, but thoughtful and free from clap-trap'. A last example from Hawkhill, Dundee, revealed a more low-key approach as this was a new initiative. The aim here was to gain an interest from local people 'more of the character of breaking up new ground and sowing the seed' that would provide more overt opportunities for evangelism on future occasions.[18] Although the responses were limited in each of these missions with only a few conversions reported, the willingness to explore a variety of approaches in communicating the faith indicated confidence in the future success of their cause.

One of the Baptist mission initiatives that had been regularly undertaken in the late nineteenth century was the work amongst fishermen during the fishing season carried out under the auspices of the Scottish Baptist Total Abstinence Society. However, from 1896 the work was jointly organised by the Evangelism Committee of the Baptist Union of Scotland. In that year Revs Joseph Burns (Clydebank), William Donald (Kilmarnock), Hugh Gunn (Merrystone,

---

[16] 'Church Extension and Evangelistic Report', *SBY 1902*, pp. 110-12.
[17] 'Church Extension and Evangelistic Report', *SBY 1902*, pp. 112-13.
[18] 'Church Extension and Evangelistic Report', 1902, pp. 114-15.

Coatbridge), John McLean (Victoria Place, Glasgow) and A.A. Milne (Cambuslang) on behalf of the latter agency held meetings from 13 July to 7 August 1896. On each of those days they organised children's meetings on the beach in the afternoons, and open air services on the streets of Fraserburgh, Peterhead and Wick in the evenings with up to 1,000 fishermen. Hugh Gunn also reported that there were a significant amount of women, many of whom had come from all over Scotland, for the herring curing. He urged the Evangelism Committee to take up the challenge of finding a lady who could undertake to visit these women in their lodgings in these fishing ports. However, it was not until 1906 that Mrs William Cooper, formerly a missionary in China, was engaged to work amongst the fisher girls of Lerwick, as a result of an appeal from the Christian Endeavour Society in Lerwick Baptist Church.[19] The Women's Auxiliary of the Baptist Union of Scotland took over the organisation of the outreach activities amongst the fishing communities in 1914.[20] They retained the link to Bible classes and Christian Endeavour Societies in many Scottish Baptist congregations whose fundraising activities had ensured that the financial needs for this work had been met. Each year from 1914 the Women's Auxiliary had produced a circular document to report back to Scottish Baptist young people on the work in the fishing communities. After World War I there was a significant reduction in the scale of the fishing industry at Lerwick with considerably less people employed in that industry. As a result by 1921 the numbers attending the mission meetings were greatly reduced compared to former years. Representatives of the various Scottish Churches also worked well together in their witness to the workers of the fishing industry. In 1923 the Baptists and the Church of Scotland held joint Sunday evening meetings for the three month duration of the fishing season.[21] The work continued steadily into the 1930s, but now there were more attractions available to the workers when off duty than the events provided by the churches. In the Baptist Mission Hall the choice of gramophone records was appreciated by the girls, especially those playing Gaelic songs. On the fisher girls' 'day off' a main meal was provided for them with the accompaniment of a Baptist Church Choir with a short evangelistic service to conclude the evening programme.[22] Here was a project that had captured the imagination of many Scottish Baptists of all ages. It was also an initiative in which different Scottish

---

[19] 'Evangelistic Report', *Baptist Union of Scotland 28th Annual Report 1895-96* (Glasgow: Baptist Union of Scotland, 1896), pp. 64-70. 'Mission to Fisher Girls', *SBY 1907*, pp. 108-109; 'Mission to Fisher Girls at Lerwick', *SBY 1910*, p. 125. In chapter three, 'Her Children Arise and Call Her Blessed', pp. 71-77, Christine Lumsden gives more information on Jane Henderson, one of the Baptist lady home missionaries involved in the work amongst the fisher girls between 1909 and 1913.
[20] 'Mission to Fisher Girls at Lerwick', *SBY 1915*, p. 150.
[21] 'The Women's Auxiliary to The Baptist Union of Scotland', *SBY 1924*, p. 158.
[22] 'Secretaries' Annual Report (of W.A.)' *SBY 1935*, pp. 185-186.

Christians, and occasionally believers from other countries too, were able to work together effectively in the promotion of the Christian faith.

The Home Mission society had seen steady rather than spectacular work carried out under its auspices by faithful men and women in the first quarter of the twentieth century. Some of its most faithful workers had given a lifetime of service for its cause. An outstanding example was Rev. Duncan McFarlane of Tiree who died aged eighty-seven in 1907. He succeeded his brother Rev. John McFarlane as pastor of the Tiree congregation and completed nearly twenty years service to add to the thirty one given by John McFarlane to that church. Duncan, pastor of Tobermory Baptist Church, Mull, from 1858 to 1879, had a powerful ministry in Tiree during the 1874 Christian Revival on that island; many people came to faith under his preaching and became members of the Tiree Baptist Church. He was seen as an obvious choice to take up the vacant charge in 1879 until his death in 1907, having completed nearly fifty years of pastoral and evangelistic ministry.[23] John Knox, minister of Lochgilphead Baptist Church served that cause faithfully from 1880 until his retirement in 1928.[24] At the October 1909 Annual Meeting of the BHMS the chair was occupied by the famous Dr Alexander McLaren, minister of Union Chapel, Manchester. He was given the honour of chairing the meeting though for a different reason, namely that he was the oldest subscribing member of the society with his name being found in subscription lists as early as 1850. McLaren, while appreciating the mention of his support for this cause, pointed out that his father David McLaren had signed an appeal to Scottish Baptists to unite in support of a Baptist Home Mission as early as 1818, nine years prior to the formation of the BHMS in 1827. At that 1909 meeting a report was given concerning the passing of Rev. Thomas Young of Sandsting and Lunnasting, the two most northerly Baptist churches in the British Isles from 1869 and 1874 respectively to 1901.[25] Dedicated service by a relatively small number of people had accomplished a great deal of working in advancing the Christian faith in the remote communities of their native land.

A snapshot picture of the work of the BHMS in its various mission stations can be drawn from the annual reports of this agency. In November 1910 after several years carrying up to as many as eight pastoral vacancies in its churches the BHMS was pleased that all its nineteen posts in eleven districts were filled.

---

[23] 'Report of the Baptist Home Missionary Society for Scotland 1908', *SBY 1909*, pp. 177-78.

[24] 'Annual Report of the Home Missionary Society', *SBY 1934,* pp. 202-203. See also J. Knox, 'Mission Work at Lochgilphead', *Scottish Baptist Magazine* (*SBM*), 17.12 (December 1891), pp. 297-300.

[25] 'Report of the Baptist Home Missionary Society for Scotland 1909', *SBY 1910*, pp. 178-79. A special tribute to Alexander McLaren was recorded at the 1909 BHMS Annual meeting in recognition of his faithful support to its work. 'Report of the Baptist Home Missionary Society for Scotland 1910', *SBY 1911*, p. 9.

In the Shetland Baptist causes, in July 1910, Laurence Scollay was pleased with growing attendances both morning and evening at Sandsting, but noted the vast majority were women as many of the men were away fishing for the summer. Lunnasting had a very small congregation in the summer due to whole families moving to Lerwick for the fishing season, though numbers were increasing during the winter months, in part due to the nearest Church of Scotland congregation being located five miles away. Burra Isle and Dunrossness were both encouraged by good congregations and a number of believers' baptisms taking place. William Gilmour reported that the Orkney congregations that year were small at Sanday, Eday and Burray with around forty people present at Baptist services though the Westray Church had a large congregation. In Caithness the small congregations at Scarfskerry, Stroma and Keiss has seen a small increase in attendance, but these causes like most of the Orkney Baptist churches were located in areas of sparse population and could not expect a large congregation. Progress in Inverness was slow amongst adults though there were a good number of children attending the Sunday School, though its further growth was limited by a shortage of Sunday School teachers. Buckie Baptist Church, by contrast had plenty of workers. It was also erecting an impressive new building and had seen significant increases in Sunday attendances, mainly from amongst the several hundred labourers engaged in the local harbour extensions. In the Hebrides there was a mixed picture. At Broadford on Skye a faithful few kept the work going but appeared to be having little impact on the wider community. On Mull, the Bunessan Church had been struggling to attract any younger people to its meetings, though the Tobermory congregation had seen significant success in attracting unchurched people to cottage meetings in different homes which indicated that a more innovative approach to outreach work could attract new people to explore the Christian faith. The Baptists of Tiree saw large congregations at their meetings. Donald McArthur reported on 25 March 1910 that at Balephuill, Tiree: 'The winter has been very busy, services being held almost nightly since October. The Sunday services are encouraging. We have after-meetings often and the people stay willingly.' The Baptists of Colonsay were also in good heart following the conversion of nine mainly younger people in a two month mission between December 1909 and January 1910. Islay Baptists had also been encouraged by the interest shown in their cottage meetings held in the district around Port Ellen. In Argyllshire the work was slow in Lochgilphead, but most encouraging at Oban where the congregation were holding outreach meetings in August 1910 on the nearby island of Kerrera and at Strontoiler where they were particularly pleased to see the high proportion of men in those congregations. The Taynult congregation had completed a seven week mission in February 1910. Many young people were in attendance at the services. There were regular baptismal services on Sunday evenings at which around two hundred people were present. Although a few of its churches were struggling to build meaningful ties with their wider communities, most of these congregations were in good heart and had reasonable grounds for optimism about their work in the next decade of the twentieth century.[26]

Home mission work amongst Scottish Baptists was never restricted to the BHMS. There had always been a variety of local, regional and occasionally national initiatives for evangelism and church planting. One example of this was the work of the Fife Joint Committee. Their report in the 1911 *Scottish Baptist Year Book* illustrates the enthusiasm they displayed for this venture. After noting that the numerical strength of several of the Fife Baptist churches

> has been greatly weakened by the emigration fever. Notwithstanding this depressing circumstance, these churches have been zealously striving to make good their losses...In February the Missions at Lochgelly and Buckhaven...were formed into churches...in the same month the Lockgelly Church entered into possession of the new church hall, built for its use by the joint committee at a cost of £700. A very central site has been secured for the prospective church buildings in Buckhaven. At Inverkeithing negotiations are in progress for a site in the High Street for the new kirk.'[27]

To put these figures in context, sixty three out of the 136 Baptist Union congregations had lost members as a result of emigration in the 1910-1911 church year, a total of 546 people.[28] It was no surprise that the total membership of the Union had declined from 20,572 in 1909-1910 to 20,359, but it was to rise again the following year to 20,703.[29] This regional Baptist Association had commenced the new century with a commitment to plant a new cause in the Pathhead district of Kirkcaldy, constituted in January 1900.[30] New church premises had been erected at Pittenweem in 1906[31], at Bowhill and for the Pathhead cause in late 1908.[32] In addition to the churches planted at Inverkeithing, Lochgelly and Buckhaven, another new congregation was planted at Rosyth in 1918, with significant progress already made that year on the erection of new premises in that town.[33] Allowing for the losses due to emigration and around 1,000 Scottish Baptist Church members killed in World

---

[26] 'Report of the Baptist Home Missionary Society for Scotland 1910', *SBY* (Glasgow: Fraser, Asher & Co., 1911), pp. 4-26.
[27] 'Fifeshire Association', *SBY* (Glasgow: Fraser, Asher & Co., 1911), p. 96.
[28] *SBY* (Glasgow: Fraser, Asher & Co., 1912, p. 69.
[29] Hunt, *Reflecting on Our Past*, 'Appendix 2: Table of Annual Statistics', n.p.
[30] G. Yuille (ed.), *History of the Baptists in Scotland* (Glasgow: Baptist Union of Scotland, 1926), pp. 148-49.
[31] Yuille, *Baptists in Scotland*, p. 155.
[32] 'Chapel Building and Enlargement', *SBY* (Glasgow: Fraser, Asher & Co., 1909), p. 51.
[33] *SBY* (Glasgow: John Cossar, 1919), p. 90.

War I[34], the steady growth in numbers in Baptist ranks up to the 1930s can only be explained by the vigorous and effective outreach strategies of bodies such as the Fife Joint Committee.

In the post war years the social context in which BHMS workers were serving had changed significantly as a result of many former service personnel returning home 'with new ideas and large expectations'. Although there were some young people more open to discuss with them about the Christian faith, others had 'a profound indifference to spiritual things which is difficult to combat and remove. The new heaven and new earth are being sought for in an improvement in material surroundings and in the quest for pleasure and amusement.'[35] However, the picture was not all bleak as the vast majority of church members returned safely after the 1914-1918 war. The regular church activities were resumed or strengthened by returning personnel and the offerings in the Mission Churches were increasing attaining a record high in 1926, which was necessary as the General Strike in England had 'interfered with the (BHMS) Travelling Agents' visitation there' and resulting in much smaller financial donations for home evangelisation work in Scotland. It was also encouraging that there were four Gaelic-speaking students in training for pastoral ministry in the Western Highlands and Islands where congregations required a minister who could preach in their native language.[36] Scottish Baptist Evangelist Thomas McQuiston noted that: 'the year 1926 has been one of the most fruitful in the history of our evangelistic enterprise' with reports of conversions in missions in the following Baptist churches: George Square and Orangefield, Greenock; Gourock, Port Glasgow, Helensburgh, Millport, Dunoon and Johnstone. Hermon Baptist Church, Glasgow, which had suffered a serious loss of members to other causes, regained its previous numerical strength after a six week mission.[37] Even though it had been a successful year in Scottish Baptist home mission, key leaders in the Baptist Union were of the opinion that even more effective work could be carried out by the merger of the BHMS with the Union's Church Extension and Evangelism Committee. At a time of sustained growth, not decline, the Union and the BHMS entered negotiations to discuss their future partnership in mission in Scotland.[38]

---

[34] S. Henry, 'Scottish Baptists and the First World War', *Baptist Quarterly*, 31 (April 1985), pp. 63-64.
[35] 'Report of the Baptist Home Missionary Society for Scotland 1919', *SBY* (Glasgow: John Cossar, 1920), p. 8.
[36] 'Report of the Baptist Home Missionary Society for Scotland 1926', *SBY* (Glasgow: Baptist Union of Scotland, 1927), pp. 6-7.
[37] T.A. McQuiston, 'The Evangelist's Report for 1926', *SBY 1927*, pp. 142-43. Similar sentiments were expressed in the 1929 Evangelistic Committee report, *SBY 1930*, p. 119.
[38] 'Report of the Baptist Home Missionary Society for Scotland 1926', p. 7; 'Home Mission' in the Sustentation Executive Report, 31 May 1926, 'Baptist Union of Scotland Minute Book 1926-1931, pp. 17-18.

The initial response of the BHMS in October 1927 to the merger proposals from the Union was a negative one, although the door to further discussions was not closed. In any case the home mission was dependent on a significant degree of financial support from the Sustentation Fund of the Baptist Union; the substantial sum of £747 had been given in that financial year alone.[39] The case for amalgamating the two bodies was strong. By 1928 of the forty-eight members of the Home Mission committee no fewer than forty-five served on the Baptist Union Council. The pastors of the aided Home Mission Stations required Union recognition and could be eligible for the Union Provident Fund. Also the long summer missionary tours had all but ceased and BHMS workers increasingly had pastoral ministries in a settled location like Baptist colleagues in the lowlands. Opposition to the merger was not due to disagreement with the above facts rather it was a concern that work in the smaller more remote communities would take a lesser priority than had been the case for the previous century of BHMS work.[40] Thomas Stewart, secretary of the Baptist Union, frustrated by the delay in considering these issues sent a stronger letter to the BHMS annual meeting in October 1928. He wished them to appoint representatives to meet with a group convened by the annual Assembly of the Union to discuss the merger of the two bodies, the position of the BHMS with respect to Union funding and 'to do this without delay so as to bring definite proposals on these matters before the Annual Meetings next year'. The home mission accepted these proposals and appointed representatives for the negotiations.[41] The catalyst for the Union proposals had been the reflection upon the Scottish Churches' Council report on the general religious situation in Scotland at the October 1927 Baptist Union Assembly. Those present agreed to set up a Commission of Enquiry with a wide-ranging remit to look at every aspect of outreach work in Baptist churches over the last seven years; to consider the detailed statistical returns submitted by the churches; to draw attention to places in towns and cities where Church Extension may be possible; to consider the present distribution of resources in workers and finance, in relation to population and need; to cover existing work in agricultural districts exploring whether itinerant evangelists might be better suited to ministry in those areas, together with a smaller number of settled pastors in those rural locations; and how Baptists could join with other Evangelical Churches in

---

[39] 'Report of the Baptist Home Missionary Society for Scotland 1927', *SBY 1928*, p. 7.

[40] 'Report of the Joint Committee appointed by the Assembly of the Baptist Union of Scotland and the Annual Meeting of the Baptist Home Missionary Society for Scotland', *SBY 1929*, p. 2 [of this Report]. D.B. Murray, *The First Hundred Years The Baptist Union of Scotland 1869-1969* (Glasgow: Baptist Union of Scotland, 1969), pp. 83-85.

[41] 'Report of the Baptist Home Missionary Society for Scotland 1928', *SBY 1929*, pp. 4-5.

extending the Christian faith in Scotland.[42] This was an extremely thorough study which revealed some clear patterns on which action needed to be taken.

In the period 1920 to 1927 Baptist Churches in Scotland had grown numerically by 5% on average, but Home Mission Churches decreased in size by the same percentage. Sunday School attendance in Baptist Churches grew by 3% in this time period, however Home Church Sunday Schools saw a fall of 15% in the number of scholars. This particular figure though corresponded with other data from the Highlands which indicated that significant numbers of younger people were leaving the Highlands in the 1920s, according to this Baptist Commission Report. Another part of the study covered financial investment in home mission work. In that seven year period the Baptist Union had invested over £20,000 in grants to the churches, of which approximately £13,438 had gone to Union Churches and £6,874 to Home Mission ones. However, the BHMS had also made grants to each of the churches under its care of just over £8,000. Home Mission congregations per annum were receiving nearly £15,000 in total. The Commission also found that the cost of living in the 1920s was 'decidedly lower' in the Highlands and Islands of Scotland. They also pointed to the need for fairness in distributing resources to the churches in proportion to the population they sough to reach with the Christian Gospel. In this connection they drew attention to the face that of the twenty-one Baptist Churches in areas with a population of less than 2,000 people, seventeen were Home Mission supported causes. It was also reported that eleven of the aided churches under the auspices of the Baptist Union, in urban areas in lowland Scotland, became wholly self-supporting during these years and recorded an increase in membership of 1012, proving the soundness of this investment, whereas the potential for numerical growth in the areas where Home Mission causes were located was extremely limited.[43] In Appendix D the report considered the needs and possibilities for church extension in the larger towns and cities.

> While not overlooking the needs and claims of the smaller towns, we are of the opinion that Church Extension should follow the movements of the population in our large cities, keeping in view the various town-planning schemes in progress and in prospect at the present time.[44]

The authors of the report named Barrhead, Montrose, Musselburgh, Saltcoats and Stevenston as five examples of towns with a population of over 10,000 people but without a Baptist Church. In this section of the study there is the clearest declaration that Scottish Baptist Home Mission ought to place a far greater priority on work in the larger urban areas. It was noted that the Church

---

[42] 'Report of Commission of Enquiry 1927-1929', *SBY 1930*, p. 1 [of this Report].
[43] 'Report of Commission of Enquiry 1927-1929', pp. 15-20.
[44] 'Report of Commission of Enquiry 1927-1929', p. 20.

of Scotland, the United Free Church, Congregationalists and the Brethren all had extensive work going on in rural areas of Scotland, in addition to the work of independent agencies such as the Faith Mission and the West Coast Mission in the 1920s[45]. If the Baptists reduced their financial input in evangelism in rural locations where all these other churches were active it might make little difference. However, there were too many larger urban centres in Scotland that had a shortage of Christian churches and ministers. It was time for more creative approaches to ministry in the countryside. Possibly the Methodist approach of joining churches in a circuit with one minister and a team of lay-preachers might be the key. In conclusion it stated the Baptist Union needed to streamline its management of home mission work by bringing all the committees dealing with it into the Baptist Union and directly responsible to the annual assembly.[46]

The Joint Committee of members from the Baptist Union and Home Mission that met in Glasgow in October 1929 unanimously recommended the union of the two bodies from the Baptist Union Assembly meetings in October 1930. Their report highlighted a number of issues. It was clear that there was no longer a clear geographical boundary separating their spheres of operations, both organisations were engaged in similar work around the country which led to an ineffective bureaucratic structure for communication with two sets of officials duplicating each others efforts. Pastors of former Home Mission charges who had become unemployed had been ineligible for assistance from the Baptist Union. This was something that had to be addressed by Scottish Baptists. The dual system of financing work was ineffective. The Joint Committee claimed that a merger was likely to result in an increase in funds to aided causes, as happened when the three Scottish Baptist home mission agencies had merged in 1827.[47] Although the figures from the financial year 1931 to 1932 did not support their expectations as donations from Scottish churches and individuals for the BHMS actually fell though English subscriptions increased slightly.[48] It is unknown but possible that the explanation for the Scottish figures was due to confusion over whether the Baptist Union of Scotland was obtaining funds from other sources to fund some of the home mission work. The Joint Committee were also convinced that there was no major legal obstacle to transferring ownership of BHMS properties to

---

[45] 'Report of Commission of Enquiry 1927-1929', p. 23. Information on the work of the interdenominational West Coast Mission can be found in F.D. Bardgett, *Devoted Service Rendered* (Edinburgh: St Andrews Press, 2002), pp, 191-99

[46] 'Report of Commission of Enquiry 1927-1929', pp. 20-22.

[47] B.R. Talbot, *Search for a Common Identity The Origins of the Baptist Union of Scotland 1800-1870* (Carlisle: Paternoster Press, 2003), pp. 161-65.

[48] 'Report of the Baptist Home Missionary Society for Scotland 1931-32', *SBY 1932*, p. 10 [of the Report].

the Baptist Union.[49] On all but the latter legal point their arguments were broadly accepted. The outstanding legal issues were resolved through the assistance of Mr J Robertson Christie K.C., an eminent authority on legal ecclesiastical issues.[50] The date of completion of the merger was 21 October 1931.[51] One chapter in Scottish Baptist Home Mission had come to an end, but equally a new one was beginning with expectations of greater evangelistic advances to come.

### Home Mission work directed by the Baptist Union 1931-1971

Fears on the part of some BHMS supporters that the Union might show less enthusiasm for mission in more remote parts of the country was seen to be misplaced in the 1930s. Following the amalgamation of the two bodies there were a series of outreach initiatives developed in those years. The Evangelistic Committee of the Union proposed that a campaign be held in every Baptist church over the winter of 1932-33. Beginning with an intensive two week mission shortly after the October 1932 Annual Assembly each local church was asked to form a Prayer Fellowship for Revival with at least one week-night service per month set apart for prayer for this purpose in the church. In addition it was suggested that home groups and family networks should also focus on this theme. Regional Associations should have quarterly conferences with speakers preaching on evangelism or revival or related themes. Each local church and association was asked to arrange services of dedication for this work. The slogan for the mission was 'Every Member a Missionary'; words taken from the motto of Gerhard Oncken, the famous German Baptist leader of the nineteenth century. In addition each church was asked to issue a quarterly four pages bulletin setting out the aims, plans and progress of this initiative and each minister in the denomination had been invited to a conference on 'the work of soul-wining' in May 1933.[52] This appeal was heeded by Scottish Baptists as almost 'all our churches are making plans for aggressive evangelistic effort'.[53] No less than five hundred conversions, for example, were reported in 1933 following three missions in the churches at Irvine, Wishaw and Tiree.[54] Former BHMS churches had also risen to the challenge. A report on the work in the Western Highlands by BHMS travelling secretary James Reid in the summer of

---

[49] 'Report of the Joint Committee', 2 October 1929, pp. 5-6.
[50] 'Home Mission – Report of Joint Commission', *SBY 1931*, pp. 118-20, 187-88; 'Report of the Baptist Home Missionary Society for Scotland 1930-31', *SBY 1931*, pp. 5-16 [of the Report].
[51] 'Report of the Baptist Home Missionary Society for Scotland 1931-32', *SBY 1932*, pp. 4-5.
[52] 'Proposed Evangelistic Campaign', *SBY 1932*, pp. 131-32.
[53] 'Evangelistic Committee', *SBY 1933*, p. 166.
[54] 'Evangelistic Committee', *SBY 1934*, p. 166.

1932 declared: 'to call my visit a pleasure would be putting it mildly. It was infinitely more than a pleasure it was an inspiration! ...to see such crowded meetings and to hear of conversions taking place and baptisms following,' though it was also reported that 'in several places the fishing industry has failed, markets have collapsed and the value of live stock has depreciated'.[55] The year, 1932, had been a transition not only for the BHMS but also for the Evangelistic Committee because its convener for the past five years, Baptist minister John Shearer, retired from its work on health grounds. In addition the Union Evangelist Thomas McQuiston also stepped down from his post as Baptist Union Evangelist in order to accept the pastorate of Cambridge Street Baptist Church, Glasgow.[56] The new era for home mission work in Scotland had begun with great expectations of further spiritual and numerical growth in Baptist ranks.

The outreach work of the denomination was aided by a variety of means in addition to the work of its ordained ministers. In 1934, for example, the Baptist Theological College of Scotland (now the Scottish Baptist College) students conducted missions in Victoria Place and John Street Baptist Churches in Glasgow and led a beach mission at Portobello, Edinburgh, for the whole of July 1937[57]. A different type of contribution was made in 1934 through the influence of the Oxford Group Movement. 'Several of our ministers and churches testify to a quickening of life and enduement of power with the Holy Spirit as a direct result of contact with the movement'.[58] A surprising number of financial donations for the work of Baptist home mission came from individuals in membership with other Christian churches in Scotland. Financial gifts from English Baptist churches were also encouraging to the travelling secretary of the home mission whose deputation work in 1936 to foster this support took him as far south as Southampton and included conducting a mission and a baptismal service for sixteen candidates in a Baptist Church in Nottingham.[59] A number of Scottish Baptist churches adopted the Scottish Churches' Council plan for simultaneous national evangelism that consisted of dedication, visitation, campaigning and shepherding, a scheme heartily commended by the Evangelistic Committee of the Union.[60] This Committee was also proposing to inaugurate a denominational outreach campaign 'immediately on the conclusion of the Simultaneous Campaign'.[61] In 1941 Scottish Baptists adopted a five-year

---

[55] 'Baptist Home Missionary Society for Scotland Annual Report 1932-33', *SBY 1933*, p. 182.
[56] 'Evangelistic Committee', *SBY 1932*, pp. 158-59.
[57] 'Evangelistic Committee Annual Report', *SBY 1935*, p. 177; 'Evangelistic Committee', *SBY 1938*, p. 174.
[58] 'Evangelistic Committee Annual Report', *SBY 1935*, p. 177.
[59] James Reid, 'Travelling Secretary's Report', *SBY 1937*, pp. 225-26.
[60] *SBY 1937*, pp. 119, 171.
[61] 'Evangelistic Committee', *SBY 1938*, p. 174.

programme entitled 'Every Member an Evangelist' that had been recommended to the Baptist family at the Baptist World Congress in Atlanta in 1939. It involved one year of preparation, a second for deepening spiritual life, a third for evangelism amongst young people, a fourth for mission in the wider community and fifth a mission to the world.[62] However, all the success in outreach initiatives was overshadowed by a gradual decrease in subscriptions to home mission work by Scottish Baptist Churches since the merger of the BHMS with the Baptist Union. As a result of expenditure greatly exceeding income James Reid had to step down as travelling secretary in 1937 with no-one appointed to take his place.[63] The advent of World War Two in 1939 also increased the challenges faced by the churches. Although only six Baptist Church buildings were damaged by German air-raids, the loss of 3,000 younger members serving in the forces[64] and a reduction of financial resources available led to the five year programme having less impact than might otherwise have been the case.[65] Overall Baptist membership figures increased to a high of 23,310 in 1935, but had declined to 21,121 by 1945. This figure was no surprise when baptismal statistics were compared from the 1920s to 1940s. In 1922 there had been 1444 believers' baptisms in Union causes, a total reduced to 570 per annum in 1939 and merely 375 in 1941. An increase to 519 baptisms in 1945[66] could not hide the underlying difficulties that Scottish Baptists would face in their outreach work in the second half of the twentieth century. Enthusiastic and creative mission initiatives had undoubtedly brought some successes but the spiritual climate in Scotland was less favourable to Christian witness than it had been earlier in the century.

The vision for further advances of the Baptist witness in Scotland was in evidence in the creation of the Church Extension Committee in 1948. Its remit was to survey the new areas of population in Scotland with a view to ascertaining the potential for evangelistic work and the planting of new Baptist congregations. The churches at Ayr and New Cumnock had sought sites for new causes within their towns; the Paisley Baptist churches had secured a site in the Glenburn district; the Glasgow Association had similarly obtained sites at Househillwood and Cranhill. Fife Baptist Association had applied for one in Glenrothes and the Baptist Union of Scotland likewise in the new town of East

---

[62] *SBY 1941*, p. 149; 1943, p. 70; 1944, p. 70.

[63] 'Annual Report of the Home Missionary Society', *SBY 1938*, p. 228.

[64] I. Balfour, 'The Twentieth Century since 1914' in D.W. Bebbington (ed.), *The Baptists in Scotland: A History* (Glasgow: Baptist Union of Scotland, 1988), p. 68; B.R. Talbot, *A Brief History of Central Baptist Association* (Glasgow: Baptist Union of Scotland, 2002), pp. 16-18; 'Annual Report', *SBY 1943*, p. 99.

[65] *SBY 1944*, p. 70; 1945, p. 70.

[66] Appendix 2: Table of Annual Statistics, in D. Hunt, *Reflections on Our Past A Statistical Look at Baptists in Scotland 1892-1997* (Hamilton: Hamilton Baptist Church, 1997), n.p.

Kilbride.[67] The Baptist Advance Campaign of 1951-52 included an action plan of the Stirling and Clackmananshire Baptist Association, led by its ministers for a year of retreats, prayer gatherings and sustained evangelistic effort in the churches from 4 November to 2 December 1952.[68] The Home Mission brought in 'Work Camps' for young people in 1952 at Tobermory and Bunessan on Mull, that combined a holiday on an island with social action that enhanced the mission work of these two local congregations.[69] Scottish Baptists were also committed to interdenominational outreach initiatives. Between 1947 and 1956 there were a series of major evangelistic campaigns led mainly by Church of Scotland ministers such as D.P. Thomson and Tom Allan entitled 'Christian Commandos' from 1947-1950;[70] the 'Tell Scotland' movement in 1952, though its activities continued until 1964;[71] and the 'All Scotland Crusade' with Billy Graham in 1955. A new form of co-operative outreach in this era were the 'Radio Missions' of 1950-52 that initiated team evangelism that was to lead to the invitation to Southern Baptist Evangelist Billy Graham for a six week crusade around Easter 1955.[72] Scottish Baptist membership figures rose from 19,263 in 1954 to 20,133 in 1955 and reached a post-war peak of 20,340 in 1956, although from 1958 the rate of decline returned to that seen in the period 1935-1954.[73] Apparently the Graham Crusade had little impact on around 70% of Church of Scotland congregations, but that may not have been surprising when so many of its clergy were opposed to that mission.[74] By contrast it had the most significant impact of any evangelistic initiative on Scottish Baptist statistics in the second half of the twentieth century.

The momentum gained by the impact of the Graham led mission in Glasgow encouraged 120 churches to join in a three year Crusade of Visitation Evangelism between 1956 and 1959.[75] These churches gained eighty new members, 112 new adherents and 506 additional children in their Sunday

---

[67] 'Church Extension', *SBY 1950*, p. 137.

[68] This initiative featured in the English periodical *The Baptist Times*, 24 January 1952, p. 1; B.R. Talbot, *Brief History of Central Baptist Association*, p. 24.

[69] 'Annual Report of the Home Missionary Society', *SBY 1953*, p. 166.

[70] *SBY 1951*, p. 136.

[71] J. Highet, *The Scottish Churches* (London: Skeffington & Son, 1960), pp. 86-87. See also D.P. Thomson, *Visitation Evangelism in Scotland 1946-1956* (Publisher Unknown, 1956). A recent thorough study of this movement is F.D. Bargett, 'The Tell Scotland Movement', *Records of the Scottish Church History Society*, Vol. 38, 2008, pp. 105-50.

[72] 'Evangelistic', *SBY 1951*, p. 136; 1952, p. 148. C.G. Brown, *Religion and Society in Scotland since 1707* (Edinburgh: Edinburgh University Press, 1997), p. 163.

[73] B. Graham, *Just As I Am* (London: Harper Collins, 1998), p. 253, for details of Graham Crusade statistics. Scottish Baptist data from Hunt, *Reflecting on Our Past*, p. 6.

[74] Brown, *Religion and Society in Scotland since 1707*, pp. 163-64.

[75] 'Evangelistic', *SBY 1959*, p. 160; 1960, p. 159.

Schools.[76] This venture was considered so successful, especially in the new congregations planted in Glenrothes and East Kilbride, that it was repeated between 1960 and 1962.[77] Another innovative approach to evangelism was an American led mission planned for February 1959 when seventy ministers and lay-people from the Southern Baptist Convention came to Britain, of which twelve came to Scottish Baptist churches. Eighty four people professed faith in Christ in missions in Greenock, Motherwell, Dundee, Fraserburgh, Ayr and Glasgow.[78] Other mission efforts that emerged in Baptist churches in the late 1950s included Youth rallies, mainly held on Saturday evenings that were a mixture of evangelism, fellowship, inspiration and teaching for young people.[79] The drive to launch new evangelistic initiatives did not slow down in the 1960s. In 1963 the 'Call to Mission' was launched[80] followed by 'Evangelism in Depth, Think Again', and 'One Step Forward', with 1,000 Baptists from 115 churches attending a conference on evangelism in 1968.[81] It was no surprise that 1969 the centenary year of the Baptist Union was marked by some special outreach ventures. On that occasion around a hundred churches committed themselves to 'Simultaneous Evangelism', a three-year programme of preparation, proclamation and preservation.[82] This initiative was a success with at least 206 conversions, together with ninety-four applications for baptism and/or membership from the forty-seven churches that reported their statistics to the Baptist Union.[83] The blessings gained from this initiative gave a new sense of unity and purpose in Scottish Baptist ranks.[84] It was no surprise that at a time when overall church attendances were falling rapidly in Scotland, in the late 1950s and 1960s, that Scottish Baptists managed to maintain or extend their work in a number of areas of Scotland.[85] Although the decline in church-going must be put in a wider social context, there was an equally steep decline in numbers in cinema audiences, dance hall attendances and in spectators at football league matches as well as commitment to a variety of voluntary organisations.[86]

Church Extension was increasingly the focus of Scottish Baptist outreach in the 1960s. The new causes at Bathgate; Broxburn; Downfield, Dundee; East

---

[76] 'Evangelistic', *SBY 1960*, p. 159.
[77] 'Evangelistic', *SBY 1960*, p. 159; 1961, p. 161; 1963, p. 166.
[78] 'Evangelistic', *SBY 1959*, p. 161; 1960, p. 159.
[79] Balfour, 'Twentieth Century since 1914', p. 71.
[80] 'Evangelistic', *SBY 1963*, p. 166; 1964, p. 166; 1965, p. 169.
[81] 'Evangelistic Committee', *SBY 1969*, pp. 36-37.
[82] *SBY 1969*, p. 58; 1970, p. 16.
[83] 'Evangelistic Committee', *SBY 1971*, p. 35.
[84] *SBY 1971*, p. 15.
[85] Central Baptist Association churches, for example, sustained steady growth in numbers from 840 members in 1952 to a peak of 1,053 members in 1970. Talbot, *Brief History of Central Baptist Association*, p. 22.
[86] Brown, *Religion and Society in Scotland*, pp. 166-69.

Kilbride; Glenburn, Paisley; Glenrothes; Granton, Edinburgh; and Pollok, Glasgow, had become established with steady growth, though the East Kilbride church had seen remarkable growth to attain a membership of 242. The most recent church-plants in Cumbernauld, Drumchapel and Easterhouse in Glasgow had also seen very encouraging increases in the numbers committed to their cause.[87] The Home Mission work continued faithfully with an encouraging new work at Forfar supported by Dundee Baptists, though sadness on Mull at the closure of the Tobermory Church and the subsequent sale of its building. Twelve ministers were serving in Home Mission charges in 1964. Bunessan, Mull, was struggling to remain open with a monthly service for the faithful few led by the minister from Oban. Eday and Sanday Churches in Orkney held only occasional services. However, Dunrossness, Shetland, had been greatly encouraged by a mission in November 1964 in which numbers rose at services for a time from 60 to 200 with six young people professing faith in Christ. Another encouragement was Buckie Baptist Church which had continued to grow with over 200 children in the Sunday School. An innovative outreach amongst younger people in September 1964 led by thirteen Inter-Varsity Fellowship Students led them into cafes and dance halls in Buckie, including a significant time spent 'in interesting discussions with many teddy boys, of which only eternity will reveal the results'.[88] The momentum for Baptist home mission work in Scotland over the first hundred years of the Baptist Union had increasingly led to a greater concentration of resources on the larger more populated districts of central Scotland. It was in these locations that the most promising opportunities for effective evangelisation and church extension were to be found.

## Home Mission from 1971-2000

The changing context for home mission in Scotland took a new form for Baptists with a decision to merge the Home Missionary Society with the Church Extension committee in 1971. Edward Campbell, in his 1971 Home Mission report, acknowledged that for the first 115 years of the society's work 'men and stations had a remoteness that no longer exists'. He also drew attention to the continuing depopulation of the more isolated rural communities as he recognised that greater attention was required to be focussed on more urban communities, although he urged that the small faithful Highland and Island churches should not be forgotten.[89] The newly formed 'Home Mission and Extension Committee' commenced its work in 1973 with encouraging reports from an evangelistic campaign amongst the Islay Baptist Churches and the

---

[87] 'Church Extension', *SBY 1965*, pp. 167-68.
[88] 'Annual Report of the Home Missionary Society', *SBY 1965*, pp. 182-89.
[89] 'Home Mission Committee', *SBY 1972*, pp. 35-36.

emergence of the newly formed causes at Erskine and Bearsden, Glasgow.[90] In 1973 the Evangelism Committee sought to promote a lay evangelism programme called WIN Schools - Witness, Involvement, Now. Andrew MacRae, General Secretary of the Baptist Union had taken part in a WIN School event in the USA in the summer of 1973. The approach to lay-witness was launched in Scotland in February 1973 at a conference in Granton Baptist Church, with a similar venture taking place in East Kilbride in November 1973.[91] After three WIN gatherings in the following year, interest in this form of training for evangelism peaked in 1975 with WIN Schools taking place in Arbroath, Carluke, Cumbernauld, Falkirk and Wishaw. New causes at Craigmiller in Edinburgh led by Harry Sprange; at Bishopbriggs, Glasgow, by David Black; Castlemilk, Glasgow by Ian Paterson; Bearsden by Gilbert Ritchie; and Alness near Inverness led by Bill Clark; all showed encouraging signs of progress in 1975. In 1977 as a result of participating in the WIN School initiative several congregations saw spectacular growth. The small church at Linwood had grown by 50% in a year; together with a 35% growth in East Kilbride, 40% in Brechin; Bank Street, Irvine by 12%; Morningside, Edinburgh by 17%; Bearsden by 34% and the Bishopbriggs Church by 68%. A further twelve congregations had exceeded the target of 10% growth in one year.[92] Although some churches had a disappointing response there were enough churches with very significant progress to enable this outreach initiative to be described as a great success in Scottish Baptist ranks.

Andrew MacRae, though, was not satisfied with the amount of Church Extension activity taking place. He noted in his 'Home Mission and Extension Committee' report that: 'new trends in Baptist witness can now be clearly observed in some areas and that by far the biggest problem is the lack of committed people.'[93] As an attempt to make further progress he had initiated discussions with the leadership of the Foreign Mission Board of the Southern Baptist Convention and subsequently met them at their headquarters in Richmond, Virginia in early 1977. It was agreed that a Southern Baptist minister would work with Scottish Baptists in the area of Church Planning and Church Growth with an option for another full-time minister to plant a cause in an 'oil-related area with considerable numbers of American personnel'. In addition some Scottish ministers would be given the opportunity to visit the USA to study American Baptist approaches to a variety of subjects including Church Growth. Dr J.D. Hughey secretary for Europe and Board President Dr Baker Cauthen were invited as guests to the 1977 Annual Assembly in Scotland.[94] Twenty-nine Scottish Baptist ministers, for example, spent time in

---

[90] 'Home Mission and Extension Committee', *SBY 1974*, p. 41.
[91] 'Evangelistic Committee, *SBY 1974*, p. 41. See also 1975, p. 40.
[92] *SBY 1978*, p. 17.
[93] 'Home Mission and Extension Committee', *SBY 1976*, p. 41.
[94] 'Home Mission and Extension Committee', *SBY 1977*, pp. 18-19.

the USA with American colleagues for a month in March and April 1979, and Americans in pastorates in Brechin and the Cults area of Aberdeen, together with other mission personnel from the USA serving for short-terms with Scottish Baptist congregations.[95] The creative and energetic Andrew MacRae ensured that Scottish Baptists had little time for complacency during his term as General Secretary of the Baptist Union between 1966 and 1980. The involvement of American Southern Baptists with the Scottish Union was a great success and led to effective work in church-planting and evangelism in Scotland and was a source of significant encouragement to Scottish Baptists.

The new enthusiasm for working with American Baptists had not lessened the commitment to engagement in mission with other Scottish Churches. Andrew MacRae as chair of the Mission, Development and Unity Committee of the Scottish Churches Council, had persuaded that body in 1977 to promote a three-year scheme entitled the 'National Initiative in Evangelism' for implementing effective forms of evangelism in the various Scottish Christian denominations by January 1978. The project began in the autumn of that year with 'Preparation including Re-appraisal and renewal'. The theme for the second year was Training 'not only in content but in the articulation of their faith verbally and through Christian lifestyle.' The culmination of these two years was to be followed by 'every possible kind of co-operative outreach' amongst churches in local, regional or national settings during 1980.[96] The 1980s had been a period of growth for Scottish Baptists, a unique phenomenon amongst the major Christian traditions in Scotland, as no other denomination that had experienced membership decline in the twentieth century had been able to reverse that trend. It was suggested that standing firm on orthodox doctrine, modernising forms of worship and engaging in outreach to younger people had been the key factors for the Baptist successes.[97] In 1980 there had been definite signs of Baptist advance in Scotland. The Bourtreehill Baptist Church was constituted at Irvine; the Alness cause likewise in the Highlands and a replanted congregation established under Brian Jago in Bo'ness. Noel Kirkman was leading a growing new church in Dalbeattie, near Dumfries and pioneer ministries were being planned for the Bridge of Don area of Aberdeen; the Whitfield estate in Dundee, together with the early stages of church-plants in

---

[95] *SBY 1976*, p. 49; 1977, p. 44; 1978, pp. 18-19, 50; 1979, p. 19; 1980, pp. 16, 19, 69, 91.

[96] 'Doctrine and Inter-Church Relations Committee', *SBY 1978*, p. 46. 1979, pp. 22, 47, 103-104.

[97] Brown, *Religion and Society in Scotland since 1707*, pp. 158-61. Undoubtedly some congregations grew as a result of participation in the charismatic renewal movement, though it is not easy to quantify its overall impact in numerical terms. I am grateful to Harry Sprange for drawing my attention to this point at the Scottish Baptist History Project, in Glasgow on 15 November 2008.

Kinross, Beith, Bridge of Don and Inverurie.[98] The most influential factor for this renewal of Baptist churches was the adoption of a three-year Simultaneous Evangelism Crusade, known as the 'Scotreach' programme in 1983, in which 144 Baptist congregations joined in three years of preparation, mobilisation and consolidation. This figure is substantially higher than the 100 churches that participated in the 1969 Simultaneous Evangelism Crusade. In fact the ownership of this mission by Scottish Baptists was greater than any previous mission since the Graham Crusade of 1955. The comprehensiveness of the planning for this initiative was crucial. There were prayer triplet schemes set up; thirty-three ministers were trained to lead church day conferences in Worship, Fellowship and Stewardship; a Scotreach newspaper produced that sold over 135,000 copies; regional rallies to promote the vision during the time of the programme; a range of publicity materials from car stickers to tee-shirts, sweatshirts, calendars, stickers and posters; local churches were required to have evangelism committees that had the task of keeping the Scotreach vision before each local church. The range of outreach events varied from big rallies to house meetings, the use of films to partnership missions with American Baptist teams and friendship evangelism over meals for invited guests. The recorded conversions took place overwhelmingly in local church events rather than at large rallies, which indicated that the effectiveness of the large-scale Crusades was being called into question.[99] When the statistics for the 1980s are compared with previous years in the Baptist Union's history it is clear that this programme was more effective than any other Scottish Baptist initiative since the early years of the twentieth century. For a healthy church to maintain its position and to replace members who died or left for a variety of reasons there is a requirement for a minimum reproduction rate of 4% of the membership total. Scottish Baptists exceeded this percentage for baptisms throughout the 1980s until 1991 with the highest figures recorded in 1986 and 1987, 5.68 and 5.59% respectively, as a result of Scotreach.[100] These impressive results were not exclusively down to the impact of Scotreach as there was a measurably significant impact on Scottish Baptist churches by the 1981 Luis Palau Glasgow Crusade, the 1989 Billy Graham Livelink Mission and his three-city 1991 Mission Scotland.[101] However, the length of impact of Scotreach was greater even than the 1955 Graham Crusade and it provided great encouragement for Scottish Baptists as they entered the last decade of the twentieth century

---

[98] *SBY 1980*, pp. 16, 18.
[99] *SBY 1983*, pp. 28, 49, 94; 1984, pp. 65-67; 1985, pp. 55-56; 1986, pp. 54-55; 1987, pp. 58-59.
[100] Hunt, 'Figure 16 Membership and Reproduction Rate', *Reflecting on Our Past*, pp. 32, Appendix 2, n.p.
[101] Hunt, *Reflecting on Our Past*, pp. 18, 34.

because not since the 1920s had there been such a consistent advance of the cause.[102]

At the start of the 1990s there had been encouraging developments in many churches such as the new Wigtown Church being able to call its first Scottish Baptist pastor and the Tiree cause its first full-time pastor for several years. New initiatives at Kinmylies and Nairn near Inverness were making good progress. The Castlehill church-plant in Bearden was constituted as an autonomous church. A denominational conference 'Toward 2000 –Scottish Baptists renewed for mission' was held in June 1990 in Stirling University.[103] 'There is Hope', an Edinburgh based interdenominational outreach initiative was taken up by churches, including Baptist ones in a number of towns in Scotland during this decade. In 1990 ten Baptist churches shared in Partnership missions with visiting teams of Southern Baptists from the USA. The Baptist Union mission fieldworker David Neil along with other Baptist ministers was exploring new ways of engaging in urban mission. He also began conversations with Operation Mobilisation and Youth with a Mission, two Christian parachurch organisations to explore the possibility of working together in evangelism in Scotland.[104] However, the momentum of the previous decade had gone by the mid-1990s. Interest in Partnership missions had diminished significantly.[105] The 'Minus to Plus' campaign of Reinhard Bonke in 1994 had produced hardly any conversions, despite the inflated expectations of its promoter and there was little interest shown by

Scottish Baptists in the 'Disciple a Whole Nation (DAWN) 2000' interdenominational church-planting initiative that same year.[106] The 1995 Evangelism and Church Extension Committee report was deeply discouraging as they could not find anyone willing to take the chair and as a group requested help to bring 'clarification of their remit'. It was significant that no report from the group was forthcoming in 1997.[107] However in that same year a Mission Strategy group had been formed with three sub-groups namely 'Urban Strategy', 'Small Towns and Rural Strategy' and 'Highlands and Islands Strategy' that were engaged in a coherent plan to regain momentum in the work of home evangelisation. The Urban Strategy Group met under the leadership of Graeme Clark in May and June 1997 and cast a vision that included: aiding existing urban causes and developing new concepts of ministry; sharing good models of growth and effective ministry; and encouraging the development of a

---

[102] Hunt, 'Figure 16 Membership and Reproduction Rate', *Reflecting on Our Past*, p. 32.
[103] *SBY 1990*, pp. 97-98.
[104] 'Department of Mission', *SBY 1991*, pp. 118-19; 1992, p. 122; 1993, p. 142.
[105] 'Mission Department', *SBY 1992*, p. 122.
[106] 'Evangelism and Church Extension Committee' *SBY* 1995, pp. 147-49.
[107] 'Evangelism and Church Extension Committee', *SBY 1996*, pp. 142-43.

course in urban theology and mission at the Scottish Baptist College.[108] The Small Towns and Rural Strategy Group was chaired by Bill Slack. Their first meeting was in May 1997. Although this body gave some attention to existing causes in these locations, its primary remit appeared to focus on identifying population centres without an evangelical witness and encouraging people in a nearby congregation to take ownership of the vision for a new church in their district.[109] The Highlands and Islands Strategy Group had met as early as May 1996 under the convenership of John Barclay. Its first meeting defined the parameters for a sabbatical study by Peter Williams, minister of Tiree Baptist Church, under the title 'Strategy for the 21$^{st}$ Century Ministry and Mission in the Highlands and Islands of Scotland'.[110] The group met to consider that study in June 1997 and later made recommendations to the Union Office-bearers concerning the appointment of Peter Williams one week per month. His remit included formulating a new strategy for the churches in the Argyll area with particular reference to Islay and Mull; seeking to encourage and support pastoral workers in remote locations; exploring the possibilities for new work in Skye, Lochalsh and/or Western Ross; together with supporting the new church plant at Brae in Shetland, in partnership with the Shetland Association.[111] 'Step Out' mission teams of young people leading several weeks of children's and youth outreach events each summer, led by the dynamic Director of Mission and Evangelism Robert Breustedt, were seeing significant growth amongst younger people in several Scottish Baptist churches in the late 1990s.[112] Baptist Union membership statistics for the 1990s, though, showed a slow but steady decline[113] and an apparent lack of confidence in the effectiveness of outreach initiatives on the part of many in the ranks could not be disguised by the busyness of its constituent congregations. However by the late 1990s a new approach to outreach involving small group Bible studies in the context of shared meals lifted morale and in the twenty-first century it was recognised as an effective tool for mission. The most popular expressions of this form of witness were called 'Alpha' and 'Christianity Explored'. A willingness to be creative in home evangelism had enabled Scottish Baptists to grow steadily in numbers for the first third of the century and to maintain its position in the 1960s long after major decline had set in within some other Christian denominations. This approach resulted in significant growth in its ranks in the 1980s. The difficulties of the 1990s were a serious problem, but not an insurmountable one for the Baptist churches in Scotland.

---

[108] Graeme Clark, 'Urban Strategy Group', *SBY 1998*, pp. 177-78.
[109] Sandy Greig, 'Small Towns and Rural Strategy Group', *SBY 1998*, pp. 173-74.
[110] Peter Williams, 'Highlands and Islands Strategy Group', *SBY 1998*, pp. 152-53.
[111] Peter Williams, 'Highlands and Islands Strategy Group', *SBY 2000*, pp. 165-67.
[112] 'Mission and Evangelism' and 'Mission Strategy', *SBY 2000*, pp. 176-81.
[113] Hunt, *Reflecting on Our Past,* 'Figure 13', p. 30 and Appendix 2, n.p.

CHAPTER 10

## *Be Not Conformed but Transformed*: Scottish Baptists and Social Action

### Derek Murray

The public image of Scottish Baptists in the twentieth century is of an aggressive evangelistic body of men and women, seeking to win Scotland for Christ. Sometimes they have co-operated with other Christians, and sometimes they have seemed to be trying to do the work on their own. While there is truth in this assumption, it only tells one side of the story. Scottish Baptists were outspoken about social questions and they were able to initiate some projects which have had both local and nation-wide effects.

While it is precarious to assume that all Scottish Baptists could be categorised as Evangelical, the great majority would accept that description. For many reasons the twentieth century, especially the earlier part of it, has been seen as a time of retreat from social concern and action by those who stressed personal conversion. Evangelicalism and the Social Gospel have appeared opposed and there were signs of withdrawal from the wider world amongst those who put personal salvation above the changing of sinful structures. Yet in 1921 Rev T.G. Dunning of the Baptist Union of Great Britain and Ireland addressed a Scottish Baptist Union Conference on the 'Social Implications of the Gospel.' 'Social obligations are,' he said, 'integral to the Gospel. Jesus commanded us to offer a cup of cold water, and to seek the extension of the Kingdom on earth. Jesus is Lord of everything. He is the one teacher who has put the Brotherhood of Man on a lasting basis.'[1] At the 1922 Assembly an enquiry was called for into industrial distress, and the place of the Christian in public life.[2] In 1924 the COPEC (Conference on Christian Politics, Economics and Citizenship) sponsored by the mainstream Protestant Churches, and roundly condemned by many evangelicals as signalling the centrality of the Social Gospel, was tentatively recommended to the Assembly.[3]

The Work of the League of Nations was mentioned from time to time in optimistic terms, as a bulwark against another World War, and in 1920 an appeal was made in the Magazine for support for the 'Save the Children Fund',

---

[1] *SBM*, 47.12 (December 1921), p. 125.
[2] *SBY 1923*, p. 99.
[3] *SBY 1925*, p. 108.

which had been set up in the aftermath of the war. At the Assembly of 1924 Rev James Hair reported that he as Convener of the Social Service Committee had represented the Baptist Union on the Anti- gambling Committee of the Churches and also on the Scottish Churches League of Nations Council, and the World's Alliance for the Promoting of International Friendship through the churches. He spoke at length of the work of the Alliance. Elsewhere he spoke of the value of meeting leaders of German churches.[4]

Alongside Scottish Baptist interest in and commitment to some aspects of the Social Gospel were other strong strands of conviction. The influence of Premillenial Dispensationalism with its inbuilt pessimism about this present age was strong, especially in churches where there was Brethren influence, and many holiness teachers, and other evangelicals, saw manmade solutions to world tensions and social issues as poor substitutes for the redemption of individuals and the desire for a speedy Second Advent and the end of the Age. Added to these convictions were fears, after the First World War, of the spread of 'godless communism' after the Russian Revolution, and with greater militancy from Trades Unions, of revolution at home. Many Baptists would have agreed with the influential Cambridge Evangelical writer, Basil Atkinson, who wrote in 1949, 'The commission of the Christian is to gather out of the world by evangelisation a people to Christ's Name. No other commission has ever been given to the Church and no other purpose for the existence of the Church is mentioned in the New Testament.' Normally, he assumed, social reform was no more than a diversion from evangelistic endeavour.[5] There were tensions evident in Assembly reports between those who saw social action as the field of the Temperance Committee only, and those who were influenced by some of the teachings lumped together as the 'Social Gospel.' That this suspicion of the Social Gospel has not disappeared is evident from James Taylor's remarks on the retiring of Janet Lacey, Director of Christian Aid in 1968, 'The Church's mission is being almost exclusively interpreted, in many quarters, in terms of action and service.'[6]

So, writing in the *History of Baptists in Scotland*, published by the Baptist Union in 1926, Rev James Hair, minister of Bristo Church in Edinburgh and Convener of the Social Service Committee of the Union, could say,

> Until recent years the social implications of the Christian Faith were not included in the programme of the Church's teaching. Any declaration of opinion on public questions, any interference with purely secular affairs, was regarded as outside of

---

[4] *SBY 1925*, p. 108.
[5] David Bebbington, 'The Decline and Resurgence of Evangelical Social Concern 1918-1980' in J. Wolffe (ed.), *Evangelical Faith and Public Zeal* (London: SPCK, 1995), p. 184.
[6] *SBM*, 94.6 (June 1968), p. 1.

her province. There was little sense of responsibility for the temporal conditions under which the people lived, or feeling of obligation to seek their improvement.

He goes on to remark of a seminal event in British history 'even during the crisis in the mining industry in this year of grace 1926, they (the Scottish Churches) have declined to follow the example of the leaders of the Churches across the Border in working for a settlement, and have stood aloof from the controversy.'

He further remarks that although for most Baptists the Churches' sole business is the saving of the individual from the forces that seek his moral and spiritual undoing, men are better than their creed and the Church has never closed its ears to the cry of distress. He mentions William Quarrier, to whom we will return, and the generous support for his work with orphans given by Sir Thomas Glen-Coats, the thread manufacturer of Paisley, and a prominent Baptist.[7]

In 1930 Hair records that the Social Service Committee 'met but once.' The Convener regrets 'that there have been no requests for speakers on Social Service topics at Association Conferences this year, and fears that this indicates a lack of interest in these questions on the part of our people. He is of opinion that the time has come when the advisability or otherwise of continuing the Committee should be considered, and suggests that the Council discuss the matter at an early date.' In 1932 he has more to report, and some optimism for the future of the Committee. There has been an Assembly Conference on 'Disarmament' with an address by Rev Henry Cook. Matters of public morality such as the Birth Control Movement, and its dangers to youth, greyhound racing and gambling generally, and the increase in unemployment- all matters which will recur in the following years, had been discussed.[8]

Nevertheless the main issue which inspired great efforts of Scottish Baptists in the first half of the century was the conflict with what he calls 'the Drink Evil.' There is no doubt that from the mid-nineteenth century or earlier the misuse of alcohol had become a real problem in Scotland and several pieces of legislation sought to deal with it. Self control and state control were demanded by temperance reformers, and by the end of the nineteenth century temperance had become identified with total abstinence, or teetotalism. The Forbes-Mackenzie Act of 1853 shut public houses in Scotland on Sundays, and introduced a closing time of 11 p.m. on weekdays. This remained in force until late in the twentieth century while on Sundays 'bona fide' travellers could travel to a hotel and drink. In 1921 a new Licensing Act relaxed some wartime restrictions and extended the closing time from 9p.m. until 10 p.m., where it remained until the liberalising Clayson Report of 1973 and its gradual

---

[7] G. Yuille (ed.), *History of Baptists in Scotland* (Glasgow: Baptist Union of Scotland Publications Committee, 1926), p 270.
[8] *SBY 1933*, p. 171.

implementation in the next few years. Membership of the Common Market in 1973, and increasing enjoyment of foreign holidays in these fairly prosperous days undoubtedly had an effect on the Scottish attitude to alcohol, and even influenced some Baptists.

By the beginning of the twentieth century organisations such as the Band of Hope, The Rechabites and the Order of Good Templars flourished, and children as well as adults were exhorted to take the pledge to abstain from all alcohol. This pledge, which read 'I agree to abstain from all intoxicating drinks as beverages, and to promote the practice of Abstinence in the community' was printed annually in the reports of the Scottish Baptist Total Abstinence Society.

The Scottish Local Veto Polls were first held in 1920 according to a complicated formula and several areas elected to enforce a no-licence policy. These were mostly smaller communities such as Kirkintilloch, Lenzie, Lerwick and Kirkwall, and a few residential suburbs in Glasgow such as Cathcart, Pollokshields and Kelvinside. Baptists in Lerwick had been active in the poll, held in 1922,[9] and were delighted with the result, which was reversed in 1947. In the same issue of the Magazine there was praise for the prohibition legislation in USA.[10] This local veto option remained on the statute book until 1976, but only a few places, such as Kilsyth had by that time remained true to their original vote.

## Baptist Efforts for Total Abstinence

Rev W.H. Millard, while he was in Wick Baptist Church for a second ministry from 1919 until 1939 'was a very active advocate of temperance and his efforts helped to ban alcohol from Wick for many years.' This activism was true for the earlier part of the twentieth century.[11] Edwin Scrymgeour of the Prohibition Party, who defeated Winston Churchill in Dundee in the General Election of 1922, was a Methodist, but he was supported by members of all the churches. His attempt to introduce an American style Prohibition Act in the commons in 1923 was heavily defeated but he was supported by members of the Independent Labour Party, and on Temperance matters Baptists were on the same side as Socialists. The well-known Communist member for West Fife, and teetotaller, Willie Gallacher, had been a member of Sir John McCallum's Bible Class in Coats Memorial, Paisley, and this crossover is not insignificant for Scottish culture.

The Scottish Baptist Total Abstinence Society had been founded in 1881 and was incorporated as the Temperance Committee of the Union in 1923. Rev Alexander A Milne served as Temperance Evangelist from 1900-1913, and was succeeded in that year by Rev J.B. Frame who served until 1923. He, in turn,

---

[9] *SBM*, 48.3 (March 1922), p. 29.
[10] *SBM*, 48.8 (August 1922), p. 90.
[11] *SBY 1971*, p. 167.

was succeeded by Rev T.A. McQuiston, now designated Union Evangelist but with a continuing interest in Temperance, from 1924-1931. These men and others conducted evangelistic missions in and beyond our churches with an emphasis on temperance and on signing the pledge.

In 1901 Rev. A.A. Milne reports, 'My first mission for the new century was held in Shiloh Hall, connected with John Street Church, Glasgow. The meetings were somewhat disappointing. Still, nine pledges were taken, and we hope other good was accomplished. My next journey was to Cupar-Fife, where several adults professed conversion…I consider the Mission to Hawick to have been one of the best during the year. Commencing on 23$^{rd}$ March we continued till 5$^{th}$ April, having altogether 27 services and taking 117 pledges, and best of all we learned of several cases of conversion.'[12]

In his first report given in 1913, J B Frame writes, 'reliable statistics show that Gladstone was right when he said, "We suffer more from the drink curse than from war, pestilence and famine."' 'Since my appointment I have conducted or addressed 158 adult and 46 children's services and about 100 pledges taken.'[13] He then gives particulars of missions in the Central belt of Scotland. It seems that sometimes signing the pledge is seen as being as important as accepting Christ, and Joseph Kemp of Charlotte Chapel comes near to saying this at the 1905 Assembly meeting of the Total Abstinence Society in Perth. The Chairman, Peter Campbell of Perth, had remarked that 'many social problems were demanding the attention of the Christian Church and Parliament, such as the proper housing of the poor, the Old Age Pension, employment for the unemployed and the obviation of the physical and mental deterioration of our children. Drink and improvidence are the causes of these problems and how rarely did we find total abstainers in want of permanent help.' Kemp's response was terse. 'Conversion leads to total abstinence.'[14]

There were several other groups, such as the British Women's Temperance Association, which were active all over the country and brought women from many churches together. In 1906 the obituary for Madame Wilhelmina Elvira Woyka, a former member of Hamburgh (sic) Baptist Church under J.G. Oncken, married to a Hungarian convert from Roman Catholicism, Mr Gustav Woyka of John Street Scotch Baptist Church, states that she was a founder of the BWTA. The Woykas were a prominent Scotch Baptist family for several generations.

The reports of the Total Abstinence Society list the Temperance activities of many churches. Bands of Hope abound, with membership in 1913, as high as 250 in Gorgie, Edinburgh and 154 in Pathhead, Kirkcaldy. Several churches had Gospel Temperance Societies, and a few reported Saturday Night Gospel Temperance meetings. By the latter part of the century such as survived had

---

[12] *SBY 1902*, C9
[13] *SBY 1914*, C6
[14] *SBM*, 31.11 (November 1905), p. 201.

become Saturday Night Tea Meetings, a useful training ground for aspirant preachers.

The denomination in Scotland which most publicly associated itself with Total Abstinence was the Evangelical Union, which by the twentieth century had united with the Congregational Union. It was fondly nicknamed the 'jeelywater Kirk' and no one in the licensed trade was allowed into membership. Some Baptist churches had provisions in their constitutions against receiving as members any who, in any way, were connected with the 'Trade.'

The reports also listed churches using unfermented wine for communion and abstaining ministers. Omissions from these lists are few. In 1913 Hillhead, Glasgow and Coats Memorial, Paisley are the only churches using fermented wine, and indeed the changeover only happened in Paisley in the early 1950's at the request of the incoming minister, Rev W.J. Grant.[15] The first minister of the Coats Church, Rev Oliver Flett had, in the great magazine controversy on the subject of wine in the scriptures in the 1880's been a fierce defender of the view that wine, to be wine, must be fermented. The minister of Hillhead, Rev J.T. Forbes, is on the list of abstainers but Rev Walter Mursell of Coats Memorial was not. I have heard the suggestion that some ministers did not sign up on conscientious grounds, as they opposed legalism. Older ministers stood for temperance, not total abstinence. The famous Dr William Landels, who had his last ministry in Dublin Street, Edinburgh, and who died in 1899, had, according to his descendants, a glass of wine (the glass is still preserved!) at dinner while the rest of the family drank water.[16] Only in 1899 had the use of 'two wines' at Communion in Dublin Street Church been discontinued.[17]

As the century moved on, the Temperance Committee and its successors kept watch on legislation, supported local option polls, and continued to press for the reduction in the number of licensed premises. That the Union had not ceased its struggle against the evil of drink is obvious in the Presidential Address for 1923. Archibald Lawson of Dundee spoke of 'the gigantic evils which are encountered in efforts to propagate the Gospel of Christ. One of the foremost is the use of alcoholic liquors as beverages. Social workers testify that the drink traffic is the greatest obstacle they have to contend with in their efforts to make life better and happier for the struggling poor.... It is the duty of every sincere Christian and patriot to plead with, urge and persuade electors to vote for 'No Licence' in November.' In 1935 the convenor of the Temperance Committee deplored the growth of cocktail drinking on social occasions among young men and women and a booklet on its evils is made available. The Temperance Committee Report for 1952 shows that there was no diminution in the cause. Rev T.A. McQuiston, the Convenor stated 'the attack on the Drink Trade has

---

[15] Personal information.
[16] Personal information.
[17] Annie Marie Baines, *History of Dublin Street Baptist Church* (Edinburgh: McLagan and Cumming Ltd, 1958), p. 16.

been both intensive and persistent. The lamentable destruction in the home, evidenced by divorce, the disruption of family life and the terrible death toll on the roads, caused largely by strong drink, has aroused the indignation of thoughtful women.'[18] In 1954 the Committee agreed with the British Women's Temperance Association's condemnation of the practice of reviving fainting heroines with alcohol at church plays.

There was a Temperance Library in the Union Offices at 113 West Regent Street, which contained among other books a Temperance Bible Dictionary which made it clear that references to wine are to grape juice. These books disappeared when the Union moved to Aytoun Road![19] D.S.K. McLeay, Secretary for many years of John Knox Street Church, Glasgow, was also Secretary of the Scottish Temperance Alliance and latterly of the Band of Hope Union. He served as President of the Union, in 1959-60.

### Scottish Baptist Initiatives in Social Service

Although most of his work had been done by the beginning of the century, it would be remiss not to mention William Quarrier, who was closely connected with Blackfriars Street Baptist Church, later in John Knox Street, and then with Hope Street Church, later Adelaide Place, Glasgow. When he died in 1903 the work at Bridge of Weir, for orphans and also for sufferers from Tuberculosis was firmly established, and had been greatly supported by Baptist people.[20] Many Baptists were involved with the Homes in the new century. Rev J.B. Coull began his Christian service there before the First World War, and went on to be minister in several churches. Rev Tom Houston, at the beginning of a varied and distinguished career, moved in 1954 from his first pastorate in Johnstone to become Chaplain to the Homes.

A notable Revival took place in Charlotte Chapel, Edinburgh in the first decade of the century. It was closely connected to the Revival in Wales and many were converted and added to the Church. In the Church's centennial year, 1908, a number of new ventures were begun. The women of the church had been concerned by the number of girls coming to the city to seek for work, and falling into bad company and prostitution. The minister, Joseph Kemp and his wife took some of the girls into their own home but it soon became apparent that something more permanent was needed. Mr J.C. Ross, a deacon of the Portobello Church offered a house in Fettes Row, in the New Town, rent-free for three years, and the church accepted the challenge. Dr Maxwell Williamson, an elder and Chief Medical Officer of Health gave practical help and Miss Bolton, a member of the Chapel, was appointed Matron. The 'White House'

---

[18] *SBY 1953*, p. 160.
[19] Personal recollection!
[20] Brian Talbot, 'William Quarrier: Philanthropist and Social Reformer', *Records of the Scottish Church History Society*, 39, (2009), pp. 89-129.

was opened in November 1908, and another member, Miss Stevenson, was appointed Institute Deaconess in the following year. Efforts were made to find good situations for the girls, and there were encouraging stories of conversions. However, many girls saw the house as a temporary refuge, and some, especially the Roman Catholic girls, were not happy at being expected to attend both Sunday services and one meeting midweek. In the end the running costs were more than the Chapel could bear, for such ambiguous returns, and the House closed in July 1910.[21]

In the earlier part of the century many churches, especially in the cities, had Mission Halls in less prosperous parts of the community. As a result of Tract distribution, Charlotte Chapel opened the Jamaica Street Mission in 1915. Jamaica Street, now rebuilt and gentrified, was a notorious part of the New Town, tucked in behind the lovely Heriot Row, and the need for evangelistic work in the area led the Chapel deaconess, Miss Boyle, to start kitchen meetings. The let of an empty shop was secured in 1916, and women's and then evening meetings commenced. Gospel activities were foremost but there was attention to social needs and of course a Band of Hope on Friday nights. The Mission was closed in 1952, although open-air meetings continued until the street was almost demolished in the late 1960's. A mission in the High Street, started privately in 1913, was given to Charlotte Chapel in 1921, and acquired premises in 1930. Most work was with women and children, and men were noticeably absent. This Mission closed during the War, in 1943. Charlotte Chapel also, in 1923, took over the Rock Mission, which had been founded in 1912 in the Grassmarket area, by Dr Maxwell Williamson. Sunday afternoon meetings, at which tea and sandwiches were served, were held until 1987. Money might be given for a bed in a Lodging House, and the Gospel was preached. The work was united with that of Carrubbers Christian Centre, which was providing for the same clientele.

Adelaide Place in Glasgow had a mission in St Clair Street for many years, and the Hillhead Missions in Partick and Port Dundas continued to have student pastors into the 1960s. There is definite evidence of a class divide, between Church and Mission. After the Thistle Street Mission of Whyte's Causeway Church in Kirkcaldy closed some of its people attended the Church, but could not be persuaded to join.[22] Missions were definitely auxiliaries to the Church and usually did not have morning services nor was communion celebrated.

The Women's Auxiliary was particularly concerned with the girls who followed the herring fleet from Shetland down the East Coast of Britain. A 'Rest Hut' was set up in Lerwick, where first-aid for injuries received during the gutting process was offered, along with tracts and open air meetings. In 1939,

---

[21] I.L.S. Balfour, *Revival in Rose Street* (Edinburgh: Rutherford House, 2008), pp. 118-119, see also *Records of the Scottish Church History Society*, Volume 39, 2009, pp. 69-89.

[22] Personal reminiscence.

owing to the failure of the herring fishing, there was less to do, but Nurse McArthur, who later served as Pastor in Home Mission churches during the war, continued to minister to medical and spiritual needs. Delegates from the WA met the minister and deacons of the Lerwick Church 'but were unable to come to any satisfactory arrangement with them.' [23] During the war the Hut was used as a canteen, and then disappears from the records.

There are many references to the recurring problem of unemployment at various crises in the century. The Tayside Association was particularly active in this field of service. In 1934 a motion was brought to the Assembly by the Ward Road Church, Dundee that more time be given to discussing social service. This produced a practical outcome. A public meeting was arranged by the Association's Unemployment Economic Committee, and a member of Ward Road, R.C. Duffin travelled to the Glasgow and Fife Associations to speak on the Church and Unemployment. The Maxwelltown Church, under the leadership of Rev David Kyles, began a craft class for unemployed men and women to make saleable items. When the Prince of Wales on a visit to Dundee in 1931 heard of this venture, which the church had withdrawn from the city-wide scheme to co-ordinate such classes, because it was partly funded by a betting shop, he insisted on visiting it. In more recent years the Falkirk Church and others have opened premises as drop-in and advice centres for the unemployed.

Some individual Baptists were deeply involved in social care during the century. John R.S. Henderson of Rattray Street Church, Dundee (President of the Union in 1961-2) succeeded his father as superintendent of the Dundee Working Boys' Home from 1936 until its closure in 1968. He was also Superintendent of the Curr Night Refuge for destitute people, and welfare officer to the Dundee Discharged Prisoners' Aid Society, and after-care officer for Borstal Services in Angus and Perthshire. His and his wife's activities in Church, Association and Union and the hospitality of his home are still remembered, and they were only one couple from our churches who worked in voluntary and statutory care agencies.

Several Churches opened their premises for the homeless, and hostel dwellers. In Glasgow in several localities such as the Grove Street Institute, Miss Irene Allan carried out for many years a caring and evangelistic ministry. 'About 1964 I began to feel a strange and insistent call to go and work with drunks, drop-outs and drug addicts,' she wrote.[24] By 1977 there were two Baptist Hostels, Greenhill and Olivehill. This enterprise developed into the work of 'The Crypt', the basement of the Hillhead Church, and was active at the end of the century. Miss Jean Laidlaw, a member of Dublin Street Church, held a Wednesday night meeting in the 1970s and 80s for 'Grassmarket men' and some women, in the Mound Centre, and later in Simpson House, an agency of the Church of Scotland. When pressure was put on her to record more

---

[23] *SBY 1940*, p. 213.
[24] *SBM*, 100.11 (November 1974), p. 4.

conversions, she was welcomed, with her friends, to the Hall of Dublin Street Church, and subsequently to Canonmills, Dublin Street's home after 1988, where the men and women became well-known, especially at Christmas. There must have been other such ventures at various times during the century, many of them almost unrecorded.

The best-known social work venture associated with a Baptist Church is surely Bethany Christian Trust. Although support and staff now come from a variety of churches, it began as the vision of Rev. Alan Berry. He, his wife Anne and their family arrived at South Leith Baptist Church in 1977, and he soon became aware of the problem of homelessness, especially among young people coming to seek work in the capital. Club premises opposite the church became available in 1979, but the church was not yet ready to commit itself to the purchase. So a Trust was formed and in 1981, when the same premises were on the market again, having in the meantime been used as a commercial hotel and so having a guest house licence and a fire certificate, they were bought and church members set about making it habitable.

The Trust, beginning as a hostel, soon found other needs to be met, and flats and other buildings were purchased, many people given help and a new start in life, a Care Van and furniture store supported. The work has spread to Fife, Aberdeen, and West Lothian, where for some years a farm was used to give city lads a taste of outdoor work. Rev. Ross Brown and Rev Ian Paterson, Alan's successors as ministers of South Leith Church have both worked for Bethany, and the church itself has been used for many Bethany purposes. The Trust has been able to employ people with a wide range of skills, many of them Baptists, and some former residents. The moving story of this complex, expanding and Christian-based work has been ably told by Anne Berry in her book *Giving Hope and a Future* published to mark the Semi-Jubilee of the Trust in 2009.[25]

In Glasgow two of the Central churches, Adelaide Place and Hillhead were concerned from the 1970's to put faith into practice and to make some contribution to caring for some victims of urban life. The Union was interested in these initiatives. In 1974 Adelaide Place Church approached the Finance and Business committee for Union support 'in a possible social work project in central Glasgow. Help was hoped for from Local and Government authorities. The Committee expressed interest and support and referred the matter to the Treasurer.' In 1977 the 'Christian Citizenship Committee has viewed with interest the opening of hostels for alcoholics at St Vincent Street and Argyle Street, Glasgow. It has agreed to support with interest and prayer the hostel for homeless girls in Buccleuch Street which has been opened by Adelaide Place Church. This is known as the Elpis Centre.'[26]

The Glasgow City Centre Ministry developed in three ways. A pioneer ministry was set up from 1975-1978, with Rev Paul Gardiner as its leader, the

---

[25] Anne E. Berry, *Giving Hope and a Future* (Fearn: Christian Focus, 2009).
[26] *SBY 1978*, p. 41.

Elpis Centre, originally a hostel for homeless girls was opened, and flats for those with addictions were maintained. In 1978 Rev Robert Gemmell as appointed as a community minister and served until 1983. There have been many changes of accommodation owing to the difficulty of registering premises and the uncertain financial support at different times, but the Elpis project has continued with some success. Rev Robert Armstrong, a member at Hillhead, and Rev Ross Campbell of the Dennistoun Church gave strong guidance and support. Marjorie McInnes, OBE, a member of Adelaide Place Baptist Church, and the only woman to be President of the Union, worked in Social Services and her Presidential Address, in 1990, was entitled 'Called to Care'.[27] She referred to new ministries in churches and chaplaincies and stressed practical Christian service.

In 1965 Rev Watson Moyes began his first pastorate at the churches at Pitlochry and Tullymet. Numbers were low, but the Pitlochry Church had ample grounds and occupied a prominent site in the main street of the town. By 1971 the Atholl Baptist Centre Limited, with a Committee which included appointees of the Baptist Union and with the well-known Baptist MP Sir Cyril Black as Honorary President, was built and opened catering for Conferences and Church groups but also very importantly for people with disabilities. Mrs Kathleen Moyes was a teacher of hearing-impaired children, and she and her husband and several other talented leaders encouraged courses for young Christians sharing holidays with the disabled and disadvantaged. Despite many challenges, the Centre has continues its work over the years.

## Accommodation for the Elderly

Churches and Associations began to see the need for specifically Christian Retirement Homes, and so did the Social Service Committee of the Union. Rev Fred. Price, Secretary of the Committee reported in 1956 that 'the Committee has been exercised during the past session almost entirely with the problem of Baptist old people. The Convener, Rev D.M. Robb (of Ward Road, Dundee) brought the matter before the committee as one of urgency. He had explored various possibilities, but the scarcity of suitable accommodation and the high cost of purchase and staffing made the matter difficult.'[28] The Women's Auxiliary had become involved, but it seems nothing further was done by the Union. The Robertson Rest Home, just across the bridge from Dundee, which was opened for members of Rattray Street Church in 1947, may have been in Mr Robb's mind. This home continued under trustees from the Church until late in the century and in 1967 is recorded as advertising also holidays with good fellowship and 'moderate terms.'

---

[27] *SBY 1991*, pp. 89-94.
[28] *SBY 1957*, p. 161.

After many years of planning and fund raising Charlotte Chapel purchased a large villa in Newhaven Road in Edinburgh in 1955, and opened it in the following year. The residents of this pleasant home were able to receive landline broadcasts from the Chapel, had family worship twice a day and were often visited by groups of young people and others from the congregation. At the end of the century it was still fully occupied by members of the Chapel, and in the 1990's four residents each attained their centenary. Only with different planning demands and social changes was it found necessary to close it in 2010.

The Church at Abbeyhill had opened a fund with a view to an eventide home in the 1950's but only in the late 1960's did the Edinburgh and Lothian Baptist Association begin to plan a venture for all the Baptist Churches in the Area. The driving force was Rev Peter Clark of the Bristo Church. The Edinburgh and Lothian Baptist Housing Association was formed in 1968, and in 1970 it purchased the former Salvation Army's Home for Mothers, the 'Tor' in Corstorphine Road. This mansion had belonged to the Chambers family of publishers and is set in extensive grounds. At first residents were chosen from applicants who were members of Baptist Churches, and, since a fund raised by Martyrs and St John's United Free Church in the city had been added to Baptist money, from members of that denomination. Two ministers, Dr Fred Cawley former Principal of Spurgeon's College and Rev G.U. Graham and an ex-president of the Union, John Grant, were among the first residents, and Sunday evening services were conducted regularly by members of all the Edinburgh churches, after which one of these men would give a gracious response.

As legislation changed, and more elderly people were maintained in their own homes, the 'Tor' was modified gradually. Incoming residents were generally older and frailer, and if there were not enough Baptist applicants, it was necessary to receive those who were referred by the Social Services. As residents became less able the change was made to Nursing Home status. At the same time the building was considerably upgraded and extended. Nevertheless the 'Tor Christian Nursing Home' maintained its links to the churches, and continued to make a notable contribution to care in Edinburgh. The Management Committee was drawn from members of Baptist Churches in Edinburgh and the Lothians, and regular services were conducted.

The Churches in Ayrshire have also maintained the Ayr Baptist Homes, at Airlie House in Ayr since 1988. This was the fruit of the vision of the Ayr Church, led by Rev Noel McCullins, and has been a notable blessing to many elderly folk.

This is not the place to chronicle the efforts to provide an adequate pension for retired ministers, but the provision of housing should be mentioned. Following the gift of New Prestwick members Mr and Mrs Bryden's house to the Union, a number of properties have been willed to the Union and others bought, in several parts of the country, greatly to the benefit of retired ministers and their widows. By 1999 there were at least eight houses belonging to the Union and occupied by retired ministers or widows.

## Care for Vulnerable People

Morningside Baptist Church was situated near the Royal Edinburgh Hospital and the members and especially the minister, Rev Peter Bowes became aware of several people with mental health issues attending the Church and its auxiliaries. Modelled to some degree on the work of l'Arche and the remarkable French Canadian inspirer of that work, Jean Vanier, the Ark Housing Association began in 1977 providing homes, firstly in Edinburgh, and later throughout Scotland, where people with mental health issues and others could live together. This venture soon embraced many besides Baptists, and its secretary, the lawyer Mrs Ruth Middleton, and other leading committee members were drawn from the Morningside Church. In the same church there was also for many years a Bible Class for those with learning difficulties.

Signing for people with hearing loss was a feature of Morningside's services for many years and in Charlotte Chapel Robin White conducted a 'Deaf Fellowship', firstly in a corner pew, and then in the Church Lounge, for 47 years, until he was 89 years old. In 1978 Rev. T. Deans Buchanan's paper on counselling the bereaved was commended to ministers by the Christian Citizenship Committee, a title dating from 1960.

Not every scheme came to fulfilment. In 1958 the Social Service Committee reported through its Secretary, Rev A.R. Hughes that a draft proposal had been submitted to the Office-Bearers of the Union for a 'Baptist Institute of Scotland', to procure suitable premises to promote welfare work among young and old members of our constituency. The Committee was told that such a proposal at the moment was impracticable owing to the ambitious nature of the scheme and the number of pressing appeals before our people. The Committee decided to raise it again another year, but there seems to be no record of this taking place. [29]

Later in the century several Baptist ministers and lay people became involved in the work of the Hospice Movement in various voluntary and paid capacities. As the Hospices in the tradition of St Christopher's in London were usually sponsored by Christian people, this is scarcely surprising. Rev James Taylor and Dr Harold Lyon of the Stirling Baptist Church were deeply committed to the setting up of the Strathcarron Hospice near Denny, and Dr Lyon became the first Medical Director of the Unit. In Paisley the Accord Hospice appointed Kenneth Jackson of Central Church as Volunteer Co-ordinator, and the Prince and Princess of Wales Hospice had as its fulltime Chaplains three successive Baptist ministers, two, Rev Alan Donald and Rev Stuart Webster in the twentieth century. St Columba's Hospice in Edinburgh opened in Edinburgh in 1977 with Rev Derek Murray of Dublin Street as part-time Chaplain, then from 1987 until 2001 as full-time in the same position.

---

[29] *SBY 1959*, p. 168.

Many lay men and women from the churches helped make up the army of volunteers that is such a remarkable feature of Hospice Care.

In the wider world of Hospital Chaplaincy Rev W.T. McGregor served for many years until 1939 as Chaplain to the Craiglockhart Poorhouse. Rev Alan Stoddart was Assistant Chaplain to Aberdeen Hospitals from 1991 and several ministers, such as Rev Robert Armstrong at Hawkhead Hospital in Paisley, Rev Harry Telfer at the City Hospital, Edinburgh and others served as part-time Hospital Chaplains along with their work in the churches.

## Peace and War

Sam Hendry gave a paper to the Scottish Baptist History Project in 1982, which was published in the Baptist Quarterly on 'Scottish Baptists and the First World War'.[30] Mainly using the SBM he traced various attitudes to the conflict which seemed to take most folk by surprise. The Office Bearers of the Union despatched a letter to the Churches –'a few words in view of the lamentable war into which so many….have been so suddenly plunged.' There was a definite conviction of the rightness of Britain's cause, and sadness at being parted from German Baptist brethren. Strong sympathy was expressed with Belgium, and the only sermon Hendry discovered on the subject was by Rev Walter Mursell of Coats Memorial published as 'The Bruising of Belgium.' War was being waged on 'brutal' Germany in the name of honour and the teaching of Jesus. There was little doubt that the British Empire had spiritual right on its side, and only one (anonymous) letter was published opposing the war, particularly the introduction of conscription.

Not surprisingly the Total Abstinence Society called for prohibition of alcohol. The drink trade was the secondary enemy, after Germany. Government control was called for. The number of men serving and the extensive list of casualties had a lasting effect on the churches, not least on those in fishing ports such as Anstruther and Pittenweem. Some who returned had found their former certainties severely challenged. 'The war,' wrote John McBeath, who had served with the YMCA, 'has made faith difficult.'

Throughout the century, then, the threat and actuality of war were inescapable. The two Great Wars of 1914-1919, and 1939-1945, and smaller but no less significant conflicts in former colonies such as Malaysia and Kenya, in Korea, in the Falklands, and at the end of the century in the Middle East, have all had their impact on the churches and have given rise to much heart-searching, discussion and many resolutions of Assembly. The threat of Atomic and Nuclear warfare has concerned our churches, and from time to time led to debates and arguments. In August 1935 there was an advertisement for the Baptist Pacifist Fellowship in the Baptist Magazine, and while I have no

---

[30] S.D. Hendry, 'Scottish Baptists and the First World War', *Baptist Quarterly*, 31.2, April 1985, pp. 52-65.

evidence that any pastors were members of that organisation, some leaders were, on conscientious grounds, pacifists.

Rev John McKendrick, well-known as an evangelist and an inspiring preacher, who had at the 1951 Assembly protested against the silence of the Social Service Committee on the subject of the armaments race, concluded his Presidential Address to the Union in 1958 entitled: 'A Plea for the Recovery of Urgency in our Witness' with these words, 'permit me a personal word here. I cannot, in view of the Cross of our Lord Jesus Christ, understand the Church of Jesus Christ countenancing modern warfare as a method of redemption, and particularly the use of nuclear warfare. Can we, dare we, as followers of Christ, whose agonising concern was to save men, even in our own self-defence, support the use of this wholesale destruction? Even God spared not His own Son, but delivered Him up for us all.'[31] Many from our churches were conscientious objectors in both World Wars, some choosing work in coal mines, some in non-combatant service and some even went briefly to prison for their convictions. Others proudly served in the armed forces, with many of our ministers being Chaplains, or working with such agencies as the YMCA in wartime, and towards the end of our period a number of ministers moved into Forces' Chaplaincy.

At the Assembly in 1961, while the situation in the gulf of Mexico and the stand off between Fidel Castro and the US government seemed to threaten the world a Council resolution, discussed in the Council meeting held just before the Assembly was put forward. It read, in part,

> 1. That this Assembly notes with horror the restarting of nuclear tests with the danger to human life by increasing fallout.
> 2. That this Assembly declares its faith in the love of God as revealed in Jesus Christ. That this love must be manifest by His disciples in all their relationships, personal, social and national.
> 3. Therefore it is incumbent upon us to work for the extension by the power of His love.
> 4. In view of the present serious world situation and the Church's ministry of intercession and reconciliation, we call on Christians everywhere to pray with renewed urgency for peace and the coming of Christ's Kingdom.

An amendment to replace paragraph three with 'Therefore it is incumbent on us to refuse to wage war but to work for the extension of Christ's Kingdom by the power of His love' was proposed. A second amendment to replace the whole motion as follows was then put forward.

> That the Baptist Union of Scotland, deploring the resumption of nuclear testing, faced with the tensions of the present world situation, affirms its belief as a Christian Church.

---

[31] *SBY 1959*, pp. 13-14.

In the sovereignty of God…
In Christ Jesus Saviour and Lord, the only hope of the world.
That in repentance to God and not in dependence on military might lies the only solution to a humanly insoluble international problem.
That the British Council of Churches be urged to arrange a Day of Prayer…

This amendment received 140 votes, and the first 13 votes, and the second amendment was duly carries 145 for, nem.con. This was one of the few occasions when the ethics of war was so clearly discussed. Both the Union Secretary, Rev George Hardie, and the President on this occasion, Rev William Whyte, had served in the First World War, and a heated exchange between Mr Whyte, who had been an officer in that war, and Mr McKendrick, who was a declared pacifist, made this a memorable occasion.[32]

During the next few years a number of ministers took part in demonstrations by the Christian section of the Campaign for Nuclear Disarmament, and towards the end of the century some Baptists were supportive of protests against Nuclear submarines in the Gareloch. Most Baptists stood apart. One minister, with pacifist sympathies, and probably speaking for many, was uncomfortable about the company he would have to keep if he joined in public demonstrations. Left wing Socialists were also against Nuclear weapons on our soil.

At the Assembly in 1967 a lively debate took place after the Citizenship report. The resolution was proposed that we ask the Government to disassociate the UK from American bombing in Vietnam and to bring whatever pressure possible on North Vietnam to stop infiltration of the South.[33] This was sent to the Foreign Office and a long explanatory reply from that Office was printed in a later Magazine.

In 1984 the Assembly debated a resolution concerning the Miners' Strike of that year. The General Secretary proposed the motion: "'as members of the Baptist Union of Scotland met at Annual Assembly in Glasgow

1. we are deeply concerned at the continuing deadlock in the mining industry and at the dissension, hardship and violence this dispute is producing;
2. We urge both restraint from violence and respect for law on the part of all concerned;
3. we call upon those on whose leadership so much depends to seek a swift settlement to this dispute by any available means;
4. we appeal to them and to all caught up in this strike to seek the way of peace and reconciliation… 'blessed are the peacemakers; for they shall be called the children of God.'

The resolution gave rise to considerable discussion, and most speakers agreed that it was not within the Assembly's competence to comment on economic,

---

[32] *SBY 1962*, p. 134.
[33] *SBY 1968*, p. 146.

industrial or political matters but to have a concern for people. Others felt that we should address the particular issues. Rev Robert Armstrong believed we needed to say something about economic issues, including the future of the coal industry, the terms on which pits should close, and about the role of the government. The Resolution was overwhelmingly carried and sent to a wide variety of interested parties.

## Gambling and Lotteries

Horse and greyhound racing and the attendant betting, football pools, gambling and lotteries all came under the condemnation of the Social Service Committee and of the Assembly. The Premium Bond Scheme in the late 1950's seemed to arouse particular disgust in Baptist circles. The Social Service Committee's report for 1956 stated that 'it is very disturbed by the proposal to issue Premium Bonds. This was regarded as a retrograde step and quite undignified. Gambling as a means of raising money for national requirements was condemned outright.' Protests to MPs were made—to no avail. In April 1968 the editor of the SBM had to apologise for an advertisement for Premium Bonds which had appeared in the previous month's Magazine as part of some publicity for National Savings. In the same issue a plea was made for members to write to MP's to discourage the adoption of a national Lottery Bill. But in 1996 the National Lottery was introduced and duly dismissed as evil. Opposition to gambling is one subject on which Scottish Baptists seem to have been unanimous. In the 1970s, under the leadership of Mrs Mary Whitehouse, the Viewers and Listeners' Association drew attention to ethical standards in the public media, especially Television. Ben Davis, then of Knightswood Church, frequently appealed in the magazine for Scottish Baptist participation in its campaigns.

## Poverty

Often mentioned in the context of opposition to alcohol and to gambling the fight against poverty at home and in the rest of the world is often mentioned, and Christian Aid and TEAR Fund often commended. In 1996 The Centre for Theology and Public Issues based at New College, Edinburgh had produced the 'Scottish Declaration on Poverty', and the Council recommended identification with it. The Assembly accepted three resolutions. The first dealt with poverty in Britain, and included the words 'we willingly accept the necessity for higher taxation to enable Government to the poor in our land.' The second condemned the low level of International Aid given by the government, deploring that the percentage allocated had diminished, and calling for the Government to aim at the target of 0.7% of GNP by 2000. A third resolution was added calling on churches 'to make their buildings more accessible and open to extend ministry to the poor in our communities.' The Union would join the Scottish Church Action on Poverty.[34]

In December 1967 Des Wilson of 'Shelter', then a new charity, wrote to describe its work, and the Citizenship Committee returned to this issue frequently. In 1998 a strong resolution on the blight of Homelessness in Scotland was introduced at the Assembly by Rev Alan Berry. He drew attention to the crisis which had now become a structural part of Scottish life and to the efforts needed to end it before the new millennium. New affordable and emergence accommodation was needed. The Scottish Churches Housing Agency was commended.

From time to time strong words were said at Assembly about immigration, and the issues surrounding it. With the strong missionary interest of the churches it is not surprising that a welcoming attitude was often taken. When the Editor, Angus McNeill, a former and subsequent missionary, remarked on 'the absurdity of Enoch Powell's latest speeches on immigration,' a letter defending Powell as 'a man who professes Christian belief and believes in the equality of all men' brought a reply referring to the BMS attitude to Powell, which was not complimentary to him.[35]

## Sex, Marriage and the Family

The century saw great changes in legislation and public attitudes to accepted standards of morality. What would have been unthinkable in 1900, at least in Christian circles, had to be confronted after the Second World War, and especially from the 60s onwards. Illegitimacy figures in some areas were quite high in previous centuries, but public morality seemed impregnable. Then changes in the law made divorce more affordable, and in Scotland it had, since the Reformation, been less difficult to obtain a divorce than in England. By 1953 mores had so changed that the Social Service Committee raised the subject of marriage and divorce. There was a current Royal Commission on marriage, and developments were awaited. In the meantime the Committee urged that 'something be done to instruct theological students in these matters and to find some way of educating our church members along these lines.

Soon such generalities had to give way to inescapable facts. In 1967 'the Medical Termination of Pregnancy Bill was closely examined, and a statement, commenting on its various clauses, prepared. In the Magazine James Taylor commented, perhaps this Bill could only exist in an age of depersonalisation like ours.'[36] Attention was paid to the danger of the so-called social clause, and stress was laid on the need for remedial measures in society to avert some of the causes of the distress that led to the demand for the termination of pregnancy.'

---

[34] *SBY 1997*, pp. 193-94.
[35] *SBM*, 102.11 (November 1976), and *SBM*, 103.1 (January 1977).
[36] *SBM*, 93.5 (May 1967), p. 1.

In 1976 a report was given of ongoing conversations between Scottish Baptists and representatives of the Roman Catholic Church, and in the section on ethics 'we found many areas of tension, in that while we find it hard to appreciate the use of ethically "questionable" things like Bingo for the benefit of Christ's Church, they found it hard to appreciate why sometimes we are not absolutely clear in our opposition say to abortion, which is the destruction of life. It is fair to say that most Baptists are against abortion except in the most extreme cases.'

In 1977 the Christian Citizenship Committee raised concern about the attack on family life, the changing attitude to divorce and abortion which ultimately brings people to a changing attitude to euthanasia, the move to lower the age of consent, and also about the lobby in Parliament to decriminalise incest. In 1984 the Assembly was informed that the Paedophile Exchange had been wound up but warned that people were being referred to foreign organisations. In 1980 the Christian Citizenship held a Conference on Pastoral Approaches to Homosexuality, but it would be fair to say that this matter has not had the prominence it has had in other churches in recent years.

End of Life issues became an increasing concern in the 1970s and later, when successive efforts were made in Parliament to permit some form of euthanasia. In October 1977 Rev Ronald Armstrong compared legal euthanasia as a step towards Hitler's concentration camps.[37] In the next issue David Fergusson, then a student and a member of Hillhead and now (2013) Principal of New College Edinburgh, replied objecting to 'hysterical outbursts against euthanasia.'

## Divorce and Remarriage

At the beginning of the century divorce, while not unknown in Scotland, scarcely concerned the members of our churches. Gradually, with social and legal changes, it did become an issue, and many ministers were uneasy about remarrying divorced persons. The distinction between the innocent and the guilty party was less easy to maintain, and there were many equivocal situations to be faced. In 1981 a report was made to the Joint Ministerial Board on the Nature of Marriage and the Problems of divorce. It concluded that here were no scriptural grounds for refusing baptism and church membership to those who had been converted after divorce, but that there were differences of opinion concerning the remarriage of divorcees.

A particularly thorny question was divorce and the ministry, which came to the same Board when men, as it was then, who had been divorced applied for ministry. In 1979 a study recommended that breakdown of marriage would normally be considered as a bar to the approval of the Board. There were long discussions on this topic, when, for example, it was suggested that as with the Levitical Priesthood, there were disqualifications for physical reasons, which were not blameworthy, so divorce or separation might be a non-blameworthy

---

[37] *SBM*, 103.10 (October 1977), p. 1.

reason for disqualification for the ministry. This raised the issue of double standards, and was not unanimously agreed. In 1981 it was agreed that a candidate whose marriage had ended before his conversion might be approved, and towards the end of the century, each case was treated on its merits. The candidate was to be interviewed by a small sub-committee and their decision, without details, was to be remitted to the Board.

## Conclusion

We have seen that Scottish Baptists have, over the twentieth century, been faced by many challenges in their social and ethical thinking and action. They have not always agreed amongst themselves, and at times they have stood with a minority of the Scottish people on certain issues. They have sought to maintain a biblical and evangelical stance, to co-operate with other Christians and others of good will and have achieved much with limited resources. To conclude this chapter I quote from T. Watson Moyes' Presidential address to the Union at the 1999 Assembly, where his theme was 'Looking Forward in Hope.'

> Whatever the answers to these questions (he has referred to the big changes in end of century society) we, as Christian people, need to offer the things that Paul calls 'true', 'noble', 'right', 'pure,' 'lovely,' 'admirable,' 'excellent,' 'praiseworthy,' And Christian leaders should renew their calling to exemplify these things. They should not allow themselves to become apparent allies of those who advocate a lesser morality.

But this is not to take away hope from those who struggle with deep personal issues, for example in the field of sexual identity. This is not to invite trite condemnation of minorities who are different. Christians like ourselves, when we look to the Scriptures, must never do so over the heads of those who honestly and decently don't fit in to the accepted frame. Calmly, Biblically, openly, we have to begin within the Baptist Union of Scotland to consider how hope is offered to those who are at present largely self-excluded from our churches.'[38]

---

[38] *SBY 2000*, p.100.

# Bibliography

**Annuals**
*Baptist Handbook* (London: Yates and Alexander, 1873).
*Baptist Union of Scotland Assembly Papers*, 2007.
*Report of the Baptist Union of Scotland*, 1869-2000.
*Report to the General Assembly of the Church of Scotland*, 1955-1959.
*Scottish Baptist Yearbook* (Glasgow: Baptist Union of Scotland, 1899-2000).

**Newspapers and Journals**
*Baptist Times*, a periodical of the Baptist Union of Great Britain and Ireland, 1916-1952.
*Life and Work*, a periodical of the Church of Scotland, 1915-2008.
*New Evangelical Magazine*, volume 2 (edited by W. Jones; London: T. Tegg, 1816).
*Radio Times*, September 1956.
*Renewal Magazine*, 1967.
*Scottish Baptist Magazine* (Glasgow: Various Publishers, 1875-2000).
*The Revival Times*, 15 May 1905.
*Time Magazine*, 18 June 1973.

**Manuscripts and Local Church Records**
Ayr Baptist Church Deacons' Meeting Minutes, 1916.
Baptist Union of Scotland Council, Executive Council and other Union Committee Minutes, 1869-2000.
*Bristo Place Baptist Church Magazine*, August 1917.
*Bristo Place Church Notes and News*, June 1920.
Stirling Street Baptist Church Meetings, Galashiels, Minutes 1913.
Stirling Baptist Church Meetings Minutes, 1911-1918.

**Books**
Allison, Neil E., *The Official History of the United Board*, volume 1, *The Clash of Empires, 1914-1939* (Great Bookham, Suffolk: United Army, Navy and Air Force Board, 2008).
—. *The Official History of the United Board*, volume 2, *The Clash of Ideologies, 1939–1945* (Great Bookham: The United Navy, Army and Air Force Board, 2012).
—. *The Scottish Thistle: Rev. Dr William 'Bill' Speirs, 10 June 1917 to 13 June 2013* (Norfolk: Privately published, 2013).

# Bibliography

*Anglican-Roman Catholic International Commission: The Final Report* (London: CTS /SPCK, 1982).
Arnott, R. Page, *History of the Scottish Miners* (London: Allen & Unwin, 1955).
Baines, Annie Marie, *History of Dublin Street Baptist Church* (Edinburgh: McLagan and Cumming Ltd, 1958).
Balfour, Ian L.S., *Revival in Rose Street: Charlotte Baptist Chapel, Edinburgh, 1808-2008* (Edinburgh: Rutherford House, 2007).
*Baptist Missionary Society: Ter-Jubilee Celebrations: 1942-44* (London: Baptist Missionary Society, 1945).
Bardgett, F.D., *Devoted Service Rendered* (Edinburgh: St Andrew Press, 2002).
Bassett, T.M., *The Welsh Baptists* (Swansea: Ilston House, 1977).
Bebbington, David W., *Evangelicalism in Modern Britain* (London: Unwin Hyman, 1989).
—. *The Baptists in Scotland: A History* (Glasgow: Baptist Union of Scotland, 1988).
—. *The Nonconformist Conscience: Chapel and Politics 1870-1914* (London: Allen & Unwin, 1982).
Beech, John, Owen Hand, Fiona MacDonald, Mark A. Mulhearn & Jeremy Weston (eds), *Scottish Life and Society, A Compendium of Scottish Ethnology*, volume 10, *Oral Literature and Performance Culture* (Edinburgh: John Donald, 2007).
Berry, Anne E., *Giving Hope and a Future* (Fearn: Christian Focus, 2009).
Brown, Callum G., *Religion and Society in Scotland since 1707* (Edinburgh: Edinburgh University Press, 1997).
Bruce, S., T. Glendinning, Iain Paterson, Michael Rosie, *Sectarianism in Scotland* (Edinburgh: Edinburgh University Press, 2004).
Burrows, Edward, *Change at Springburn: A Centenary History of Springburn Baptist Church* (Glasgow: Springburn Baptist Church, 1992).
—. *From Faith to Faith: Kirkintilloch Baptist Church 1887-1987* (Kirkintilloch: Kirkintilloch Baptist Church, 1987).
—. *'To me to live is Christ': A Biography of Peter H. Barber* (Milton Keynes: Paternoster, 2005).
Byford, C.T., *Peasants and Prophets: Baptist Pioneers in Russia and South Eastern Europe* (London: Kingsgate Press, 2$^{nd}$ edition, 1912).
Campbell, Iain, *Fixing the Indemnity: the Life and World of Sir George Adam Smith* (Carlisle: Paternoster Press, 2004).
de S. Cameron N.M., et al (eds), *Dictionary of Scottish Church History and Theology* (Edinburgh: T. & T. Clark, 1995).
Capon, John, *Evangelical Tomorrow* (London: Harper Collins, 1977).
Carey, George, *The Meeting of the Waters* (London: Hodder & Stoughton, 1985).
*Churches Together in Pilgrimage* (London: British Council of Churches, 1989).

Cheyne, A.C., *The Transforming of the Kirk* (Edinburgh: Saint Andrew Press, 1983).
Coats, George H., *Rambling Recollections* (n.p.: printed privately, 1920).
Coats, Olive Mary & Victoria Coats, *Dr and Mrs Joseph Coats: A Book of Remembrance compiled by their daughters* (Glasgow: Jackson, Wylie & Co., 1929).
Coffey, David, *Build that Bridge* (Eastbourne: Kingsway, 1986).
Cooper, Alan, *Old Inverurie and Kemnay in Pictures* (Catrine, Ayrshire: Stenlake, 2003).
Dekur, Paul R., *For the Healing of the Nations: Baptist Peacemakers* (Georgia: Smyth & Helwys, 1993).
Denny, James, *Studies in Theology* (London: Hodder & Stoughton, 1894).
Ehrenstron N. & G. Gassman, *Confessions in Dialogue: Survey of Bilateral Conversations Among World Confessional Families, 1959-1974* (Geneva: WCC, 1975).
Ellis, Christopher J., *Together on the Way* (London: British Council of Churches, 1990).
Ewan, Elizabeth, Sue Innes & Sian Reynolds (eds), *The Biographical Dictionary of Scottish Women* (Edinburgh: Edinburgh University Press, 2007).
*Evangelical Union Jubilee Conference Memorial Volume* (Glasgow: T. Morison, 1892).
Finney, Charles, *Lectures on Revivals of Religion* (edited by William G. McLoughlin; Cambridge, Mass.: Belknap, 1960).
Fisher, John S., *Impelled by Faith: A Short History of the Baptists in Scotland* (Stirling: Scottish Baptist History Project, 1996).
Gammie, A., *The Churches of Aberdeen* (Aberdeen: Aberdeen Daily Journal Office, 1909).
Gordon, Eleanor & Gwyneth Nair, *Public Lives: Women, Family and Society in Victorian Britain* (New Haven & London: Yale University Press, 2003).
Gordon, James M., *James Denny (1856-1917): An Intellectual and Contextual Biography* (Carlisle: Paternoster, 2006).
Graham, Billy, *Just As I Am* (London: Harper Collins, 1998).
Green, B., *Crossing the Boundaries: A History of the European Baptist Federation* (Didcot: Baptist Historical Society, 1999).
—. *Tomorrow's Man: A Biography of James Henry Rushbrooke* (Didcot: Baptist Historical Society, 1997).
Haldane, R.B., *Autobiography* (London: Hodder & Stoughton, 1929).
Hardesty, Nancy A., *Your Daughters Shall Prophecy: Revivalism and Feminism in the Age of Finney* (New York: Carlson, 1991).
Hewat, E.G.K., *Vision and Achievement, 1796-1956: A History of the Foreign Missions of the Churches united in the Church of Scotland* (London: Thomas Nelson, 1960).
Highet, J., *The Scottish Churches* (London: Skeffington & Son, 1960).

# Bibliography

Hobhouse, Mrs Henry, *I Appeal unto Caesar* (London: George Allen & Unwin, 1917).
Hocken, P., *Streams of Renewal: Origins and Early Development of the Charismatic Movement in Great Britain* (Exeter: Paternoster, 1986).
Holman, B., *F.B. Meyer. If I had a Hundred Lives* (Fearn: Christian Focus, 2007).
Holmes, Janice, *Religious Revivals in Britain and Ireland 1859-1905* (Dublin: Irish Academic, 2000).
Hoover, A.J., *God, Britain and Hitler in World War II: The View of the British Clergy 1939-1945* (Westport, Connecticut: Praeger, 1999).
Hossack, George, *Ayr: Our Baptist Story* (Ayr: Ayr Baptist Church, 1986).
Houseman, Henry, *John Ellerton, A Sketch of His Life and Works* (London: S.P.C.K., 1896).
Hudson, Kate, *CND Now More than Ever: The Story of a Peace Movement* (London: Vision, 2005).
Huebner, A, *The Truth of the Pre-Tribulation Rapture Recovered* (Millington, N.J.: Present Truth Publishers, 1976).
Hudson, W.S., *Religion in America* (New York: Harper and Row, 1955).
Hunt, D., *Reflections on Our Past: A Statistical Look at Baptists in Scotland 1892-1997* (Hamilton: Hamilton Baptist Church, 1997).
Hunter Alistair G. & Steven G. Mackie, *A National Church in a Multicultural Scotland* (Dunblane: Scottish Churches Council, 1986).
Ireland, Lockhart Landels, *Pte. John Maclean. The Black Watch* (Kirkcaldy: Fifeshire Advertiser, 1917).
Irving, Edward, *The Coming of Messiah in Glory and Majesty, by Juan Josafat Ben-Ezra a converted Jew, Translated from the Spanish, with a Preliminary Discourse* (London: L.B. Seeley & Sons, 1827).
Jeffrey, Kenneth S., *When the Lord Walked the Land: The 1858-62 Revival in the North-East of Scotland* (Carlisle: Paternoster, 2002).
Jeremy, D., *Capitalists and Christians* (Oxford: Clarendon, 1990).
Johnstone, William (ed.), *William Robertson Smith: Essays in Re-assessment* (Sheffield: Sheffield Academic, 1995).
Kaye, Elaine, *For the Work of Ministry: A History of Northern College and Its Predecessors* (Edinburgh: T. & T. Clark, 1999).
—. *Mansfield College, Oxford: Its Origin, History and Significance* (Oxford: Oxford University Press, 1996).
Kemp, W., *Joseph W. Kemp: The record of a Spirit-filled life* (London: Marshall Morgan & Scott, n.d. [1936]).
Knox, W., *Scottish Labour Leaders 1918-1939* (Edinburgh: Mainstream, 1984).
Leitch, James & Edward Burrows, *From Faith to Faith: Kirkintilloch Baptist Church 1887-1987* (Kirkintilloch: Kirkintilloch Baptist Church, 1987).
Lewis, Jessie Penn, *War on the Saints* (Thomas E. Lowe, 1994).
Lillie, D., *Beyond Charisma* (Exeter: Paternoster, 1981).
Lomax, E., *The Railway Man* (London: Vintage, 1995).

Lord, F.T., *Baptist World Fellowship: A Short History of the Baptist World Alliance* (London: Carey Kingsgate, 1955).
McBain, Douglas, *Fire over the Water* (London: Darton, Longman & Todd, 1997).
MacGregor, S., *The Myrtle and Ivy* (Edinburgh: Macdonald, 1967).
McLachlan, Matthew, *Whyte's Causeway Baptist Church: The First Hundred Years 1852-1952* (Kirkcaldy: For the Church, 1952).
McVicar, M. (ed.), *The Great Adventure: Scotland and the BMS* (Glasgow: Baptist Union of Scotland, 1992).
Mair, C., *Stirling: The Royal Burgh* (Edinburgh: John Donald, 1990).
Marchant, James, *Dr John Clifford* (London: Cassell, 1924).
Matthews, H.C. & Brian Harrison (eds), *Oxford Dictionary of National Biography* (volume 1; Oxford: Oxford University Press, 2004).
Middlebrook, Martin, *The First Day of the Somme* (Barnsley: Pen & Sword, 2006).
Moyes, T.W., *Our Place Among the Churches: Scottish Baptist Ecumenical Relations in the Twentieth Century* (n.p.: SBHP, 2013).
Murray, Derek B., *Scottish Baptist College Centenary History 1894-1994* (Glasgow: Scottish Baptist College, 1994).
—. *The First Hundred Years* (Glasgow: Baptist Union of Scotland, 1969).
Novotny, J., *The Baptist Romance in the Heart of Europe: The Life and Times of Henry Novotny* (East Orange, New Jersey: Czechoslovak Baptist Convention in America and Canada, 1939).
Oliphant, M.O.W., *The Life of Edward Irving* (London: Harper, 1862).
Palmer, Derek, *Strangers No Longer* (London: Hodder & Stoughton, 1990).
Polland, D. & R. Polland, *Great is Your Faithfulness: A History of Irvine Baptist Church* (Irvine: Irvine Baptist Church, 2006).
Pope, R. (ed.), *Religion and National Identity: Scotland and Wales, C.1700-2000* (Cardiff: University of Wales Press, 2001).
Prestige, Lucina (ed.), *Today, Tomorrow* (Edinburgh: Polygon, 2001).
Randall, Ian M., *Spirituality and Social Change* (Carlisle: Paternoster, 2003).
—. *The English Baptists of the Twentieth Century* (Didcot: Baptist Historical Society, 2005).
Reith, George M., *Reminiscences of the United Free Church General Assembly 1900-1929* (Edinburgh: Moray, 1933).
Rushbrooke, J.H. (ed.), *First European Baptist Congress* (London: Baptist Union, 1908).
Schweitzer, Richard, *The Cross and the Trenches. Religious Faith and Doubt among British and American Great War Soldiers* (Westport C.T: Praeger, 2003).
Scroggie, G., *The Unfolding Drama of Redemption* (Glasgow: Pickering & Inglis, 1957).
Sell, Alan P.F., *Defending and Declaring the Faith* (Exeter: Paternoster, 1987).

# Bibliography

Semlyen, Michael de, *Ecumenism: Where is it leading us?* (Gerrards Cross, Bucks: Dorchester House, 1989).

Shawcross, William, *Deliver us from Evil: Warlords and Peacekeepers in a World of Endless Conflict* (London: Bloomsbury, 2000).

Shearer, John, *Modernism: The Enemy of the Evangelical Faith* (1st edition; n.p.: n.d. [early 1940s]).

—. *The Baptist Confession of Faith* (Stirling: Jamieson & Munro, n.d. [1937]).

—. *The Evangelical Faith* (2nd edition; Glasgow: John Shearer, 1946).

Shepherd, P., *The Making of a Modern Denomination: John Howard Shakespeare and the English Baptists 1898-1924* (Carlisle: Paternoster, 2001).

Silber, Laura and Allan Little, *The Death of Yugoslavia* (London: BBC /Penguin, 1995).

Slaven, A. & S. Checkland, *Dictionary of Scottish Business Biography* (volume1; Aberdeen: Mercat, 1986).

Smout, T.C., *A Century of the Scottish People 1830-1950* (London: Collins, 1986).

Snape, Michael, *God and the British Soldier: Religion and the British Army in the First and Second World Wars* (London: Routledge, 2005).

—. (ed.), *The Back Parts of War: The YMCA Memoirs and Letters of Barclay Baron, 1915–1919* (Woodbridge, Suffolk: Boydell, 2009).

Spurr, Frederic C., *Some Chaplains in Khaki* (London: Kingsgate, 1916).

Staley, Philip H., *The Scottish Baptist Lay Preachers' Association A Historical Review* (n.p.: Scottish Baptist History Project & Scottish Baptist Lay Preachers' Association, 1993).

Stanley, B., *The History of the Baptist Missionary Society 1792-1992* (Edinburgh: T. & T. Clark, 1992).

*Statement by Principal and Lecturers* (Glasgow: The Baptist Theological College of Scotland, June 1944).

Stead, W.T., *The Story of the Welsh Revival* (New York: Fleming H. Revell, 1905).

Strachan, G., *The Pentecostal Theology of Edward Irving* (London: Darton, Longman & Todd, 1973).

Talbot, Brian R., *A Brief History of Central Baptist Association 1909-2002* (Glasgow: Baptist Union of Scotland, 2002).

—. *Search for a Common Identity: The Origins of the Baptist Union of Scotland 1800-1870* (Carlisle: Paternoster, 2003).

—. *Standing on the Rock: A History of Stirling Baptist Church* (Stirling: Stirling Baptist Church, 2005).

*The Baptist Who's Who* (London: n.p., n.d. [1934?]).

*The Baptist World Congress, London, July 11-19, 1905* (London: Baptist Union, 1905).

*The Centenary Brochure of the Free Communion Baptist Church, Crown Terrace, Aberdeen* (Aberdeen: Crown Terrace Baptist Church, 1939).

*The Pope in Britain: Collective Homilies and Speeches* (London: St Paul's, 1982).
Thomson, D.P., *Visitation Evangelism in Scotland 1946-1956* (Publisher Unknown, 1956).
Torrance, D., *The Scottish Secretaries* (Edinburgh: Birlinn, 2006).
Tuttle, G.S., *So Rich a Soil* (Edinburgh: Handsel, 1986).
Urquhart, J., *Modern Discoveries and the Bible: From the Creation to Abraham* (London: Marshall, 1898).
—. *The Inspiration and Accuracy of Holy Scripture* (Glasgow; Pickering and Inglis, 1895).
Wallis, A., *In The Day of Thy Power* (London: CLC, 1956).
Wardin, A.W., *Baptists Around The World: A Comprehensive Handbook* (Nashville: Broadman and Holman, 1995).
Werkner, Ines-Jacqueline & Christine R. Barker, *Der Militarpfarrer im Auslandsein: Gestig-religioser Beistand oder nur Sozialarbeiter?Zur Funktion von Religion in einer zunehmend sakularen Welt, in Diener zweir Herren* (Berlin: Sonderdruckk, 2005).
White, R.E.O., *The Biblical Doctrine of Initiation* (Grand Rapids: Eerdmans, 1960).
Wilkinson, Alan, *Dissent or Conform? War, Peace and the English Churches 1900-1945* (London: SCM, 1986).
—. *The Church of England and the First World War* (London: S.P.C.K., 1978).
Wootton, Janet (ed.), *This is Our Story: The Free Church Women's Ministry* (London: Epworth, 2007).
Yuille, G. (ed.), *History of the Baptists in Scotland* (Glasgow: Baptist Union of Scotland, 1926).

**Articles & Book Chapters**
Allison, Neil E., 'Free Church Revivalism in the British Army during the First World War' in Michael Snape & Edward Madigan (eds), *The Clergy in Khaki: New Perspectives on the British Army Chaplaincy in the First World War* (Farnham: Ashgate, 2013).
—. 'Operation Agricola: Our Entry into Kosovo', *RAChD Journal*, 39.1 (January 2000).
—. 'Shakespeare's Man at the Front. The Rev. W.C. Charteris O.B.E. M.C.', *Baptist Quarterly*, 41.4 (October 2005).
—. 'T.N. Tattersall D.S.O: His War Experience and Medals', *The RAChD Journal*, 45 (2006).
Allison, Ruth, 'A Wife's View of Ministry', *Caring and Sharing*, The Magazine of the Scottish Baptist Ministers' Wives' Fellowship (Spring 2001).
Bardgett, F.D., 'The Tell Scotland Movement', *Records of the Scottish Church History Society*, 38 (2008).

# Bibliography

Bebbington, David W., 'Baptist Members of Parliament 1847-1914', *Baptist Quarterly*, 29 (April 1981).
—. 'Baptist Members of Parliament in the Twentieth Century', *Baptist Quarterly*, 31 (April 1986).
—. 'Baptist Members of Parliament, A Supplementary Note', *Baptist Quarterly*, 42 (April 2007).
—. 'The Decline and Resurgence of Evangelical Social Concern 1918-1980' in J. Wolffe (ed.), *Evangelical Faith and Public Zeal* (London: SPCK, 1995).
Brown, Stewart J., 'A Solemn Purification by Fire: Responses to the Great War in the Scottish Presbyterian Churches, 1914-1919', *Journal of Ecclesiastical History*, 45.1 (January 1994).
Coffey, John, 'Democracy and popular religion: Moody and Sankey's mission to Britain, 1873-1875' in Eugenio F. Biagini (ed.), *Citizenship and Community* (Cambridge: Cambridge University Press, 1996).
Craske, Jane, 'The Grounds of Dispute: Theologies of Leadership, Ministry and Ordination and Women's Ministry' in Janet Wootton (ed.), *This is Our Story: The Free Church Women's Ministry* (London: Epworth, 2007).
Cuthbertson, Greg, 'Pricking the "nonconformist conscience": Religion against the South African War' in Donal Lowry (ed.), *The South African War Reappraised* (Manchester: Manchester University Press, 2000).
Forsyth, P.T., 'G.A. Smith's Yale Lecture', *British Weekly*, No.756 (25 April 1901).
Hale, Frederick, 'Captives of British Imperialism?' *Baptist Quarterly*, 39.1 (January 2001).
Hamilton, I., 'D.L. Moody' in N.M. de S. Cameron et al (eds), *Scottish Dictionary of Church History and Theology* (Edinburgh: T. & T. Clark, 1993).
Henry, S.D., 'Scottish Baptists and the First World War', *Baptist Quarterly*, 31.2 (April 1985).
Hillyer, P.N., 'Albert Ritschl' in Sinclair B. Ferguson (ed.), *New Dictionary of Theology* (Leicester: IVP, 1988).
Hoyle, R. Birch, *The Teaching of Karl Barth: An Exposition* (London: Student Christian Movement, 1930).
Lumsden, Christine, 'George Yuille "Grand Old Man" of Scottish Baptists' in D. Polland & R. Polland (eds), *Great is Your Faithfulness: A History of Irvine Baptist Church* (Irvine: Irvine Baptist Church, 2006).
McConnachie, John, 'The Teaching of Karl Barth', *Hibbert Journal*, 25 (1926-1927).
McCracken, Robert J., 'How Barth has influenced Me', *Theology Today*, 13 (October 1956).
McCracken, Robert J., 'Let the Preacher Preach the Word', *Theology Today*, 2.1 (April 1945).

Macdonald, L.O., 'Women in Presbyterian Churches' in N.M. de S. Cameron et al (eds), *Dictionary of Scottish Church History and Theology* (Edinburgh: T. & T. Clark, 1995).

McIntyre, John, 'Karl Barth's Predestination', *British Weekly*, No. 2917 (24 September 1942).

Mackintosh, Hugh R., 'Leaders of Theological Thought: Karl Barth', *Expository Times*, 39 (1927-1928).

MacLeod, James Lachlan, '"Greater Love Hath No Man than This": Scotland's Conflicting Religious Responses to Death in the Great War', *The Scottish Historical Review*, 81.211 (April, 2002).

Meek, D.E., 'Religious Life 8: Highlands since the Reformation' in M. Lynch (ed.), *Oxford Companion to Scottish History* (Oxford: Oxford University Press, 2007).

Randall, Ian M., 'Graham Scroggie and Evangelical Spirituality', *Scottish Bulletin of Evangelical Theology*, 18.1 (Spring 2000).

—. 'The Role of Conscientious Objectors: British Evangelicals and the First World War', *Anabaptism Today* (February 1996).

Read, D.H.C., 'Forward with Calvin: A Glance at the New Orthodoxy', *British Weekly*, No. 2666 (2 December 1937).

Rennie, Ian S., 'Fundamentalism and the Varieties of North Atlantic Evangelicalism' in Mark Noll, David W. Bebbington and George Rawlyk (eds), *Evangelicalism: Comparative Studies of Popular Protestantism in North America, the British Isles, and Beyond 1700-1990* (Oxford: Oxford University Press, 1994).

Roberts, Richard H., 'The Reception of the theology of Karl Barth, in the Anglo-Saxon world: history, typology and prospect' in S.W. Sykes (ed.), *Karl Barth: Centenary Essays* (Cambridge: Cambridge University Press, 1989).

Robbins, Keith, 'The British Experience of Conscientious Objection' in Hugh Cecil & Peter Liddle (eds), *Facing Armageddon: The First World War Experience* (Barnsley: Pen & Sword, 2003).

Roxburgh, Kenneth B.E., 'Edinburgh behind closed doors: The Edinburgh and Lothian Baptist Association Fraternal 1947-1987', *Baptist Quarterly*, 38.1 (January 1999).

—. 'Eric Roberts and Orthodoxy among Scottish Baptists', *Baptist Quarterly* 39.2 (April 2001).

—. 'James Morison (1816-1893)', *Records of the Scottish Church History Society*, 32 (2002).

—. 'Revival: An Aspect of Scottish Religious Identity' in R. Pope (ed.), *Religion and National Identity: Wales and Scotland c1700-2000* (Cardiff: University of Wales Press, 2001).

—. 'The Fundamentalist Controversy Concerning the Baptist Theological College of Scotland', *Baptist History and Heritage*, 36.1/ 36.2 (Winter /Spring 2001).

# Bibliography

Sell, Alan P.F., 'An Englishman, An Irishman and a Scotsman...', *Scottish Journal of Theology*, 38 (1985).

Smith, George Adam, 'Recent Literature on the Old Testament', *The Expositor*, 3rd series, No.10.

Smith, Karen E., 'British Women and the Baptist World Alliance', *Baptist Quarterly*, 41 (January 2005).

Speirs, William, 'Their Name Liveth', *R.A.Ch.D Journal*, 19.97 (June 1964).

Stowe, David, 'Re-thinking 10 /West Yorks at Fricourt', *Standto! The Journal of the Western Front Association* (August / September 2008).

Strachan, G., 'Edward Irving and Regent Square: A Presbyterian Pentecost', *Journal of the Presbyterian Historical Society*, 14 (1968-72).

Talbot, Brian R., 'Fellowship in the Gospel: Scottish Baptists and their relationships with other Christian Churches 1900-1945', *Evangelical Quarterly*, 78.4 (2006).

—. 'William Quarrier: Philanthropist and Social Reformer', *Records of the Scottish Church History Society*, 39 (2009).

—. 'Unity and Disunity: Scotch Baptists, 1765-1842' in R. Pope (ed.), *Religion and National Identity: Wales and Scotland c1700-2000* (Cardiff: University of Wales Press, 2001).

Tatham, Meaburn & James E. Miles (eds), *The Friends Ambulance Unit 1914–1919. A Record* (London: Swarthmore, 1919).

Thompson, J.H., 'The Nonconformist Chaplain in the First World War,' in Michael Snape & Edward Madigan (eds), *The Clergy in Khaki: New Perspectives on the British Army Chaplaincy in the First World War* (Ashgate: Surrey, 2013).

Torrance, Thomas F., 'Karl Barth', *Expository Times*, 66 (1955).

Turner, Max, 'Ecclesiology In The Major "Apostolic" Restorationist Churches in the United Kingdom', *Vox Evangelica* 19 (1989).

White, R.E.O., 'Theology and Logic', *Baptist Quarterly*, 16.8 (October, 1956).

Wright, Elizabeth F., 'Thomas Hadden: Architectural Metalworker', *Proceedings of the Society of Antiquaries of Scotland* 121 (1991).

Ypersèle, Laurance van, 'Making the Great War great: 1914-18 war memorials in Wallonia' in William Kidd and Brian Murdoch (eds), *Memory and Memorials* (Aldershot: Ashgate, 2004).

**Unpublished Theses, Essays & Papers**

Armstrong, Robert, 'The Lower Fifth', an unpublished paper given to the Scottish Baptist History Project, 19 April 2008.

Black, David, unfinished 'Autobiographical Memoir', 2003.

Hicks. David, 'Memoirs of World War Two', unpublished paper, 2008.

MacRae, Andrew, 'Reflections on the Baptist Union of Scotland 1966-1980', January 2008.

Robinson, Alan C., 'The Role of British Army Chaplains during World War Two' (unpublished Ph.D. thesis, University of Liverpool, 1999).
*Tokens of the Church of Scotland, 19$^{th}$ and 20$^{th}$ Centuries*, PSAS 77, 1943.
*Tokens of the Free Kirk,* PSAS 79, 1945.
*Unpublished Tokens of the Church of Scotland, 17$^{th}$ and 18$^{th}$ Centuries*, PSAS 75, 1941.